BIG IDEA, INC. PRESENTS

VeggieTales
VeggieConnections™
Connecting to a Powerful Relationship with God.

ELEMENTARY LEADER'S GUIDE

INTEGRITY®
PUBLISHERS
family

www.bigidea.com

www.integritypublishers.com

Managing Editor/Program Creator: Cindy Kenney
Project Managers: Laura Minchew, Dawn Woods
Writing and Creative Team: Linda Bredehoft, Karen Brothers, Lynda Freeman, Joyce Gibson, Natalie Gillespie, Betty Hayes, Kim Gunderson, Linda Hartzler, Renae Johnson, Cindy Kenney, Linda McGee, Mary Murray
Editors: Patty Crowley, Joyce Gibson, Judy Gillespie, Jim Hawley, Linda McGee, Dawn Woods, Laura Minchew, Jennifer Stair, Stephanie Terry
Illustrators: Larry Nolte, Big Idea Design
Design: Big Idea, Inc., Blum Graphic Design, and Frankel Design
Art: Larry Nolte and Big Idea Design
Music and Puppet Tracks: Chris Davis, Renae Johnson, Cindy Kenney, Mike Nawrocki, and Phil Vischer

ISBN: 1591452635
06 07 08 CHG 6 5 4 3 2

CONTENTS

WELCOME TO *VEGGIECONNECTIONS*™
Connecting to a powerful relationship with God

THE
DIRECTOR'S GUIDE

Kids will have an opportunity unlike any experience they've had before as they plug in to a powerful relationship with God. Kids know that *VeggieTales* means fun. During the 52 weeks of **VeggieConnections**, they will learn to connect with the Lord in every part of their lives. This curriculum will provide a foundation from which a life-long relationship with God can take place. Each lesson will take the Bible message from the head to the heart, joining the heart of a child to the heart of God.

VeggieConnections: **Connecting to a powerful relationship with God** is all about helping kids connect to a closer relationship with God. It is based on the Bible verse from James 4:8: "*Come near to God and he will come near to you.*"

Children will be introduced to and encouraged to adopt a catch phrase that can help to build and process their relationship with God every day of the year. That catch phrase is:

THiNK-LiNK-ACT

Each session will help kids focus on various THINK–LINK–ACT activities that help children to walk the walk and talk the talk, hopefully opening doors for the Holy Spirit to enter in and build meaningful relationships that will carry kids through every day of their lives. This catch phrase will help children who are new to learning about God and those who already know all about him connect to God as they make decisions and walk through life. Hand motions to accompany the catch phrase, along with the *THINK–LINK–ACT* song with motions, have been developed to help children learn and adopt this phrase as their own. Leaders will teach kids to:

THiNK:
Stop and think about what God wants you to do.

LiNK:
Link God's Word and what you've learned to your choices.

ACT:
Go and act on what God wants you to do!

STEPS TO SUCCESS

Big Idea wants to make your job easier while providing the most quality experience available. These Steps to Success will guide you toward providing the best program possible!

LESSON OVERVIEWS

The lesson overviews for the six *VeggieConnections* units can be found on the following pages. This will provide you with a look at:
- the theme unit (such as The Love Connection).
- the Unit Memory Verse used throughout each session in that unit (one memory verse per unit/ eight sessions)
- the model Bible person for each unit theme (such as Jesus).
- the six unit session reviews with the:
  - Lesson Focus
  - Bible story
  - Connection Word

The Faith Connection at the Veggie Lagoon
Connecting to **Faith** using **Moses** as our example

Unit Verse: *"Now faith is being sure of what we hope for and certain of what we do not see,"* Hebrews 11:1.

Lesson 1: God has a purpose for everyone.
The birth of Moses: Exodus 2:1–10
Connection Word: faith

Lesson 2: My faith helps me overcome challenges.
Moses escapes into Midian: Exodus 2:11–25
Connection Word: challenge

Lesson 3: I have faith that God is in control.
God talks to Moses from a burning bush: Exodus 3:1–4:17
Connection Word: control

Lesson 4: My faith helps me do what is right.
Moses returns to Egypt: Exodus 5:1–11:10
Connection Word: plague

Lesson 5: My faith helps me to persevere.
Moses helps the Hebrews prepare: Exodus 12:1–13:16
Connection Word: persevere

Lesson 6: My faith helps me to trust in God.
Moses leads God's people through the Red Sea: Exodus 13:17–14:31
Connection Word: chariot

Lesson 7: My faith helps me to be obedient.
Moses receives the Ten Commandments: Exodus 19:1–20:21
Connection Word: commandment

Lesson 8: I will share my faith with others.
Moses shares his faith: Deuteronomy 11:1–21; Hebrews 11:24–28
Connection Word: witness

The Communication Connection at Snoodleburg
Connecting to **Communication** through Paul's Ministry

Unit Verse: *"Ask and it will be given to you, seek and you will find; knock and the door will be opened to you,"* Matthew 7:7.

Lesson 1: God knows me; I want to know him.
Jesus speaks to Saul: Acts 9:1–19
Connection Word: communication

Lesson 2: Connect with God through prayer.
Paul prays for the church in Colosse: Colossians 1:1–14
Connection Word: prayer

Lesson 3: Connect with God by listening to him.
Paul listens to God: Acts 16:6–10
Connection Word: listen

Lesson 4: Connect to God through worship.
Paul and Silas worship God from prison: Acts 16:16–36
Connection Word: worship

Lesson 5: Connect to God through the Bible.
Paul explains about the armor of God: Ephesians 6:10–20
Connection Word: armor

Lesson 6: Connect to God through the Holy Spirit.
Paul explains how to live by the Spirit: Galatians 5:16–26
Connection Word: Holy Spirit

Lesson 7: Connect to God by letting him help me solve my problems.
Paul sails for Rome: Acts 27:1–44
Connection Word: help

Lesson 8: Connect to others with God's help.
Paul tells others about God: Acts 9:20–31
Connection Word: preach

The Love Connection at Flibber-o-loo
Connecting to Love through Jesus

Unit Verse: "'*Love the Lord your God with all your heart and with all your soul and with all your mind.' This is the first and greatest commandment. And the second is like it: 'Love your neighbor as yourself,'*" Matthew 22:37-39.

Lesson 1: **God is love**
Jesus and Nicodemus: John 3:1–21
Connection Word: love

Lesson 2: **I have Jesus as my Savior and Counselor.**
Jesus and the Holy Spirit: John 16:5–15
Connection Word: counselor

Lesson 3: **I have Jesus to teach me how to love.**
Jesus teaches the Beatitudes: Matthew 5:1–12
Connection Word: teach

Lesson 4: **I have Jesus as my daily source of love.**
Jesus and his disciples: Matthew 14:22–36
Connection Word: source

Lesson 5: **I have Jesus to show me how to forgive others.**
Jesus and others: Luke 15:11–32
Connection Word: forgive

Lesson 6: **I have Jesus to show me how to love my neighbor.**
Jesus and the parable of the good Samaritan: Luke 10:25–37
Connection Word: neighbor

Lesson 7: **I show my love to Jesus, because he loves me.**
Jesus tells us how to show love: John 14:23–31a
Connection Word: obey

Lesson 8: **I show my love to others through service.**
Jesus and his people: Matthew 20:20–28
Connection Word: servant

The Trust Connection at Dodgeball City
Connecting to Trust with life examples from Joseph

Unit Verse: *"May the God of hope fill you with all joy and peace as you trust in him so that you may overflow with hope by the power of the Holy Spirit,"* Romans 15:13.

Lesson 1: God knows what's best for me.
The story of Joseph: Genesis 37:1–50:26
Connection Word: trust

Lesson 2: I will trust God to help me with my problems.
Joseph is sold into slavery: Genesis 37:3–36
Connection Word: slavery

Lesson 3: I will show my trust in God by obeying him.
Joseph is tempted to do wrong: Genesis 39:1–20a
Connection Word: temptation

Lesson 4: I will trust God is with me in hard times.
Joseph in prison: Genesis 39:20b–23
Connection Word: attitude

Lesson 5: I will trust God to give me courage.
Joseph and the cupbearer and baker: Genesis 40:1–23
Connection Word: courage

Lesson 6: I will strengthen my trust in God by building my
    relationship with him.
Joseph interprets Pharaoh's dreams: Genesis 41:1–10
Connection Word: interpret

Lesson 7: I will trust in God's plan.
Joseph is in charge of Egypt: Genesis 41:41–45:15
Connection Word: plan

Lesson 8: I will show my trust in God to others.
Joseph reassures his brothers: Genesis 50:15–21
Connection Word: reassure

The Time Connection at the Chocolate Factory
Connecting to **Time** through the writings of the disciple **John**

Unit Verse: *"Teach us to number our days aright, that we may gain a heart of wisdom,"* Psalm 90:12 (NIV).

Alternate Version: *"Teach us to make the most of our time, so that we may grow in wisdom,"* Psalm 90:12 (NLT).

Lesson 1: God is eternal.
John writes about how God became human: John 1:1–18; 1 John 5:13–18
Connection Word: eternal

Lesson 2: God is with me all the time.
John writes about the Holy Spirit: John 14:15–29
Connection Word: Holy Spirit

Lesson 3: I will spend time with God.
John writes about walking in the light: 1 John 1:5–2:6
Connection Word: light

Lesson 4: I will set godly priorities with my time.
John writes about Jesus' teachings: John 15:1–17
Connection Word: priority

Lesson 5: I will trust in God's timing.
John writes about Lazarus: John 11:1–44
Connection Word: patience

Lesson 6: I will make good use of my time.
John writes about what Jesus does in Cana and Jerusalem:
    John 2:1–11; John 4:46–5:17
Connection Word: effort

Lesson 7: I will look for times to share God's Word with others.
John writes about the woman at the well: John 4:1–38
Connection Word: living water

John 8: I will use my time to serve others.
John writes about Jesus washing the disciples' feet: John 13:1–20
Connection Word: serve

The Joy Connection at Madame Blueberry's Tree House

Connecting to Joy by looking at David's Life

Unit Verse: *"You have made known to me the path of life; you will fill me with joy in your presence, with eternal pleasures at your right hand,"* Psalm 16:11.

Lesson 1: God is my source of joy.
David shares his joy in the Lord; Psalms 24; 103; 104
Connection Word: joy

Lesson 2: I find joy in whom God created me to be.
Samuel anoints David: 1 Samuel 16:1–13
Connection Word: anoint

Lesson 3: I can find joy even in times of trial.
David fights both criticism from others and a big giant: 1 Samuel 17:1–50
Connection Word: trial

Lesson 4: I find joy in being content.
David waits to be king in God's time: 1 Samuel 26:1–25
Connection Word: content

Lesson 5: I find joy in being thankful.
David's prayer of thanksgiving: 2 Samuel 7:18–29; Psalm 100
Connection Word: thankfulness

Lesson 6: I find joy in being kind.
David shows kindness to Mephibosheth: 2 Samuel 9:1–13
Connection Word: compassion

Lesson 7: I find joy in walking with God.
David's song of praise: 2 Samuel 22
Connection Word: praise

Lesson 8: I want to share my joy in the Lord with others.
David's psalm of praise: Psalm 145
Connection Word: psalm

A ROTATIONAL CURRICULUM

Kids get to travel to six, fun Veggie sites for eight week sessions during the year to help build excitement, hold their interest, and allow them to benefit from a change of pace.

This rotation is not only great for kids, but it's also terrific for leaders as this curriculum style will also require fewer teaching volunteers, adaptable programming, and less burnout for the staff.

At each Veggie site, the children will enter a fun lesson experience that helps them process their relationship with God through a biblical message. This new, cutting-edge approach to learning will engage kids each step of the way!

Flibber-o-loo: Kids will connect to a loving relationship with Jesus! Flibber-o-loo and Jibberty-lot are fun Veggie communities whose citizens wear shoes and pots on their heads! But these two Veggie towns have a problem: they don't get along with each other. At this site, kids will work through the problems of getting along with others as they learn that being different just means that God made each one of us special.

Madame Blueberry's Tree House: Kids will celebrate their relationship with the Lord by connecting to what it means to be joyful. At this fun site, kids will look at all the "stuff" in their lives and visit a place called StuffMart! By the end of their visit, kids will discover what it means to be content, thankful, kind, and sharing. And they'll celebrate it all with great joy!

Veggie Lagoon: When kids travel to the Veggie Lagoon, they'll have a chance to connect to their faith by looking at Moses as their role model. At this site, kids will not only have some seaside fun, but they'll dig into what it means to be faithful and discover how their faith is reflected in their lives.

Snoodleburg: Kids will learn the importance of good communication from the apostle Paul. Each child will discover that he or she is wonderful and unique! Snoodleburg is a fun atmosphere for kids to find out how and why God wants us to communicate in loving ways. Kids will not only realize the value of communicating with each other, but they'll discover how important their communication with God is, too.

Dodgeball City: Kids will arrive at a rootin' tootin' place to corral their feelings and learn what a trusting relationship with God is all about. By looking at the life of Joseph, kids will soon find that God not only wants us to trust him, but that he has placed a great deal of trust in us!

The Chocolate Factory: What child wouldn't want to visit the Chocolate Factory? Through the writings of the apostle John, kids will learn how to set priorities and use their time to worship and serve others!

HOW THE CONNECTION WORKS

Veggie Connections is your solution to children's programming! There are two kits, the *VeggieConnections Preschool Curriculum Kit* and the *VeggieConnections Elementary Curriculum Kit*. These kits include:

Program Leader's Guide: This provides an overview of the Director materials along with each Site Leader responsibilities. It helps with determining a daily schedule, training staff, overview of the program, how the rotational program works, and how to help kids connect to a closer relationship with God.

VeggieConnections CD-ROM: This provides Directors with Leader Devotions, student take-home pages, promotional materials and clip art, *VeggieConnections Shepherd* pages, holiday lessons and Opening Countertop Connections. All material on this CD-ROM is reproducible.

VeggieConnections Music CD and Puppet Tracks: This two disc CD provides leaders with two program-specific songs, 13 applicable Veggietunes, and 48 puppet tracks from Bob and Larry to open each day's activities.

Veggie Bible Dictionary: This amazing book is filled with fun definitions that will help kids understand words from the Bible. Kids will also be introduced to all the characters from VeggieTales, and they'll discover what some of the wacky words in the Veggie world mean, too!

VeggieConnections Program DVD: This wonderful resource provides leaders with 52 VeggieTales clips to help introduce kids to the lessons they will learn as they discover new ways to connect with God.

Bob and Larry's Clues to Good News: These outreach booklets are perfect for leaders to distribute to new children being introduced to God as well as to every child in church programs. In these books, Bob and Larry help kids uncover various questions they may have about what it means to have a relationship with God.

VeggieConnections Coloring and Activities Book: This resource for Site Leaders can be used for further fun and activity during kids' visits to each site or as a take-home resource.

Bob and Larry puppets: These delightful puppets will enable Leaders to tell children delightful messages to help them connect with God every day.

***Compassion International* Bank Template:** This bank template can be used to construct a bank that can be used to collect funds for the sponsorship of a child from a developing country. This project will enable kids to participate in a mission program either with their church family or at home.

CONNECTION TO YOUR VEGGiE WORLD

Countertop Connections: Where It Begins

Kids gather with Bob and Larry for Countertop Connections each session for an Opening Assembly filled with fun! Kids will meet with their *VeggieConnections Shepherds* to:

- See a puppet skit from from Bob and Larry (with recorded skits and the real voices of Bob and Larry)
- Sing
- Hear about how to have a connection with God
- Watch a five to seven minute clip from *VeggieTales*
- Participate in a mission project with *Compassion International*

How It Works

Estimate the number of children that will attend *VeggieConnections* and divide them into six groups. These groups can be identified with Veggie nametags (*found on the CD-ROM*) like this:

- Bob the Tomato Connection Group
- Larry the Cucumber Connection Group
- French Peas Connection Group
- Junior and Laura Camp Connection Group
- Mr. Nezzer Connection Group
- Madame Blueberry Connection Group

Divide each large group into smaller *VeggieConnections Groups* of six to eight children. Each of these groups will be led by a *VeggieConnections Shepherd* who will stay with their group throughout the program. *VeggieConnections Groups* work together to discuss, process, and participate in various activities at each site.

Each of these *VeggieConnections Groups* will visit one **VeggieConnections** site for eight consecutive weeks of the program, then rotate to a new site for the next eight weeks. Over one year, kids will visit the six sites (eight weeks per site) plus four holiday lessons. Your Site Leader is the teacher for each unit. *VeggieConnections Shepherds* work with the children but do not have preparation outside of class.

It looks something like this:

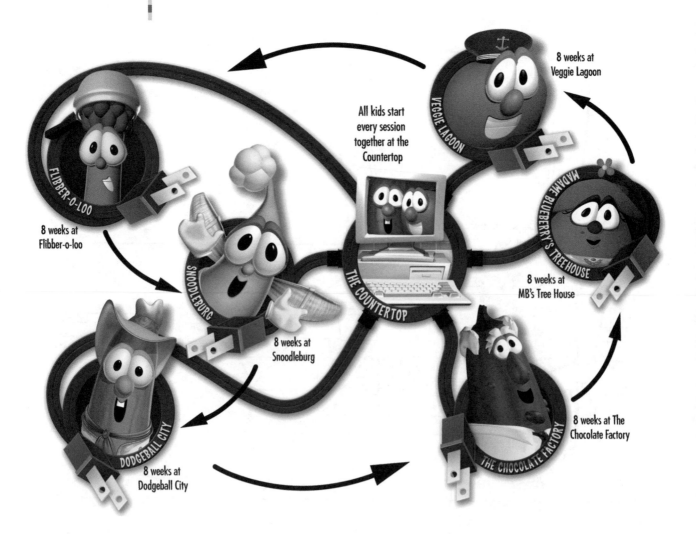

8 weeks at Veggie Lagoon

All kids start every session together at the Countertop

8 weeks at Flibber-o-loo

8 weeks at MB's Tree House

8 weeks at Snoodleburg

8 weeks at Dodgeball City

8 weeks at The Chocolate Factory

Rotational Schedule
(each session = 8 weeks)

Session	Veggie Lagoon	Chocolate Factory	Madame Blueberry's Tree House	Snoodleburg	Flibber-o-loo	Dodgeball City
1	Bob's Kids	Larry's Kids	Nezzer's Kids	J&L's Kids	French Pea Kids	Madame B's Kids
2	Larry's Kids	Nezzer's Kids	J&L's Kids	French Pea Kids	Madame B's Kids	Bob's Kids
3	Nezzer's Kids	J&L's Kids	French Pea Kids	Madame B's Kids	Bob's Kids	Larry's Kids
4	J&L's Kids	French Pea Kids	Madame B's Kids	Bob's Kids	Larry's Kids	Nezzer's Kids
5	French Pea Kids	Madame B's Kids	Bob's Kids	Larry's Kids	Nezzer's Kids	J&L's Kids
6	Madame B's Kids	Bob's Kids	Larry's Kids	Nezzer's Kids	J&L's Kids	French Pea Kids

Connections Sessions

The Sites. Every session in *VeggieConnections* encourages kids to connect to a powerful relationship with God. Each site has a different connection that will help kids to build that relationship and process the Bible message. Through this process, kids will:

- be introduced to a new way in which kids can build a relationship with God
- be presented with an interactive, engaging Bible story
- be invited to explore the message with practical, everyday life applications
- be encouraged to remember the message theme with fun crafts and games
- be empowered to apply the message to everyday life and learn a catch phrase, THINK—LINK—ACT, to encourage them to remember, process, and put their relationship with God into action every day

Leaders will be provided with a menu of activities to accomplish each of these goals. Activities can be selected that will best fit each church's program needs based on time, budget, space available and personal preference. Specific instructions for each site leader can be found at the start of each *VeggieConnections* site section.

Daily Sessions. After children gather together for Opening Countertop Connections, they will be dismissed to one of the six Veggie sites. Each site is set up in the following format and contains three main parts:

- PART ONE: Plugging In at the Site (VeggieConnection and Prayer Connection)
- PART TWO: Plugging In to God's Word (God Connection and Activity)
- PART THREE: Plugging In to My Life (Cucumber Connection, Kid Connection, and Prayer Connection)

Countertop Connection
All children gather at the opening of each session at the Countertop Connection. Countertop Connections can be lead by two to three volunteers who just create this portion of the lesson (approximately 10 minutes) and then leave. Or the Director of Children's Ministry can rotate and lead each session with support from two *VeggieConnections Shepherds*.

Site Set-Up
Each unit begins with a title page and site overview to prepare leaders so that they can help lead children to the God Connections at that site.

The remainder of this section will provide the Site Leader with information to create the site itself and to prepare for leadership, along with a few starters for teaching:

- **Connection Goals**
- **Welcome to the Site**
- **Site Leader's Role**
- **How to Build the Site**
- **Life Application Memory Tools**
- **THINK—LINK—ACT**
- **Music Suggestions**

Plugging In at the Site

PART ONE: Plugging In at the Site has two sections to help kids enjoy the Veggie site:

> **A. Veggie Connection**
> **B. Prayer Connection**

During this time, kids will be greeted by the Site Leaders and introduced to the site Lesson Focus. Site Leaders will have a simple, fun costume or the prop to identify themselves as the Veggie Site Leader. This part of the lesson will then help introduce kids to the Veggie site, to prayer, and to the God Connection the lesson will focus on. It will also help kids to think, "What does this have to do with me?"

Plugging In to God's Word

PART TWO: Plugging In to God's Word has two main sections with a few subsections to help kids experience the Bible:

> **A. God Connection**
> **B. Activity Connection**
> **1. High - Powered Game**
> **2. Low - Powered Game**
> **3. Craft**

This is the Bible presentation and exploration of each session. During this time, kids will experience an interactive Bible presentation and then have a variety of ways to explore and remember what they have learned. Each Bible story will focus on a role model from the Bible— Jesus, Paul, Moses, Joseph, David, or John— to help mentor kids to build their own relationship with the Lord.

When the Bible presentations are over, kids can explore what they have learned in a variety of ways.

James 4:8 ("*Come near to God and he will come near to you.*") is the overarching Bible verse for this program that ties everything together.

In addition, each Veggie site will have a Unit Memory Verse for kids to focus on as they connect with God. Having one memory verse per site will help kids to memorize, apply, and own this verse as they explore each Bible story and their relationship with God. This Scripture passage will then remain in their hearts and minds forever.

Leaders will then have an opportunity to pick and choose from several game and craft activities to help kids explore and remember what they have learned. Leaders can select from these activities to build a program that best fits time, budget, and participant needs.

Plugging In to My Life

PART THREE: Plugging In to My Life has three different sections that provide life application for the kids:

> **A. Cucumber Connection**
> **B. Kid Connection**
> **C. Christ Connection**

The closing portion of each session helps kids to personalize what they have learned. It encourages kids to apply the God Connection to everyday life by putting it into practice right away!

Life Application Activities

Bob and Larry puppets will come to life as they talk to kids in short puppet skits within each lesson. These skits end with a question that helps children to process their budding relationship with God as they use the Bible message they've just learned to help Bob and Larry with a problem.

Leaders can provide kids with an ongoing activity that will relate to each God Connection. This activity will build from week to week and culminate in a memory tool children can take home with them at the end of each eight-week site visit.

At the end of each session, kids are provided with a take-home page that will help them to remember the Lesson Focus.

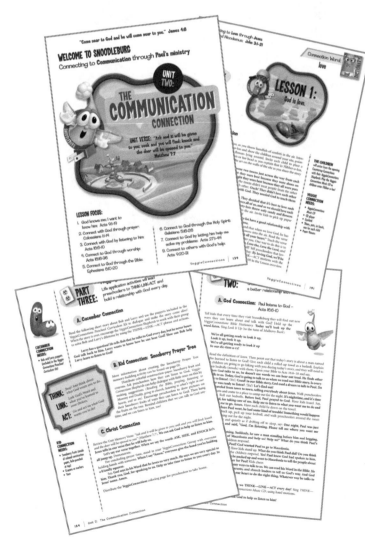

◆ VEGGIE FUN

◆ CONNECTING TO OTHERS

◆ INTERACTIVE BIBLE STORIES

◆ HIGH-POWERED GAMES

◆ LOW-POWERED GAMES

◆ FUN ACTIVITIES

◆ CRAFTS

◆ PUPPET SKITS

◆ MEMORABLE SONGS

◆ BIBLE EXPLORATION

◆ CONNECTING TO CHRIST

Releasing children from poverty
Compassion
in Jesus' name

MISSION PROJECT: COMPASSION INTERNATIONAL

VeggieConnections will encourage kids to:

CONNECT TO CHILDREN ALL OVER THE WORLD!

The Opening Countertop Connections and various **VeggieConnections** sessions will provide specific direction and mission emphasis for leaders and children.

Our experience has shown that program directors are looking for mission projects that will help make an impact on the lives of others. *Big Idea, Integrity,* and *Compassion International* have partnered together to provide you, the church, with an opportunity to make a difference. This provides a very practical way for kids to impact lives and reach out with what they are learning by connecting to kids all over the world!

Compassion International bank templates can be copied and made into banks for each classroom, or for individual children to take home and use with their families. *Compassion* child packets can be obtained free of charge by contacting *Compassion* for as many children in your program as you desire. A child packet contain the biography and photo of a child awaiting a sponsor. You may opt for having the entire class sponsor a child as a group, or you may want to encourage children to sponsor a child with their families.

Depending upon your decision, children may construct banks to take home, along with a child packet and a letter describing what *Compassion International* does for children all over the world. Or they may simply be instructed to contribute to the sponsorship of the group-sponsored child by bringing funds to the classroom to deposit in the *Compassion* bank. In that case, the letter from *Compassion International* describing what *Compassion* does for children all over the world should be sent home with the child so the parent understands what the group is participating in.

Compassion International links resourceful, caring Christians like the children and families in your program to children in need throughout the world. *Compassion* works closely with Christ-centered, evangelical churches in front-line communities to identify and register children who urgently need care. Each child gets to participate in a church-based program that offers life-changing benefits and opportunities, including educational assistance, health care, positive interaction with Christian adults, supplemental food (if necessary), and so much more. But most importantly, every sponsored child learns about Jesus and is encouraged to develop a lifelong relationship with the Lord.

Big Idea is confident in asking you to participate with *Compassion International* because we have seen their work firsthand. We believe in what they do and how they do it. For more information, visit www.compassion.com. To order your free child packets, simply call 800-336-7535 and tell them that you are calling to help children through the *VeggieConnections* curriculum.

Or request child packets by writing to:
Compassion International
Attn: **VeggieConnections** Project/Volunteer Network
12290 Voyager Parkway
Colorado Springs, CO 80921

CONNECTION PLANNING

Big Idea's **VeggieConnections** will provide you with a quality children's ministry program that will work in a variety of settings for a number of needs. The start of each Site Leader's section provides set-up and decoration options that will allow you to keep things simple, or go all out!

To help you get ready for this program, we have provided you with a number of tools to make your job easier:

- Planning Calendar
- Customizing **VeggieConnections** for various programs
- Connections training session

Follow the Planning Calendar to make your job easier, chart your course and plug in to a **VeggieConnections** program you won't forget! The Planning Calendar is divided into potential leadership responsibilities. Please keep in mind that you do not need all these positions to offer a successful program. Instead, these different leadership roles allow you to separate various duties and help volunteers to work in an area that best fits their needs if your church is large enough.

NOTE: If you are preparing this program for the fall, be sure to take advantage of preparation time prior to the start of school. Utilize the time that most parents, teens, and children have during summer breaks to set up the Veggie sites. Once they are done, your sites are ready to go for an entire year!

Planning Calendar: Plan with Prayer

Leader	Four Months Before Program	Two Months Before Program
Director	1. Decide on usage for *VeggieConnections*. 2. Set Leader meetings. 3. Decide where Leaders meet. 4. Outline use of space. 5. Set a budget. 6. Recruit Site Leader/ Teachers & Coordinators and Train. 7. Estimate enrollment – plan *VeggieConnections* groups. 8. Order additional materials.	1. Have a parent meeting to explain *VeggieConnections* program (and recruit any outstanding volunteers!). 2. Continue regular planning meetings. 3. Keep leaders informed of updated information. 4. Obtain reports from leaders and do budget checks. 5. Check on orders of additional curriculum or supply needs. 6. Begin publicity. 7. Send out program invitations. 8. Reevaluate space needs.
Site Leader (The Site Leader prepares lessons for one unit/ site of study)	1. Attend planning meetings. 2. Attend training session. 3. Put together lesson from menu of activities. 4. Determine supply list. 5. Collect needed supplies.	1. Finalize lesson plans. 2. Refine adjustments to different age groups. 3. Check supply collections. Determine what is still needed for supplies and crafts. 4. Check in with Decorations Coordinator on preparations.
VeggieConnections Shepherds (Leaders of *Veggie-Connections Groups*)	1. Attend training session. 2. Review lessons. 3. Become familiar with age-group shepherding requirements.	1. Pray about lessons and how to develop relationships.
Decorations Coordinator	1. Attend training session. 2. Evaluate decoration needs. 3. Brainstorm ideas. Develop a site plan (with Site Leaders). 4. Recruit decoration help, if needed. 5. Plan Countertop Connections setting.	1. Finalize decoration plans. 2. Begin any major set construction. 3. Obtain needed supplies. 4. Assign decorating leadership of different sites.
Countertop Connections Leaders (may be Children's Minister or Director)	1. Attend training session. 2. Recruit puppeteers, Music Leader and emcee. 3. Obtain *Compassion International* materials. 4. Make supply lists.	1. Begin learning music. 2. Begin rehearsing puppet shows. 3. Create lyric sheets for participants.
Publicity Coordinator	1. Review publicity needs. 2. Outline a plan and execution needs. 3. Recruit publicity skit leaders.	1. Begin publicity: (See CD-Rom) - Newsletters - Church bulletins - Posters and lawn banner - Skits, displays, radio
Registration Coordinator	1. Set preregistration date. 2. Set registration deadline (if needed). 3. Determine registration process.	1. Create registration form and distribute. 2. Hold preregistration.

Planning Calendar (Cont.)

Two Weeks Before Program	One Week Before Program	One Day Before Program
1. Hold last big planning meeting. 2. Obtain reports from leaders and do budget checks. 3. Continue publicity. 4. Make Closing Celebration plans. 5. Check contingency plans: rain, safety/first aid, substitute backup leaders.	1. Touch base with Site Leaders. 2. Update registration lists. 3. Check in with all leaders. 4. Do budget check. 5. Create signage for first aid, restrooms, check-in, pick-up.	1. Offer support to leaders. Do any last minute troubleshooting. 2. Provide final registration lists. 3. Hang necessary signage. 4. Distribute Leader Devotions or designate place for devotional before class. 5. Ask all leaders to arrive early to greet children. 6. Be sure registration check-in is ready to go.
1. Check in with Decoration Coordinator to make final site set-up preparations. 2. Create supply list and supply bin for each activity. 3. Make sample crafts. 4. Prepare life-application activity starter for each child.	1. Test object lessons, rehearse Bible presentations, review activity directions. 2. Be sure to have a Bible for each child. 3. Review schedule so you are clear on all final plans. 4. Call Shepherd who will be with the first *VeggieConnection Groups* in your site on week one.	1. Do final supply check. 2. Set up for first day activities. 3. Review schedule. 4. Be sure site is ready with Decorations Coordinator. 5. Distribute any needed information to Shepherds. 6. Check schedule.
1. Obtain initial group list from Director. 2. Pray for each participant. 3. Create attendance chart.* 4. Prepare student journal.	1. Obtain updated group list. 2. Complete attendance chart.* 3. Create program nametags.*	1. Obtain final group list. 2. Complete journal page for each participant. 3. Complete nametags.* 4. Prepare backpack. 5. Check schedule.
1. Continue with major set construction (if any). 2. Create character stand-ups and wall murals. 3. Check in with Site Leaders.	1. Complete final set construction. 2. Create final sites and Opening Countertop Connections.	1. Do final site and room assembly with Site Leaders. 2. Do final Opening Countertop Connections set-up.
1. Rehearse music with pianist and/ or band, and/or CD. 2. Rehearse puppet skits. 3. Collect props.	1. Check on final music and sound equipment needs. 2. Do final rehearsal of skits. 3. Check props.	1. Do sound checks. 2. Check in with Director for any last-minute changes.
1. Continue publicity. 2. Display crafts, offer program snack tastes, perform skits.	1. Provide each child with *Bob and Larry's Clues to Good News*.	
1. Recruit Registration Coordinators for opening day. 2. Define registration and check-in process for opening day. 3. Create needed signage.	1. Complete preregistration. 2. Touch base with Registration Coordinators. 3. Complete signage.	1. Be sure registration and check-in is well marked with procedure. 2. Have extra forms and pencils.

*can be done by the Registration Coordinator

CUSTOMIZING *VEGGIECONNECTIONS* FOR VARIOUS PROGRAMS

VeggieConnections can be customized to meet a variety of your programming needs. The material can accommodate a small class with an individual leader; same day lessons; and both small and large church programs, and is adaptable to space available, for example, churches without a permanent classroom space.

VeggieConnections can provide a great curriculum for:

- **Sunday School:** Here's a year - round resource to offer your Sunday School program a boost! No matter what program you are currently using, it's rare to find a program that will help focus on a relationship with God. By taking a year off to offer *VeggieConnections*, you'll provide kids with a new focus that it sure to enhance any other program you're doing!
- **Midweek Clubs:** This program can provide great fun, significant outreach, and solid Bible teaching between Sunday services all year long.
- **Preschool Programs:** A great opportunity to provide an everyday experience kids will never forget.
- **Homeschooling:** A new, creative way to present lessons to children at home. Not only will *Veggie-Connections* meet many needs for Christian parents, it will provide a wonderful avenue for kids to invite their friends to join in, too.

Midweek Program

VeggieConnections can be customized to a Midweek Program that will last for a year or even for two years if you meet for 24 weeks during the year.

This can be done in one of two very effective ways:
- Offer the full rotational program, exactly as the curriculum suggests;
- Divide your midweek program into eight-week sessions, and offer just one fun Veggie site per session.

The following schedule ideas may help you in using *VeggieConnections* for your midweek program:

3 Hour Format
5:00 Opening Countertop Connections
5:15 *VeggieConnections Shepherds* take their **VeggieConnections** group to the appropriate site
5:20 Veggie and Prayer Connections
5:40 God Connections
6:00 Meal
7:00 Activity Connection game
7:20 Activity Connection craft
7:45 Plugging In to My Life
8:00 Dismissal

2 Hour Format
6:30 Opening Countertop Connections
6:45 *VeggieConnections Shepherds* take their **VeggieConnections** group to the appropriate site
6:50 Veggie and Prayer Connections
7:10 God Connections
7:30 Snack Time
7:40 Activity Connection game
8:00 Activity Connection craft
8:15 Plugging In to My Life
8:30 Dismissal

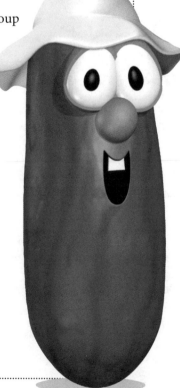

Sunday School

VeggieConnections has been written to a 52-week Bible class format. There are six rotations of eight - week sessions, in addition to four large-group holiday lessons. (Holiday lessons can be found on the *VeggieConnections* CD-ROM)

Every session will provide leaders with more material than actually needed. This allows leaders to select from a menu of activities that will best suit the needs of your church and the children who attend.

If you are offering *VeggieConnections* for Bible class, you may find it valuable to offer a schedule that looks something like this:

8:45	Opening Countertop Connections
8:55	*VeggieConnections Shepherds* take their *VeggieConnections* group to the appropriate site
9:00	Veggie and Prayer Connections
9:15	God Connections
9:30	Activity Connection
9:45	Plugging In to My Life

After School Programs

VeggieConnections can be customized to a preschool program that will last you for a one-year program or even for two years if you meet for 24 weeks during the year (or less).

Consider using the following schedule with your little ones:

K thru 2nd grade		**3rd grade thru 5th grade**	
3:00	Opening Countertop Connections	3:00	Opening Countertop Connections
3:15	Veggie and Prayer Connections	3:15	Veggie and Prayer Connections
3:30	God Connections	3:30	God Connections
3:45	Free Time	3:45	Free Time
4:15	Activity Connection	4:15	Activity Connection Game
4:30	Plugging In to My Life	4:30	Activity Connection Craft
4:45	Snack Time	4:45	Snack Time
5:00	Free Time	5:00	Plugging In to My Life
		5:15	Free Time

Homeschooling

VeggieConnections can be customized to a homeschool program that will last you for an entire year! Here's how:

1. Offer just one Veggie site a time. Decorate one room of your home, as desired.
2. Begin your school day with the opening materials, allowing your kids to enjoy a simple puppet show with Bob and Larry. Then view the short *VeggieTales* video and sing one of the program songs with the accompanying music *CD*.
3. Move into the Veggie and Prayer Connections.
4. Present the God Connection. Follow it up with a short review and answer any questions your kids may have.
5. Move on to your schoolwork for that day.
6. After lunch, allow your kids to do one or more of the Activity Connections.
7. Complete any schoolwork for the day.
8. Conclude with one or more of the Plugging In to My Life.

Connecting to a Traditional Lesson Plan

VeggieConnections can be adapted to a traditional lesson and rotation plan with great ease. While we would still encourage you to try the new approach toward learning, we certainly understand if you are unable for whatever reason. Here's how:

Step 1: Instead of recruiting Site Leaders, you will need teachers for each grade level.

Step 2: Order a Leader's Guide for every teacher. You may also wish to provide them with a music *CD* and *CD-ROM*. Preschool teachers will most likely want to have Bob and Larry puppets.

Step 3: Instead of setting up each site, encourage teachers to decorate their rooms for just one site (if desired). Start with Session in the Leader's Guide: THE FAITH CONNECTION.

Step 4: Decorate your gathering area for the Opening Countertop Connections. Encourage children to gather the same way, as if you were offering the rotational sites. Kids can meet their teachers at this time, hear the Bob and Larry skit, and watch the video. Then kids can be dismissed to their classrooms.
OR: If you do not have a gathering time, consider obtaining the puppet tracks and *VeggieTales* videos for your teachers to show in the classroom.

Step 5: Follow the guidelines for each lesson, keeping in mind that you will most likely have more information than needed. Simply pick and choose from the menu of activities that will best fit your needs.

Time-Saver Suggestion: If you set up a site in each classroom, have the Teacher and their class changes rooms every eight weeks so that you don't have to recreate site set-up.

MODIFY THE VEGGiECONNECTiONS FOR CHURCH SiZE

VeggieConnections can be modified to meet the needs of small, medium, and large churches. Follow these suggestions as you build your program:

Small Churches or Starter Churches at a Temporary Facility

Simplify recruitment needs by combining or sharing the following positions:
- Site Leaders can assume individual site decorations and eliminate the need for a Decorations Coordinator.
- *VeggieConnections Shepherds* can provide help with opening puppet skits, publicity, and music and create registration materials for their *VeggieConnections Group.*

Countertop Connections can be presented by different pairs of *VeggieConnections Shepherds* or Site Leaders. Offer this gathering time in your church sanctuary before or between services, in your fellowship area, a designated learning room, a foyer, or even on the front lawn. Use the music CD to provide accompaniment with *VeggieConnections* music.

Decrease decoration needs so that your volunteers don't feel overly taxed. Each site set-up offers two options. Follow option 2. If you do have some volunteers who wish to be creative, allow them to go all out—while providing others with the option to keep it simple.

Reduce multiple site needs by offering only two sites at a time. Allow your group to rotate through each site, then take them down and create two new ones, and so on until you've completed the number of units desired.

Select the game or craft that requires less preparation and fewer supply needs. There are several options to choose from.

Medium to Large Churches

Medium to large churches often have a larger talent pool to draw from, but a smaller budget due to large registration numbers. To address these needs, follow these guidelines:

Match volunteer abilities and interests to coordinate with program needs. You will get more people involved, with less responsibility. Write detailed job descriptions for each position, using the staffing needs described in the chart on pages 30-31. Help volunteers identify their strengths and weaknesses so that each leader is matched with a position that will be beneficial to everyone.

Identify volunteers who want to help part-time. Utilize these positions to fulfill helper roles, nursery needs, substitute positions, puppeteers, music leaders, registration, and traffic help.

Let volunteers with creative talents go for it! Provide them with the site decoration transparency art and set-up directions. Encourage them to brainstorm some of their own ideas. Let them feel ownership in the project and watch the Veggie sites unfold before your eyes!

Show the *VeggieTales* **video clips** on a large screen, or bring in several small televisions and hook them up together so that every child can see the video clip and experience the fun.

Create a large puppet stage that shows a miniature countertop for Bob and Larry puppets to appear on. If you have a large-screen projector, you may wish to show your puppet skits on a big screen, too. Be sure puppeteers for the Countertop Connections practice working the Bob and Larry puppets to coordinate with the puppet CD.

Adjust the Connections for Special - Needs Children

VeggieConnections encourages kids to work together, promotes relationship building, and focuses on overcoming everyday challenges. Follow these simple tips to welcome children with special needs.

- Make rooms, gathering area, and registration places wheelchair accessible.
- Recruit additional Shepherds or high school students to work with children who are handicapped or have a learning disability. Inform these helpers about each child's individual needs and provide them with further information that will help the *Veggie-Connections Shepherds* gain further insight to help each child succeed.
- Be aware of all allergies and medication needs.
- Talk with each special - needs child's parent to obtain information on exactly what the child can do, needs help with, or likes do.
- Encourage these children to succeed by pointing out their strengths at each Veggie site.
- Provide large motor activities and variety for children who experience learning disabilities.
- Allow children a chance to work at their own pace. Provide optional activities that may not require reading or writing, if that's a problem.
- Don't spotlight these children. Just welcome them and help them to build relationships as you normally would within each small group.
- Praise children and affirm positive behavior and relationship building.

CONNECTIONS STAFFING

VeggieConnections offers a wide variety of opportunities for volunteers to get involved and support the children's ministry program. Use this chart to determine the volunteers you need and help each volunteer to be matched with a position that will beneficial to everyone. *VeggieConnections* offers a full year of curriculum. Each Site Leader prepares one eight week unit and then repeats that unit every eight weeks for an entire year. If year long recruitment of six (one per site) will be an issue, consider a tag-team approach of pairing two Site Leaders per site. the two Site Leaders work together in the setup, decoration, and lesson planning. Then they each teach for eight weeks, thus requiring a six-month commitment for your teachers.

Staff Titles	Program Director/ Project Coordinator	Site Leaders	VeggieConnections Shepherds
Gifts and Skills Needed	1. Well organized 2. Assertive and people-oriented 3. Administrative skills 4. Able to lead children and adults 5. Good communication abilities 6. Budget-conscious	1. Well organized 2. Good planner 3. Good communication skills 4. Effective speaker 5. Budget conscious 6. Able to lead children in a loving manner and keep them engaged and interested	1. Loves children 2. Excellent relational skills 3. Good communication skills 4. Strong prayer leadership
Time Commitments	1. 4-5 months for planning, organization, and preparation 2. Daily management of program 3. Program follow-up	1. 2-3 months for planning, organization, and preparation 2. Daily curriculum presentation	1. 1-2 months before for prayer 2. 1 week before to identify group 3. Daily program Shepherd 4. Follow up with group
Responsibilities	1. Planning 2. Recruiting 3. Training 4. Communication 5. Budget control 6. Program management 7. Program trouble-shooting 8. Program follow-up 9. Volunteer appreciation	1. Site decoration and setup (with Decorations Coordinator if one is appointed) 2 Plan and presenting one unit lesson that is repeated to different age groups as they rotate through the site through the direction of the *VeggieConnections* program	1. Shepherd a group of 6-8 children through program 2. Relationship building w/children 3. Guide message processing and small group discussion 4. Assist as needed with games, puppets skits and crafts 5. Lead children in prayer and encourage prayer development 6. Help participants to personalize each session and apply to everyday life

Staff Appreciation

Don't forget to show appreciation to your leaders at *VeggieConnections* for all their efforts and dedication to helping kids build a relationship with God. Use the following ideas:

- Pray for your leaders. Let the leaders know that God, the kids, and you value what they do. Ask God to lead them through each connection.
- Provide ongoing support. Distribute the Leader Devotions on the *VeggieConnections CD-ROM* and offer a time of prayer and devotion each day of your program. (Offer nursery care for their children.) This can be done 15 minutes before the start of each session or at the end of the day.
- Touch base with each volunteer on a weekly basis. Provide a *VeggieConnections Staff Newsletter* with notes of encouragement and upcoming information. Leave a space called: "Connection Problems!" where leaders can jot down any troubleshooting needs and leave it with you at the end of the session (in case they don't have time to stay and discuss things with you). Make follow-up calls, if necessary.

Games and Craft Leaders	Music and Puppet Leaders	Registration and Publicity Leaders
1. Well organized 2. Good planner 3. Good communication skills Crafts: - Good with hands Games: - Lots of energy - Enjoy variety	1. Good communication skills 2. Good people skills Drama: - Good speaker - Animated - Good voice projection Music: - Understand how to read and lead music	1. Registration: - Well organized - Detail person 2. Publicity: - Good planner - Knowledge of church promotional avenues and schedules 3. Clean-Up: - Servant heart
1. 2-3 months for planning, organization, and preparation 2. Daily or part-time curriculum presentation, if working in teams	1. 2-3 months for planning, organization, and preparation. 2. Daily or part-time curriculum presentation if working in teams	1. Registration: - 2 months (Coord.) - 1 or 2 days (workers) 2. Publicity: - Clean Up - Part-time daily and after-program needs
1. Prepare and present crafts and games (See Leaders Guide) 2. Gather supply needs 3. Lead craft or game directions	1. Music: - Plan and learn music - Recruit band or piano accompaniment, if needed 2. Drama: - Recruit skit performers - Memorize lines or learn them well - Rehearse skits 3. Both: - Gather audio needs	1. Registration: - Plan and organize registration - Hold pre-registration - Assemble group lists - Design registration form - Send out invitations - Participate in registration and check-in 2. Publicity: - Plan and organize publicity opportunities (Newsletter, bulletin, invitations, phone-tree, posters, radio, lawn banner, photography) 3. Clean-Up: - Daily clean-up and overall church clean-up

- Leave a *VeggieConnections* treat where leaders will find it at the start of each session (snacks, notes, flowers, and so on).
- Build a *VeggieConnections* staff album. This will be a fun reminder of the experience, provide affirmation of leader's work, and be a great tool to generate excitement for kids moving to a new site or children just entering the program! You might recruit a photographer to help.
- Distribute *VeggieConnections* appreciation certificates. These can be reproduced using the pattern on page 42.
- Create thank-you cards. Use the *VeggieConnections* clip art and attach a flower, coupon for ice cream, or invite them to a Closing Connections party at the end of the year.
- Provide a baby-sitter one night per session so that leaders can take the night off and enjoy some fun and relaxation!
- Ask parents to sign up to provide any full-time volunteers with a meal one night during a session. This will be a greatly appreciate treat. Parents who are not involved with the children's program in any other way often are delighted to prepare a meal.

STAFF TRAINING CONNECTIONS

Provide your leaders with the best possible experience by offering a quality training event. The training workshop outlined on the following pages can be done efficiently and effectively, and you can have fun in the process. Here's how:

Training Workshop

Getting Ready
Gather all necessary materials and display them for your leaders. Be sure that you have:
- A *Preschool Leader's Guide* for all preschool Site Leaders
- An *Elementary Leader's Guide* for all elementary Site Leaders
- *VeggieConnections Shepherd* (small group) leader pages from the CD-ROM and pages 34–35 from this guide.
- VeggieConnections take-home pages from the CD-ROM
- Game and Craft booklets from the CD-ROM
- *Veggie Bible Dictionary*
- *Bob and Larry's Clues to Good News* outreach book
- *VeggieConnections Music CD* and music lyrics and piano scores from the CD-ROM
- *VeggieConnections Openings and Puppet Tracks* from the CD and CD-ROM
- Program Rotation and Overview
- How *VeggieConnections* Works pages 14–19
- Attendance roster (if ready)
- *Compassion International* sample banks and brochures found on the CD-ROM.
- Site clip art to create transparencies, and Veggie clip art from the Leader Guides and *CD-ROM*
- *VeggieConnections DVDs*
- Bob and Larry puppets
- Veggie nametags you can create from the *CD-ROM*
- Staff list with phone numbers
- Refreshments

Preparing the Room

Make your leaders feel welcome and appreciated, and be sure they know you want this to be a positive experience during which they, as well as the children, will grow in faith and have plenty of fun in the process. Create a fun, *VeggieConnections* atmosphere.
- Play program music.
- Create Bob and Larry stand-ups using the clip art. Create into a transparency, shine onto large cardboard sheets, outline, and color in. Then take photos of each of the leaders with Bob and Larry to give away and post on a bulletin board to show appreciation and generate excitement.

- Serve a menu of refreshments to reflect each of the sites:
- Veggie Lagoon: Tiny umbrellas in slushees (smoothies or fruit punch)
- Snoodleburg: Snooberry Jell-O (Jell-O Jigglers©)
- Flibber-o-loo: Pot pies
- Dodgeball City: Cornbread
- Madame Blueberry's Tree House: Blueberry pie
- The Chocolate Factory: Small chocolate candies
- Have candy kisses to distribute as Leaders arrive
- Create some simple "connections" by hanging colorful crepe paper and cross–connecting them all throughout the room
- Create a banner that says, "Welcome to Veggie-Connections" and include the Program Verse. (You can also use this at your Opening Countertop Connections, too.)
- Create a stop sign (or several) that includes the THINK—LINK—ACT catch-phrase that everyone will learn.

Meeting Schedule

20 minutes	Welcome and Prayer
30 minutes	How the *VeggieConnections* Works
30 minutes	Specialty Training (Break into groups) a. Site Leaders b. *VeggieConnections* Shepherds c. Specialty Coordinators
20 minutes	Refreshments, Questions, and Prayer

Welcome, Prayer, and Opening Activity

- Welcome everyone to *VeggieConnections*. Open in prayer, and go through one of the Leader Devotions from the CD-ROM.
- Introduce the program and offer a sample activity from one of the sites.
- Read the Program Verse together from James 4:8. Point out that this is the guiding verse in the program that will connect to everything that is done!

How the *VeggieConnections* Works

1. Explain that *VeggieConnections* is all about:
   a. Helping kids build a relationship with God.
   b. Helping kids to stop and THINK—LINK—ACT so that they can connect to their relationship with God in everything they do.

2. Distribute:
    a. The Unit overviews on pages 5–7.
    b. Staff list with phone numbers.
    c. Student rosters (if ready)
    d. Any other applicable material for leaders present

3. Talk about the unique nature of this program. Point out that children will be encouraged to build a relationship with God each step of the way in every session.

4. Distribute pages 8–13 of this guide and a *Veggie Bible Dictionary* to each leader. Point out that each session has a Connection Word that relates to what the kids will be learning that day. The dictionary is a wonderful place for kids to look up the word—or use to look up other Bible words and Veggie meanings!

5. Talk about how your church will present the Opening Countertop Connections provided in the *CD-ROM*.
    a. Emcee or lead this gathering time, using guidelines on the *CD-ROM*.
    b. Explain how children will find and meet their *VeggieConnections Shepherd*.
    c. Watch one of the fun puppet shows, using the Bob and Larry puppets and the puppet *CD*.
    d. Enjoy an Opening VeggieTales Countertop Connections clip to introduce one of the session lessons.
    e. Introduce the *Compassion International* mission opportunity so that kids can connect to kids around the world!

6. Describe each Veggie site and your vision for how it will look like and work within your church program.
    a. Distribute a rotation schedule.
    b. Distribute the program overview.
    c. Distribute a program calendar and time schedule for everyone to follow.

7. Explain when and how your Leader Devotion time will work.

8. Go over program details:
    a. Introduce the *Veggie Bible Dictionary* and how that works in the program. Also convey whether or not you are going to offer the dictionaries to your church families at a group discount.
    b. Go over *Bob and Larry's Clues to Good News* and when to distribute to children who are new to the church or just learning about having a relationship with God. Be sure to discuss how to order more books and make them available to friends of the children in your congregation. These are great giveaways for outreach events, family nights, etc.
    c. Safety, health, and children with special needs
    d. First aid
    e. Registration
    f. Day care for leader's children
    g. Openings
    h. Decorations
    i. Leader materials
    j. Dismissal time

Specialty Training

Designate a training leader for each specialty group. Working in small groups will provide an efficient and meaningful experience for everyone involved. Be sure to provide each specialty group with the following:

1. Necessary materials to carry out their responsibilities.
    a. Distribute Leader's Guides to all Site Leaders.
    b. Distribute information about how to lead a child to Christ found on pages 36.
    c. Age-level information sheets utilized in your Children's Ministry program.
    d. Any denominational materials needed for your program.

2. Allow leaders time to discuss responsibilities, brainstorm ideas, and ask questions.

3. Outline a support system, budget plans, important dates, and contact names for troubleshooting problems and questions.

Refreshments, Questions, and Prayer

Thank leaders for their time, energy, creativity, and devotion. Assure them that you are there to encourage them as they lead children in building a relationship with God.

Close your time together in prayer.

VEGGIECONNECTIONS SHEPHERDS

What Is a *VeggieConnections Shepherd*?

A *VeggieConnections Shepherd* will guide a small group of children (generally six to eight children in each group) through the entire program. *VeggieConnections Shepherds* work with the same group of children each session and do not have to prepare any lesson materials. They simply show up to build relationships, guide lesson processing, and help participants personalize each lesson so they can apply it to their everyday lives.

VeggieConnections Shepherds Guidelines

1. Shepherd an age-related group of six to eight kids through the program.
    a. Escort kids from place to place in the program.
    b. Greet each child at the Opening Countertop Connections.
    c. Stay with each child until he or she is picked up at the end of a session.
    d. Distribute the *VeggieConnections Shepherd* pages from the *CD-ROM*.

2. Maintain attendance records and children's supplies.
    a. Fill in an attendance chart (if your church uses one).
    b. Bring a backpack to the program for use throughout. Backpack should be large enough to keep a *Veggie Bible Dictionary*, *VeggieConnections Shepherd* pages, take-home pages, *Bob and Larry's Clues to Good News*, and Bibles.
    c. Keep kid's nametags and redistribute at each Countertop Connections.

3. Encourage relationships between children and God. . .
    a. as children meet, play, and study.
    b. as children process everyday dilemmas found at each Veggie site, using the THINK—LINK—ACT catch-phrase.
    c. as children think about how they can connect to the lives of needy children in the *Compassion International* mission project.

4. Assist Site Leaders with activities in the program.
    a. Participate with kids in each activity. Don't be a passive observer.
    b. Listen carefully to instructions, so that you can answer individual questions that kids have.
    c. Help Site Leaders distribute supplies, facilitate activities, and provide help.
    d. Assist children with craft activities as needed.
    e. Facilitate games.
    f. Talk and listen to the kids, getting to know them.
    g. Help to clean up after activities.
    e. Line kids up and keep your group together to move from place to place quickly and efficiently.

5. Help kids process the Bible messages.

6. Guide participants toward personalizing each lesson so they can apply it to their everyday lives.

7. Keep a journal page for each child. This can be done very simply in a spiral notebook. Shepherds should record each child's name, age, address, and phone number. This page can be used to add interesting notes, characteristics, and prayer requests.

VeggieConnections Shepherds Connection Tips

1. Look for teachable moments and discussion opportunities while working through each activity. Engage kids in the THINK—LINK—ACT method of thinking whenever possible.

2. Use the lesson overview on the *VeggieConnections Shepherd* pages (from the *CD-ROM*) to review the upcoming lesson before you gather with your group each day. Read the stories and pray. Ask God for guidance in reaching children where they are in their own faith journeys.

3. Watch for real-life situations that will apply to your sessions. Check the news, and read up on the subjects that kids will talk about.

4. Include everyone in discussion opportunities, but don't ever pressure anyone into sharing a story when he or she may feel uncomfortable. Accept kids' answers and opinions for what they are, and let them decide when and how to grow in their faith.

5. Be ready to lead a child to Christ when he or she is ready. Distribute *Bob and Larry's Clues to Good News* or use the guide on page 36. Be especially sensitive and aware of children who are new to your program, may have never gone to church, or may not know who Jesus is. Help these children connect with other adults and kids who can share their own faith with children.

6. Be cautious about letting the more talkative kids dominate a discussion or activity. Take a mental inventory of who has shared opinions and whether or not everyone has had an equal chance to participate. Pave the way for quieter kids to open up when they are ready.

7. Kids often fear embarrassment or teasing when sharing real-life stories, yet they long to do so. Model acceptance, friendship, and the importance of honesty while kids share. Reassure kids that they are not alone in the way they feel or the problems they encounter. When children don't want to share, let them know that God can help whether they talk to him alone or within the group.

8. Arrive early each day. This will make kids feel welcome and will show your enthusiasm and sincerity for working with them.

HELPING CHILDREN COME TO FAITH IN CHRIST

Children cannot be made to trust and follow Christ as their Savior. It is something that can happen only with the Holy Spirit's help and intervention when a child is ready. We suggest that you follow the teachings of your own church regarding helping children come to a relationship with Jesus Christ. But if that kind of help is not available, here are some guidelines to follow.

Excitement and enthusiasm must be caught rather than taught. Children can feel love only through experience, not by reading about it in a book. Faith is a lot like that, too. We can provide opportunities for positive faith experiences by sharing God's Word, by communicating excitement about our own faith, by accepting kids for who they are, and by modeling our joy as Christians.

When we help kids apply God's Word in their own lives, we are creating possibilities for the Spirit of God to work through us. Let kids feel what it's like to be loved as God's children, to be forgiven through Jesus' sacrifice, and to receive Christ's promise of everlasting life. Pray for children when they struggle with how to become followers of Jesus. Encourage kids to ask questions, explore the Bible, and discuss their feelings openly. Doors will open, and kids will feel the invitation of the Spirit when the time is right. Take advantage of teachable moments, particularly when you see a child seeking more information in a given situation. Allow that child an opportunity to explore his or her faith with you. Invite children to talk with you after class, and encourage them to talk with their parents at home.

If you are looking for a particular time to invite children to share their faith experience, you might consider giving them *Bob and Larry's Clues to Good News*. There is a sample of this book in the kit, but more can be ordered.

When children express a readiness to commit to Christ, you will want to be sure they understand certain biblical truths before they take this most important step.

1. God loves us even though we have sinned by acting in ways that displease him.

2. Jesus, the Son of God, never did anything wrong. He is the only One who can take away our sins, and he did this when he died on the cross.

3. We receive Jesus as our Savior when we believe that Jesus died for us and ask him to forgive our sins and commit to follow and obey God's ways.

4. God gives us the gift of eternal life so that we can be with him forever.

5. The Holy Spirit guides us and helps us live as Christians.

You will want to acquaint children with verses that will help them understand the decision they are making. The following verses are good Bible passages to use for this purpose.

"But God demonstrates his own love for us in this: While we were still sinners, Christ died for us" (Romans 5:8).

"For God so loved the world that he gave his one and only Son, that whoever believes in him shall not perish but have eternal life" (John 3:16).

"For all have sinned and fall short of the glory of God" (Romans 3:23).

"That if you confess with your mouth, 'Jesus is Lord,' and believe in your heart that God raised him from the dead, you will be saved. For it is with your heart that you believe and are justified, and it is with your mouth that you confess and are saved" (Romans 10:9-10).

"Repent and be baptized, every one of you, in the name of Jesus Christ for the forgiveness of your sins. And yu will receive the gift of the Holy Spirit" (Acts 2:38).

Safety Issues

All the leader materials in **VeggieConnections** provide specific safety tips for various activities. But as you plan and prepare for your program, there are some general concerns that you'll want every leader to be made aware of.

1. Be sure to offer a first aid station in your program. You may want to staff this station with a volunteer nurse—but even a mom or dad can provide needed help in most circumstances.
    a. Stock with needed supplies for cuts, scrapes, bee stings, and insect repellant.
    b. Provide registration forms so that Site Leaders will have contact information if a call for a parent or ambulance is needed.
2. Identify food allergies for all children. Provide a space on your registration form and pass this information onto Site Leaders and *VeggieConnections Shepherds*.
3. Check your church's insurance policy to make sure you have up-to-date policies that protect you in all situations. While it's unlikely a situation will occur, you want to make sure that your church and volunteers are protected.
4. Be sure that children are supervised by more than one person in any given room at all times.
5. Ask a volunteer to do a facility check to make sure that rooms and hallways are free of clutter and debris.
6. Provide guidelines to leaders for what to do:
    a. in emergency situations
    b. in cases of extreme discipline problems

Connection Promotions

Good publicity and positive promotion of **Veggie-Connections** will make the difference in who will choose to participate.

Publicity Ideas

1. **Church Opportunities.** Use your church's newsletter, bulletin, flyers, and announcement boards to inform your congregation about the program. For your convenience, you can obtain the following items through the *CD-ROM* or by reproducing some of the pages from this guide:
    a. Bulletin Announcements – *CD-ROM*
    b. Invitation Postcards – *CD-ROM*
    c. Registration Form (page 40)
    d. Program Flyers – *CD-ROM*
2. **Rotation Opportunities.** Each site rotation includes an eight-week session. This is a great chance to:
    a. Encourage children who have been absent a lot to come back to the program.

b. Renew enthusiasm for the program by inviting kids to an all-new, fun, Veggie site.
c. Provide an opportunity for children in the program to invite their friends.
d. Welcome new children from the community.

3. **Dates**. Put program dates on the church calendar early. Publicize these dates well in advance of each session start date so that families can make plans to participate.
4. **Announcements.** Take advantage of church programs to make announcements or present a skit to promote the fun.
5. *VeggieConnections* **Booth.** Decorate with clip art and Veggie stand-ups. Place it in a high-traffic area. Include:
    a. Opportunities to have a picture taken with Bob and Larry stand-ups.
    b. *VeggieConnections* craft samples
    c. Veggie site background images
6. **Lawn Banner.** Publicize what, when, and how to get more details.
7. **Radio Commercial.** Include a few program highlights along with pertinent program information and a number to call for more details.
8. *VeggieConnections* **Coupons.** Encourage registration by offering treats.

Remember to publicize your program in a variety of ways to appeal to a broad range of participants. Repetition is the key!

Fund-Raising Ideas

Keeping a budget is an essential part to any successful program. After you determine your program needs, participant costs (if any), and available church contributions, you may discover the need to raise money for your program. Follow these tips to help reach your program dreams so that you can reach a maximum number of children with an opportunity to build a relationship with God!

1. **Create *VeggieConnections* Stand-ups.** Use the clip art on the *CD-ROM* to create Veggie character stand-ups. Transfer the art onto transparencies and copy onto cardboard. Color and cut out. Let kids get their pictures taken with their favorites and charge a small fee for each photo. Use the Veggie frame on the CD-ROM.

2. **VeggieConnections Party.** Invite families to a fun-filled party to raise money for the program. Charge a small admission fee or ask for donations. Offer some of the **VeggieConnections** games!

3. **VeggieConnections Pickle Pot.** Church families and parents are longing for children to connect to a relationship with God! Many will want to show their support in a monetary way. Create a large Pickle Pot with a sign that says, "We're in a pickle and need financial help. Help kids connect to a powerful relationship with God!"

4. **VeggieConnections Supply Exchange.** Make a list of the needed supplies, write each supply on a 3" x 5" index card, and post them on a bulletin board. Encourage families to take a card in exchange for a Veggie coupon. Coupons can be offered for baked goods, babysitting, cleaning services, raking, office help, decorating ideas, organizational help, and so on.

Supporting Connections
Opening Countertop Connections

Set the stage for a very Veggie welcome! Create a Veggie countertop for kids to gather at and discover ways to build a relationship with God. You'll find the materials for this part of the sessions on the *CD-ROM*.

Each day, participants will gather together with their friends from *VeggieTales* to discover a variety of ways to build a relationship with God. They will:

1. Pray
2. Sing
3. Learn the Program Verse
4. Listen to fun puppet skits that provide kids with an introduction to each session
5. See a fun clip from *VeggieTales* that introduces each Lesson Focus.
6. Participate in the mission project with *Compassion International*.

Veggie Bible Dictionary

Every session in **VeggieConnections** offers a CONNECTIONS WORD. This word is selected from the God Connection of the day. Kids are encouraged to look up the meaning in the dictionary to help them to better understand what they are learning. At times, some of these words will be a small challenge for kids; however, it will build a lifelong foundation from which to understand the Bible and build a relationship with God.

The *Veggie Bible Dictionary* will also help kids to understand some of the fun, wacky words in the

world of *VeggieTales*!

There is one dictionary provided in the kit. Additional dictionaries are available for purchase for use in each site, for church, classroom, and for home use.

Bob and Larry's Clues to Good News

Children have many questions about God, the Bible, and what it means to have a relationship with him. *Bob and Larry's Clues to Good News* is an outreach guide that meets kids at their level. Each section of the book is broken down with a child's question that is addressed by two favorite characters from *VeggieTales*, Bob and Larry.

These two, fun personalities will search for the answers to kid's questions and find clues to God's Good News…right in the Bible. These clues will provide children with an introductory foundation that will help them to go to the Bible for future answers and reading. The messages encourage a budding relationship with God and enforce the message that God made each child special, and he loves them very much!

VeggieConnections CD-ROM

To make the leadership positions easier, along with creating a tool to keep costs down for the church, the *CD-ROM* will provide program directors with a great resource that includes the following:

- Game and Craft guide for activity specific leaders
- *VeggieConnections Shepherd* pages to provide them with a tool that educates them on each session's theme, message, Bible story, and leadertips.
- Leader Devotions that will help leaders to focus on the message and reflect upon their own lives before the session begins. This will encourage leaders to center themselves in God's Word and spend time in prayer before the sessions begin.
- Holiday Lessons have been developed for large group learning on four major holidays during the year: New Year's, Easter, Thanksgiving, and Christmas. These four lessons complete the year-round cycle of the curriculum and provide churches with an easy-to-do program that helps kids focus on the meaning of each holiday.
- Opening Countertop Connections, complete with puppet tracks to help leaders introduce each day's session and present a Bob and Larry skit.
- *Compassion International* activities. Added materials to provide churches with additonal ways to help participants connect to kids all over the world.
- Promotional materials and clip art to help directors and publicity leaders promote *VeggieConnections*.
- Sheet music, lyrics, and hand motions. On the *CD-ROM* and page 43–53.

Follow-Up Connections

After a successful *VeggieConnections* experience, it is our prayer that many children have developed a meaningful relationship with God.

Even though these *VeggieConnections* have ended, there are many ways to show continuing connections! Show appreciation to your volunteers, make new invitations, and use this experience to make next year's program even better!

Appreciation

Say thank you to kids and leaders who have been connected to the program. Use the appreciation ideas for leaders found on pages 30–31 of this guide to say thank you.

Ask *VeggieConnections Shepherds* to send follow-up notes to kids who were in their group. This will let each child know he or she is still being thought about, prayed for, and cared for. Include a photo to recall a special memory.

Evaluation

Ask both parents and leaders to provide you with program feedback. This will help to strengthen your future programs, show participants that you value their opinion, and help to plan your program next year. Use the Evaluation Form on the *CD-ROM*.

_____

(Insert church's name here.)

_____

(Insert church's address here.)

_____

(Insert program dates here.)

Parent/Guardian Name_____

Address_____

Phone Number_____Work or Cell Number_____

Would you like more information about the church?_____

Emergency Contact_____Phone_____

Child's Name_____

Date of Birth_____Grade_____

Allergies or Other Concerns_____

Child's Name_____

Date of Birth_____Grade_____

Allergies or Other Concerns_____

Child's Name_____

Date of Birth_____Grade_____

Allergies or Other Concerns_____

Volunteer Information:

Name of Volunteer_____

___ *VeggieConnections Shepherds*   ___ Clean-Up Helper
___ Publicity Leader/Helper   ___ Nursery Worker
___ Games Leader/Helper   ___ Registration Helper
___ Refreshments Helper

THANKS FOR CONNECTING WITH US!

We're so glad you joined this year's *VeggieTales* experience.
Hope to see you again very soon! Please join us for:

_____

_____

_____
Program Director

THANKS FOR CONNECTING WITH US!

We're so glad you joined this year's *VeggieTales* experience.
Hope to see you again very soon! Please join us for:

_____

_____

_____
Program Director

Certificate of Appreciation

When it comes to helping kids plug into a relationship with God,
you helped to provide kids with an experience they'll never forget!

Thanks for making **VeggieConnections** such an amazing encounter.

_____
Leader

_____
Connections Director

_____
Date

Certificate of Appreciation

When it comes to helping kids plug into a relationship with God,
you helped to provide kids with an experience they'll never forget!

Thanks for making **VeggieConnections** such an amazing encounter.

_____
Leader

_____
Connections Director

_____
Date

Piano/Vocal

Think, Link, Act

Words by Cindy Kenney
Music by Christopher Davis

Think, Link, and Act, that is what I'm gon - na do.

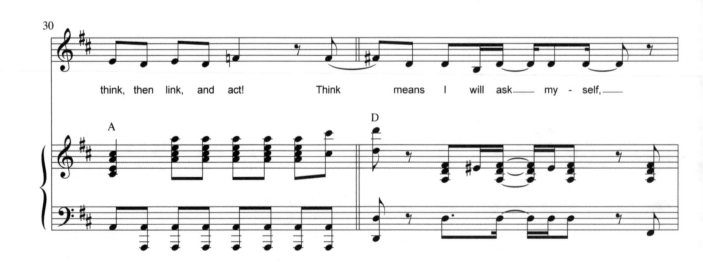

Music Motions

THINK—LINK—ACT

When I have a problem (Hands outstretched; point to self; point to forehead)
I know that God keeps track. (Point to self; point to God; write on pretend tablet)
I'll remember what I need to do. (Point to forehead; point to self; hands outstretched)
It's THINK, then LINK, then ACT! (Point to forehead; hook fingers together with one palm facing up and one palm facing down; hands outstretched)

Chorus:
THINK means I will ask myself (Point to forehead; point to self while shrug shoulders)
"What would Jesus do?" (Hands to cheeks; then hands outstretched above head)
LINK is trusting that God's Word (Hook fingers together with one palm facing up and one palm facing down; hands open in shape of a book)
Will tell me what is true. (Both hands point to self; then point and shake finger in air)
ACT means I'll connect with God (Hands outstretched; hook fingers together with one palm facing up and one palm facing down; point upward)
And show it all to you! (Spread outstretched arm across body and sweep to the side)
THINK, LINK, and ACT, that is what I'm gonna do. (Point to forehead; hook fingers together with one palm facing up and one palm facing down; hands outstretched; point to self and nod head yes.)

God knows more than I do (Both hands outstretched upward; nod yes; point to self)
When stuff gets of whack. (Roll hands in front of self)
I'll remember what I need to do. (Point to forehead; point to self; hands outstretched)
It's THINK, then LINK, then ACT! (Point to forehead; hook fingers together with one palm facing up and one palm facing down; hands outstretched)

When I have to make a choice (Point to self; point to side of temple)
I will, yep, that's a fact! (Point to self; nod yes; swing fisted arm in front of chest)
I'll remember what I need to do. (Point to forehead; point to self; hands outstretched)
It's THINK, then LINK, then ACT! (Point to forehead; hook fingers together with one palm facing up and one palm facing down; hands outstretched)

Piano/Vocal

God Connection

Words by Cindy Kenney
Music by Christopher Davis

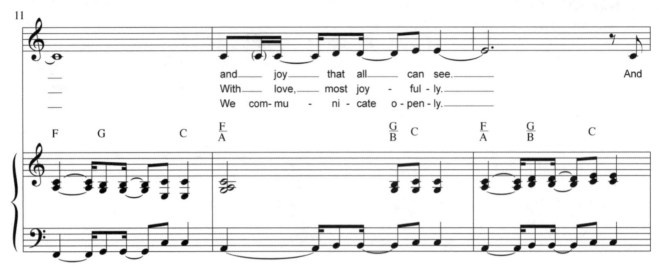

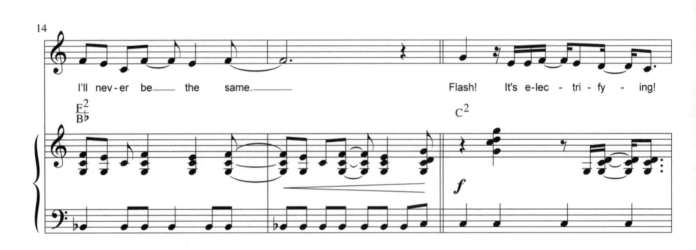

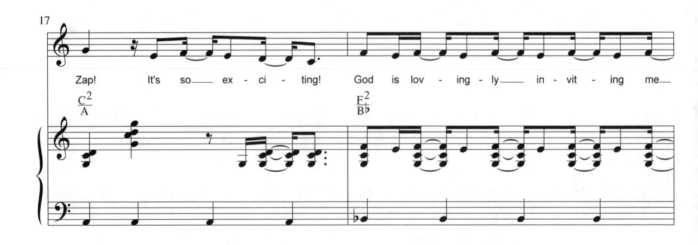

to con - nect____ with him.____ It's e - lec - tri - fy - ing!

Zap! It's so ex - ci - ting! God is lov - ing - ly____ in - vit - ing me

1., 2.

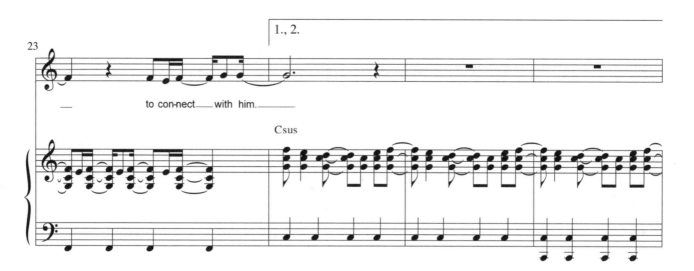

to con-nect____ with him.____

To con- nect___ with him.

To con- nect___ with him.___

It's e - lec - tri - fy - ing! Zap! It's so___ ex - ci - ting!

God is lov - ing-ly— in-vit - ing me— to con-nect— with him.—

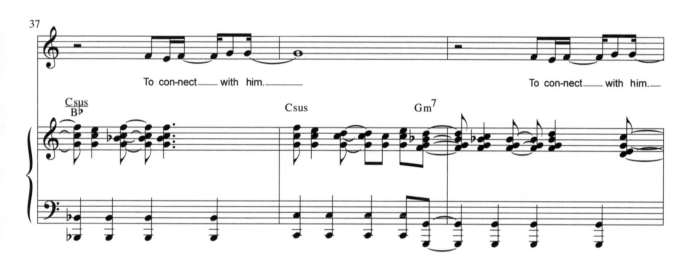

To con-nect— with him.— To con-nect— with him.—

Veggie Lagoon Backdrop

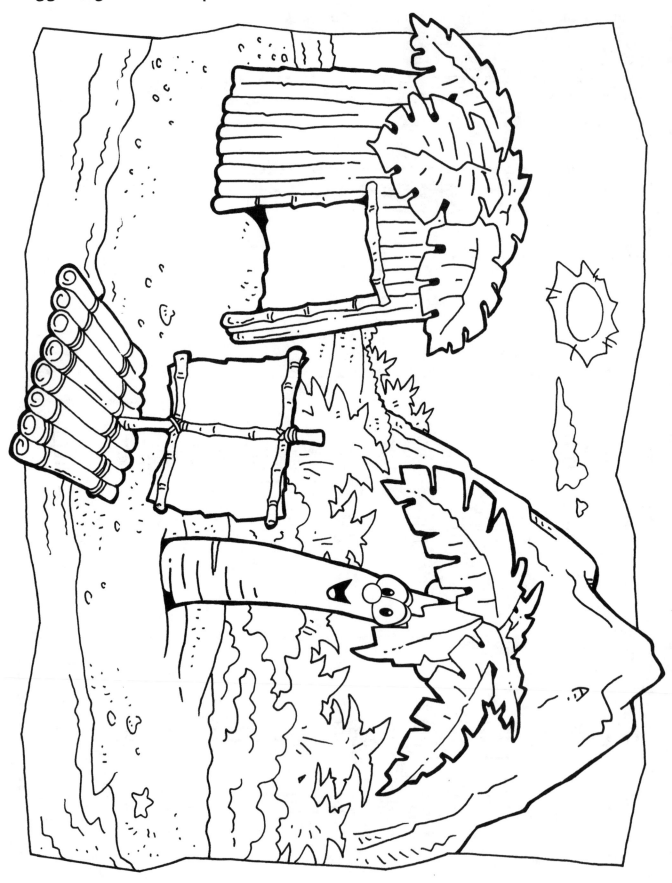

Snoodleburg Backdrop

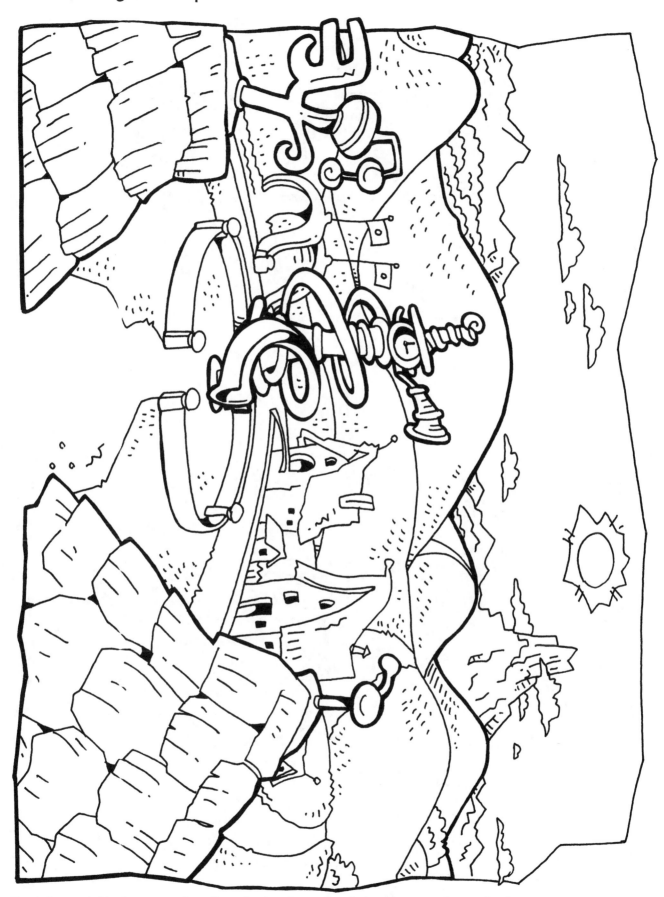

Flibber-o-loo Backdrop

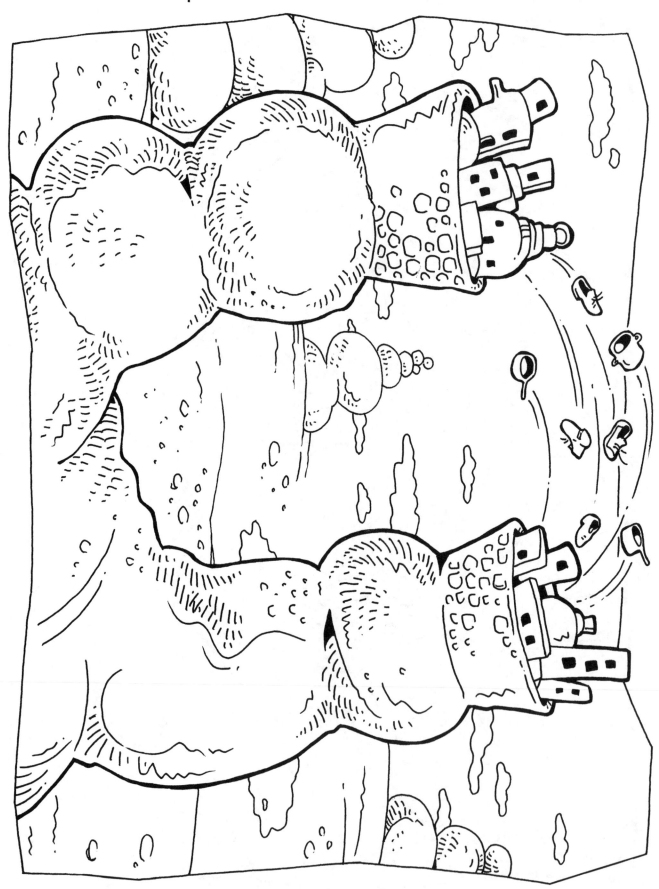

Dodgeball City Backdrop

Chocolate Factory Backdrop

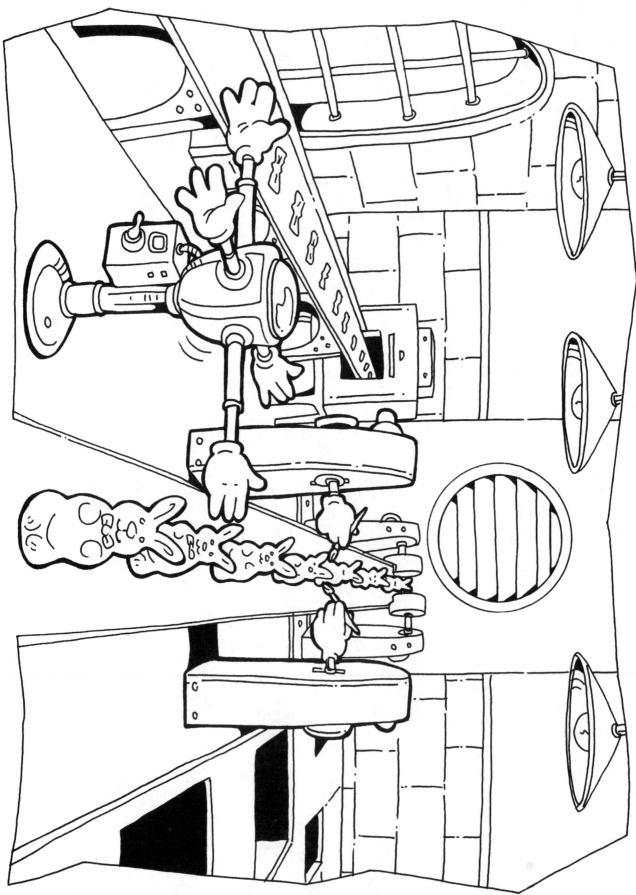

Madame Blueberry's Tree House Backdrop

Countertop Backdrop

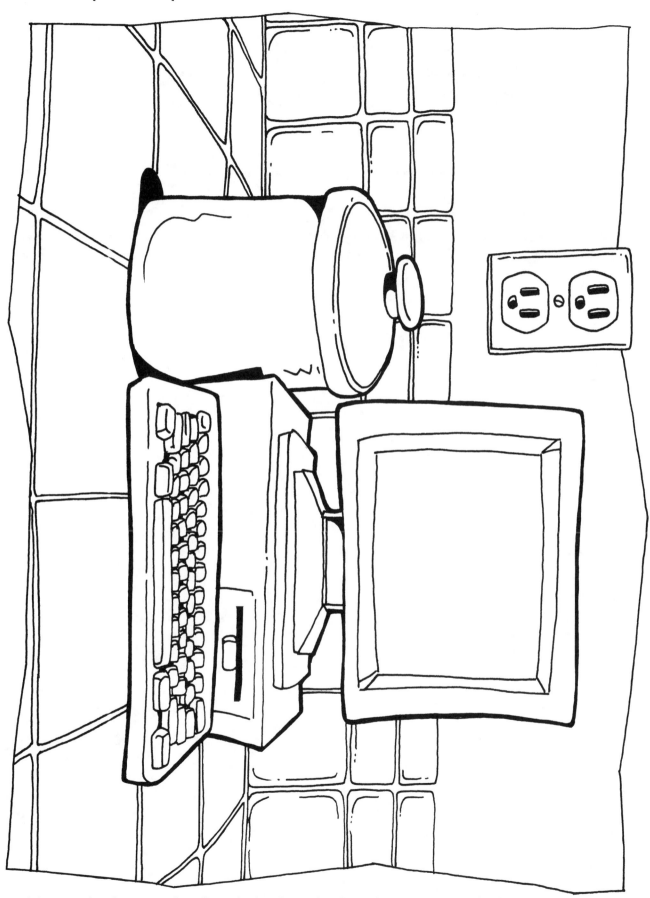

Clip Art - Program logo

Clip Art - Bob and Larry

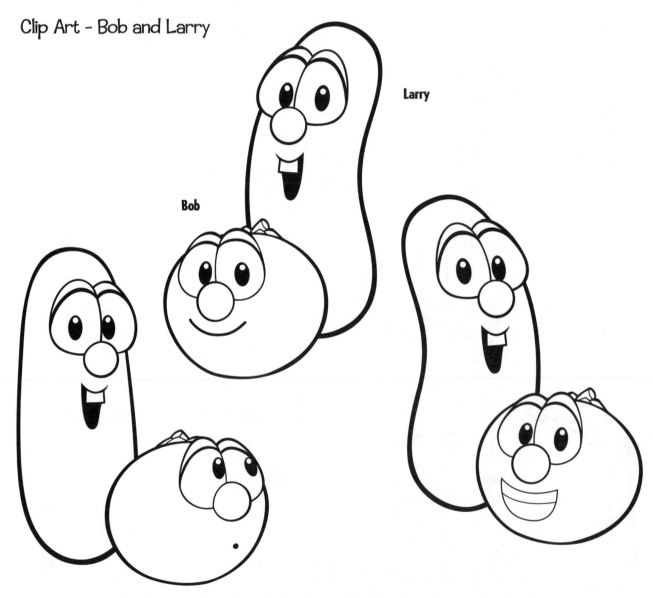

Larry

Bob

Permission granted to photocopy and use clip art for the sole use of producing this program in your church.

Clip Art - Veggie Characters

Larry

Bob

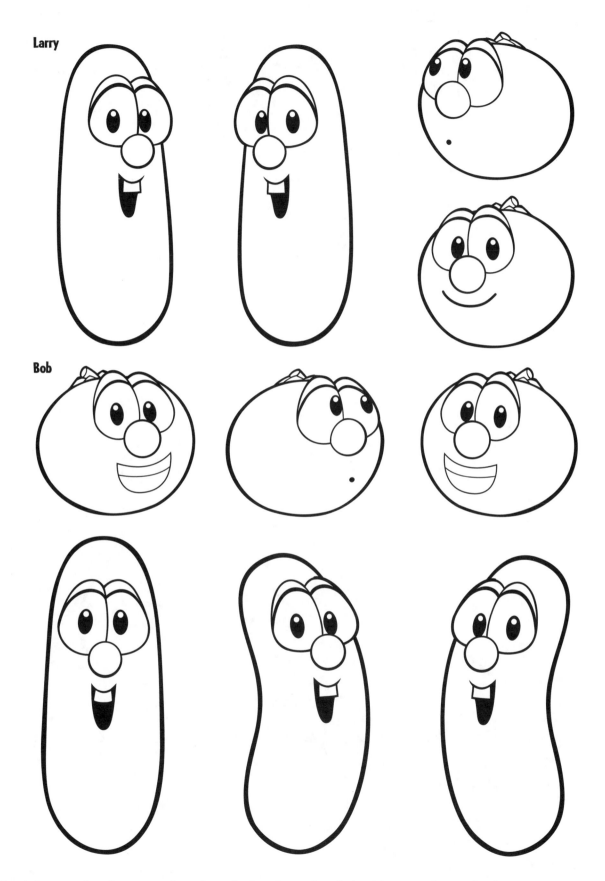

Clip Art - Veggie Characters

Laura

Junior

Jerry

Jimmy

Permission granted to photocopy and use clip art for the sole use of producing this program in your church.

First Mate
Larry

Skipper
Bob

The
Professor

Snoodle Doo

Snoodle 1

Snoodle 2

Farmer Snoodle

The Clock Tower

Permission granted to photocopy and use clip art for the sole use of producing this program in your church.

Clip Art - Flibber-o-loo / Unit 3: Love

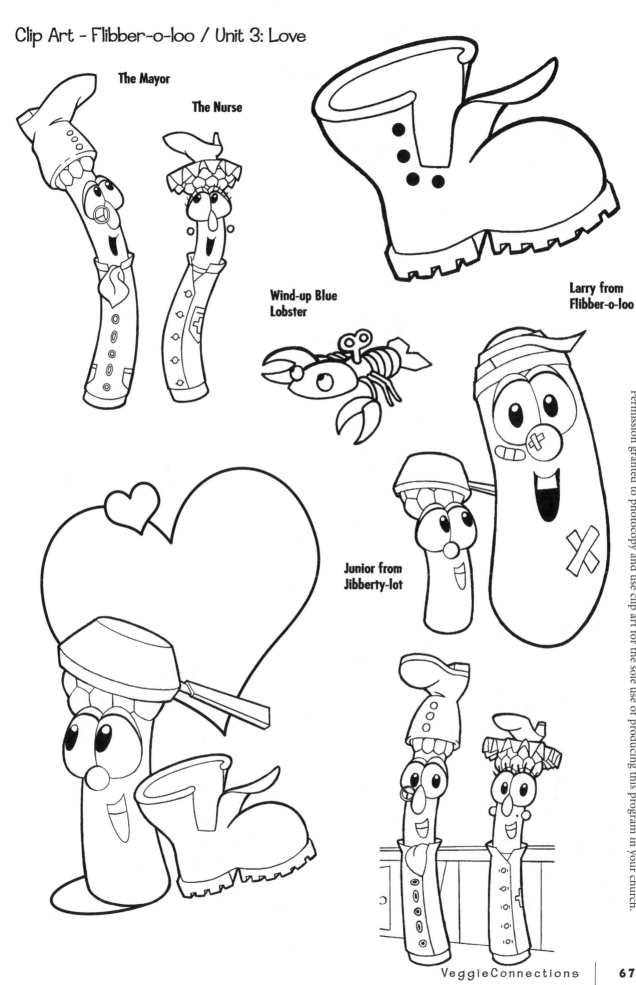

The Mayor

The Nurse

Wind-up Blue Lobster

Larry from Flibber-o-loo

Junior from Jibberty-lot

Clip Art - Dodgeball City / Unit 4: Trust

Pea Brothers

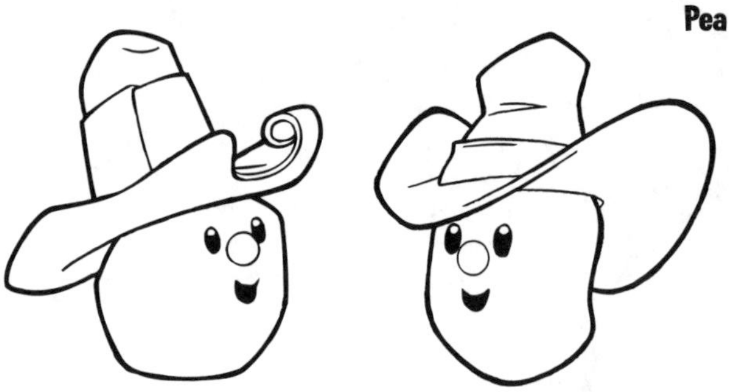

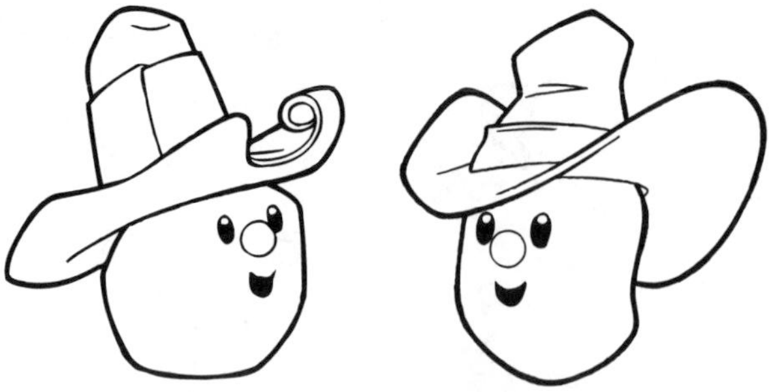

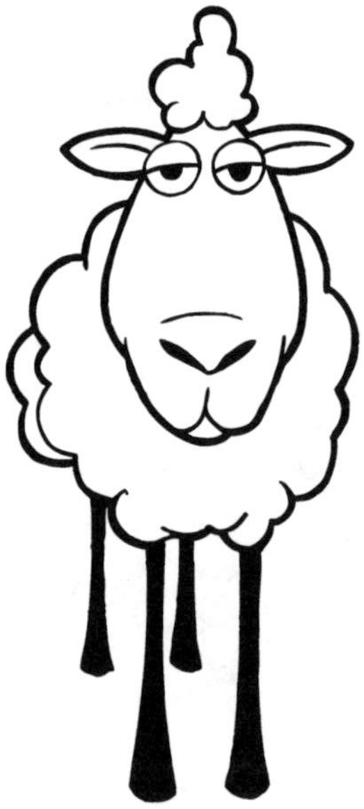

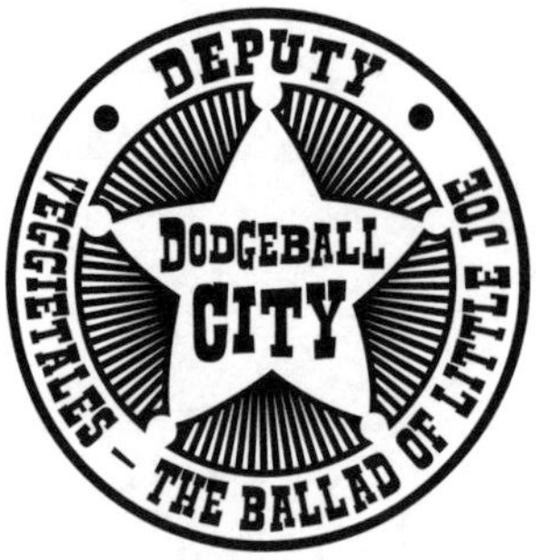
DEPUTY
DODGEBALL CITY
VEGGIETALES – THE BALLAD OF LITTLE JOE

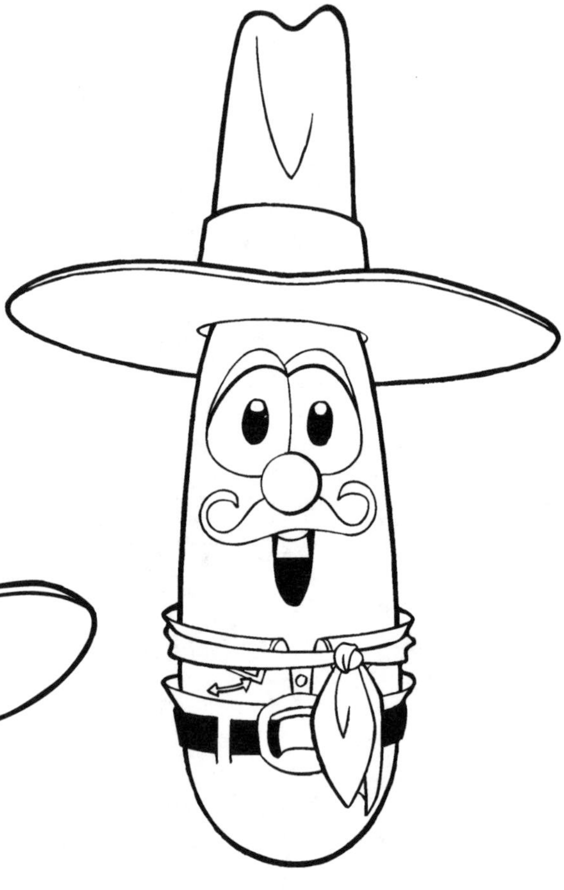

Sheriff Bob

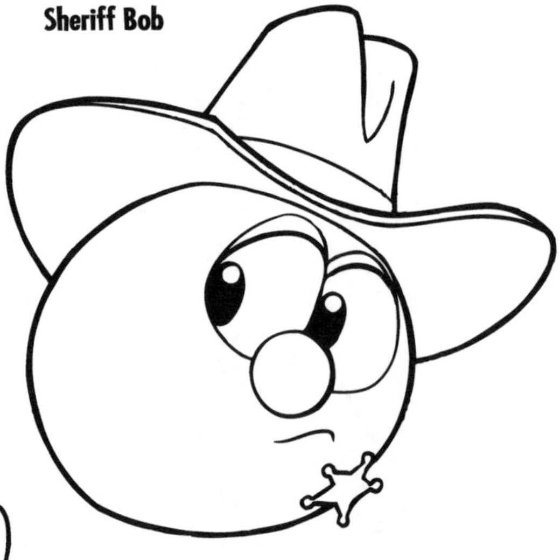

Madame Blueberry as Miss Kitty

Larry as Little Joe

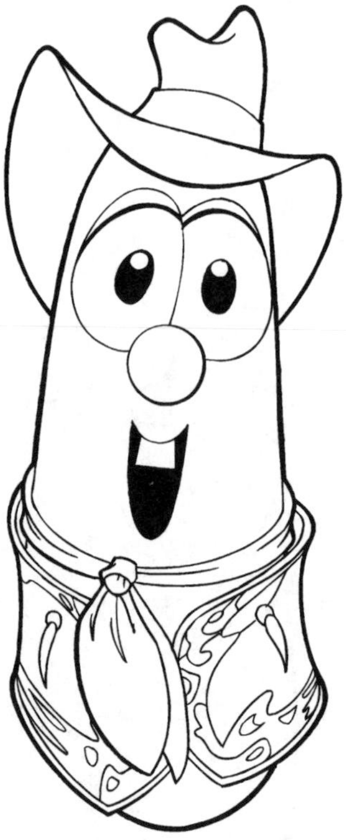

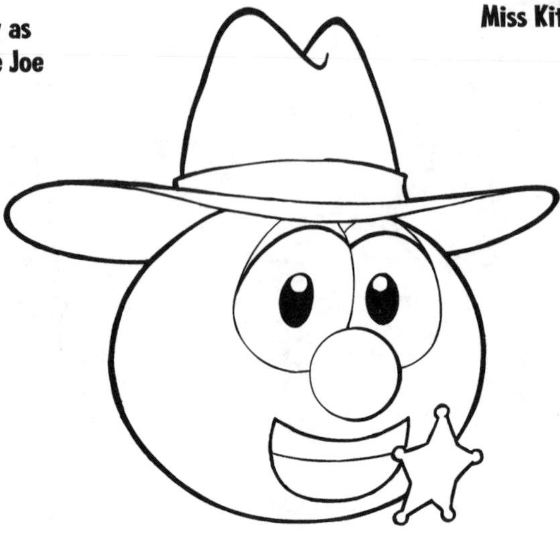

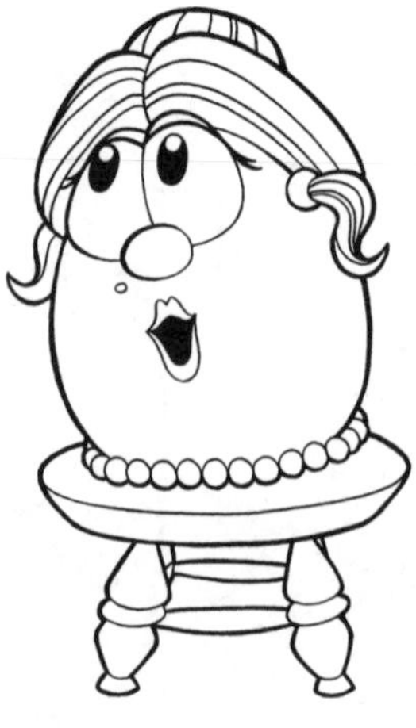

Laura

Mr. Nezzer

Mr. Lunt

Larry as Benny

Bob as Rack

Chocolate Bunny

Junior as Shack

Larry

Bob

Scallion
Salesman

Madame
Blueberry's
Tree House

Madame
Blueberry

"Come near to God and he will come near to you." James 4:8

WELCOME TO VEGGIE LAGOON

Connecting to **Faith** using **Moses** as our example

UNIT ONE:

THE **FAITH** CONNECTION

UNIT VERSE: "Now faith is being sure of what we hope for and certain of what we do not see." Hebrews 11:1

VEGGIE LAGOON

LESSON FOCUS:

1. God has a purpose for everyone: Exodus 2:1-10

2. My faith helps me overcome challenges: Exodus 2:11-25

3. I have faith that God is in control: Exodus 3:1-4:17

4. My faith helps me do what is right: Exodus 5:1-11:10

5. My faith helps me to persevere: Exodus 12:1-13:16

6. My faith helps me to trust in God: Exodus 13:17-14:31

7. My faith helps me to be obedient: Exodus 19:1-20:21

8. I will share my faith with others: Deuteronomy 11:1-21; Hebrews 11:24-28

Faith Connection Goals

The Faith Connection is all about helping kids understand what faith is and how to develop a relationship with God. This will develop some new relationships among the children, and it will strengthen others.

Each Lesson Focus will take kids on a journey toward various ways they can grow closer to our Lord. The Countertop Connections opening sessions with Bob and Larry will introduce the concept of having a relationship with God. It will be supported with the Program Verse from James 4:8: **"Come near to God and he will come near to you."**

When kids are dismissed to the Veggie Lagoon, they will have the chance to actually explore what it means to have faith in God. Kids will be challenged to build a relationship with God, deepen their faith commitment, and put their faith into action in everyday life.

The first lesson in the session explores God's purpose for everyone and helps children to understand that their faith relationship begins with the fact that God made each of them special and unique. Lessons 2–7 will help kids to delve into what a relationship with God means.

Lesson 8, the faith unit, will encourage young people to take what they have learned and share it with others.

Warning: Activities in these lessons may call for foods containing wheat, dairy, or nuts. Please be aware that some children may have medically serious allergic reactions to these foods. Let parents know that their kids will be offered snacks that may include these items, and post a list of ingredients each week for any snacks offered during the lesson. Whenever foods containing wheat, dairy, and nuts are suggested in these lessons, be sure to have safe alternatives on hand.

Welcome to the Veggie Lagoon!

In this unit, kids will travel to the Veggie Lagoon to explore their faith. One of the VeggieTales videos that Bob and Larry will present to the children during the Countertop Connection time is called *God Wants Me to Forgive Them?* In that video, Bob and Larry travel to enjoy a fun parody of an old television favorite, *Gilligan's Island.* The Veggie Lagoon is modeled somewhat after this island.

In this delightful seaside setting, kids will have a great opportunity to explore the faith lessons and develop their relationship with God.

Your Role in the Veggie Lagoon: A Castaway

As a castaway at the Veggie Lagoon, you will act as the host to each group of elementary kids as they rotate through your site every eight weeks.

It is suggested that you appear as a fun, shipwrecked survivor with ragged jeans or pants, a red shirt, and a fisherman's cap. Another alternative is simply to wear tropical attire.

How to Build and Prepare the Veggie Lagoon

OPTION 1:

If you have more time and a permanent space

Create the Veggie Lagoon as a tropical paradise that kids won't soon forget! Feel free to utilize these ideas or add others of your own.

Use the Veggie Lagoon transparency art and the Veggie Lagoon clip art included in the Director's Guide to create a backdrop and a life-sized Bob and Larry. Do this by projecting the Veggie Lagoon backdrop transparency onto a large bedsheet or mural-sized paper, and trace the island scene. Paint or color it, and fasten the background to the wall of your site.

To further create the feel of a lagoon, create a makeshift shelter out of a large refrigerator box, or set up a tent. Anchor tiki torches in large coffee cans or small buckets. You can purchase these at party stores or make them out of broom handles and tissue paper. Add blue glitter or crepe paper to the water area of the mural and/or along the bottom portion of another wall in your room. Add paper fish.

Hang fishing nets filled with the catches of the day from various areas in your room. Create a campfire area by making a small circle with large rocks. In the center, fill it with sand and/or dirt. If you wish to have a "campfire," you might consider making a "fire" by placing a flashlight underneath some red, orange, and yellow tissue paper. Fill a small wading pool with clean sandbox sand and add shells, smooth pieces of driftwood, and other ocean-related objects to it.

Create a wall mural for the Veggie Lagoon using art found on page 54.

The Veggie Lagoon

Fill a suitcase or trunk with assorted clothing, food staples, beaded necklaces, and other items spilling out of it. String a clothesline across part of your site and hang an old T-shirt or cutoff jeans from it. Place extra clothespins on the line for later use.

Create a gathering spot by setting up a table and chairs under a large tarp, by using a large beach blanket to sit on, or by using your tent.

OPTION 2:

*If you are short on time
or do not have a permanent space*

Even if you are short on time or space, you can create a great Veggie Lagoon that children will enjoy for the eight weeks they visit this site.

Use the Veggie Lagoon transparency art and the Veggie Lagoon clip art included in the Director's Guide to create a backdrop and a life-sized Bob and Larry. Do this by projecting the Veggie Lagoon backdrop transparency onto a large bedsheet or mural-sized paper and trace the island scene. Paint or color it, and hang the background on the wall of your site.

Simply fold up the sheet and replace it each week if you are short on time or need to share the space with others.

Use a suitcase or a trunk to easily store seaside items from week to week. Fill it with assorted nets, fish, shells, and a clothesline.

Life Application Memory Tools

The most important part about a lesson that encourages children to build a relationship with God is the life application. It is imperative that we provide kids with the tools they need to carry what they have learned into everyday experiences.

In this curriculum, there are three main ways we will encourage kids to do this:

1. Kids will discover ways to share their faith development with other kids in each session.

2. Kids will learn a catch-phrase that will help them to remember what they should do in real-life experiences.

The catch-phrase we have created is THINK—LINK—ACT. There is a song built on this principle on the *VeggieConnections Music CD* in your kit that will help kids remember this important tool. In addition, each session will focus on various THINK—LINK—ACT activities to help children build meaningful relationships with the Lord that will carry kids through every day of their lives. Here's what it means:

THINK:
Stop and think about what God wants you to do.

LINK:
Link God's Word and what you've learned to your choices.

ACT:
Go and act on what God wants you to do!

Now add some fun hand motions!

THINK: Touch head with fingertip two times.
LINK: Left hand out, right hand out.
 Clasp your hands together, fingers intertwined.
ACT: Release grip and roll hands three times.
 Finish with arms outstretched.

3. Kids will also create a weekly life application memory tool as a reminder of the unit to help them remember the focus of each lesson.

PLANNING TUBE:

At the Veggie Lagoon, kids will create their own lifetime roadmap. Just like a captain needs a map so he doesn't wind up as a castaway on an island, kids, too, need a roadmap for their lives.

This roadmap is like an architectural plan and a timeline. Each child will need a paper towel tube and a photocopy of the bamboo wraparound on page 115. If you can't get enough tubes donated, you can always create them by rolling up card stock and taping it together.

Allow kids to decorate the bamboo wraparound and fill their names in on the appropriate blank that says, "God has a purpose for _____." Then cover the tube by taping or gluing the bottom edge of the wraparound onto the tube, rolling it around the tube, and then gluing the end that has the writing on it in place.

This tube will be utilized every week to hold a different part of each child's plan in his or her faith development process. At the end of the unit, kids can take their tubes home as an excellent reminder of what they learned and their faith development in each session.

Suggested Music for the Veggie Lagoon

Use these songs from the *VeggieConnections Music CD* in your sessions:

1. *THINK—LINK—ACT*
 Music motions found on page 48
2. *God Connection*
3. *You Are the One!*
4. *God Is Bigger*
5. *Stand Up!*

Connecting to **Faith** using **Moses** as our example
The birth of Moses: **Exodus 2:1–10**

PART ONE:

**Plugging In
at the Veggie Lagoon**

Introduction to the site
and lesson focus

LESSON 1:
God has a purpose for everyone.

A. Veggie Connection

Before kids arrive, use the Bob and Larry clip art (found on the *VeggieConnections CD-ROM*) to create a page of five duplicate Bobs and five duplicate Larrys for each child. You will utilize these during this session.

Dressed as the Castaway, greet the kids at the entrance to the Veggie Lagoon. Introduce yourself to them. Invite them to explore the site, look through the trunks, examine shells, and play with the sand for a few moments. If you were not able to set up the more elaborate site option, bring in pictures of tropical islands for the kids to see.

Call kids together and sit under the shelter or in your gathering area. **Welcome to the hot and sunny Veggie Lagoon! I'm the Castaway here at the lagoon, and I've been stranded for . . . I don't even remember how long! At least I have Bob and Larry with me.** Look around for a minutes. **Well, they're usually with me. They're probably out collecting wood for the fire.** As the session goes on, continue to make excuses for where Bob and Larry might be on the island.

Since you're stranded here with me, we're going to explore what it means to have faith in God. Let's take a look at what the word *faith* **means in the** *VeggieConections Bible Dictionary.*

Ask a volunteer to look up today's Connection Word, *faith*, and read it aloud. Ask kids what the word *faith* means to them. Encourage interaction within the small group.

Distribute the clip art of Bob and Larry. Ask kids to cut each of them apart so each has five Bob characters and five Larry characters. Then introduce kids to the concept of faith and encourage relationship building in this game.

One person in each small group begins by stating something he or she has done that he or she doesn't think anyone one else in the group has done (*Visit Europe, get straight A's, do a belly flop, and so on*). Anyone else in the circle who has done it gets a Bob or Larry from that person. Continue going around the circle as many times as time allows.

Afterward, talk about the importance of believing each other in order for the game to be successful. Then say: **Faith is all about believing in God. If we are going to have a good relationship with God, we have to believe in him. God believes in *us,* too! He created each one of us special, and he has a purpose for everyone! Let's find out what that means.**

THE CHILDREN
will arrive with their
VeggieConnections Shepherds
from the opening
Countertop Connections
featuring Bob and Larry.
Play the *VeggieConnections
Music CD* as children enter
the Veggie Lagoon.

**VEGGIE
CONNECTION
NEEDS:**

- *VeggieConnections
  Music CD*
- CD player
- *VeggieConnections
  Bible Dictionary*
- Bob and Larry clip art
  on the *VeggieConnections
  CD-ROM,* five of each
  per child
- Scissors

B. Prayer Connection

Let's talk with God about our faith and discover how God has a purpose for everyone.

Allow a few minutes for kids to share something that happened to them this week—either good or troubling—and then start the prayer by sharing it in this way:

God, I know you have a purpose for everyone. This week . . .

Plugging In to God's Word

Connecting to God's Word in the Bible and understanding how that can help us to have a better relationship with him

A. God Connection: The birth of Moses – Exodus 2:1-10

Say: **Once upon a time, there was a man named Moses who had a lot of faith.** (*Hurray! sign*) **Every time Moses came near to God, God came near to Moses.** (*Hurray! sign*) **That's what our Program Verse tells us to do in James 4:8. Do you remember that verse? Let's say it together!** Allow everyone to say the verse they have been learning during the Countertop Connections time. **A long, long time ago, Moses was born.** (*Hurray! sign*) **Moses' mom was an Israelite who had great faith in God.** (*Hurray! sign*) **But the Israelites were slaves.** (*Oh no! sign*) **There was an Egyptian king, called Pharaoh, who did not believe in God.** (*Boo! Hiss! sign*) **He had many riches and armies to make the Israelites be his slaves.** (*Boo! Hiss! sign*)

The Egyptian slaves had to work hard in the hot sun all day and not get paid for it! (*Oh no! sign*) **Pharaoh did not care that the Israelites had faith in God, because he did not.** (*Boo! Hiss! sign*)

One day, Pharaoh decided that there were too many new baby Israelites being born. (*Oh no!*) **Pharaoh was afraid that the Israelites would soon outnumber the Egyptians and decide not to be his slaves anymore.** (*Wow! sign*) **So Pharaoh made a horrible rule that all the baby Israelite boys must be killed.** (*Boo! Hiss! sign*)

Moses' mom was worried about him, but she had faith in God. She knew that God made him special and for a purpose. (*Hurray! sign*) **Moses' mom had heard many stories of how God helped his people.** (*Hurray! sign*) **So she made a little basket, placed Moses in it, and floated him down the river, hoping that he would be saved for God's purpose! It was really scary!** (*Oh no! sign*) **But even though Moses' mom was afraid to let her baby float down the river, she had faith that God would save him.** (*Wow! sign*) **She told her daughter, Miriam, to walk along the riverbank and see what happened. Even though Miriam was frightened, she had faith that God would watch over her, too.** (*Wow! sign*)

Baby Moses floated near a place where Pharaoh's daughter was wading in the water. (*Oh no! sign*) **When the princess saw the floating basket, she fell in love with this sweet, little baby and rescued him.** (*Wow! sign*) **Miriam bravely ran up to the princess and volunteered to find a woman to nurse the baby and take care of him for her. The princess said okay!** (*Wow! sign*) **So Miriam ran to get her own mother. Moses' mom was able to keep Moses alive and even take care of him!** (*Wow! sign*) **Moses grew up to help the Israelites, just the way that God had planned.** (*Hurray! sign*)

God had a purpose for Moses' mom. God had a purpose for Miriam. God had a purpose for Moses. And God has a purpose for you!

After the story, be sure that kids understand that Moses' mom had to make a very important decision but had faith in God, knowing that he had a special purpose for both her and Moses. Point out that in order to have a strong faith, you must also have a relationship with God.

Ask kids to share a recent decision that they have had to make. Knowing that God has a purpose for them, ask how God may have . . . or could have . . . made any difference in their decision-making process.

If this is the start of the *VeggieConnections* program, introduce the kids to the THINK—LINK—ACT concept. If the group already understands this concept, reinforce it here. Tell kids that every time we have to make a decision, big or small, God wants us to THINK—LINK—ACT.

God has a purpose for everyone. And we can live out that purpose when we stay connected to God through faith. Lead the kids in reading the Unit Memory Verse from Hebrews 11:1 and ask them to repeat it with you.

B. Activity Connection

Choose from the following activities to help kids explore and remember that God wants us to know him and has a purpose for everyone (approximately 10–15 minutes each).

1. High-Powered Game: A Faith Relay With Purpose

Provide each child with five to ten pieces of paper. Use tape to mark a starting and ending point slightly longer than the distance of all the papers lined up together in a row.

Divide kids into even teams. Give each first person in line the same number of sheets and a marker. Each child must get from the starting line to the ending line and back by using each of the papers as steppingstones to get there. Place the stones one in front of the other.

But there is a purposeful catch! Kids must write down something or draw something that describes themselves on each page before they can set the paper down as a stepping-stone! When the child reaches the ending line, he or she turns around and picks up each piece of paper on the way back, reading each description. Team members should cheer each other on by saying: **Have faith!**

This game is not so much a competition as a fun discovery of how God can fulfill each child's purpose.

2. Low-Powered Game: Wrapping Up Your Purpose

Write down a list of various talents, interests, and traits on a piece of paper in an easy-to-cut-out grid. Photocopy and cut them out. Sample characteristics:

· Smile a lot	· Soccer player	· Singer	· Energetic	· Like to cook
· Caring	· Fashionable	· Like math	· Game player	· Like to bicycle
· Kind	· Neat	· Huggable	· Writer	· Organized

Place all the descriptions into a pile and tell the kids to find a partner. Kids begin by sorting through the pile to find three descriptions that describe him or her. Then, using only *one hand*, partners grab a box, place the descriptions into the box, and then work together to wrap it up. This will encourage kids to build relationships with each other, too. After the wrapping paper is on, kids can add ribbon or Veggie clip art. It will be a very fun—and funny—experience!

Allow kids to "show off" their gifts! Point out that these presents are truly a gift from God because God created each one of us special and made us for a special purpose.

Encourage kids to discuss ways God can use them for his purpose in the future!

3. Craft: Made for a Purpose

Each child was created special and unique and made for a wonderful purpose by God. Let kids create a fun, imaginative reflection of themselves, encouraging each child to remember that he or she was created very special in God's eyes.

Provide each child with a plastic bottle and a Styrofoam ball. Allow kids to fill bottles with different colors of sand. Use a funnel to pour the sand in the bottle. Push the Styrofoam ball into the top of the plastic bottle to create a body and head. Glue in place.

Provide a variety of decoration items and allow kids to create unique designs and imaginative reflections of themselves. Chenille wires work well for arms, and forks are a clever way to create hair, but let kids do their own thing!

Afterward, ask kids to explain why each created his or her reflection the way it was done. Celebrate each one and remind kids they were created unique and each one has a special purpose for God. Write "I am special" on a construction-paper triangle and glue it to the front.

HIGH-POWERED GAME NEEDS:

- Full sheets of scrap paper
- Markers

LOW-POWERED GAME NEEDS:

- Boxes (one for every two kids)
- Wrapping paper
- Paper
- Tape
- Glue
- Optional: ribbon; Veggie clip art (on the *VeggieConnections* CD-ROM)

OPTION:

You can use the same boxes over and over as different kids rotate through your site every eight weeks.

CRAFT NEEDS:

- Small soda or water bottles, plastic (one per child)
- Styrofoam balls (one per child)
- Colored sand
- Funnel
- Plastic forks
- Chenille wires
- Colored markers or crayons
- Construction paper
- Scissors
- Glue
- Other decorative items (yarn, beads, toothpicks, felt, sequins, and so on)

PART THREE:

Plugging In to My Life

Life application of the lesson to lead kids to THINK–LINK–ACT and build a relationship with God every day

A. Cucumber Connection

CUCUMBER CONNECTION NEEDS:

- Pickle jar
- Pickles artwork from the *VeggieConnections Shepherd* pages (on the *VeggieConnections CD-ROM*)
- Green construction paper

Before kids arrive, enlarge and copy the pickles from the *VeggieConnections Shepherd* pages on the *VeggieConnections CD-ROM* included in the *VeggieConnections Elementary Curriculum Kit* onto green construction paper. Cut them out and put into a pickle jar.

Have kids sit with their *VeggieConnections Groups*. Let a volunteer draw a pickle from the Pickle Pot. Written on each pickle is an everday dilemma that kids face, related to this lesson. Either the child or a Shepherd reads the pickle aloud. Shepherds then help their group talk through possible solutions, using the THINK—LINK—ACT way of looking at it.

B. Kid Connection: Planning Tube

KID CONNECTION NEEDS:

- Paper towel tube (or card stock)
- Bamboo wraparound on page 115
- Bamboo frame on page 116
- Glue or tape
- Crayons or markers

Kids will create an architectural-like plan as a longtime reminder of what they learned at the Veggie Lagoon. Distribute a paper towel tube or card stock to create a tube. Color and fill in the name on the bamboo wraparound artwork found on page 115. Wrap around the tube and tape or glue in place, taking care that the name is the last portion showing. Explain that this is a combination timeline and planning tool to encourage a lifelong faith relationship with God.

Copy and distribute the bamboo frame from page 116. Encourage kids who are writers to jot down today's Lesson Focus. Then tell kids to create a timeline that indicates, or pictures, various highlights in their lives, from the time they were born, right up to the present. Point out that God had a special purpose for each of the events in their lives!

While at the Veggie Lagoon, kids will learn more about that special purpose and how to build their faith in God. Roll up the page and place it in the planning tube. Keep it from week to week to add new pages.

C. Christ Connection

CHRIST CONNECTION NEEDS:

- Building blocks

OPTION:

If you don't have building blocks, even something like marshmallows and toothpicks will work for this activity. Be creative!

- *VeggieConnections* take-home newspaper (one per child)

Provide each group with a supply of blocks to build a tower. As each child takes a turn, he or she must: a) give a reason why he or she has faith in God, for example something God has done or something known from the Bible and then place a block onto the tower; or b) ask a question relating to faith in God and remove a block from the tower. Blocks can be added back on if someone from the group can help answer a question that takes a block away. Reinforce that faith questions are never bad! They help us to build our tower and our relationship with God!

Afterward, encourage the groups to build something of their choice. Tell kids to think about what they want to build and then work together to build it. After structures are built, say: **Before you began building you decided what your building plan would be. In the same way, before you were born, God loved you and made you for his special purposes. One big part of his plans for you was that you and he would have a close relationship. He wanted you to love him and to come near to him, just as he is always near to you.**

Encourage kids to name one thing they'd like to have faith in God for this week. It may be a tough situation they are facing, a choice they have to make, or a worry that's been on their mind. Or it might simply be wanting to have faith in God for his purpose for them. Then begin your prayer time together.

Dear Lord, we know you have a purpose for each one of us. We want to have faith in you this week for . . .

Thank the kids for visiting the Veggie Lagoon with Bob and Larry and invite them back next week to discover more about their relationship with God!

Distribute the take-home newspaper, **VeggieConnections**.

Connecting to **Faith** using **Moses** as our example
Moses escapes into Midian: **Exodus 2:11-25**

PART ONE:

Plugging In at Veggie Lagoon

Introduction to the site and lesson focus

LESSON 2:
My faith helps me overcome challenges.

A. Veggie Connection

Dressed as the Castaway, welcome the kids to Veggie Lagoon. Ask the kids to have a seat under the shady shelter. Let a volunteer look up today's Connection Word, *challenge*, in the *VeggieConnections Bible Dictionary* and read the definition aloud. Ask a few volunteers to briefly tell about a challenge they have faced.

I've got a challenge for you! Gather over here on the "beach." Have the kids gather around the wading pool or basins with sand. Each *VeggieConnections Group* becomes a team. Be sure each team has access to sand, and give each team a jug and every child a spoon. The goal is for the teams to each fill their jug with sand, using only their spoons. This will present a challenge because the jug opening is small, they will all be trying to dump spoonfuls in at the same time, and time is limited. Give the signal to begin and allow about two minutes for kids to work. When time is up, let teams compare how much sand they managed to get into their jugs. Praise kids for the way they worked together to accomplish their task.

What did you think of this challenge? Allow for responses. **What are some other challenges—some real ones—you have faced?** Kids might share anything from a sports competition to a problem at home or school.

B. Prayer Connection

Have the kids get into a circle with their *VeggieConnections Groups*, taking one plastic spoon with them. Kids may pass the spoon around the circle, letting whoever is holding it have a turn to pray. Encourage the kids to say sentence prayers, thanking God for something that happened during the past week, and asking his help to grow in faith and their connection to God.

THE CHILDREN
will arrive with their *VeggieConnections Shepherds* from the opening Countertop Connections featuring Bob and Larry. Play the *VeggieConnections Music CD* as children enter the Veggie Lagoon.

VEGGIE CONNECTION NEEDS:
- *VeggieConnections Music CD*
- CD player
- *VeggieConnections Bible Dictionary*
- Empty quart jug (one per group)
- Plastic spoons (one per child)
- Pool or basins of sand (if not already at the site)

OPTION:
If you are not able to have sand at your site, play the game using bowls of uncooked rice mixed with paper clips. The task is to sort out the paper clips from the rice using hands while blindfolded.

PART TWO:

Plugging In to God's Word

Connecting to God's Word in the Bible and understanding how that can help us to have a better relationship with him

A. God Connection: Moses Escapes into Midian – Exodus 2:11-25

BEFORE YOU START:

Recruit three *Veggie-Connections Shepherds* or older kids to play the parts of Think, Link, and Act. Play the Reporter yourself. Copy the script below for each actor. Make a sign for each actor to wear labeled "Think," "Link," "Act," and "Reporter." Save the signs for use in *Lesson 5*.

Have the kids sit where all can see the drama. Show the kids where today's Bible story is found, in Exodus 2.

Reporter: The THINK—LINK—ACT undercover agents are on a mission to learn how faith works in the lives of real people to help them overcome challenges. Think, Link, and Act are on location in Egypt, where they have just found the famous man named Moses.

Think: There he is. There's the guy that floated down the river in a basket when he was a baby. Remember? The Egyptian princess found him and saved his life.

Link: Yeah, he's been a pretty lucky guy. He grew up as the son of a king, while all of his people—Israelites—worked as slaves in the hot sun.

Act: Can you see what he is doing?

Think: It looks like he's out watching his people work.

Link: He looks sad, and—wait a minute—kind of angry, too.

Act: It looks like he spotted that Egyptian beating up the Israelite slave. Ouch! That's gotta hurt.

Think: I wonder what Moses thinks about this?

Link: I wonder if he'll link his thoughts to the stories his mother told him when he was just a boy, before he went to live in the palace, about how his people are really God's chosen people—even though they are slaves now.

Act: I wonder how he'll act when he realizes what that Egyptian is doing. Oh, I guess we didn't have to wonder long. Looks like Moses knocked him down—and he's not getting up! I'm not sure that was a good way to handle that challenge. Are you?

Think: He should have stopped to think about what God would have wanted him to do, that's for sure. But God can still forgive him and help him overcome this, just as he helps us overcome our challenges.

Link: I know God can still use Moses, even after something bad like this.

Act: I wonder what happens next.

Reporter: I've got the report on that, Think, Link, and Act. Word got out about what Moses did, and then Pharaoh—that's the Egyptian king—came after him. So Moses had to run away!

Think: He left Egypt—his home?

Reporter: Yes, and he had to stay away for a long, long time.

Link: Was God taking care of him?

Reporter: Yes! Moses found a safe place to live in the desert. He married a shepherd girl and had a son.

Act: Wow, he must have been in the desert a long time.

Reporter: Moses had to wait for the Pharaoh to grow old and die before he could even think about going home to see his family in the palace. He couldn't see his Israelite mother Jochebed, his sister Miriam, or his brother Aaron. Back then, they didn't have phones, e-mail, pagers, or even post offices. Moses could not keep in touch. His challenge was that he just had to wait and wonder.

Think: What was happening back in Egypt all that time?

Reporter: The Israelites had their own challenges. They were still slaves, and even when the Pharaoh died, another one replaced him who made them work just as long and hard.

Link: Had God forgotten them?

Reporter: God never forgets his people. He heard their prayers. He had a plan—and Moses would be part of that plan—when the time was right.

Act: That sounds like something *we* should remember!

Reporter: That's right. God never forgets us. He's with us to help us overcome our challenges. And our relationship with God grows when we let him help us with our challenges.

Thank the actors for helping you. Invite the kids to say the Unit Memory Verse with you, Hebrews 11:1.

Have the kids gather in their *VeggieConnections Groups* to discuss these three questions: **What kinds of challenges are you facing now? How can it help to know that God is with you? What is something you can do to connect with God that will help you have faith in him during your challenge?**

B. Activity Connection

Choose from the following activities to help kids explore and remember that God is with them at all times to help them have faith to overcome their challenges (approximately 10–15 minutes each).

1. High-Powered Game: Picture Challenge

Have kids form six groups. Randomly assign one of the six scenes from the Bible story to each group, but don't reveal the number of the scene:

1. Moses as a prince of Egypt, watching the Israelite slaves working
2. Moses watching an Egyptian hurting an Israelite slave
3. Moses attacking the Egyptian
4. Moses running away from Egypt
5. Moses with his shepherd wife and son
6. Israelites praying to God for freedom from slavery

Provide paper and markers to groups. Explain to groups they need to illustrate the Bible story on their papers. Have *VeggieConnections Shepherds* encourage kids to draw enough detail to make their part of the story recognizable, but not to worry about making great art! Each group needs to draw their picture twice, making the two pictures as similar as possible.

While groups are working on their scenes, tape posterboard or mural paper on two opposite walls, if possible. Number six spaces for kids to place their scenes. You want the numbers to still be visible when the six pictures are taped in place.

After groups are finished with their two scenes, collect the pictures, making two sets of the six scenes. Divide the kids into two groups and give each group one set of pictures. Explain that groups are to look through the pictures and determine the order of the six scenes from the Bible story. Have kids use a Bible, open to Exodus 2, for help.

Once kids think they have the correct order, have six kids each take a picture, run up to the posterboard or mural paper and tape their picture on the correct place. Once a group has all six pictures in place, check the order as listed above. The group who completes the larger picture in the correct order wins the game. Have the other team place their pictures in order and then volunteers from that group briefly tell what is happening in each part of

HIGH-POWERED GAME NEEDS:

- Paper
- Markers
- Tape
- Posterboard or mural paper
- Bibles

the Bible story. Say: **Your groups had a challenge to put the pictures of the Bible story in the correct order. Just as Moses faced a challenge in this story, you will also face challenges in your life. And just as God helped Moses, he will help you handle the challenges you face.**

2. Low-Powered Game: Knot Challenge

Begin by asking the kids to think of some challenges they face, maybe ones they named earlier. **Now think about how those challenges can make you feel sometimes. A really hard challenge can make us feel worried or scared or tied up in knots!**

Have the kids stand in circles with an equal amount of kids in each circle. Assure there is a *VeggieConnections Shepherd* available to help each circle.

Instruct the kids to each reach their right hands out in front of them and at the same time call out a challenge they face in one word, such as, **math**, **piano**, or **sister**. Then they grab the right hand of the person across the circle from them, as if shaking hands.

Then instruct the kids to hold left hands with the person standing next to them. When they grasp hands, they should call out another challenge they face. Each person should now be holding the hands of two different people, and the group will look like a giant knot.

The goal is to try and unwind the group without letting go of any hands, not even for a second. Kids may need to duck under someone's arm, carefully step over someone, or twist around backward, but the group will end up in an unknotted circle.

As each group finds itself back in a circle, they should call out together: **My faith helps me overcome challenges!** Say: **When we remember what happened to Moses and how God helped him through some very tough challenges, our faith can grow as we wait to see how God will help us through our own challenges!**

3. Craft: Sailboat Challenge

CRAFT NEEDS:
- Full sheets of paper to be recycled
- Colorful construction paper
- Markers
- Scissors
- Stickers or Veggie clip art (on the *VeggieConnections CD-ROM*)

Before kids arrive, create a finished sailboat utilizing the directions below.

Distribute a piece of paper to be recycled and a colorful sheet of construction paper to each child. Hold up your finished sailboat so that everyone can see the front and the back without touching it, and challenge kids to try to fold their piece of paper to be recycled to see if they can create the finished image. It will be quite a challenge!

Assure kids they shouldn't feel bad if they can't do it. It's not as easy as it looks! Remind kids that's why we need God to help us through our real challenges in life! Life problems aren't always easy, but we can rely on God to guide us through what to do. If the outcome isn't what we want, remind kids that God can see the *big* picture, and we also must trust in what he has planned for us. That's what having a relationship with God is all about!

To create the sailboat, fold a piece of 8½" x 8½" square construction paper in half, corner to corner, then fold it in half the same way again.

Next, unfold the paper one time so that you have a triangle. Hold the triangle so that the middle point is facing your left. Then fold the bottom half in half so that the edge of the paper fold meets with the paper fold in the center of the first triangle. (See illustration on page 83.)

Turn the boat around so that you can see the back side of the boat and the point of the triangle that was originally facing your left is now on your right. Fold the bottom point of the boat up so that it meets the halfway line of the original triangle. Then take the far left point that is remaining and fold it to the right so it creates a straight line on the left-hand side of the boat. Tuck the tip of the point under the fold that is already there. This will hold the entire boat in place.

Decorate the boat as desired with markers, stickers, and Veggie clip art. Write the words, "God helps me overcome challenges" along the bottom.

Lesson 2 – Sailboat Folding Diagram

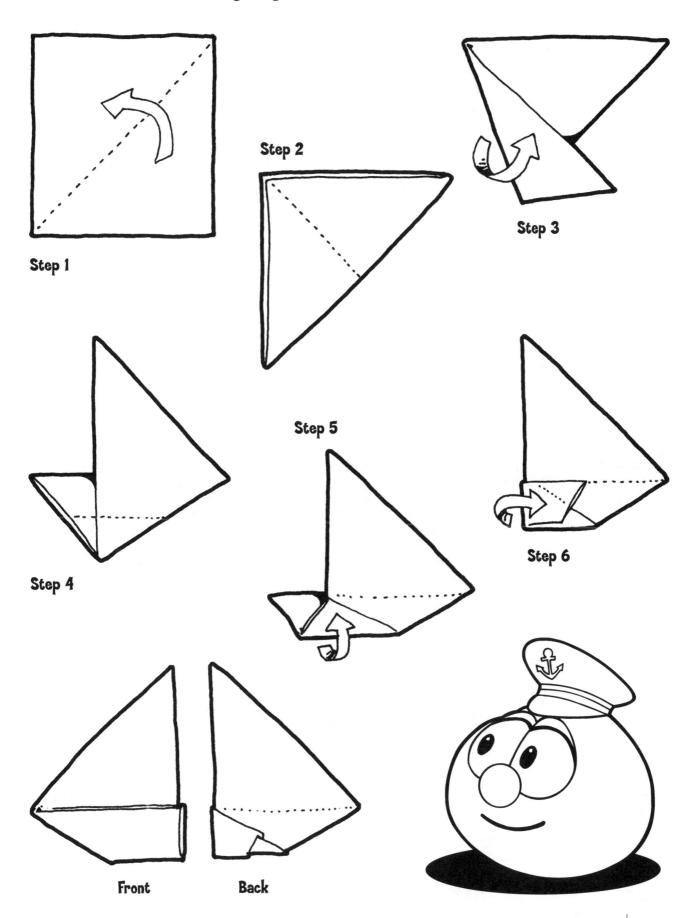

Step 1

Step 2

Step 3

Step 4

Step 5

Step 6

Front

Back

PART THREE:

Plugging In to My Life

Life application of the lesson to lead kids to THINK-LINK-ACT and build a relationship with God every day

A. Cucumber Connection

CUCUMBER CONNECTION NEEDS:

- Pickle jar
- Pickles artwork from the *VeggieConnections Shepherd* pages (on the *VeggieConnections CD-ROM*)
- Green construction paper

Before kids arrive, enlarge and copy the pickles from the *VeggieConnections Shepherd* pages on the *VeggieConnections CD-ROM* included in the *VeggieConnections Elementary Curriculum Kit* onto green construction paper. Cut them out and put them in a pickle jar.

Have the kids sit with their *VeggieConnections Groups*. Let a volunteer draw a pickle from the Pickle Pot. Written on each pickle is an everyday dilemma that kids face, related to this lesson. Either the child or a Shepherd reads the pickle aloud. Shepherds then help their group talk through possible solutions, using the THINK—LINK—ACT way of looking at it.

Jessica's friends are going to a movie on Friday night. Jessica wants to go, too, but it's a movie her parents won't allow her to see. Her friends think she should go anyway. What should Jessica do?	Chelsea's little brother, Kevin, wants to tag along wherever she goes. Her mom tells her to include her brother, but Kevin messes up everything. How can she keep her frustration from pouring out on her little brother?	Jason can't do math. He thinks it's confusing and that the numbers just don't connect. No one seems to understand. How can he "link" his problem to the right "acts"?

B. Kid Connection: Planning Tube

KID CONNECTION NEEDS:

- Index cards (one per child)
- Locking plastic snack bags (one per child)
- Plastic spoons
- Sand
- Optional: packing tape
- Planning Tubes (made in *Lesson 1*)

In *VeggieConnections Groups*, have kids pick one challenge that they face. Have groups plan how to act out the challenge, showing how they would handle it using the THINK—LINK—ACT approach. Allow groups to act out their challenges for the others.

Having faith in God is a very important thing, especially as we face challenges. What would you like to say to God about some of the challenges you face? Invite kids to brainstorm some ideas. After discussing, distribute index cards and have each child write a note to God on his or her card.

Give each child a locking plastic snack bag and a plastic spoon. Help kids place their index cards in the bag, then spoon in some sand and seal. You may wish to tape bags closed with packing tape to ensure they cannot be opened. Say: **We started out today working on a challenge, putting some of this sand into a jug. That's not normally a challenge we face, but this sand can remind us of that challenge and of how God can help us with our challenges. We need to keep our faith in him, and ask for his help.**

Help kids roll up their bags and put them in their planning tubes. Collect the tubes for next week.

C. Christ Connection

CHRIST CONNECTION NEEDS:

- *VeggieConnections* take-home newspaper (one per child)

Lead the kids in singing the *THINK—LINK—ACT* song. Then lead everyone in saying the Unit Memory Verse, Hebrews 11:1.

Have the *VeggieConnections Shepherds* ask their group members about special prayer requests, challenges they will face before they come together again, and other needs. Then encourage the kids to pray for one another about the challenges they just discussed. The Shepherds may close the prayer time by praying for any child who wasn't mentioned and by thanking God for the great stories of challenges he gave us in the Bible.

When finished, encourage the kids to pray for these friends during the week. Distribute the take-home newspaper, **VeggieConnections**.

Connecting to **Faith** using **Moses** as our example
God talks to Moses from a burning bush:
Exodus 3:1–4:17

control

PART ONE:

Plugging In at Veggie Lagoon

Introduction to the site and lesson focus

LESSON 3:
I have faith that God is in control.

A. Veggie Connection

Dressed as the Castaway, welcome the children to the Veggie Lagoon, and hand each one a wrapped candy. Tell the kids they are not to eat it yet, and invite them to be seated around the beach.

Ask for a volunteer to look up today's Connection Word, *control*, in the *Veggie-Connections Bible Dictionary* and read the definition. **What parts of your day do you have control over?** *(What I wear, what I play at recess or after school, how hard I practice my sport/instrument.)* **What parts of your day do you have no control over?** *(What subjects I take in school, what I eat for supper, when I have to go to bed.)*

As a Castaway of this island, I have control over the food. I've given each of you Bob and Larry's favorite Veggie Lagoon candy, and now you can control what to do with it. You can eat it, you can give it away, or you can trade it for something else! Bring out the paper grocery bag of fruit candy rolls. **You can trade your candy for what ever is in this bag. You have to choose if you want to give up control of your candy for something else.**

Open the empty plastic bag and let kids who have chosen to give you control of their candy to stand and drop their candy in the bag. They should remain standing. After all the kids have made their choice, open the large bag and give each of the standing child a fruit candy roll.

For kids who remained sitting, ask if they are now willing to hand over control of their candy. Hand out the candy rolls to the rest of the group. Allow the kids to eat their "island fruit."

As they eat, explain: **This was a little experiment about control. It's probably pretty easy to give up control of candy. But we face bigger things in our lives. Today we're going to look at how we can trust God and give him control of our daily lives. Sometimes God asks us to trust him with something we can't see—like you couldn't see what was in my bag. But when we give control to God by following his ways, our lives are much better!**

THE CHILDREN
will arrive with their
VeggieConnections Shepherds
from the opening
Countertop Connections
featuring Bob and Larry.
Play the *VeggieConnections
Music CD* as children enter
the Veggie Lagoon.

**VEGGIE
CONNECTION
NEEDS:**

- *VeggieConnections Music CD*
- CD player
- *VeggieConnections Bible Dictionary*
- Wrapped candy (one per child)
- Fruit candy rolls (one per child) hidden in a paper grocery bag
- Paper grocery bag

B. Prayer Connection

Take time for kids to connect to one another and to God by briefly discussing their week. Gathered in *VeggieConnections Groups*, let the kids tell of anything they've prayed about that they saw an answer to, especially if it's something their small group has prayed about in the last two lessons. Then take time to thank God for answered prayers and ask for his help in challenges that continue.

PART TWO:

Plugging In to God's Word

Connecting to God's Word in the Bible and understanding how that can help us to have a better relationship with him

A. God Connection: God talks to Moses from a burning bush – Exodus 3:1–4:17

GOD CONNECTION NEEDS:

- Bible
- Medium-sized cardboard box
- Utility knife
- Tissue paper in red, orange, and yellow
- Green construction paper
- Personal size battery-operated fan
- Posterboard, to prepare signs (one per *Veggie-Connections Group*)
- Markers
- Bedsheet, or small tarp
- Tape
- Long stick, for a walking stick
- Bible-time cloak (cape or robe or draped cloth)
- Glue

BEFORE YOU START:

Place a medium (18"–24" sides) cardboard box on the floor. If the box has writing or colors on it, fold it inside out, so the brown sides face out. Lift up the top flaps and temporarily tape them together. Using a utility knife, cut branchlike shapes down three sides of the box, extending about 2/3 the way down each side. They need to be thick enough to stand upright on their own. You should have two to three branches per box side. Cut out leaf shapes using the green construction paper and glue to the branches. Then tear strips of red, orange, and yellow tissue paper. Tape some smaller strips to the branches, and tape larger strips to the inside of the box. Place a personal fan inside the box, facing it toward the front of the box. You could use stacked paperback books to adjust the angle. Turn the fan on and add more colored tissue paper strips to give the desired fire effect. Place the prepared box where you will be using it and cover it with the bedsheet or tarp. You will also need to prepare a sign for each *VeggieConnections Group* that reads: "Excuses, excuses!"

OPTION:

For a more realistic-looking burning bush, use a real or fake potted plant that has branches. Tape red, orange, and yellow strips of tissue paper to the branches and place the personal fan near the bottom of the plant, pointing up to make the tissue "flames" move like real flames.

While kids are in their *VeggieConnections Groups* praying, set the burning bush prop at the front of the story area, and cover it with the sheet to hide it for now.

Have groups sit in a semicircle around you. Give each *VeggieConnections Shepherd* one of the "Excuses, excuses!" signs. Say: **I want you to think about a time you've been told to do something, but you made excuses for why you didn't want to do it.** Have Shepherds encourage kids to share. When a child shares, have the Shepherd hold up the sign and lead their group in saying: **Excuses, excuses!** If kids are having a hard time thinking of a situation, have the Shepherd share one and everyone respond as above. Allow a few kids in each group to share. Then say: **Some of you shared with your group excuses you've given. Why do you think we make excuses?** Allow responses. **Today we're going to see that we're not the only ones who make excuses. I will tell you the Bible story two times. The first time, you will listen very carefully. Then the second time, I'll give you instructions for something fun you can do. Whenever you hear Moses make an excuse in our story today, I want all groups to stand up and call out, "Excuses, excuses!"**

Open your Bible to Exodus 3. **Who remembers where we left Moses last week?** (*He had run away from Egypt and was living in the desert. He married into a shepherding family.*) While kids are responding, put on the cloak and pick up the walking stick. Uncover the "burning bush" and turn on the fan. As you tell the following story, walk around the bush and show dramatic effect where indicated. Begin by standing a good distance from the bush.

Moses was in the desert. He had been there for many years. He still loved God, but he wasn't quite sure what God was doing in his life. After all, Moses had been raised as a prince of Egypt but was an Israelite by birth—one of God's chosen people. Yet here he was, taking care of sheep a long way from Egypt.

One day, Moses was on the far side of the desert, near what was called the mountain of God—Mt. Horeb. Moses saw the strangest thing. Point to the "burning bush" prop. **A bush on fire! Moses walked up to it and saw an even stranger thing—it wasn't burning up! It just stayed on fire! When Moses walked closer, a voice came out of the bush! The voice told Moses that he was standing on holy ground. The fire in the bush meant that God was right there!**

Moses hid his face! He knew God was awesome and powerful. Moses was amazed. And even more amazing was that God had something to say to Moses.

God told Moses that he was still in control. Even though the Israelites were still slaves, even though Moses was stuck in the desert, God was still in control. In fact, God laid out a plan for Moses to go to the Egyptian king, called Pharaoh, to free God's people. And you know how Moses responded? He said to God, "Who am I, that I should go to Pharaoh and bring the Israelites out of Egypt?" Prompt Shepherds to have kids stand and say: **Excuses, excuses!**

Then God said to Moses, "I will be with you." God told Moses the Israelite people would come to this mountain they were on, and that the people would all worship God. Sounds like God was in control, doesn't it? But Moses worried about what he would say to the Israelite people about God's message. Have a Shepherd read Exodus 3:13–14 aloud. Prompt Shepherds to have kids stand and say: **Excuses, excuses!**

The problem Moses had was that he forgot God was in control. He thought the people would be trusting in him—not God. If God could make a bush burn without burning up, he could surely free his people from slavery in Egypt.

Then God told Moses how he would go the older leaders of the Israelite people and they would go with Moses before Pharaoh and demand to be freed to worship God in the desert. God also told Moses that Pharaoh would refuse until God sent wonders upon them, and the Israelites would even take the Egyptian's stuff when they left. Really sounds like God was in control, right?

But then Moses said, "What if they do not believe me or listen to me?" Prompt Shepherds to have kids stand and say: **Excuses, excuses!**

So God showed Moses how he was in control. Hold up the stick. **God told Moses to throw his walking stick down on the ground. So Moses did.** Throw the stick down. **He could hardly believe it—the stick turned into a live snake!** Jump back as if scared. **But all Moses had to do was reach down and grab the snake by the tail, and it turned back into a stick again.** Pick up the stick.

Then God told Moses to put his hand inside his cloak. Put your hand in your cloak. **When he took it out again, it was horribly pale and crusty from a skin disease called leprosy.** Look at your hand in disgust and fear. **But when Moses put his hand back in his cloak, it was healed.** Put your hand back in and then out of your cloak; look relieved and happy. **God told Moses to perform these miracles if the Israelite elders didn't believe that he was sent by God.**

Then God told Moses that if the people still didn't believe him, he would make Moses able to turn the water of the Nile River into blood. Do you think God is still in control?

But Moses told God he wasn't a good speaker. Prompt Shepherds to have kids stand and say: **Excuses, excuses! God told Moses he would help him speak. But Moses was still having trouble trusting that God was in control. Then Moses told God to send someone else.** Prompt Shepherds to have kids stand and say: **Excuses, excuses!**

Finally, God told Moses he would send his brother Aaron to go with him. Aaron would do the speaking for Moses. So Moses obeyed God and decided to trust that God was in complete control.

Have kids discuss the following question in their *VeggieConnections Groups*:
What things in our lives can we trust that God is in control of? Allow responses.

B. Activity Connection

Choose from the following activities to help kids explore and remember that God is in control (approximately 10–15 minutes each).

1. High-Powered Game: Out of Control Relay

BEFORE YOU START:

You'll need pairs of relay teams for this game. It is best if each team is no more than eight kids. You will want to have 2, 4, 6, or 8 teams. Prepare a set of 8 cards for each team. On 2 cards, write "Out of Control!" and on 1 card write, "God's in Control!" Shuffle each 8 card set, but make sure the "God's in Control!" card is near the bottom of the stack for the first round of the game. Tape a masking tape starting line and a finish line. At the finish line, put the cards facedown lined up with each relay team.

HIGH-POWERED GAME NEEDS:

- Prepared index cards (one per child)
- Masking tape

Divide the kids into two relay teams, with up to eight kids on each team. Team members will walk backward to the finish line, pick up a card, and return to their team, again walking backward, and tag the next player. If a player picks up a card that has "Out of Control!" on it, that player must join the other team. Explain the object is for each team to end the game with their same team members. Also explain there is one "God's in Control!" card per team, and that if a player picks up that card, his or her team immediately should reform to their original team, winning the game.

Play the game several times, reshuffling the cards each time. These rounds may end early because the "God's in Control!" card may come earlier in the game. After a few rounds, talk about how the game was like kids trying to control things in their lives. Be sure to point out how kids couldn't win the game without the "God's in Control!" card, and how that is true about their lives as well.

2. Low-Powered Game: Control the Ball

BEFORE YOU START:

Tape off four large squares in four sections of the site, each large enough for about a third of your class to fit inside. With a marker, label the squares (writing on the tape): "Start," "Home," "School," "Hobbies." Place all the balls in the Start square. You will need enough balls for about a third of your class.

LOW-POWERED GAME NEEDS:

- Numerous small balls (such as table tennis or golf balls)
- Numerous medium-sized balls (such as softballs or tennis balls)
- Numerous large balls (such as basketballs, volleyballs, soccer balls)
- Masking tape
- Marker

Explain to the kids that they have several areas of life where they need to trust that God is in control. Three of those are home, school, and hobbies. Point out the squares with these areas labeled.

Divide the kids into three equal groups, and have each group stand in one square, either School, Home, or Start. The Hobbies square is empty for now. Explain that at your signal, the kids in the Start square will get on their hands and knees and use their noses or heads to push the balls (one ball per child) over to the Home square. They must carefully control their ball or it will get away from them and end up taking longer. As soon as they get their ball to stay in the Home square, they jump up and call out: **I give God control at home!**

As soon as a child calls that, another child waiting in the Home square takes over the ball, pushing it in the same manner over to the School square. As they arrive, they jump up and call out: **I give God control at school!**

The kids in the School square then take over the balls as they arrive, pushing them to the Hobbies square. Upon arrival, they call out: **I give God control of my hobbies!** Or they may name a specific hobby, such as karate or piano.

See how quickly and efficiently the kids can control all the balls and move them through the squares. If time permits, play again, letting the kids each choose a different size ball to try pushing. Ask: **Were some balls easier to control than others? Which ones? Did any of you totally lose control of your ball, so that it was hard to get back to where you were supposed to be? That is the way our lives are, if we allow things to get way out of control, it's harder than ever to allow God to help us.**

3. Craft: Burning Bush Candles

Say: **In our Bible story, God appeared to Moses in the burning bush. Let's make our own burning bush candles to remind us that God was in control with his plan for Moses and his people and that we can trust God with control of our lives.**

Provide each child a baby food jar and a cotton ball. Show kids how to pour a small amount of white glue on a cotton ball and smear a thin layer of glue on the outside of their jars. Then have kids place red, orange, and yellow pieces of tissue paper onto their jars in a random pattern, creating a "fire" look. Have kids completely cover the outside of the jar, but tear any loose paper away from the top or inside of the jar. This creates the burning bush.

Give each child a "God is in control" strip of paper to glue to the outside of their jar. Provide a tea light candle for kids to put inside their jars.

CRAFT NEEDS:

- Baby food jars (empty and clean), (one per child)
- Small, torn pieces of orange, red, and yellow tissue paper
- White glue
- Cotton balls
- Strips of white paper with "God is in control" written on them
- Small tea light candles (one per child)

PART THREE:

Plugging In to My Life

Life application of the lesson to lead kids to THINK-LINK-ACT and build a relationship with God every day

A. Cucumber Connection

Before kids arrive, enlarge and copy the pickles from the *VeggieConnections Shepherd* pages on the *VeggieConnections CD-ROM* included in the *VeggieConnections Elementary Curriculum Kit* onto green construction paper. Cut them out and put them in a pickle jar.

Have the kids sit with their *VeggieConnections Groups*. Let a volunteer draw a pickle from the Pickle Pot. Written on each pickle is an everyday dilemma that kids face, related to this lesson. Either the child or a *VeggieConnections Shepherd* reads the pickle aloud. Shepherds then help their group talk through possible solutions, using the THINK—LINK—ACT way of looking at it.

CUCUMBER CONNECTION NEEDS:

- Pickle jar
- Pickles artwork from the *VeggieConnections Shepherd* pages (on the *VeggieConnections CD-ROM*)
- Green construction paper

Your brother told a lie to your parents about you that got you into a lot of trouble. You want to get even with him. What should you do?	Felicity believes in Jesus and she "thinks" she wants to be his friend. But she's not very interested in learning how to be like him or obey what the Bible teaches. What should Felicity do?	Sarah and Alyssa are good friends, but Sarah is always bossing Alyssa around. Alyssa is tired of it. How can Alyssa "think" of a way to "link" her desire for God to be in control with kind "actions" toward Sarah?

B. Kid Connection: Planning Tube

KID CONNECTION NEEDS:

- Strips of red, orange, and yellow tissue paper
- Transparent tape
- Bamboo frame on page 116 (one per child)
- Red and orange crayons or markers
- Planning tubes (made in *Lesson 1*)

God appeared to Moses in a burning bush that didn't burn up. But Moses still had a hard time trusting that God was in control. Probably none of us will ever see a miracle like Moses did, but we can remember Moses' story and trust that God is in control. When we see God working in our lives, we can trust him with control, just as Moses did.

Distribute the planning tubes to the children, ensuring each child gets his or her tube. Provide copies of the bamboo frame to kids, and make tissue paper strips, tape, and crayons, or markers available to everyone.

Today we are going to write in bright firelike colors on our Bamboo Frames and tape them closed with a strip of bright tissue paper. This will help us remember the burning bush and that we know that God is in control, and we can trust him with what is happening in our lives.

Invite kids to think of an area where they need to see that God is in control in their own lives. Have the kids write a prayer on their bamboo frames asking God to take control. Help the kids roll up their prayers, wrap a tissue paper strip around them, and tape them shut. Have kids put their prayers in their planning tubes and collect the tubes for use next week.

C. Christ Connection

Sing the *THINK—LINK—ACT* song, using the motions below. Then lead the kids in saying the Unit Memory Verse, Hebrews 11:1.

Invite the kids to get into their *VeggieConnections Groups* again. Have *VeggieConnections Shepherds* begin a prayer time by saying: **Dear Lord, we want to have faith in you even when we don't think things are in control. Help us to have faith this week by . . .** Kids may choose to finish the sentence with their own prayer. The Shepherd should close the group in prayer, praying for each child by name.

Distribute the take-home newspaper, **VeggieConnections**.

THINK:
Stop and think about what God wants you to do.

LINK:
Link God's Word and what you've learned to your choices.

ACT:
Go and act on what God wants you to do!

Now add some fun hand motions!

THINK: Touch head with fingertip two times.

LINK: Left hand out, right hand out.
Clasp your hands together, fingers intertwined.

ACT: Release grip and roll hands three times.
Finish with arms outstretched.

Connection Word:

plague

PART ONE:

Plugging In at Veggie Lagoon

Introduction to the site and lesson focus

LESSON 4:

My faith helps me do what is right.

A. Veggie Connection

BEFORE YOU START:
Spread out the bugs and frogs all over Veggie Lagoon as if an infestation happened overnight.

Dressed as the Castaway, look upset as you welcome the kids at the entrance to Veggie Lagoon. Explain that a strong ocean wind came through last night and brought "thousands" of bugs to the island and that a huge ocean tide brought "hundreds" of frogs. **I don't know how I'm ever going to get our beautiful lagoon in shape for our games and activities today! I could really use your help. Will you help me? Great! But we're in a hurry so we won't miss any fun today—and there's one problem.**

Explain that the bugs and frogs might be "poisonous"—or they might not; you haven't had time to examine them. So just to be safe, the kids have to pick them up in this manner only: With the paper lunch bag open, bend down and use the craft stick to push one bug or frog at a time into the bag. The kids may not use their hands. But promise the kids that for their hard work, the top three collectors will receive a prize. Stress that no matter what, they may not pick up the critters in any other way. Also emphasize that you're in a hurry, and the biggest collectors get that wonderful prize.

Give each kid a paper bag and a craft stick. Send them off to scour the lagoon for bugs and frogs, reminding them about the reward. Pretend you are timing the kids, allowing several minutes for them to collect most of the bugs and frogs.

Then ask the kids to gather together and be seated. Thank them for picking up the critters from the lagoon.

Then stop and look closely at the kids. Ask: **Did you all *really* follow my instructions? I told you the right way to handle these critters. Did any of you feel like doing it a different way?** Pause for a show of hands. **Raise your hand if you followed my instructions exactly and you didn't cheat at all.** Pause for a show of hands. **Great work! I have a prize for you!** Give each child with a raised hand a sticker. **You know what? It's hard to do what's right when the things you're supposed to do are really hard—or really strange, like this. It doesn't really matter who collected the most bugs; you all helped, and that's what counts. So I'm going to give you all a sticker, even those of you who gave in to not wanting to do**

THE CHILDREN
will arrive with their *VeggieConnections Shepherds* from the opening Countertop Connections featuring Bob and Larry. Play the *VeggieConnections Music CD* as children enter the Veggie Lagoon.

VEGGIE CONNECTION NEEDS:

- *VeggieConnections Music CD*
- CD player
- Dozens of plastic bugs and frogs (to be used throughout the lesson)
- Paper lunch bags (one per child)
- Craft sticks (one per child)
- Stickers (one per child)
- *VeggieConnections Bible Dictionary*

the right thing. As you give stickers to all the rest of the kids, let volunteers tell why it was easy or hard to so the right thing and what made them want to break the rules (*Wanting the prize, feeling lazy, not paying attention.*)

Our Bible story is about some really strange things that happened, along with some really hard instructions for the people to follow. And not only are having all these bugs and frogs strange, they also have something to do with today's Connection Word. Have a child find *plague* in the *VeggieConnections Bible Dictionary* and read the definition. Explain that bugs and frogs were two plagues in the Bible story, and the kids should be on the look-out for more.

B. Prayer Connection

Have the kids gather with their *VeggieConnections Groups*. Let the kids briefly share what's been going on in their lives during the week, especially any hard things they've had to do. Let the kids pray for one another, asking God to make each other strong to do what's right and thanking him for his love, even when they do what's wrong.

PART TWO:

Plugging In to God's Word

Connecting to God's Word in the Bible and understanding how that can help us to have a better relationship with him

A. God Connection: Moses returns to Egypt – Exodus 5:1–11:10

BEFORE YOU START:

Ask three Shepherds or older kids to play the parts of Moses, Aaron, and Pharaoh, and make copies of the skit for them. If you want to choose younger students, pair them with a reader and let the reader read the lines while prompting the younger students to act them out. Plan on playing the role of the reporter yourself. Set out containers with frogs in one, bugs in another, and paper balls in a third.

Invite the kids to sit where all can see the drama. Show the kids in a Bible where today's story is found, in the book of Exodus.

GOD CONNECTION NEEDS:

- Bible
- Stick or cane, one each for Moses and Aaron.
- Toy snake
- Bible-time clothes for Moses and Aaron to wear
- Crown for Pharaoh to wear
- Plastic frogs and bugs
- Wadded up paper balls
- Three large bowls or containers

Reporter: Today we're watching eighty-year-old Moses and his older brother Aaron as they get ready to go to Pharaoh, the king of Egypt. God had told Moses to tell Pharaoh that he needs to let the Israelite slaves go. No more free labor, no more big bricks, unless he gets his own people to do it. Let's watch and see how it goes.

Moses: You know the situation, don't you, Aaron?

Aaron: The Israelite leaders are very angry with us already. Ever since we told Pharaoh to let the Israelites go, he got so mad he made the Israelites work even harder.

Moses: Let me get your staff. (*Moses picks up a stick or cane and hands it to Aaron, who should also have the toy snake hidden in his hand or in a pocket. They walk a short distance as if approaching the Pharaoh's palace.*) Well, we're here. Go on in and tell the king what we came for.

Aaron: Oh, no. I may have to do the talking, but we're going in together, just as God told us. We're going to do the right thing.

(*Aaron pretends to knock on a door and then go in. Moses and Aaron approach Pharaoh, who is sitting on a chair like a throne.*)

Pharaoh: So you're back? There's nothing you can do to convince me to let the Israelites go. Nope. Not gonna do it.

(Aaron pretends to throw his stick down but actually throws the snake. Have the actor try to "hide" the stick so that it appears the stick has turned into the snake.)

Pharaoh: Hey, your snake just ate my wise guys' snakes. What's up with that?

Aaron: *(Reach down to pick up the snake. Hide the snake and hold up the stick.)* Well, Pharaoh, God is just trying to show you that you should do the right thing and obey God. He wants you to let our people go.

Pharaoh: Nope, not gonna do it. Get out of my sight! *(Moses and Aaron leave.)*

Reporter: The next day, God told Moses to go down to the Nile River to where Pharaoh was taking his bath.

Moses: *(To Aaron as they approach Pharaoh, who is sitting on the floor pretending to scrub himself.)* I am NOT going to talk to Pharaoh while he's in the tub!

Aaron: Don't worry. He's in the Nile River and has lots of servants there. Just keep faith in God, and we'll be able to do what is right. *(They walk up to Pharaoh.)*

Pharaoh: So you're back? There's nothing you can do to convince me to let the Israelites go. Nope. Not gonna do it.

(Moses strikes the water with his staff. Pharaoh looks around disgusted and jumps up out of the "water.")

Pharaoh: Ew! That's gross! You turned the water into blood! My beautiful Nile River!

Aaron: Well, Pharaoh, this is just another way God is trying to show you that you should do the right thing and obey God. He wants you to let our people go.

Pharaoh: Nope. Not gonna do it. Get out of my sight! *(They leave.)*

Reporter: Moses and Aaron kept going back to Pharaoh as the days went by. *(Moses and Aaron walk back to Pharaoh, who sits on his chair "throne" again.)*

Aaron: Let God's people go!

Pharaoh: Nope. Not gonna do it.

Reporter: This time God sent a plague of frogs. *(Moses takes a handful of frogs from the nearby container and tosses them in the air.)*

Aaron: Let God's people go!

Pharaoh: Nope. Not gonna do it.

Reporter: Then God sent a plague of gnats. *(Aaron takes a handful of bugs from the container and tosses them in the air.)*

Aaron: Let God's people go!

Pharaoh: Nope. Not gonna do it.

Reporter: This time God sent a plague of flies. *(Moses takes another handful of bugs and tosses them into the air.)*

Aaron: Let God's people go!

Pharaoh: Nope. Not gonna do it.

Reporter: Then God sent big, oozing sores—first to the animals and then to the people. *(Pharaoh moans and scratches himself.)*

Aaron: Let God's people go!

Pharaoh: Nope. Not gonna do it.

Reporter: For the next plague, God sent a huge hailstorm! *(Moses and Aaron both pick up paper balls from the container and throw them at Pharaoh.)*

Aaron: Let God's people go!

Pharaoh: Nope. Not gonna do it.

Reporter: For the next plague, God sent a swarm of hungry locusts! *(Moses takes a handful of bugs from the container and tosses them in the air.)*

Aaron: Let God's people go!

Pharaoh: Nope. Not gonna do it.

Reporter: For the next plague, God made the land totally dark for three days. *(Turn off the room lights for a few seconds. Pharaoh makes sounds and motions as if he can't see.)*

Aaron: Let God's people go!

Pharaoh: Nope. Not gonna do it.

Reporter: For the last plague, God was fed up with Pharaoh and his heartless people because they refused to do the right thing. He made all the firstborn animals and sons of every Egyptian family die. But the sons of the Israelites were all safe. *(Pharaoh covers his face with his hands and cries.)*

Pharaoh: *(Looks up, mad.)* Go! Get out of here! Take all your Israelite people and ever thing you own! For that matter, take everything we Egyptians own, too! Just leave us!

Reporter: It was very hard for Moses and Aaron to keep doing the right thing, because each plague made Pharaoh angrier and so he made the Israelites work harder. But the two brothers had faith that God was going to see them through if they continued to listen to him and do the right thing.

Thank the actors. Then have *VeggieConnections Shepherds* discuss these questions: **What did Moses and Aaron keep doing that was the right thing to do? What are some times that you've had to face something hard—and how did you do what was right?** Let volunteers share.

THINK:
Stop and think about what God wants you to do.

LINK:
Link God's Word and what you've learned to your choices.

ACT:
Go and act on what God wants you to do!

Now add some fun hand motions!

THINK: Touch head with fingertip two times.

LINK: Left hand out, right hand out. Clasp your hands together, fingers intertwined.

ACT: Release grip and roll hands three times. Finish with arms outstretched.

B. Activity Connection

Choose from the following activities to help kids explore and remember that their relationship with God helps them do what's right (approximately 10–15 minutes each).

1. High-Powered Game: Pharoah, Will You Let My People Go?

Have all the kids stand at one end of the playing area. One child begins as "Pharaoh" and stands at the opposite end. The group of kids say: **Pharoah, Pharaoh, will you let my people go?** The child playing Pharaoh yells: **No!** All the kids take a giant step or two forward. The kids repeat their question, Pharaoh repeats his answer, the kids take another step forward. Play in this way until the kids draw near Pharaoh. At any point in the game, Pharaoh may instead answer the question: **Yes, you may go!** and immediately chases the kids back to their starting line. Whoever Pharaoh tags first becomes the next Pharaoh, and the game starts again.

2. Low-Powered Game: Avoid the Plagues!

Divide the kids into two teams and have each team blindfold one player. This person is to be guided by another who walks behind them and calls out which way to move so the blindfolded player avoids stepping on the plagues.

Have the blindfolded team members and their guides negotiate the course. Players must reach the finish line and return to the start before giving the blindfold to the next team member. The next pair then goes out on the course. If teams are uneven, one child can repeat one of the two game roles. Continue until each person has negotiated the course. The first team to finish wins.

To make the game more difficult, have *VeggieConnections Shepherds* watch as kids negotiate the course and add one point for every plague players step on. The team with lowest score wins, regardless of who finishes first.

In this game, you tried to avoid the plagues. In the actual Bible event, Pharaoh could have avoided the plagues by choosing to do right and obey God. When we face hard times in our lives, let's all remember to have faith in God and know that he will help us get through tough times.

3. Craft: THiNK–LiNK–ACT Pyramid

Encourage kids to create their own Egyptian pyramid, to display the THINK—LINK—ACT phrase to help them to remember to do what's right.

Provide each child with a craft foam pattern of an equilateral triangle 5 inches on each side. Tell kids to trace three additional patterns onto craft foam. Cut them out. Use dark markers to write the words THINK, LINK, ACT, one on each side of the triangle. Or write each of the words on a different colored, small rectangle piece of craft foam that is then glued onto each triangle. Then ask each child to sign each triangle, under the words THINK, LINK, ACT, indicating their willingness to do what's right every day!

Last, punch a hole in each corner of the triangles. Then take a small piece of yarn and tie each of the bottom corners of the triangles together. Then bring each of the triangles upward to create the pyramid. Use one more piece of yarn and tie each of the tops of the triangles together and create a looped tie so that the pyramid can hang.

Say: **Hang your pyramid in a spot at home to remind you to THINK—LINK—ACT so that you can remember to do what God wants you to do.**

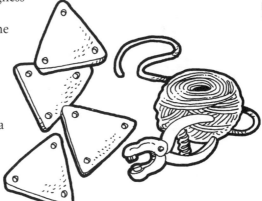

LOW-POWERED GAME NEEDS:

- Crumpled paper balls
- Plastic frogs and bugs
- Blindfolds
- Masking tape

BEFORE YOU START:

Tape a starting line and a finish line and tape off game borders on both sides between the start/finish lines. In your playing area, evenly scatter crumpled paper balls, plastic frogs, and bugs.

CRAFT NEEDS:

- Craft foam
- Scissors
- Equilateral triangle pattern
- Hole punch
- Markers
- String or yarn

PART THREE:

Plugging In to My Life

Life application of the lesson to lead kids to THINK—LINK—ACT and build a relationship with God every day

A. Cucumber Connection

CUCUMBER CONNECTION NEEDS:

- Pickle jar
- Pickles artwork from the *VeggieConnections Shepherd* pages (on the *VeggieConnections CD-ROM*)
- Green construction paper

Before kids arrive, enlarge and copy the pickles from the *VeggieConnections Shepherd* pages on the *VeggieConnections CD-ROM* included in the *VeggieConnections Elementary Curriculum Kit* onto green construction paper. Cut them out and put them in a pickle jar.

Have the kids sit with their *VeggieConnections Groups*. Let a volunteer draw a pickle from the Pickle Pot. Written on each pickle is an everyday dilemma that kids face, related to this lesson. Either the child or a *VeggieConnections Shepherd* reads the pickle aloud. Shepherds then help their group talk through possible solutions, using the THINK—LINK—ACT way of looking at it.

| Jasmine doesn't like it when her best friend Kayla says things that are not nice about their other friends. What could Jasmine do? | Tyler has to give a report in front of his class, and he is afraid. He wants to do a good job, but he is really scared. What can he do? | Kyle saw his teenage sister doing something she shouldn't do. Kyle doesn't want to be a tattletale, but he doesn't want his sister to do wrong things. What could Kyle do? |

B. Kid Connection: Planning Tube

KID CONNECTION NEEDS:

- Crumpled paper "hailstones" (one per child)
- Planning tubes (made in *Lesson 1*)
- Pencils and/or crayons

Have each child pick up a "hailstone" from the earlier plagues and gather in their *Veggie-Connections Groups*. Say: **Moses and Aaron had faith that God would do as he said, and they did what was right. Pharaoh didn't do what was right, so God sent plagues on his land. These "hailstones" can help us remember that we need to do what is right. In your groups, talk about some of the times when it's hard for you to do what is right.** Allow time for groups to discuss.

Once kids have talked about some situations, discuss some "links" to things the Bible says that might help them in these situations. Then talk about how they they what would be the right way to "act" in these situations. Have kids flatten out their hailstone papers, and write or draw a picture of them doing the right thing. Help kids roll up their pictures and place them in their planning tubes. Collect the tubes for use next week.

C. Christ Connection

CHRIST CONNECTION NEEDS:

- *VeggieConnections* take-home newspaper (one per child)

Sing the *THINK—LINK—ACT* song. The lead the kids in saying the Unit Memory Verse, Hebrews 11:1. Remind kids that their faith in God will help them to do what is right if they stop to THINK—LINK—ACT.

In *VeggieConnections Groups*, have kids tell what's coming up this week that they might need God's help with. Have the *VeggieConnections Shepherds* start the prayer by saying: **Lord, we want to have faith to do the right thing in every situation. Help us to have faith this week when . . .** Let volunteers tell God the things they were just talking about. Close by thanking God for loving each of us.

Distribute the take-home newspaper, ***VeggieConnections***.

Connecting to **Faith** using **Moses** as our example
Moses helps the Hebrews prepare:
Exodus 12:1–13:16

PART ONE:

Plugging In
at Veggie Lagoon

Introduction to the site
and lesson focus

LESSON 5:
My faith helps me
to persevere.

A. Veggie Connection

Dressed as the Castaway, welcome the kids as they enter Veggie Lagoon and look disgusted at the mess. Say: **You've been visiting my island for a while now, and I think it's time to put you to *work*!**

Provide plastic grocery bags and have kids in groups of two or three walk around the island and clean up the mess. Have one or two groups of kids pick up and stack the Bibles and other books. Don't say anything to the kids while they are working.

When kids are done, tell them to line up and remain standing. Then have the group who stacked the Bibles and books give one or two Bibles to each child. For younger children, give only one book. Have kids spread out and hold their books out in front of them while you review. Ask for any volunteers to tell you what has happened to Moses and the Israelite people. Explain to the kids how the Egyptian king forced the Israelite people to build things and work very hard. Stop several times and ask how it feels to hold the books. After kids are showing obvious strain from holding the books or have dropped them, have them sit down.

When you came in today, I told you to clean up the lagoon. Then I made you hold the books until it hurt. I did this to help you feel what it might have been like to worked as a slave in Egypt, under Pharaoh. I only had you hold the books a few minutes. Do any of you know how long the Israelites were slaves in Egypt? *(Over 400 years.)* **That's a long time! How hard do you think that would be?** Allow responses. **But God hadn't forgotten his people in Egypt. He wanted the Israelites to have faith in him. And that brings us to our Connection Word for today.**

Ask for a volunteer to get the *VeggieConnections Bible Dictionary* and look up *persevere* and read it aloud. **You preserved by following my instructions. And today we'll see how the Israelites persevered as God freed them from Egypt.**

B. Prayer Connection

Have kids divide into *VeggieConnections Groups*. Have *VeggieConnections Shepherds* encourage kids to share areas where they need to persevere. Lead a prayer asking for kids to trust in God when they face hard times.

THE CHILDREN
will arrive with their *VeggieConnections Shepherds* from the opening Countertop Connections featuring Bob and Larry. Play the *VeggieConnections Music CD* as children enter the Veggie Lagoon.

VEGGIE CONNECTION NEEDS:

- *VeggieConnections Music CD*
- CD player
- Crumpled paper balls
- Plastic bugs and frogs (used in *Lesson 4*)
- Bibles and other hardback books (one or two per child)
- Plastic grocery bags (one per every two or three kids)
- *VeggieConnections Bible Dictionary*

BEFORE YOU START:

Scatter the Bibles, other books, paper balls, and plastic bugs and frogs around the Veggie Lagoon. You can also spread other clean trash around the site for a more messy look.

Plugging In to God's Word

Connecting to God's Word in the Bible and understanding how that can help us to have a better relationship with him

A. God Connection: Moses helps the Hebrews prepare – Exodus 12:1–13:16

BEFORE YOU START:

Recruit three *VeggieConnections Shepherds* or older kids to play the parts of Think, Link, and Act, and have them wear the name signs used in previous weeks. Copy the skit for each of them.

Invite the kids to sit where all can see the skit. Show the kids where today's Bible story is found, in Exodus 12 — 13.

GOD CONNECTION NEEDS:

- Bible
- "Think," "Link," "Act" signs from lesson 2

Think: Boy, just think! The Israelites were slaves in Egypt for hundreds of years!

Link: They had to persevere a lo-o-o-ong time to get through that!

Think: Persevere? What's that?

Act: I think one of these kids can tell me! (*Points to a volunteer, who explains.*)

Link: They also had to persevere while God was convincing Pharaoh to let the people go. Moses and Aaron really had to persevere to keep going back to Pharaoh, over and over again.

Act: Let's have a look at what the Israelites are up to now. (*The three pretend to walk. As they describe what they see, they gesture at imaginary Israelites.*)

Think: Here we are, back in Egypt. What are those Israelites doing? They're rushing around like they're preparing for something. Link, have you figured it out?

Link: It looks like they're packing! I heard Moses tell the people that God was going to send one final, awful plague to convince Pharaoh to let the slaves go. The Israelites have faith in God so they're finally trusting Moses, and they're preparing to leave!

Act: They're preparing special food—just the way God told them. They're making food they can eat as they quickly pack and travel.

Think: You mean, fast food?

Act: Something like that! The main dish is roast lamb, and they're supposed to put the blood of the lamb on their outside doorposts. Then when the Lord sees the blood on the doorposts, he will pass over the Israelites' homes.

Link: That's because when the Lord brings death to the Egyptians, he'll see which Israelites have faith in him.

Act: Right. And they're also preparing bread without the yeast. The yeast makes bread rise and be light and fluffy, but it takes a lot of time—and that's what the Israelites don't have! So they'll eat flat bread, like tortillas or pita bread.

Think: What's that awful, crying sound?

Link: It's the Egyptians crying! They're sad because of the horrible plague God brought on them. Now they probably understand just who is the one true God.

Think: And the Egyptians are giving the Israelites gold and food and fancy clothes—anything to get them out of town faster!

Act: It's really happening! After persevering through years of slavery, the Israelites are finally free! Their faith helped them to persevere!

You may want to further discuss how hundreds of years after the first Passover, Jesus talked about himself being the Passover sacrifice when he went to the cross to forgive our sins. Just as God saved the Israelite people from Egyptian slavery, he saved us from our slavery to sin with Jesus' death.

Thank the actors. Say: **When the Israelites left Egypt, God told the people to celebrate with a special ceremony, called the Passover. Each year, God's people were told to celebrate the Passover as reminder of how God brought them out of Egypt.**

Have kids divide into *VeggieConnections Groups* and discuss ways they can persevere in their faith.

B. Activity Connection

Choose from the following activities to help kids explore and remember that their faith in God will help them to persevere through difficult times (approximately 10–15 minutes each).

1. High-Powered Game: My Faith is in God!

Place a chair in the middle of the playing area. Place a set of index cards in alphabetical order faceup on the chair. Select one volunteer to be Moses. "Moses" will call out: **My faith is in God, who is . . .** When a child can think of a reason to have faith in God that starts with the top letter of the stack, he or she should run to grab that card. Several may try to get the card. The one who gets it first calls out the word or phrase they thought of, such as *amazing!* (for the first letter, *A*). That player then places the card facedown and goes behind Moses, with hands on Moses' waist. Moses then begins to jog around the playing area, with one person following.

Moses again calls out: **My faith is in God, who is . . .** and kids will try to get the *B* card. Once an answer that starts with *B* is called out, that child joins the line. Continue play until they reach a letter that no one can answer. At that point, Moses joins the playing field and the second in line becomes Moses. They then may call on a *VeggieConnections Shepherd* for help. If the Shepherd is stumped, everyone agrees to turn that letter over and go on to the next letter.

2. Low-Powered Game: Plates of Perseverance

Have kids divide into *VeggieConnections Groups*. Give each group one small plastic or foam plate. Have each group choose one person to hold the plate on their fingertips. Once the plate is balanced, kids slowly add cotton balls, trying not to upset the balance of the plate. Kids keep adding cotton balls. See which group can balance the longest. When a plate falls, have another child take his or turn balancing the plate. Play until each group member has had a chance to balance the plate.

You had to have perseverance when balancing the plate in this game. And just like balancing a plate is hard, sometimes it's hard to have faith in God that perseveres. But God rewarded the Israelites' perseverance in their faith, and he will reward yours, too.

3. Craft: Traveling Lunch Pouch

BEFORE YOU START:
Prepare several 12" circle patterns out of card stock. Punch 12 holes 1" from the edge of the circle, in a pattern like numbers on a clock. Cut the fabric into 12" squares. Place the individual trail mix ingredients in separate containers.

VeggieConnections Shepherds will need to help younger kids with this craft. Provide cord pieces, beads, fabric squares, scissors, markers, and circle patterns to kids. Show the kids how to trace a circle on their fabric, cut it out, and mark the holes using the 12-inch circle pattern. Punch holes around the perimeter of the fabric, where the holes are marked.

Have the kids thread the cord in and out of the holes and pull the cord ends, closing the fabric into a pouch. Have kids tie a double knot a few inches from the end of the cord, slip one bead on the cord, and fasten it with another double knot. Repeat for the other end, after cutting off the excess cord.

Give each child a piece of the brown construction paper. On it, have them write a prayer of thanks that an Israelite might write to God for how he rescued them after they had persevered for so long. Place the paper in the fabric pouch.

Next, have the kids make some trail mix, putting in their bowls ingredients that they like. Once mixed, put some of the mix in the plastic bags and allow kids to enjoy some.

While kids are eating, say: **When the Israelites were packing, they realized that their perseverance had been worth it. God had come to their rescue by freeing them from Egyptian slavery!** Discuss some things that could have helped the Israelites persevere, like praying, singing praises to God, and talking to others about God. Have kids put the remainder of their trail mix in their lunch pouches and tie them shut.

HIGH-POWERED GAME NEEDS:

- Index cards
- Marker

BEFORE YOU START:

Write the letters of the alphabet on index cards, one letter per card. If your group is large, you may need to make more than one set and set up more than one game area.

LOW POWERED GAME NEEDS:

- Small plastic or foam plates
- Cotton balls

CRAFT NEEDS:

- Plastic snack bags with zipper closing
- Disposable bowls
- Ingredients for trail mix (such as raisins, dried fruit, dry cereal or small crackers, nuts, and sunflower seeds)
- 1' square natural-colored fabric (one per child)
- 3' long jute or heavy cord (one per child)
- Large wooden beads (two per child)
- Hole punches
- Scissors
- Card stock circle patterns
- Pens
- Markers
- Light brown construction paper

PART THREE:

Plugging In to My Life

Life application of the lesson to lead kids to THINK–LINK–ACT and build a relationship with God every day

A. Cucumber Connection

CUCUMBER CONNECTION NEEDS:

- Pickle jar
- Pickles artwork from the *VeggieConnections Shepherd* pages (on the *VeggieConnections CD-ROM*)
- Green construction paper

Before kids arrive, enlarge and copy the pickles from the *VeggieConnections Shepherd* pages on the *VeggieConnections CD-ROM* included in the *VeggieConnections Elementary Curriculum Kit* onto green construction paper. Cut them out and put them in a pickle jar.

Have the kids sit with their *VeggieConnections Groups*. Let a volunteer draw a pickle from the Pickle Pot. Written on each pickle is an everyday dilemma that kids face, related to this lesson. Either the child or a *VeggieConnections Shepherd* reads the pickle aloud. Shepherds then help their group talk through possible solutions, using the THINK—LINK—ACT way of looking at it.

Carter signed up to run in a race at his school's Track & Field Day, but now he "thinks" it's too hard. He doesn't feel like going to the practices, and he still gets out of breath easily. What should Carter do?	Mollie is having a hard time in art class. Her projects are not very neat or nice looking, and her teacher keeps telling her she needs to try harder. She is trying, but it is taking too much work. What can she do?	Alison wants to believe that God really loves her, but she just isn't sure. How can she persevere in her faith in order to believe that she is special to him?

B. Kid Connection: Planning Tube

KID CONNECTION NEEDS:

- Bamboo frame on page 116 (one per child)
- Planning tubes (made in *Lesson 1*)
- Pencils

Ask for volunteers to stand and say the Unit Memory Verse, Hebrews 11:1 by memory, either by themselves or in pairs.

Ask the kids to name things they "hope for" and "are certain of" that they can't see. These things will be very different for different kids, depending on their circumstances. They might name things like passing the grade they're in, getting a promised puppy, earning a special reward, and so on. Others might name even more "sure" things, such as the sun being in the sky on a cloudy day, the seasons continuing, or gravity holding them down.

Another thing we can be sure of is God himself. We can't see him, but we can see how he works in our lives and in our world. Because we have faith in God, we can persevere in following his ways.

Invite kids to identify where they need to depend on their faith in God to persevere in difficult situations. Have the kids write a prayer on their bamboo frames asking God to help them in these situations, roll it up, and put it in their planning tubes. Collect the tubes for next week.

C. Christ Connection

CHRIST CONNECTION NEEDS:

- *VeggieConnections* take-home newspaper (one per child)

Sing the *THINK—LINK—ACT* song, using the motions. Then have the kids sit with their *VeggieConnections Groups* and talk about what they might have to persevere through before they come together again. Have the *VeggieConnections Shepherds* open a prayer time with this prayer starter:

Dear Lord, thank you that you love us and that you love to help us. We praise you for being so wise and understanding everything we go through. Please help us to persevere with these things that we're dealing with . . . Let the kids take turns finishing the prayer in their own words.

Distribute the take-home newspaper, **VeggieConnections**.

Connecting to **Faith** using **Moses** as our example
Moses leads God's people through the Red Sea:
Exodus 13:17–14:31

chariot

PART ONE:

Plugging In
at Veggie Lagoon

Introduction to the site
and lesson focus

LESSON 6:
My faith helps me
to trust in God.

A. Veggie Connection

BEFORE YOU START:
Attach mural paper to a long wall, with the bottom edge at kids' knee-height. Draw a waterline or waves across the middle of the whole paper so that the bottom half is "underwater."

OPTION:
If you have access to a TV and VCR or DVD, show a clip of the chariot race in the film *Ben Hur* to show kids chariots in action.

Dressed as the Castaway, welcome the kids to Veggie Lagoon. Invite them over to the mural paper, and ask them to decorate the ocean scene by drawing at least two things. One thing that might be found underwater should be drawn under the waves, and one thing that might be found on top of or over water should be drawn floating on the waves or in the sky above them. As kids work, you might mention strange things that have been found on the bottom of the sea or a river, such as sunken boats, cars, jewelry, and so on. Compliment the kids on their artwork.

When all have had a chance to contribute to the mural, ask the kids to have a look at what the others drew. Then gather the kids together.

In our Bible story, something very strange ended up at the bottom of a sea. I won't tell you yet how it got there yet, but to understand the story, you need to know this word. Ask a volunteer to get the *VeggieConnections Bible Dictionary* and look up *chariot*. Explain that a chariot was like a tall cart or wagon a soldier stood in, that was pulled by horses. Show a picture of a chariot, or a film clip if you have one. Chariots play an important part in our story today.

B. Prayer Connection

Ask the kids to get into their *VeggieConnections Groups* and take a few minutes to catch up on the week. Kids may share any answers to prayer they have seen and any new concerns. Then have the *VeggieConnections Shepherds* lead a prayer where the kids can thank God and ask for his help.

THE CHILDREN
will arrive with their
VeggieConnections Shepherds
from the opening
Countertop Connections
featuring Bob and Larry.
Play the *VeggieConnections
Music CD* as children enter
the Veggie Lagoon.

**VEGGIE
CONNECTION
NEEDS:**

- *VeggieConnections
  Music CD*
- CD player
- Mural Paper
- Markers or crayons
- *VeggieConnections
  Bible Dictionary*
- Picture of a chariot

PART TWO:

Plugging In to God's Word

Connecting to God's Word in the Bible and understanding how that can help us to have a better relationship with him

A. God Connection: Moses leads God's people through the Red Sea - Exodus 13:17–14:31

BEFORE YOU START:

Make a poster of the pillar of fire using red, orange, and yellow markers. Make a pillar of cloud poster with a dark blue marker showing puffy, cloud outlines stacked on top of each other. Also draw a poster of a chariot and a rider. Spread out two bedsheets in an area near where you tell the Bible story. Recruit four *VeggieConnections Shepherds* and show them how to raise and lower the sheets like walls of water. If you have a small area, have the Shepherds wait until you march around the room before laying out the sheets for the "crossing the sea" part of the story.

GOD CONNECTION NEEDS:

- Bible
- Two sheets of posterboard
- Markers (red, orange, and yellow)
- Two plain bedsheets (blue, if possible)
- Stick, such as broom handle

Ask for some volunteers to help with the Bible story. You'll need one child to hold the pillar of cloud poster, one to hold the pillar of fire poster, and one to play Moses and carry the stick. Recruit a *VeggieConnections Shepherd* to represent the Egyptians using the chariot poster. Have this Shepherd stand behind the group of kids and hold the poster. Have your recruited Shepherds stand next to the sheets. Also have a Shepherd by the lights or blinds to respond as the story dictates.

Last time we gathered together, we saw how Pharaoh finally decided to allow God's people, the Israelites, to leave Egypt for good. We're going to act out the rest of the story together.

Gather all the kids together. Have Moses and the kids with the two posters join the front of the group.

There were over a million people leaving Egypt. Have kids turn around and wave and say: **See ya, Pharaoh!** Then begin marching as a group around your room.

God was with the people as they marched in the desert. He led the people with a pillar of cloud during the day. Have the "pillar of cloud" child come out in front of the group and hold up his or her poster. **When night fell, God was with the people by having a huge pillar of fire guide the people at night.** Signal the Shepherd to turn off the lights or close the blinds. Have the "pillar of fire" child take the place of the "pillar of cloud" child. Then march a bit in the "darkness."

Signal to have the room brightened and have the "pillar of cloud" child replace the "pillar of fire" child, while continuing to march. Make a slow circle around your room, avoiding the sheets.

Did you notice we marched in a circle just now? Well, that is exactly how God told Moses to lead the people. God wanted Pharaoh to think the Israelites were lost and were stuck in the desert. When Pharaoh was told all the Israelites had left, he changed his mind and ordered his army to go after them. He had hundreds of fancy chariots and horses and troops chasing the Israelites across the desert.

Have the group march over to the place where the sheets are while the chariot Shepherd follows behind you. **God led the Israelites to edge of the sea.** Have the chariot Shepherd call out: **Hi there, used-to-be slaves! When the Israelites saw the Egyptian chariots racing toward them, they complained to Moses that it would have been better to have been slaves in Egypt than to die in the desert! But God told Moses to wave his hand over the sea.** Have Moses hold his stick out over the sheets while the Shepherds lift up both sheets, forming a "wall of water" on either side. Then have the group march between the sheets and turn around and face the sea they just crossed through.

Some one million Israelites crossed the sea on dry ground, walking between two huge walls of water. By the time the last Israelite had crossed, Pharaoh's chariots reached the edge of the sea. They headed into the dry land, but God made the wheels of Pharaoh's

fancy chariots fall off! Then he had Moses wave his hand over the sea again. Have Moses wave his hand and have the chariot Shepherd toss his poster into the "sea" while the sheet Shepherds throw the sheets down to cover the poster. **So God stopped the Egyptian army from reaching the Israelites, and all of Pharaoh's fancy chariots took a dive in the sea!**

Thank kids for participating in the Bible story.

B. Activity Connection

Choose from the following activities to help kids explore and remember that God wants us to trust him (approximately 10–15 minutes each).

1. High-Powered Game: Chariot Races

Divide the kids into *VeggieConnections Groups* and have groups line up behind the tape start line. **When Pharaoh's chariots went after the Israelites, God caused their wheels to fall off! Hopefully you won't have this problem for our game!**

Have kids in each group line up in pairs for wheelbarrow (chariot) races. The "driver" stands behind the "chariot" and holds the chariot's legs, while the chariot moves with his or her arms down the course. Note: if you have girls wearing skirts, have them play the "drivers."

Have groups play a few rounds of the game.

HIGH-POWERED GAME NEEDS:

• Masking tape

BEFORE YOU START:

Tape start and finish lines at about 20' apart. The lines should be about 6' long for each *VeggieConnections Group*.

2. Low-Powered Game: Red Sea Faith Jump

Lay out two long ropes parallel, about one foot apart. Tell the kids this is the Red Sea and they are to jump over it. Have all the kids line up on one side. They are to jump over to the other side, without touching the "water" in between the two ropes. But before jumping, kids should call out a time or situation when it can be hard to have faith in God. *(When I'm disagreeing with my parents, when I have a test at school, when I'm having a hard time learning something new, when my pet died.)* After all the kids call out something and jump over, move the two ropes about six inches farther apart.

Continue calling and moving the ropes. Eventually kids will start "falling into the Red Sea" by landing on the ropes. Those kids must stand outside the sea while the others continue to play. Once the ropes are too far apart for most of the kids to successfully jump, remind the kids that the Israelites certainly couldn't "jump over" the Red Sea, and they didn't even get their feet wet. Instead of being blocked by the Red Sea, God opened a path through the water for them. Have all the kids go to one end of the ropes, which now form the path through the sea, and let them walk the path between the ropes calling out: **My faith helps me to trust in God!**

LOW-POWERED GAME NEEDS:

• Two long pieces of rope or clothesline per two or three *VeggieConnections Groups*

3. Craft: Faith Visors

Say: **When God's people were in the desert, they were guided by a pillar of cloud during the day, and a pillar of fire by night. God did this so the people would continue to have faith in him. But when they reached the sea they saw the Egyptian army and got scared. The people had already forgotten that God had freed them from Egypt. They were looking at the Egyptians instead of having faith in God. Let's make something that will remind us to have faith in God, when things don't look very good.**

Provide foam visors and have kids spell "FAITH" on their visors with glitter glue pens. Have *VeggieConnections Shepherds* help younger children. Then have kids decorate their visors with foam shapes using craft glue to fasten the shapes to their visors. Have them use the glitter glue pens to finish decorating their visors. Set the visors aside to dry until the end of class.

CRAFT NEEDS:

• Plain craft foam visors (one per child)
• Foam shapes
• Craft glue
• Glitter glue pens in a variety of colors
• Colored permanent markers

CUCUMBER CONNECTION NEEDS:

- Pickle jar
- Pickles artwork from the *VeggieConnections Shepherd* pages (on the *VeggieConnections CD-ROM*)
- Green construction paper

PART THREE:

Plugging In to My Life

Life application of the lesson to lead kids to THINK–LINK–ACT and build a relationship with God every day

A. Cucumber Connection

Before kids arrive, enlarge and copy the pickles from the *VeggieConnections Shepherd* pages on the *VeggieConnections CD-ROM* included in the *VeggieConnections Elementary Curriculum Kit* onto green construction paper. Cut them out and put them in a pickle jar.

Have the kids sit with their *VeggieConnections Groups*. Let a volunteer draw a pickle from the Pickle Pot. Written on each pickle is an everyday dilemma that kids face, related to this lesson. Either the child or a *VeggieConnections Shepherd* reads the pickle aloud. Shepherds then help their group talk through possible solutions, using the THINK—LINK—ACT way of looking at it.

Calvin's dog died, and he doesn't think it was very fair. He had prayed that God would heal his dog. Now Calvin isn't sure he trusts God anymore. What can Calvin do?	Theresa "thinks" everything has gone wrong this week, even things she prayed about. She is frustrated with schoolwork, her schedule is too busy, and her friends are mad at her. What can Theresa do?	Thom's grandma has been sick. He feels sad for her, and he is afraid it might get worse. What can Thom do?

B. Kid Connection: Planning Tube

KID CONNECTION NEEDS:

- Paper mural from Veggie Connection activity
- Planning tubes (made in *Lesson 1*)
- Markers

Remove the mural from the wall, used in the Veggie Connection opening activity. Recruit two *VeggieConnections Shepherds* to each hold one end of the mural in an open area. Have kids gather in front of the mural. Say: **We used this mural earlier because the Red Sea was an important part of our Bible story. The Red Sea was a barrier to the Israelites' faith in God. When they saw the Egyptians coming after them, they lost their faith in God. But God parted the Red Sea and showed the people they should always have faith in him.**

Encourage kids to think of one way they can express their faith in God. Then have kids run and "break through" the mural while calling out their faith expression. **Let's use this mural as a reminder to have faith.** Have kids each tear a section of the mural for their planning tubes. Give each child his or her own tube and markers. On the back of their mural pieces, have kids write prayers of how God can help them overcome the "Red Sea" faith barriers they face. Allow kids to roll up their prayers and put them inside their tubes. Collect the tubes for next week's use.

C. Christ Connection

CHRIST CONNECTION NEEDS:

- *VeggieConnections* take-home newspaper (one per child)

Sing the THINK—LINK—ACT song. Ask the boys to stand up and say the Unit Memory Verse, Hebrews 11:1, by memory. Then have the girls do the same.

Have the *VeggieConnections Shepherds* gather their group members and ask about special prayer requests, challenges they will face before they come together again, and other needs. Have the Shepherd begin a prayer by saying: **Dear God, thank you for the great examples of faith in the Bible. We love to hear the Bible stories! We'd like to learn to trust you as the people in the Bible did. Please help us. Especially help us to trust you this week with . . .** Let volunteers complete the sentence in their own words. The Shepherds should make sure all the kids' requests are mentioned.

Distribute the take-home newspaper, ***VeggieConnections***.

Connecting to **Faith** using **Moses** as our example
Moses receives the Ten Commandments:
Exodus 19:1–20:21

PART ONE:

Plugging In at Veggie Lagoon

Introduction to the site and lesson focus

LESSON 7:
My faith helps me to be obedient.

A. Veggie Connection

Dressed as the Castaway, greet the children as they arrive at Veggie Lagoon. Give them some outlandish or silly rules they have to follow at the lagoon today. Examples: **Don't step on any lines on the floor** (if you have a tile floor); **Say hello to every palm tree and toy fish; You have to tiptoe so you don't disturb the sand crabs; We need more ocean breezes, so flap your hands at three other people to make wind; No smiling, laughing, or giggling— we've been having entirely too much fun here!**

Once the kids have had a few minutes to experience these rules, gather them together and ask: **What do you think of our new Veggie Lagoon rules?** *(They're silly, don't make any sense, and so on.)* **Do you think we should have no rules at all here?** Encourage the kids to ponder this and discuss what might happen if there were no rules at all.

Invite the kids to think of a few rules that would be really good for the lagoon—and why. Are these rules to make sure that visitors are safe? To make sure they're having fun? Encourage kids to think of rules outside the usual classroom rules. They might want to come up with some that would be useful only at a lagoon. **I made up some rules for the lagoon today because we're going to be looking at rules.**

Bring out the *VeggieConnections Bible Dictionary* and have a volunteer look up *commandment* and read the definition. Let several kids try putting the definition into their own words. **God gives us rules because he loves us and wants the best for us. Let's find out more about these rules.**

B. Prayer Connection

Today pray "popcorn" prayers. Invite the kids to take turns popping up and thanking God for a rule that's helped them, then popping back down again. *("Thanks, God, that we have to use kind words with each other"* or, *"I'm glad no one's allowed to shove me.")*

Offer a prayer, including some of the kids' rules, and thank God for the rules he gives us.

THE CHILDREN
will arrive with their *VeggieConnections Shepherds* from the opening Countertop Connections featuring Bob and Larry. Play the *VeggieConnections Music CD* as children enter the Veggie Lagoon.

VEGGIE CONNECTION NEEDS:
- *VeggieConnections Music CD*
- CD player
- *VeggieConnections Bible Dictionary*

Plugging In to God's Word

Connecting to God's Word in the Bible and understanding how that can help us to have a better relationship with him

A. God Connection: Moses receives the Ten Commandments – Exodus 19:1–20:21

GOD CONNECTION NEEDS:

- Bible
- Paper
- Pencils

Have the kids be seated under the shelter. Show them where today's Bible story is found, Exodus 19—20.

After the Israelites escaped from Egypt, they traveled for three months and then came to the Desert of Sinai. Here, God stopped them and came to visit them by coming down to a mountain called Mt. Sinai. God's presence was so mighty and awesome that the whole mountain looked like it was on fire!

God wanted the Israelites to have a good relationship with him so much that he came in a way that they could see him. And he gave them special commandments to live by, so they would know how to obey him. The most famous commandments he gave are called the Ten Commandments.

When Moses went up on the mountain, God promised that if the Israelites obeyed him and kept the commandments, they would always be his special people. They would have a great connection with him. Because Moses had faith in God, he agreed to obey.

Moses told the people what God said, and they promised, "We will do everything the Lord has said." They agreed to obey because they had faith in God.

We also can choose to obey God—because we want to have a friendship relationship with him. Let's learn these Ten Commandments that God gave. Have kids divide into *VeggieConnections Groups.* Give each child a sheet of paper and pencil. Instruct the kids to listen to the commandments. After each they should write the number of the commandment and sketch a picture of what it means. Have *VeggieConnections Shepherds* help kids if they can't think of ideas to draw.

The first commandment is, "You should have no God but me." Have the kids write the number one and spend a brief time drawing their picture.

God said in the second commandment to not make any idols or false gods. Pause while the kids write number two and draw a picture. Explain an idol is any human-made object people worship instead of God.

The third commandment is to not misuse God's name. That means to always speak God's name with respect and kindness. Pause while the kids write number three and draw a picture.

The fourth commandment says to remember to keep the Lord's Day holy. Explain that we set apart one day to belong to God and his purposes. Pause while the kids write number four and draw a picture.

The fifth commandment says to honor your father and mother. Pause while the kids write number five and draw a picture.

The sixth commandment is to not murder anybody. Pause while the kids write number six and draw a picture. They may want to turn to the back of their papers by now.

The seventh commandment says that people should always be faithful to their wife or husband and not fall in love with anybody else. Pause while the kids write number seven and draw a picture.

The eighth commandment says, "Do not steal." Pause while the kids write number eight and draw a picture.

The ninth commandment tells us not to lie. Pause while the kids write number nine and draw a picture.

And the tenth commandment explains that we shouldn't envy other people's things or be jealous of what they have. Pause while the kids write number ten and draw a picture.

Briefly review these Ten Commandments again by naming them and having the kids hold up their pictures for others to see each one.

Moses gave God's commandments to the Israelites. Because they had faith that God's rules were good, they promised to be obedient. They learned that their lives were much better when they did obey. We can learn the same thing!

God will help us keep his rules if we remember to THINK—LINK—ACT every time we feel like doing the wrong thing. Our faith in God helps us to be obedient.

Take a few minutes to discuss these questions with the kids: **What did God give Moses and the Israelites?** *(Special commandments to obey.)* **Why did God give these commandments?** *(Because he loved them, and so their lives would be better.)* **What can help us to be obedient and keep God's commandments?** *(Our faith and trust in him and our desire to stay connected to him.)*

B. Activity Connection

Choose from the following activities to help kids explore and remember that their faith in God helps them to be obedient to God's commandments (approximately 10–15 minutes each).

1. High-Powered Game: Ten Commandments Kickball

Tape four paper "bases" in a baseball diamond pattern and have a *VeggieConnections Shepherd* be the pitcher. Tell the group that they are going to play "Ten Commandments" kickball. **In this game, the ball represents things that might make you want to disobey what the Bible says. When the Shepherd rolls the ball to you on your turn, you need to kick that disobedience away! If you shout one of the Ten Commandments as you run the bases, then no one can tag you out.**

Explain that they can say the commandment in their own words, such as: **I won't lie** or **Married people should love each other** or **I'll put God first.** Kids may say a commandment that another player has said, but if they get a second turn, they have to say a different commandment. They can also say something based on a commandment, like: **I won't cheat in school.**

Have kids take off their shoes so they won't kick the ball too hard. Place about eight kids in the "field," and line up the rest as kickers. Keep the game moving quickly, with the "outfielders" just retrieving the ball. Most kids will be able to call out a commandment and run around the bases without slowing down the game by being tagged.

While playing this game you had to quickly think of God's commandments to avoid being tagged. In real life, there may be times when you have to think quickly when facing tough choices. Keeping God's commandments in your heart can help you obey God.

HIGH-POWERED GAME NEEDS:

- One rubber playground ball
- Paper
- Masking tape

2. Low-Powered Game: Changing Rules Game

BEFORE YOU START:

You'll need three same-sized boxes. Tape a 10' starting line. Tape the bottom of the boxes closed and cut off the top flaps. Place the boxes 3' apart and 10'–15' away, open end facing the starting line.

Say: **Let's play a game where you can see the importance of rules.** Divide kids into three teams. Divide the first team into three groups, having each group line up at the starting line, across from one of the three boxes. Give the first player in each line a can of tennis balls. Each player gets three tries. **To score a goal in this game you need to get your tennis balls into the box. The team that gets the most goals, wins. I'll keep track of the goals with the help of the coaches** *VeggieConnections Shepherds.* Give Shepherds paper and markers to track the goals. Have the other two teams cheer on their opponents.

For the first team, have the players simply roll the tennis ball down the course, trying to get it in the box. Each player gets three tries. Have a leader from each team keep score of the goals and announce Team 1's score.

LOW-POWERED GAME NEEDS:

- Masking tape
- Three cans of tennis balls (nine balls total)
- Three medium-sized cardboard boxes, about 1' square
- Three paper towel tubes
- Paper
- Markers

After Team 1 has played, say: **Wait a minute. This game is too hard! Let's change the rules!** For the Team 2 players, turn the boxes upright and give the first player in each line a paper towel tube. Have players put the ball on the end of the tube and quickly walk down to the box and drop the ball in the box. Give each player three tries as before. You should have a much higher goal-count for the second team. But you probably had some kids who dropped the ball. Announce the goals scored for Team 2. **This game is still too hard! New rules!**

Have Team 3 line up. Give the first player in each line three balls and have players walk to the box and drop the balls in the box. This should result in the highest score yet. Ignore any protests at this point. Ask for the score and announce Team 3 as the winner, most likely. **Congratulations to Team 3! You outplayed the other two teams!** Show a look of concern. **Wait a minute! Something wasn't right about this game.** Ask kids to talk about how the game wasn't played with the same rules for everybody. **This game wasn't fair to everybody. Rules in games are made so everyone has fair chance in the game. You can't play a game without rules. And we can't live life without rules that protect us. God gave us his commandments so we can live together fairly and not hurt others.**

3. Craft: Ten Commandments Parchment

BEFORE YOU START:

Photocopy a Ten Commandments page (p. 110) for each child. Prepare strong tea for each *VeggieConnections Group*.

OPTION:

If your class is large, you could have some small groups do this craft while the others play the games, and then switch places.

CRAFT NEEDS:

- Copies of the Ten Commandments on page 110 (one per child)
- Shallow pans (one per *Veggie-Connections Group*)
- Strong tea in pitchers (one per group)
- Blow-dryers (at least one per group)
- Newspapers
- Twine
- Pencils

Explain that old documents often turn yellow with age and develop wrinkles from much use. Tell the kids that they will make their own copy of the Ten Commandments, making the paper look old and well-read.

Place newspapers around the work area to protect the tables and floor. Have kids gather around the shallow pans, with a *VeggieConnections Shepherds* to help at each. Have Shepherds carefully pour tea into the pans, so paper will be fully covered when placed inside.

Instruct the kids to put their name on the back of their Ten Commandments paper, and then tear the edges to make it look well-used. Then have the kids crumple up their papers into a ball, then smooth them back out again.

Show the kids how to lay their papers gently in the pan. When the paper begins to take on some color, help the kids carefully lift it out, letting it drip on the protective newspaper. Then, have kids place their papers on newspaper and pat them dry with a wad of newspaper to soak up excess water.

Have Shepherds use blow-dryers as kids carefully hold up their parchment and dry it thoroughly. Make sure Shepherds don't let the heating element get too close to the papers. You could also clip the damp papers to the Veggie Lagoon fishing net and place a floor fan to blow on them. While the first parchments are drying, have more kids dye their papers. When the tea gets low, refill the pan.

While the parchments are drying, talk with the kids about which commandments they find easy to follow and which ones they think are hard. When the papers dry, have the kids roll up their parchment and tie it with a piece of twine.

PART THREE:

Plugging In to My Life

Life application of the lesson to lead kids to THINK–LINK–ACT and build a relationship with God every day

A. Cucumber Connection

Before kids arrive, enlarge and copy the pickles from the *VeggieConnections Shepherd* pages on the *VeggieConnections CD-ROM* included in the *VeggieConnections Elementary Curriculum Kit* onto green construction paper. Cut them out and put them in a pickle jar.

Have the kids sit with their *VeggieConnections Groups*. Let a volunteer draw a pickle from the Pickle Pot. Written on each pickle is an everyday dilemma that kids face, related to this lesson. Either the child or a *VeggieConnections Shepherd* reads the pickle aloud. Shepherds then help their group talk through possible solutions, using the THINK—LINK—ACT way of looking at it.

Kailey's dad told her to do her chores, but she sees her friends outside and really wants to go out and play. She really dislikes doing chores. Which commandment does she need to obey, and what should she do?	Jonathan's teacher told him to come in for detention after school for talking in class. Jonathan didn't want to get in trouble at home, too, so he told his mom he had an after-school sports practice. Which commandment does Jonathan need to remember, and what should he do?	Rachel saw a man drop some money when she was at the gas station with her aunt. She wants to keep it. What should she do?

CUCUMBER CONNECTION NEEDS:
- Pickle jar
- Pickles artwork from the *VeggieConnections Shepherd* pages (on the *VeggieConnections CD-ROM*)
- Green construction paper

B. Kid Connection: Planning Tube

Divide the kids into groups of three. Have the kids in each threesome decide who will be Think, Link, or Act. Assign each threesome a commandment. (You may skip the ones that are harder for kids, such as adultery and idols.) Each group needs to quickly think of a situation where they might run into that commandment this week and work out the THINK—LINK—ACT for it. (*Think—I don't always feel like going to church; Link—I remember the commandment to put God first; Act—I'll go to church and really try to learn and praise God. Or, Think—I wish I had that game my friend has; Link—the Tenth Commandment tells me to not be jealous of what others have; Act—I'll stop focusing on what my friend has and thank God for what I do have.*)

Allow a few minutes for threesomes to discuss. Have *VeggieConnections Shepherds* circulate to help the groups. Then have each group stand and tell their solution, with THINK—LINK—ACT motions with each child saying their assigned Think, Link, or Act answer.

Distribute the planning tubes to the children, ensuring each child gets his or her own. Provide a sheet of gray construction paper and a black, fine-tipped marker to each child. Have kids tear their paper into a stone tablet shape.

God gave us his commandments so we would be faithful to him and live the way he wants us to live. God's plan for your life is to be faithful to him. On your paper tablet, write one or two of the commandments you struggle with. Then write a brief prayer asking God to help you be faithful to his commandments.

Allow kids time to write their prayers. Have them roll up their paper tablets and put them in their tubes. Collect the planning tubes for use in the next lesson.

KID CONNECTION NEEDS:
- Gray construction paper
- Planning tubes (made in *Lesson 7*)
- Black fine-tipped markers

C. Christ Connection

Sing the *THINK—LINK—ACT* song with the motions. See if the threesomes can stand and say the Unit Memory Verse, Hebrews 11:1, by memory.

Have *VeggieConnections Groups* sit together and share prayer requests. The *Veggie-Connections Shepherd* could lead the kids in a prayer like this: **Dear God, thank you for showing us the best way to live. Help us always to Think about these commandments, Link them to what we want to do, and Act they way you want us to. In Jesus' name, amen.**

Distribute the take-home newspaper, *VeggieConnections*.

CHRIST CONNECTION NEEDS:
- *VeggieConnections* take-home newspaper (one per child)

Commandment 1:
I am the Lord your God.
Commandment 2:
You shall have no other gods before me.
Commandment 3:
You shall not misuse the name of the Lord your God.
Commandment 4:
Remember the Sabbath day by keeping it holy.
Commandment 5:
Honor your father and your mother.
Commandment 6:
You shall not murder.

Commandment 7:
You shall not commit adultery.

Commandment 8:
You shall not steal.

Commandment 9:
You shall not give false testimony against your neighbor.

Commandment 10:
You shall not covet your neighbor's house. You shall not covet your neighbor's wife, or his manservant or maidservant, his ox or donkey, or anything that belongs to your neighbor.

NIV BIBLE TRANSLATION

Connecting to **Faith** using **Moses** as our example
Moses shares his faith: **Deuteronomy 11:1–21;
Hebrews 11:24–28**

PART ONE:

Plugging In at Veggie Lagoon

Introduction to the site and lesson focus

LESSON 8:
I will share my faith with others.

A. Veggie Connection

Dressed as the Castaway, welcome the kids back to Veggie Lagoon. Invite them to wander around the lagoon and examine or play with any favorite parts or pieces. For example, some may enjoy the variety of ocean items hanging in the net, some might like playing in the sand, and others might enjoy lying on a beach towel under the shelter in the "ocean" breeze. If you were not able to set up the more elaborate site option, bring in books of tropical islands for the kids to look through.

After a few minutes, ask the kids to all find someone else to go to and explain what they like best about Veggie Lagoon and why. As the Castaway, wander around and listen in, and ask the *VeggieConnections Shepherds* to watch and listen as well. See which kids can make their favorite lagoon item sound the most interesting to someone else. See if any of the listeners were so intrigued by the description that they went to see for themselves.

Then have everyone sit down where they are and listen as you and the Shepherds give examples of things you saw or overheard that made Veggie Lagoon sound great.

When you tell someone else about something you've seen or experienced, you are being a witness. We sometimes hear the word *witnessing* **used in church. What do you think that word might mean?** Listen to suggestions. Then ask a volunteer to look up *witness* in the *VeggieConnections Bible Dictionary* and read the definition to the group. Then ask the kids again to think about ways to witness about their faith. Let volunteers share their ideas.

Have the kids gather with their *VeggieConnections Groups*. Ask them to tell about times they've told someone why they like being friends with Jesus or times they've heard someone talk about their faith in a personal way.

B. Prayer Connection

Still seated in their groups, invite the kids to pray by finishing the following prayer starter that you begin: **Dear God, we're thankful that we get the chance to come near to you. There's so much we like about you! We want to praise you by telling you why we love you and like being your friend . . .** Let the kids take turns saying what they like about God. **In Jesus' name, amen.**

THE CHILDREN
will arrive with their
VeggieConnections Shepherds
from the opening
Countertop Connections
featuring Bob and Larry.
Play the *VeggieConnections
Music CD* as children enter
the Veggie Lagoon.

**VEGGIE
CONNECTION
NEEDS:**

- *VeggieConnections
  Music CD*
- CD player
- *VeggieConnections
  Bible Dictionary*
- Optional: tropical
  islands pictures

Plugging In to God's Word

Connecting to God's Word in the Bible and understanding how that can help us to have a better relationship with him

PART TWO:

A. God Connection: Moses shares his faith – Deuteronomy 11:1-21; Hebrews 11:24-28

GOD CONNECTION NEEDS:

- Bible
- Sign Language Words (below)

BEFORE YOU START:

Copy one Sign Language Words bookmark below for each child. You'll use the ones you don't use in this activity later in this lesson.

Sign Language Words

Love

Faith

Obey

Let the kids sit under the shelter. Begin by asking kids to tell about things that happened to Moses and the people of Israel that they have been learning about. When something bad is mentioned, ask: **How do think he/they felt?** When something he/they did right is named, ask: **Why do you think he/they did that?** Allow a few minutes for the kids to remember the life of Moses and the experiences of the Israelites in Egypt and after they left.

Have kids divide into *VeggieConnections Groups*. Give *VeggieConnections Shepherds* a copy of the Sign Language Words and have them hold it out for kids to see while they practice the motions.

Tell the kids that these are three important words that can help us remember the life of Moses: faith, love, and obedience. Teach the kids the American Sign Language for these three words:

Faith—Point to the head, then bring fists together on top of each other as if building.

Love—Cross arms over top of the heart with hands in fists as if hugging tight.

Obey—Place both sets of fingertips at forehead as if pulling something out; then lay hands open flat in front of self (palms up) as if setting something out.

First teach the kids the sign for *faith*. Then read Hebrews 11:24–28 aloud, pausing to help the kids do the sign for faith at every mention of the word.

Then explain: **When Moses led the Israelites to the border of the land God had promised them, he sat them down to have an important talk—before they ever set foot in their new country. Moses had been following God for years and years and years. He had grown to have a very deep faith in God. He loved God very much. And because of that, he really wanted to share his faith in God, to tell them how important God is and what God had done for him. Moses was eager to share his faith with others. Here is some of what Moses said.**

Teach the kids the signs for *love* and *obey*. As you read the following summary of Deuteronomy 11:1–21, lead the kids in signing *love, obey,* and *faith* when indicated in parentheses.

Moses said to the Israelites, "Love *(sign love)* **the Lord your God and obey** *(sign obey)* **all his laws and commands—every single one of them. Why? Because you have seen God do many amazing and great things! And that makes your faith** *(sign faith)* **in him strong. So be sure to tell everyone!**

"An important way to show your faith *(sign faith)* **in God and your love** *(sign love)* **for him is to obey** *(sign obey)* **him. And if you carefully obey** *(sign obey)* **him, if you keep your promise to love** *(sign love)* **him, then God will be with you in this new land.**

"How can you stay away from temptation and keep on obeying *(sign obey)* **God? Study and learn and listen to God's Word so much that it becomes part of your heart** *(sign love)* **and part of your mind. How can you build your faith** *(sign faith)* **and keep growing in love** *(sign love)* **for God? Teach God's Word to others. And think about God's Word all the time! When you're at home and when you're out. When you're going to bed at night and when you're getting up in the morning. Keep God's Word where you'll see it all the time. And then your faith** *(sign faith)* **will grow and your love** *(sign love)* **will grow and then you'll really want to obey** *(sign obey)* **God."**

Tell the kids that Moses' talk to the Israelites was written down, and many things that Moses did and said, along with the things he saw God do and heard God say, are written down in the Bible.

Discuss these questions with the kids: **What kinds of things did Moses do to share his faith?** *(He obeyed God, he showed that he loved God, he told others what he had experienced with God, he taught others about God—he shared his faith in God with others.)* **What are ways you can share you faith in God with others?** Let the kids brainstorm ideas. More will be explored as the lesson continues.

B. Activity Connection

Choose from the following activities to help kids explore and remember that God wants us to get to know him and share my faith with others (approximately 10–15 minutes each).

1. High-Powered Game: Shell Friends

Divide the kids into teams for a relay. At your signal, the first player on each team runs to the sand and uses a sifter to find a shell. When one is found, the player has to stand up and call out the first name of a friend he or she would feel comfortable talking to about Jesus. Then he or she runs back to the team with it. Then the next player does the same thing. While the other players are sifting, the kids already back at their teams use a black permanent marker to write the first initial of that friend's name on the shell.

The winning team is the first group that finds a shell and a name for every player. But let all the teams continue playing until everyone has a shell. Encourage the kids to keep their shells and pray for the friend whose initial they wrote. They can put their shell in their planning tube at the end of the lesson.

2. Low-Powered Game: Following God Trios

Have kids divide into *VeggieConnections Groups* and give each *VeggieConnections Shepherd* a Sign Language Words page. Have Shepherds review and practice with their kids one of the words you assign. Assign a different word to each group. If you don't have groups in multiples of three, have some kids join other groups so you'll either have three, six, or nine groups. After groups have practiced their signed word, have them gather together.

We've learned how *faith, love,* and *obey* were words that Moses lived out in his life. And all three of these words are important for us. Have kids scatter out in the playing area. Explain to kids the object of the game is to go around the room signing the word they practiced in their group. When a player finds another that has a sign different from theirs, the two join together and continue signing, looking for the third different sign from another player. When kids have formed word trios, they can talk about how they can live out their word in sharing their faith.

Have Shepherds join the game and help any singles or pairs having trouble making a trio. If you have time, have groups reform and practice a new word and have kids play again. After everyone has formed trios, ask for some volunteers to share what they talked about in their trios.

3. Craft: Colorful Faith Snowboards

Give each child a foam plate, and help them draw an oval the size of a fingerboard toy on it (about 3" x 1"). You may want to make the shape larger for younger students. Have them cut out the shape to make a snowboard.

Have the kids draw four lines to divide their snowboard into five equal parts. They put glitter glue into each of these areas, working from left to right, in this order: gold, dark blue, red, white, green, from one tip of the board to the other. Encourage kids to be creative applying the glitter glue to each section.

While these are drying, teach the kids that they can use their snowboards to share the message of Jesus' love with others, using these colors:

Gold—God lives in heaven, where he wants us to live with him forever.

Dark blue—But we can't live with him there, because we have all done wrong things. This makes us "blue" or sad.

Red—So God sent his son, Jesus, to die for our sins on the cross. Red reminds us of his blood that paid the price for our sin.

White—If we tell God we are sorry for our wrongdoing and ask him to live in our hearts, our sins are washed away like clean, white laundry.

Green—Then we have a brand-new life, and we can grow closer to God, just as green plants grow. We grow by learning the Bible and praying.

You can use these snowboards to tell your friends about Jesus!

HIGH-POWERED GAME NEEDS:

- Sandbox sifters, colanders, or pie tins
- Play sand in containers (from the Veggie Lagoon site)
- Small seashells mixed into the sand
- Black fine-tipped permanent markers

OPTION:

If you don't have sand, use boxes of packing peanuts and have kids look for hidden table tennis balls.

LOW-POWERED GAME NEEDS:

- Sign Language Words (used earlier)

CRAFT NEEDS:

- Disposable foam plates (one per child)
- Scissors
- Pens or markers
- Glitter glue in gold, dark blue, red, white, and green

OPTION:

Have kids make skateboards instead of snowboards. Let the kids draw their boards off the edge of the plate so that one end angles up. Use a cut toothpick for axles and glue two wood wheels (with holes) onto the ends of the toothpicks. Then kids glue these wheel sets under the board.

PART THREE:

Plugging In to My Life

Life application of the lesson to lead kids to THINK–LINK–ACT and build a relationship with God every day

A. Cucumber Connection

CUCUMBER CONNECTION NEEDS:

- Pickle jar
- Pickles artwork from the *VeggieConnections Shepherd* pages (on the *VeggieConnections CD-ROM*)
- Green construction paper

Before kids arrive, enlarge and copy the pickles from the *VeggieConnections Shepherd* pages on the *VeggieConnections CD-ROM* included in the *VeggieConnections Elementary Curriculum Kit* onto green construction paper. Cut them out and put them in a pickle jar.

Have the kids sit with their *VeggieConnections Groups*. Let a volunteer draw a pickle from the Pickle Pot. Written on each pickle is an everyday dilemma that kids face, related to this lesson. Either the child or a Connection Shepherd reads the pickle aloud. Shepherds then help their group talk through possible solutions, using the THINK—LINK—ACT way of looking at it.

Savannah wants to tell her friends that she loves Jesus, but she is nervous. She knows some of her friends don't go to church, and she doesn't know how to get started. What should she do?	Everyone thinks that DeShawn has a lot of faith. He goes to church every week, and he knows a lot about the Bible and what Jesus did for him. But deep in his heart he is not really sure he has a good relationship with God. How can he be sure?	Matthew wants his friendship with God to get stronger, but his parents don't go to church very often. What can he do?

> There is a word that helps us share
> Our friendship with the Father.
> F-A-I-T-H
> F-A-I-T-H
> F-A-I-T-H
> It's faith that helps us share.

B. Kid Connection: Planning Tube

KID CONNECTION NEEDS:

- Planning tubes (made in *Lesson 1*)
- Sign Language Words bookmark (used earlier)
- Pencils

Lead the kids in singing the *F-A-I-T-H* song (to the tune of *Bingo*):

Have each *VeggieConnections Group* stand in a circle and say the Unit Memory Verse, Hebrews 11:1. Let every child within their group state one way they'd like to share their faith this week.

Distribute the planning tubes to the children, ensuring each child gets his or her own. Provide a copy of the Sign Language Words bookmark and pencil to each child. **We've been learning about faith in God here at Veggie Lagoon with Bob and Larry. And you've been creating special reminders to have faith in God. Now your planning tubes are getting pretty full, but there's one more thing we need to add.**

Invite kids to identify who they know that needs to connect with God. Have the kids write these names on their bookmarks. Then have kids write brief prayers for these people. Have them roll up their bookmarks and put them inside their planning tubes. Also have kids put the shells—if you did the High-Powered Game—in their tubes.

During your time with God, look through the things in your planning tube and ask God to give you more faith to live out these things.

C. Christ Connection

CHRIST CONNECTION NEEDS:

- *VeggieConnections* take-home newspaper (one per child)

Sing the *THINK—LINK—ACT* song.

Have the *VeggieConnections Shepherds* lead their groups in prayer for friends the kids would like to share their faith with and for any other requests that require faith. Shepherds may want to use a prayer starter like this: **Dear Lord, thank you so much for the great friends we have. And because we like them—and we love you—we want our friends to know about you and how much you love them and can help them. Please help these friends to become friends with you** ... Let kids name friends. **And Lord, thank you for giving us faith to believe in you. Please help us to trust you this week with these things** ... Let kids talk to God about things they are facing. When finished, have the Shepherds close the prayer time by thanking God for each child.

Distribute the take-home newspaper, *VeggieConnections*.

God has a purpose for:

Tape this edge to tube first.

"Come near to God and he will come near to you." James 4:8

WELCOME TO SNOODLEBURG

Connecting to **Communication** through **Paul's Ministry**

UNIT TWO:

THE
COMMUNICATION
CONNECTION

UNIT VERSE: "Ask and it will be given to you; seek and you will find; knock and the door will be opened to you." Matthew 7:7

LESSON FOCUS:

1. God knows me; I want to know him: Acts 9:1-19

2. Connect to God through prayer: Colossians 1:1-14

3. Connect to God by listening to him: Acts 16:6-10

4. Connect to God through worship: Acts 16:16-36

5. Connect to God through the Bible: Ephesians 6:10-20

6. Connect to God through the Holy Spirit: Galatians 5:16-26

7. Connect to God by letting him help me solve my problems: Acts 27:1-44

8. Connect to others with God's help: Acts 9:20-31

Communication Connection Goals

The Communication Connection is about helping kids learn how to talk to God—and to listen to him.

Each Lesson Focus will take kids on a journey toward various ways they can grow closer to our Lord. The Countertop Connections opening sessions with Bob and Larry teach that God already knows us, and he wants to help us know him better! This concept will be reinforced by the Program Verse from James 4:8: "*Come near to God and he will come near to you.*"

When kids are dismissed to Snoodleburg, they will have exciting opportunities to explore a variety of ways of communicating with God. Kids will be encouraged to put this concept into daily practice. They will be challenged to build their faith as they grow closer to God.

The first lesson in the session begins with the foundational truth that God knows everything about us—and challenges kids to get to know God. The next six lessons will focus on a variety of ways kids can connect to God.

The last lesson explores how God can help kids connect to others.

Warning: Activities in these lessons may call for foods containing wheat, dairy, or nuts. Please be aware that some children may have medically serious allergic reactions to these foods. Let parents know that their kids will be offered snacks that may include these items, and post a list of ingredients each week for any snacks offered during the lesson. Whenever foods containing wheat, dairy, and nuts are suggested in these lessons, be sure to have safe alternatives on hand.

Welcome to Snoodleburg!

In this unit, kids will travel to Snoodleburg to learn how to communicate with God. One of the VeggieTales videos that Bob and Larry will present to children during the Countertop Connections time is called *A Snoodle's Tale.* In the video, Bob reads this delightful rhyming story about Snoodles and the creator who made them. Snoodleburg is the charming little town where the story takes place, and nearby is Mt. Ginchez, where the Snoodles' creator lives. Be sure to watch *A Snoodle's Tale* before you prepare your class lessons.

Kids will have fun in Snoodleburg exploring the communication lessons while learning to know God better.

Your Role in Snoodleburg: The Mayor

As the Mayor of Snoodleburg, you will act as the host to each group of elementary kids as they rotate through your site every eight weeks.

It is suggested that you dress in pastel colors as the Mayor. You could wear a flower in your lapel. You might want to wear a party hat in a pastel color and adorned with cotton balls or pom poms.

How to Build and Prepare Snoodleburg

If you have more time and a permanent space

Snoodleburg is a little town filled with beautiful pastel-colored houses, green fields, fruit-bearing trees, and colorful flowers. Next to the town are the tall gray peaks of Mt. Ginchez. Feel free to use the following decorating ideas or come up with ideas of your own!

Use the Snoodleburg transparency art and the Snoodleburg clip art included in the Director's Guide to create a backdrop and a life-sized Snoodle. Copy the art onto a transparency, and shine the backdrop on a large bedsheet or mural-sized paper. If you use a pastel-colored sheet such as yellow, pink, or blue, you'll save time coloring or painting the additional colors on the sheet. Paint or color it, then fasten the background to the wall of your site. For the end of the tower chute, use red construction paper curled in the chute shape. Fasten it to the sheet or mural for a real-looking Snoodle chute!

You may color a Snoodle on the sheet or make a free-standing one with heavy cardboard covered with mural paper, painted in pastel colors. You could add the backpack craft (see p. 124 for instructions) to the Snoodle for a more realistic look. You may want to place the Snoodle near the door to greet the children.

Hang puffy white clouds and create red-snooted finches from red construction paper and hang them from the ceiling. Around the borders of the ceiling and in the doorway, create the tops of the Snooberry trees by hanging garlands of greenery, available from a craft store. Attach colorful flowers and red pom poms to represent the Snooberry fruits.

Create the Mountains of Ginchez on another wall. Create a mountain shape by piling boxes against

Create a wall mural for Snoodleburg using transparency art found on page 55.

The Snoodleburg Clock-tower

the wall. Drape a dark or gray-colored sheet onto the "mountain" and secure with tape. This will give a 3-D effect for the shape of the mountain.

On a third wall or a bulletin board, create a map of Paul's travels. Make a transparency of the map on page 134 to create your map. This map will also be photocopied and used in several of the lessons.

Cover the floor with colorful leaf petals or paper flowers. Use inexpensive, pastel-colored plastic table covers to keep the tables clean and add to the festive feeling of the room.

If you are short on time or do not have a permanent space

Even if you are short on time or space, you can create a colorful Snoodleburg that children will enjoy for the eight weeks they visit this site.

Use the Snoodleburg transparency art and the Snoodleburg clip art included in the Director's Guide to create a backdrop and a life-sized Snoodle. Copy the art onto a transparency, and shine the backdrop on a large bedsheet or mural-sized paper. If you use a pastel-colored sheet such as yellow, pink, or blue, you'll save time coloring or painting the additional colors on the sheet. Paint or color it, then fasten the background to the wall of your site.

You will also need a map of Paul's travels. Make a transparency of the map on page 134 to make your map.

Simply fold up the sheet and map each week if you share the space with others.

Life Application Memory Tools

VeggieConnections will teach an important Bible lesson to kids each week. Knowing the Bible is the beginning of a relationship with God. Putting that learning to practice through life application really solidifies a child's relationship with the Lord. It is imperative that we provide kids with the tools they need to carry what they have learned into everyday experiences through life application.

In this curriculum, there are three main ways we will encourage kids to do this.

1. Kids will discover ways to share their prayers with other kids in each session.
2. Kids will learn a catch-phrase that will help them to remember what they should do in real life experiences.

The catch-phrase we have created is to THINK—LINK—ACT. There is a song built on this principle on the *Veggie Connections Music CD* in your kit, which will help kids remember this important tool. In addition, each session will focus on various THINK—LINK—ACT activities that help children to build meaningful relationships with the Lord that will carry kids through every day of their lives. Here's what it means:

THINK:
Stop and think about what God wants you to do.

LINK:
Link God's Word and what you've learned to your choices.

ACT:
Go and act on what God wants you to do!

Now add some fun hand motions to the catch-phrase!

THINK: Touch head with fingertip two times.

LINK: Left hand out, right hand out.
Clasp your hands together, fingers intertwined.

ACT: Release grip and roll hands three times.
Finish with arms outstretched.

3. Kids will also create a weekly life application memory tool as a reminder of the unit to help them remember the focus of each lesson.

Snoodle Backpack

In Snoodleburg, kids will create a Snoodle backpack. The instructions for this memory tool are also found in *Lesson 1* on page 124. Each week, kids will add prayers and activities that can be rolled up and put in their backpacks.

Distribute supplies, and have the kids follow these instructions as you demonstrate: Remove the top from a cereal box. Open the bottom of the box. Wrap the box with wrapping paper, using tape or glue sticks. Leave the top open. Wrap the bottom flaps with paper, but leave the bottom open until the elastic straps are attached. Attach the elastic strips on the right and left side of the box, right top to right bottom, left top to left bottom, both on the side closest to the child's body; use staples then duct tape to reinforce the connections. Tape the bottom of the box shut.

Follow the craft illustration to trim the poster board to look like wings and have kids decorate the wings with the markers. Carefully cut two 8" vertical slits in each side of the box closest to the child's body. Show kids how to slide the wings through until there are equal lengths of the wing showing on both sides of the box. Reinforce the wings by using pieces of duct tape on the inside of the box.

Each child will need a photocopy of the Snoodle on page 155. Using glue sticks, have children glue the picture of the Snoodle to their backpacks. On an index card, let children write "God loves [their name]." Use tape or a glue stick to attach the card to one side of the backpack.

The Snoodle backpacks will be used throughout the unit lessons to encourage kids in their prayer lives. At the end of the unit, kids can take their backpacks home as an excellent reminder of how they learned to connect with God and to challenge them to keep praying.

Suggested Music for Snoodleburg

Use these songs from the *VeggieConnections Music CD* in your sessions:

1. *THINK—LINK—ACT*
   Music motions found on page 48
2. *Help Me Listen*
3. *Standin' in the Need of Prayer*

Connection Word:

communication

PART ONE:

Plugging In at Snoodleburg

Introduction to the site
and lesson focus

LESSON 1:
God knows me;
I want to know him.

A. Veggie Connection

Dressed as the Mayor of Snoodleburg, greet the kids at the entrance to Snoodleburg. Introduce yourself to them. Invite them to explore the town and the curious Snoodle characters. Call kids together around Mt. Ginchez. Say: **Welcome to Snoodleburg! I am the Mayor of this fine town. The large tower you see here is where Snoodles are created. The mountain in the distance is Mt. Ginchez. One of our most well-known residents, Snoodle Doo, actually climbed to the top of Mt. Ginchez. It was there that he met his creator, and discovered that the creator knew all about him. This creator even painted a picture of Snoodle Doo that showed him how special he was.**

God, our creator, knows all about each one of us, and he made everyone special and unique. Knowing this encourages us to want to know God better and build our relationship with him. That's what we'll do here in Snoodleburg!

And we also get to eat yummy Snoodleburg food. One of our favorite foods is pancakes with noodles. What do you think about that? Invite responses. **Let's have some fun with our favorite food!**

Have the kids sit in their *VeggieConnections Groups*. Give each child a pancake on a paper plate. Place a container of cooked spaghetti where all can reach it. Instruct kids to make the pancake a self-portrait, using noodles for facial features. This is a good opportunity for *VeggieConnections Shepherds* to get to know the children in their small groups better. While kids work, walk around to groups and affirm the work of each child. Say: **As I walked around and looked at your pancake and noodle pictures, I noticed one thing. Every pancake was different! And as I look at every one of you, I notice that you are each different from each other.** Begin asking questions about how kids are different from one another. They will probably notice things such as gender, race, height, color and length of hair, eye color, and clothes. **You've noticed some differences, but there are some differences that are even more important. What do you think those could be?** Kids might mention skills or abilities. **The most important difference is that every one of you is unique, a one-of-a-kind creation of God. And God knows everything about you and he loves you very much, as our favorite tomato tells us. And God wants us to love him and learn about him. That brings us to today's Connection Word.**

Ask for a volunteer to look up today's Connection Word, *communication*, from the *VeggieConnections Bible Dictionary* and read the definition aloud. **God told us in the Bible that he knows us because he made us. And when we want to know God better, we can talk to him and read about him in the Bible. That's *communication*.**

THE CHILDREN
will arrive with their *Veggie-Connections Shepherds* from the opening Countertop Connections featuring Bob and Larry. Play the *Veggie-Connections Music CD* as children enter Snoodleburg.

VEGGIE CONNECTION NEEDS:

- *VeggieConnections Music CD*
- CD player
- Paper plates
- Frozen pancakes, thawed (check with parents about food allergies)
- Cooked, rinsed, and cooled spaghetti
- Wet wipes
- *VeggieConnections Bible Dictionary*

Before we learn about *communication* in our Bible story today, we can communicate with God through prayer.

Have kids clean their hands with wet wipes before moving to the prayer time.

B. Prayer Connection

Say: **So let's have some communication with God right now. A great way to connect with him is by talking to him by praying.** Invite *VeggieConnections Groups* to sit in a circle and take turns praying around their circle. Encourage each child to think of one thing they're happy about and that they can thank God for. Then encourage the kids to think of one special thing they'd like to communicate with God about, such as a choice of a new after-school activity, a fear they're facing, a problem with another kid, or anything else on their minds.

After allowing time for *VeggieConnections Groups* to pray, close by thanking God for what Snoodle Doo learned—that God knows and loves each child and made everyone special.

PART TWO:

Plugging In to God's Word

Connecting to God's Word in the Bible and understanding how that can help us to have a better relationship with him

A. God Connection: Jesus speaks to Saul – Acts 9:1–19

GOD CONNECTION NEEDS:

- Map of Paul's travels (on page 134)
- Bible
- Bible-time costumes (optional)
- Flashlight

TEACHER TIP:

Younger children may benefit from hearing the story before interacting with it. Explain to kids you'll read the story twice. For the first reading, they should listen carefully. For the second reading, kids will help tell the story.

Gather the kids at the base of Mt. Ginchez for the Bible presentation.

Bring the map of Paul's travels down to where the kids can gather around and touch it. Have one of the kids locate Jerusalem; then have a strong reader read Acts 9:1–2 aloud. Explain that Saul went to the most powerful religious leaders in Jerusalem and that early Christianity was called "the Way." Have another volunteer find Damascus on the map. Explain that Saul was later called by another name, Paul.

Saul hated everyone who believed in Jesus. He wanted to arrest them and kill them. He thought God would be pleased with this. He didn't understand that God loved these people.

Ask for at least three volunteers to help act out the rest of the story. If possible, give them Bible-time costumes to wear. One person will play Saul, one will play Ananias, and several kids can play Saul's friends. Tell the actors to silently walk through the actions as you narrate. Have Ananias initially stand apart from Saul and his friends and wait for a cue from you.

Saul left Jerusalem with some friends to go to Damascus to arrest believers there. Read Acts 9:3–9 aloud. At the point of the flash of light, shine the flashlight on the head of the child playing Saul.

Read Acts 9:10–19 as the actors walk through the actions. Have the actors take a bow on completion. Thank the actors and have them sit with the group.

At first, Saul believed God wanted him to hurt believers. But when Saul met God's son, Jesus, and believed in him, he learned what God really wanted. Explain that Jesus came to tell people what God wanted them to know. Without Jesus, people thought they knew what God wanted for them.

But how can someone get to know God? Do you remember our VeggieConnections Program Verse? *"Come near to God, and he will come near to you."* **In this story, we saw that God came near to Saul first, and then Saul came near to God, as he obeyed Jesus.**

Have the kids gather in their small groups. *VeggieConnections Shepherds* should help their groups discuss how Saul followed the THINK—LINK—ACT process after he was blinded: THINK—He knew he did not want to remain blind. LINK—He had just received instructions from the Lord. ACT—He decided to trust the Lord's instructions; he went to Damascus and met with Ananias, and was healed. Then have the Shepherds take a minute to discuss with the kids: **What does God know about you? How can you get to know God as a friend?**

B. Activity Connection

Choose from the following activities to help kids explore and remember that God wants us to get to know him (approximately 10–15 minutes).

1. High-Powered Game: Blind Balloons

BEFORE YOU START:

Print characteristics of God on separate slips of paper. Each statement should begin with "God is . . ." Some examples are: loving, faithful, helping, just, holy, a friend, powerful, and creative. You may want to use a Bible concordance or dictionary for additional ideas. Put each slip of paper inside a balloon, inflate it and tie it off. Prepare one for each child. Place all the balloons in a large garbage bag.

To play, divide kids into teams of three or four. Give each child a plastic grocery bag. Move all teams to the perimeter of the playing area. Blindfold one child in each team. Release the balloons in the center of the playing area. At your signal, the blindfolded kids try to capture one balloon by holding the handles of the grocery bag and scooping a balloon into it. The other team members help by calling instructions to their blindfolded team member. When a team member catches a balloon, have him or her return to her team and blindfold the second team member and repeat the above. Continue playing until all team members have a balloon.

Have kids pop their balloons and read their slips of paper aloud to their team members. Then have teams discuss these questions: **How do these statements about God make you want to get to know God better? How do these words "communicate" to us about God? Give an example of a time Jesus was _____ [word on paper slip].** Encourage *Veggie-Connections Shepherds* to assist the discussion as needed. If time permits, let teams share their answers with other teams.

2. Low-Powered Game: Communication Lite

To play, divide kids into teams of three or four. One member of each team should choose an object in the room and keep it a secret. Give a flashlight to another member of each team. Turn off the lights and begin this "I Spy" type of game.

The member with the flashlight will point to an item in the room, and the team member who chose an item will simply say whether they are "hot" or "cold." Then pass the flashlight to another player on the team and repeat the process until the chosen item is guessed. Turn on the lights when most of the teams have finished and allow another player on each team to choose an object.

After a couple of rounds, bring the teams together and say: **You could only use a few words in this game, and that made it hard to find the objects. Would it have been easier to find the objects if people had been able to communicate with you? Think about how well you know God. How hard is it to know God if we don't talk to him?** Allow responses. **How can we communicate with God?**

Reinforce the lesson focus that God knows us and wants everyone to know him better.

3. Craft: Created Special Collage

Say: **Snoodle Doo was sad because the other Snoodles painted pictures of him that put him down. But the Snoodle creator painted a beautiful picture of Snoodle Doo, telling him he was very special. And God created each one of us very special, too! One way we communicate with God is thanking him for the special way he made us. Let's create a collage that shows how special we are to God.**

Encourage kids to think of something special about themselves, such as a talent or skill, a personality trait, or some way they feel God's love. Provide shoebox lids or a shallow box to each child. Spread out the crafts supplies and allow children to create colorful collages. Have *VeggieConnections Shepherds* assist kids if they don't know what to create, or to help with the craft supplies.

After kids have created their pictures, have kids share what they created and why. Be sure to enthusiastically affirm their responses.

HIGH-POWERED GAME NEEDS:

- Slips of paper
- Bible reference tools (optional)
- Balloons (one for each child)
- Large garbage bag
- Blindfolds
- Plastic grocery bags (one per child)

LOW-POWERED GAME NEEDS:

- A variety of classroom or personal items (at least a dozen)
- Flashlight or penlights (one for every three or four kids)

BEFORE YOU START:

You'll need an area that can be darkened, about like dusk. If needed, place at least a dozen objects around the room, such as classroom or personal items (the more unusual the better). Kids will use flashlights to point to objects in the area.

CRAFT NEEDS:

- Shoebox lid or other shallow box (one per child)
- White glue and glue sticks
- Variety of uncooked noodles, such as shells, spirals, and bowties
- Markers
- Paint pens or craft paint and brushes
- Glitter glue
- Beads and other craft items

PART THREE:

Plugging In to My Life

Life application of the lesson to lead kids to THINK–LINK–ACT and build a relationship with God every day

CUCUMBER CONNECTION NEEDS:

- Pickle jar
- Pickles artwork from the *VeggieConnection Shepherd* pages on the *CD-ROM*
- Green construction paper

A. Cucumber Connection

Before kids arrive, enlarge and copy the pickles from the *VeggieConnections Shepherd* pages on the CD-ROM included in the *VeggieConnections Elementary Curriculum Kit* onto green construction paper. Cut them out and put into a pickle jar.

Let a volunteer draw a pickle from the Pickle Pot and either the child or a Shepherd should read the dilemma out loud. Each Shepherd should then process the question with his or her small group using the THINK—LINK—ACT phrase.

Amy keeps calling herself "stupid." She doesn't think she can do anything right. You are her friend and want to help her. What can you do?

Yana is put down by the other girls in her class because she has trouble speaking. She wonders if God loves her, how come he doesn't help her talk better. You want to encourage Yana. What can you do?

Jose thinks no one likes him because he's not very good at sports. He is good at other things, but he doesn't think they're very important. Jose is your friend, so what can you do?

KID CONNECTION NEEDS:

- Cereal boxes, medium size (one per child)
- Pastel-colored wrapping paper
- Clear tape or glue sticks
- Elastic strips (like the kind used for waistbands), at least 1" wide, 18" long (two per child)
- Duct tape
- Posterboard, 3' x 8' section for each child
- Scissors
- Markers
- Snoodle on page 155 (one per child)
- Pastel-colored index cards
- Pencils or pens
- Snoodle Journal on page 156 (one per child)
- Yarn

BEFORE YOU START:

Copy one Snoodle (page 155) and one Snoodle Journal page (page 156) for each child.

B. Kid Connection: Snoodle Backpack

Distribute supplies, and have the kids follow these instructions as you demonstrate: Remove the top from a cereal box. Open the bottom of the box. Wrap the box with wrapping paper, using tape or glue sticks. Leave the top open. Wrap the bottom flaps with paper, but leave the bottom open until the elastic straps are attached. Attach the elastic strips on the right and left side of the box, right top to right bottom, left top to left bottom, both on the side closest to the child's body; use staples then duct tape to reinforce the connections. Tape the bottom of the box shut.

Follow the craft illustration to trim the poster board to look like wings and have kids decorate the wings with the markers. Carefully cut two 8" vertical slits in each side of the box closest to the child's body. Show kids how to slide the wings through until there are equal lengths of the wing showing on both sides of the box. Reinforce the wings by using pieces of duct tape on the inside of the box.

Give kids a Snoodle and have then use glue stick to attach the picture to the back side of the pack. On an index card, let children write "God loves [their name]." Use tape or a glue stick to attach the card to the side of the backpack.

Give kids a Snoodle Journal page and pencils or pens. **Each time we gather in Snoodleburg, you'll make something to go into your backpack. For today, communicate with God by writing or drawing a prayer telling God how you want to grow closer to him.**

Allow time for kids to create their prayers. Then have kids roll them up, tie yarn around them, and put them in their backpacks.

C. Christ Connection

Have kids sing along to the *THINK—LINK—ACT* song from the *VeggieConnections Music CD*.

Communication is an important part of our lives. We communicate with others to let them know our needs. God wants us to communicate with him about our needs and what we are thankful for. While we are in Snoodleburg, we are going to be learning Matthew 7:7, a verse from the Bible: *"Ask and it will be given to you; seek and you will find; knock and the door will be opened to you."* **Have the kids repeat the verse once or twice.**

Let's pray. It's exciting God, to realize how well you know us. You created us! We are so glad that you love every part of us and want to be closer to us. Be with us Lord as we ask, seek, and knock on your door. In Jesus' name, amen.

Distribute the take-home newspaper, ***VeggieConnections***.

CHRIST CONNECTION NEEDS:

- *VeggieConnections Music CD*
- CD player
- *VeggieConnections* take-home newspaper (one per child)

Connection Word:

prayer

PART ONE:

Plugging In at Snoodleburg

Introduction to the site and lesson focus

LESSON 2:
Connect with God through prayer.

A. Veggie Connection

Dressed as the Mayor of Snoodleburg, greet the kids as they arrive and invite them to be seated in a semicircle near the base of Mt. Ginchez.

    I have two magnets. Demonstrate as you speak. **If I hold them together, the positive side connects to the negative side. If I try to touch positive to positive, they push each other away.** Pass the two magnets around so kids can quickly experiment with the magnets' actions.

    Now let's play a game, where you all get to act as magnets! Give each child a half construction paper sheet, which they should attach to their shirts with a binder clip. At your signal, they roam around Snoodleburg. Whenever you call: **Connect!** kids should try to match with another child with the color you call out. For example: **Pink match blue, green match orange, yellow match red!** Give them a quick moment to connect by linking arms. After a few seconds call: **Stop!** Those kids not matched should sit down on the sidelines. Play a few rounds, calling **Stop!** much faster each time. After a brief playtime, have kids return to the semicircle.

    Ask for a volunteer to get the *VeggieConnections Bible Dictionary* and look up today's Connection Word: *prayer*. Say: **Thinking about magnetic connections can tell us a little about connecting with God in prayer. When we draw near to God**—hold up one magnet—**he will draw near to us**—connect second magnet to the first. **When we have a close connection to God, we will want to communicate with God through prayer. Today we will focus on keeping that prayer connection with God strong!**

B. Prayer Connection

Have the kids gather with their *VeggieConnections Groups* and link arms. Give each *Veggie-Connections Shepherd* an index card with a prayerstarter written on it. Have the *Veggie-Connections Shepherds* begin sentence prayers below, pausing to let the kids call out their own answers to the Lord.

        God, thank you today for . . .
        We love you because you are . . .
        Please forgive us for . . .
        Please help us with . . .
        In Jesus' name, amen.

THE CHILDREN
will arrive with their *Veggie-Connections Shepherds* from the opening Countertop Connections featuring Bob and Larry. Play the *Veggie-Connections Music CD* as children enter Snoodleburg.

VEGGIE CONNECTION NEEDS:

- *VeggieConnections Music CD*
- CD player
- Two strong magnets
- Construction paper sheets cut in half in a variety of colors
- Small binder clips (one per child)
- *VeggieConnections Bible Dictionary*

PRAYER CONNECTION NEEDS:

- Index cards with prayer starters written on them (one per *Veggie-Connections Group*)

Plugging In to God's Word

Connecting to God's Word in the Bible and understanding how that can help us to have a better relationship with him

A. God Connection: Paul prays for the Church in Colossae – Colossians 1:1-14

GOD CONNECTION NEEDS:

- Map of Paul's travels (on page 134)
- Bibles
- Posterboard or large paper for each group
- Markers

Say: **Paul prayed a lot. He had a close connection with God, which he knew was very important. He prayed for people who didn't know about Jesus, for his work in spreading the good news, for other Christians, and for many churches. Many books in the New Testament are actually letters that Paul wrote to churches, and these letters include many prayers. Today let's look at one special letter Paul wrote to the believers in the city of Colossae, while he was in prison in Rome. Point out the cities of Colossae and Rome on the map.**

Divide into *VeggieConnections Groups*. Alternate assigning groups one of these pairs of verses: Colossians 1:1–8 and 9–14. Provide groups posterboard or mural paper and markers. Have them make two vertical columns on their poster. At the top of the first column kids should write the question: "What did Paul pray for?" At the top of the second column, they should write the question: "What can we pray for?"

Explain to groups they should read through their assigned verses and list in the first column answers to the question, "What did Paul pray?" Have *VeggieConnections Shepherds* encourage involvement of all their group members. Then have kids look at their answers on their posters and use these statements to help list possible answers to the second question, "What can we pray for?"

After groups have finished listing their prayers, allow groups to share their responses. **One way we can learn about prayer is by looking at people in the Bible who prayed. Paul's prayers give us examples of things we can pray about. Just as Paul connected to God through his prayers, we can grow closer to God when we pray to him. What is one thing you learned about prayer today?** (*Paul prayed for people who know Jesus, Paul prayed for other Christians, Paul prayed for churches, and so on.*)

B. Activity Connection

Choose from the following activities to help kids explore and remember that God wants us to pray to him (approximately 10–15 minutes each).

1. High-Powered Game: Target Practice

HIGH-POWERED GAME NEEDS:

- Piece of plain paper (one per child)
- Pens or pencils
- Hula-Hoop® or similar large target
- Label for target: "God, your Creator"

Provide each child a piece of paper. Have children write a prayer on the paper and then help them make paper airplanes. They should write their initials on their plane so they can identify it. Have the children stand together about fifteen feet away from you as you vertically hold your Hula-Hoop®. They should try to send their airplane through the hoop. After the first try, allow them to stand five feet closer, then five feet closer.

Encourage the kids whether their airplane makes it through the target or not. **The closer you get the easier it is to hit the target isn't it?** Have kids all gather back at the fifteen foot range from the target. Then remove the target and say: **The good news is that with God no matter where you stand or how good your aim is, he will always hear your prayers. For this last time, just launch your airplane and think of your prayer. Remember that the moment it leaves your hands, God hears it.**

2. Low-Powered Game: Unscrambled

BEFORE YOU START:

On two sets of different colored index cards write each word of Matthew 7:7, one word for each card, including the verse reference "Matthew 7:7". You'll also have two blank cards in each color. Stack the cards and shuffle them to mix them up. Tape the index cards all around the room.

Divide the kids into two teams, assigning each team one of the two index card colors. Have each team take turns sending one team member to retrieve one card, relay style, but they must walk backward. Remaining team members will put the cards in the correct order. Have a volunteer from each team look up Matthew 7:7 in their Bible and read it aloud for their team as members put the cards in order. The first team done wins. Practice saying the verse as a group and then ask if anyone would like to try part of it alone.

The more you work with a verse the more familiar it will become. For example, did you notice that one way to remember, ask, seek, knock, is to just start with the word ASK—A is for ask, S is for seek, K is for knock. What a great verse to remember that when we pray to God, he hears us and answers our prayers!

LOW-POWERED GAME NEEDS:
- Two colors of index cards, 25 of each color
- Tape
- Bible (one per team)

3. Craft: Snoodle

Have kids create a Snoodle to remind them to listen to God, just as Snoodle Doo listened to his creator. Using a funnel, let kids help fill a balloon with sand, tying off the top with a rubber band. Have kids draw a mouth with markers. Then have them add cotton-ball hair, construction-paper wings, and googly eyes. Have *VeggieConnections Shepherds* assist their kids as needed.

As children work, talk about ways they can talk to God. **The Snoodle went to his creator and had a conversation with him. And God is our loving Creator. We can talk to God whenever we need to. All we need to do is pray.**

As background music, you may want to play the song *Help Me Listen* on the *VeggieConnections Music CD.*

Allow children to take their Snoodles home to remind them to talk to God because they are loved by him.

CRAFT NEEDS:
- Clean sand and funnel
- Small light blue balloons (one per child)
- Rubber bands
- Black permanent markers
- Cotton balls
- White construction paper
- Googly eyes (two per child)
- Glue
- *Help Me Listen* song on *VeggieConnections Music CD;* CD player

PART THREE:

Plugging In to My Life

Life application of the lesson to lead kids to THINK-LINK-ACT and build a relationship with God every day

A. Cucumber Connection

Before kids arrive, enlarge and copy the pickles from the *VeggieConnections Shepherd* pages on the CD-ROM included in the *VeggieConnections Elementary Curriculum Kit* onto green construction paper. Cut them out and put into a pickle jar.

Let a volunteer draw a pickle from the Pickle Pot and either the child or a Shepherd should read the dilemma out loud. Each Shepherd should then process the question with his or her small group using the THINK—LINK—ACT phrase.

CUCUMBER CONNECTION NEEDS:
- Pickle jar
- Pickle artwork from the *VeggieConnections Shepherd* pages on the CD-ROM
- Green construction paper

You want to spend some time in prayer, but you get too busy during the day, and at bedtime you realize you haven't prayed. What can you do?	You see a slide presentation from a missionary family that your church supports. What could you do?	Your grandmother has been very sick. What can you do?

B. Kid Connection: Snoodle Backpack

BEFORE YOU START:

Copy the "Prayer Types" on page 157. Make a set of enlarged pictures for your use. Cut apart and put sections in a basket for kids to draw one. Also copy another set and leave intact.

KID CONNECTION NEEDS:

- Prayer Types on page 157 (two per child); one enlarged set for you
- Basket
- Snoodle backpacks (made in *Lesson 1*)
- Pens or pencils
- *VeggieConnections Music CD*
- CD player
- Rubber bands

Use the larger pictures as you demonstrate. Say: **There are different kinds of prayers. Some prayers tell God how wonderful he is.** Show one of the papers with a heart on it. **Some prayers thank God for something he's done.** Hold up a paper with the gift on it. **Some prayers tell God we're sorry for some behavior.** Show a paper with tears on the face. **Some prayers ask God to do something.** Show a paper with hands and a question mark.

Put all the separated sheets facedown in a basket and place the basket in the middle of the room. Have kids in their *VeggieConnections Groups* gather around the basket. **When it's your turn, go to the basket and take out a piece of paper. Name a time that you might need to say a prayer like the one pictured on the paper, and then say that prayer.** Give an example, such as, "A time I'd feel sad is when I fight with my brother, and I might pray: God, I'm sorry I fought with my brother." **Then keep the paper and return to your group.** Have one child from each group alternate going to the basket and removing a paper. Continue until each child has an opportunity to participate, and each child has all four prayer pictures.

Remember, our Unit Memory Verse reminds us of God's promise to answer the prayers of those who are connected to him. Let's say it together. Lead the kids in reciting Matthew 7:7: **"Ask and it will be given to you; seek and you will find; knock and the door will be opened to you."**

Have the kids sit down with their *VeggieConnections Groups*. Then direct the groups to talk about times this week that they might say the prayers they came up with during the activity.

Distribute the Snoodle backpacks to the children, ensuring each child gets his or her pack. Then hand out an intact copy of "Prayer Types" to each child. Review what the four prayer pictures mean. Have kids write an example of each prayer they might pray by each picture. Have *VeggieConnections Shepherds* help the younger children in their groups. While kids work, play *Standin' in the Need of Prayer* from the *VeggieConnections Music CD*. Give kids rubber bands to band their rolled up prayer pictures and place them in their backpacks. Collect backpacks for use next week.

C. Christ Connection

CHRIST CONNECTION NEEDS:

- *VeggieConnections Music CD*
- CD player
- *VeggieConnections* take-home newspaper (one per child)

Have everyone stand and sing the *THINK—LINK—ACT* song from the *VeggieConnections Music CD*.

Have the kids sit in a circle and ask them what they would like to pray about (THINK). Explain you'll play *Standin' in the Need of Prayer*. As soon as a child has a prayer he or she should quickly stand up and say the request, then sit down. After each request, focus on God's promise to answer the prayers of those who are connected to him (LINK). Pray together about the request (ACT). Continue until all kids who have a request have been prayed for.

Distribute the take-home newspaper, **VeggieConnections**.

Connecting to **Communication** through **Paul's Ministry**
Paul listens to God: **Acts 16:6–10**

PART ONE:

Plugging In at Snoodleburg

Introduction to the site and lesson focus

LESSON 3:
Connect with God by listening to him.

A. Veggie Connection

BEFORE YOU START:

Copy the following phrase on index cards. You'll need one card for each *VeggieConnections Shepherd:* "The Biggle-bag trees are growing purple Biggle-bag fruits, and the Far-lilly flowers are yellow this year."

Dressed as the Mayor of Snoodleburg, greet the kids with these comments: **Welcome back to Snoodleburg! I'm glad you've come back to visit me! In Snoodleburg, we have some colorful trees and plants this time of year.**

Have kids divide into their *VeggieConnections Groups* and sit in circles. Give each *VeggieConnections Shepherd* an index card with the printed phrase you prepared before the lesson. Instruct them to play a simple game of "telephone" with their kids. The Shepherd will whisper the phrase into the ear of the first child, and each child will whisper the phrase to the person on the child's right. When the last person has heard the message, he or she says it aloud. For younger children, the Shepherd may only read the first part of the phrase (the "Biggle-bag tree fruits" part). Most likely by the time the phrase has gone around the circle it will not be the same as the original. Repeat the game a second time, and see if kids retain more of the original message the second time.

It was probably easier for you to get the message the second time you heard it. The more you listen to someone, the easier it is for you to hear what they are telling you. We're going to be talking about listening today. Invite a child to look up *listen* in the *Veggie-Connections Bible Dictionary* and read the definition. **This Connection Word today is a clue for understanding our Bible story about Paul.**

B. Prayer Connection

Say: **For our prayer time today, let's whisper our prayers to give our ears practice in listening carefully.** Have the kids gather in their *VeggieConnections Groups* and each whisper a one-sentence prayer.

THE CHILDREN
will arrive with their *Veggie-Connections Shepherds* from the opening Countertop Connections featuring Bob and Larry. Play the *Veggie-Connections Music CD* as children enter Snoodleburg.

VEGGIE CONNECTION NEEDS:

- *VeggieConnections Music CD*
- CD player
- Index cards
- Pens
- *VeggieConnections Bible Dictionary*

PART TWO:

Plugging In to God's Word

Connecting to God's Word in the Bible and understanding how that can help us to have a better relationship with him

A. God Connection: Paul listens to God – Acts 16:6-10

BEFORE YOU START:

Cut five red construction paper sheets into a stop sign shape, and write "Do not enter" on them. Cut one green sheet into a circle, and write "Come over and help us" on it. On separate sheets of paper, print the places mentioned in today's Bible passage: Phrygia, Galatia, Mysia, Bithynia, Troas, and Macedonia. Post these visibly around Snoodleburg. At all the spots except Macedonia, place a red stop sign, face down on the floor. At the Macedonia spot, place the green sign face down on the floor. If it isn't already displayed, hang the map of Paul's travels where kids can easily point out the places on it.

GOD CONNECTION NEEDS:

- Construction paper sheets (five red, one green)
- Paper
- Marker
- Map of Paul's travels (on page 134)
- Bible

Gather the kids around Mt. Ginchez and open your Bible. Say: **When God talks to us, we don't always hear his words out loud. How do you think God talks to us?** *(Through the Bible, through people who love and serve him, through things that happen to us, through good ideas in our minds.)* **In our Bible story today, he used another way to talk to Paul.**

Read Acts 16:6–8 aloud, having volunteers trace Paul's travels on the map as they are mentioned. **Can you think of one way the Spirit might have kept Paul from going to these places?** With each suggestion given, walk to one of the places in the order mentioned in the story and hold up the stop sign. *(Authorities prevented them, they could have had problems getting transportation, the weather could have been difficult, perhaps Paul felt uncomfortable with the travel plans as he prayed, and so on.)* **The Bible doesn't say how, but Paul was paying attention to God's direction. Remember, God talks to us in many ways, including through things that happen to us.**

Read Acts 16:9, and walk to the Macedonia spot. **I'm sure Paul was wondering what God had in mind for him, so he was listening for God's direction. God spoke to Paul in his dream, and Paul listened to God.** Read verse 10. Hold up the green sign, and have a child point out Macedonia on the map.

Remember that God uses many ways to talk to you. He could remind you of a Bible verse. You could ask someone like your parents or a teacher at church to help you, because sometimes God uses people to help you know what he wants. Something may happen that makes you think that God wants you to do something. You need to be listening for him.

Or you might get a feeling in your heart that God wants you to act. Remember, feelings that come from God can be found in what the Bible teaches. God will never give you a feeling about something that goes against his Word.

Assign each *VeggieConnections Group* one of the signs to go and sit near. **Have you ever felt like God was connecting especially with you? For example, when you heard or read a Bible verse, did you feel like God meant it to say something to you? Or maybe you had been praying about something and looking for how God would answer—then something happened that seemed to be his answer. Share your experience with your small group.** Allow any who wish to share to do so. *VeggieConnections Shepherds* should be ready to give an example.

Remember our Program Verse: "*Come near to God, and he will come near to you,*" *James 4:4*. When we pray, we come near to God. He will come near to us to respond. We should expect to hear an answer from God. He probably won't answer out loud to us, and he may not answer at that moment. But God will answer us when we pray. Take a few minutes to talk about things you have recently prayed for, and talk about how God has answered you. Be sure Shepherds include the idea that God could answer yes, no, wait, or with a different plan of his. If it seems appropriate, groups may pray again for the things that the kids mention.

B. Activity Connection

Choose from the following activities to help kids explore and remember that God wants us to listen to him (approximately 10–15 minutes each).

1. High-Powered Game: "I Can't Hear You!" Obstacle Course

BEFORE YOU START:

Prepare several signs using paper or card stock: face with an angry expression, picture of a tornado, picture or drawing of a computer game. Place tables, chairs, and other objects in random places in the open area in such a way that kids will have to walk around them to get across the room. On these obstacles place the objects from the Needs list on the right. With masking tape, tape off an area on the floor and tape arrows to help direct them, instructing kids that they cannot go out of bounds to avoid the chairs.

Say: **Sometimes we allow things to keep us from listening to God. We can get too busy, or we watch too much TV, or we are angry, or we just don't pay attention to God at all! These things become obstacles. An obstacle is something that keeps us from doing something that we need or want to do. An obstacle to prayer is anything in our lives that makes us feel or say to God, "I don't have time for you!"**

Explain that the object of the game is to cross the obstacle course quickly. Walk through the course, explaining that the placed arrows will point the way for them to go. Explain that at each obstacle, they must completely run around it, calling: **I will not let _____ (***TV, anger, busyness, computer games, toys, sports, books***) keep me from listening to God!**

Divide kids into two equal teams. Have team one line up on one side of the playing area, and the second team on the opposite side. Have kids form groups of up to four kids and have these groups enter the course from both sides of the playing area. Once these groups have passed the first obstacle, send the next group of kids to begin the course. The course will become more difficult as more groups move through in opposite directions. Give stopwatches to *VeggieConnections Shepherds* and have them time the teams going through the course. Allow all groups from both teams to finish the course. Have Shepherds announce the fastest time.

After the game, gather the kids around. **Just as these obstacles make it hard to get to the other side easily, these same kinds of things can keep us so busy that we don't take time to listen to God. We may miss what he wants to say to us. How did it feel to spend so much time going around each obstacle?** Allow for responses. **We need to get quiet sometimes to allow ourselves to hear God.**

2. Low-Powered Game: Come Over to Help Us!

Divide the group into two teams. One side will be Paul and his friends, which will have the newspapers. The other side will be Macedonians, which will have the baskets, boxes, or paper bags. The two teams line up on opposite sides of the playing area. The Macedonians will call out: **Come over to help us!** The other side will make paper wads to represent Paul) and try to toss them into the baskets. The Macedonian side should try to catch the paper wads. After a while, collect all paper wads and switch sides.

After the game, say: **Let's look at what Paul did using THINK—LINK—ACT.** Do the motions:

THINK—Paul wanted to go where God wanted him to go, and he expected God to tell him.

LINK—Paul was prevented to go a number of places. Paul had a dream to go to Macedonia.

ACT—Paul listened to God and went to Macedonia.

HIGH-POWERED GAME NEEDS:

- Paper or card stock to make several signs
- Masking tape
- Small cardboard box, decorated to look like a TV
- A stuffed animal
- A piece of kids' sports gear
- Storybooks
- Stopwatches

LOW-POWERED GAME NEEDS:

- Newspapers
- Large baskets, boxes, or paper bags

OPTION:

To play a less active version of this game, you can use cotton balls instead of paper wads, and shoe boxes instead of baskets; and you can play the game at a table, instead of the entire playing area.

3. Craft: Listening Tubes

CRAFT NEEDS:

- Card stock or lightweight posterboard strips
- Long tubes, such as narrow mailing tubes, gift wrap tubes, or two paper towel tubes connected with duct tape to make a longer tube (one per child)
- Scissors
- Clear tape
- Dried rice, small beans, lentils, unpopped popcorn (any assortment large and small), one-half cup per child
- Assorted generic gift wrapping paper
- Stickers
- Colored markers
- Labels (one per child)
- Colored electrical tape
- Rulers

Kids will create a craft that will also serve as a reminder to be listening for God. Give each child a tube and help him or her tape a cardboard circle to one end of the tube, making sure the end is completely taped closed. Give each child a handful of card stock strips to fold accordion style. They should drop their folded strips into their tube. Let kids cut and fold more strips until their tube is full. Then they should pour in a half cup of rice and beans. Help the kids securely tape the top of the tube closed with the second circle. Then have kids decorate their tubes with gift wrap and stickers. Have the kids tape the label at the midpoint of their tube. Show the kids how to gently turn their tubes on end and listen to how it sounds like rain.

Moses wrote a song that compared the teaching of God to gentle rain that plants need, in Deuteronomy 32:2: "Let my teaching fall like rain and my words descend like dew, like showers on new grass, like abundant rain on tender plants." As you listen to the rain sound that these tubes make, let it remind you to eagerly listen for God.

God, your words are like the gentle rain. I am listening Lord, speak again.

PART THREE:

Plugging In to My Life

Life application of the lesson to lead kids to THINK-LINK-ACT and build a relationship with God every day

A. Cucumber Connection

CUCUMBER CONNECTION NEEDS:

- Pickle jar
- Pickles artwork from the *VeggieConnections Shepherd* pages (on the *VeggieConnections CD-ROM*)
- Green construction paper

Before kids arrive, enlarge and copy the pickles from the *VeggieConnections Shepherd* pages on the CD-ROM included in the *VeggieConnections Elementary Curriculum Kit* onto green construction paper. Cut them out and put into a pickle jar.

Let a volunteer draw a pickle from the Pickle Pot and either the child or a Shepherd should read the dilemma out loud. Each Shepherd should then process the question with his or her small group using the THINK—LINK—ACT phrase.

Coralee loves to sing. She feels God is telling her to use her talent. What should she do?	Felix wants to join the park district's soccer program, but he also wanted to learn how to play the trumpet. His mom said he could only do one. What should Felix do?	Lately you have been feeling inside that you want to know Jesus better. What should you do?

B. Kid Connection: Snoodle Backpack

Ask for a volunteer with a strong voice and give this person a Bible with Matthew 7:7 highlighted or marked. Gather the rest of the kids into a large group in the middle of your room. Place the Bible reader away from the group. Tell the kids in the group to begin talking to each other in soft, low voices. Have the Bible reader read Matthew 7:7 aloud strongly. Stop the kids in the group from talking and ask if anyone heard the Bible verse being read. Allow kids in the group to repeat the Bible verse.

Then repeat the activity, having kids talk louder in the group. Again, see if anyone heard the Bible verse. If anyone did, repeat the activity a third time, having kids talk loudly to one another, and having the Bible reader read, but not shout, the Bible verse. Ask if anyone heard the verse this time. **The louder it got, the harder it was for you to hear the Unit Memory Verse. Sometimes, we need to get quiet to be able to listen to God.**

Divide into *VeggieConnections Groups.* In your groups, take a few minutes to talk about times that it is hardest for you to listen to God. *VeggieConnections Shepherds* should encourage the kids to share what is going on in their lives. This is the THINK part of the process. The LINK and ACT part will be verbalized in "Christ Connection" below.

Distribute the Snoodle backpacks to the children, ensuring each child gets his or her own. Provide popular kid's magazines, posterboard or mural paper, glue sticks, and scissors to each group. Have kids create a mural by cutting or tearing out magazine pictures of kids' activities or things that take up their time, and gluing them to the posterboard or mural paper. After the murals are finished, have kids cut them into pieces, one per person. Shepherds should make sure each child has one large piece. Then have kids cut their piece in half, placing one half in their backpacks, and keeping the other half. Collect the backpacks for next week.

Have kids look at their mural pieces. **These pictures show things that can take up your time and make it hard to find time to listen to God.** Have kids turn their pictures over. **But on this back side, there is nothing. Take a minute and write one way you will take time to listen to God this week. Keep this as a reminder for you to be listening to God.**

KID CONNECTION NEEDS:

- Bible
- Snoodle backpacks (made in *Lesson 1*)
- Popular children's magazines
- Posterboard or paper
- Glue sticks
- Scissors
- Pencils or pens

C. Christ Connection

Sing the *THINK—LINK—ACT* song, with the motions.

Explain that the THINK—LINK—ACT process requires that we listen to God for it to work. **When we say: What would Jesus do? we expect God to show us. We need to pay attention for his answer. He may remind us of Bible stories or words. He may put an idea in our head. Listen to what God may be saying to you! In your group discussion, you just went through the "Think" step; you thought of times you could be listening for God. What is the next step?** *(Link!)* **That's right! Now we remember that God wants to come near to us when we come near to him, by listening for him, by paying attention to what he might be trying to show us. Then, the first part of "Act" is to decide what to do.**

Encourage *VeggieConnections Groups* to take time for prayer, finishing this prayer-starter: **God, we want to connect to you by listening to you. Sometimes it's hard to be quiet and patient. To listen better, God, I want to . . .** Kids name their own ideas. **In Jesus' name, amen.**

Distribute the take-home newspaper, *VeggieConnections.*

THINK:
Stop and think about what God wants you to do.

LINK:
Link God's Word and what you've learned to your choices.

ACT:
Go and act on what God wants you to do!

CHRIST CONNECTION NEEDS:

- *VeggieConnections Music CD*
- CD player
- *VeggieConnections* take-home newspaper (one per child)

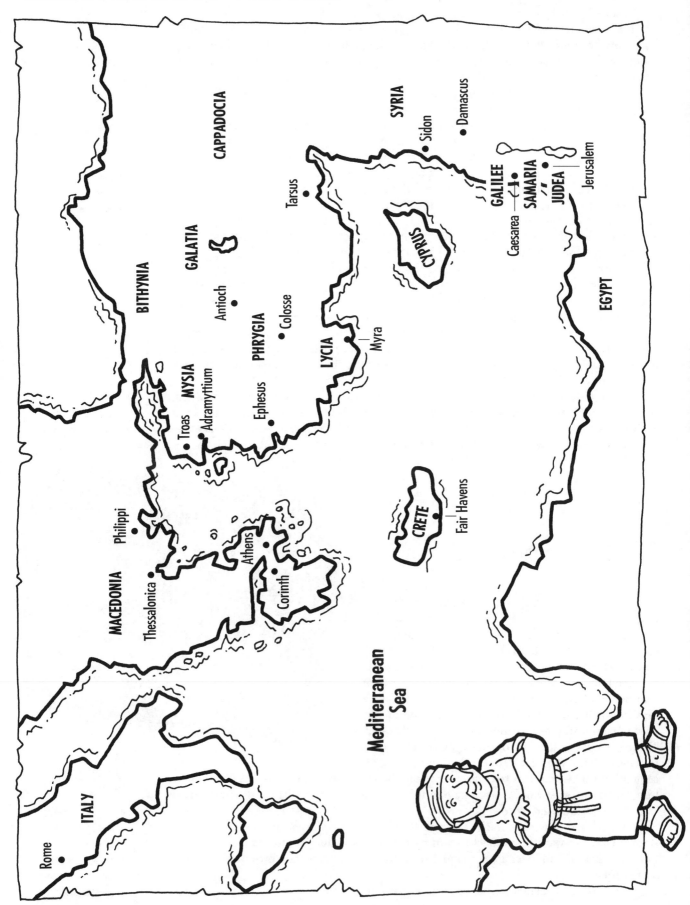

Connection Word:

worship

PART ONE:

Plugging In at Snoodleburg

Introduction to the site and lesson focus

LESSON 4:
Connect to God through worship.

A. Veggie Connection

Dressed as the Mayor of Snoodleburg, welcome the kids to Snoodleburg. **Welcome back to Snoodleburg! Since we are learning** *VeggieConnections,* **let's begin by thinking about connections. Everyone form a circle. I will say something like: Connect elbow to hip. In the circle, everybody connect with those on both sides of you—somebody's elbow to another person's hip. Make sure you are connected on both sides!** Give the kids these connections:

- **Hand to head**
- **Foot to foot**
- **Elbow to hand**
- **Hand to knee**
- **Arm to arm**

That was fun! There are so many ways we could connect to each other. And today we're going to learn an important way to connect to God—through worship. Have a volunteer look up *worship* in the *VeggieConnections Bible Dictionary* and read the definition. *Worship* **means telling God how great he is, thanking him for all he's done for us, giving him our hearts, talking to God, singing, giving an offering, serving God, and promising to know him better.**

B. Prayer Connection

Say: **Let's tell God how great he is right now!** Gather the kids in one big circle. Encourage them to call out a short sentence of praise, such as: **God, you are strong!** or **Lord, you are loving!** If kids need ideas, ask them to think of something good that happened to them this week and how they could praise God for it.

THE CHILDREN
will arrive with their *Veggie-Connections Shepherds* from the opening Countertop Connections featuring Bob and Larry. Play the *Veggie-Connections Music CD* as children enter Snoodleburg.

VEGGIE CONNECTION NEEDS:
- *VeggieConnections Music CD*
- CD player
- *VeggieConnections Bible Dictionary*

PART TWO: Plugging In to God's Word

Connecting to God's Word in the Bible and understanding how that can help us to have a better relationship with him

A. God Connection: Paul and Silas worship God from prison – Acts 16:16-36

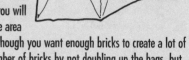

BEFORE YOU START:

Create various sizes of "bricks" and "boulders." To create a brick, open two paper lunch bags, face the open ends toward each other, and insert one into the other. To create a boulder, do the same with brown paper grocery bags. Stack the bags in one corner of the room, to make a semi-enclosed dungeon. If you anticipate that you will need a large space to accommodate all the kids at the site, you can enclose the area by using the chairs in the room and using the paper bricks more sparingly, although you want enough bricks to create a lot of chaos when they are tossed during the "earthquake." You can increase the number of bricks by not doubling up the bags, but by simply opening them and standing them up, top down.

GOD CONNECTION NEEDS:

- Brown paper lunch bags
- Brown paper grocery bags
- Bible

Remember, we can worship God in many ways. We can sing, pray, or think about a Bible verse or story. We can give an offering or praise him.

In our Bible story, Paul and his friend Silas were in jail. They hadn't done anything wrong. But they sang praises to God while they were there! Let's go over to this corner. **Let's imagine it's the jail Paul and Silas were in.** Guide the children to sit close together within the "brick" walls. If possible, dim the lights of the room.

The Bible tells us it was around midnight when Paul and Silas were singing praises to God. Everyone, link arms to imagine that the prisoners were chained together. Everybody in the jail could hear them singing about Jesus. Let's sing a praise song, too, while we're linked together. Lead the kids in singing a short, familiar praise song, such as *Hallelu, Praise Ye the Lord.*

Then motion the kids to get still. **Suddenly, the jail began to shake!** Invite everyone to shake with you. **The ground began to quake!** Motion everyone to sway back and forth with you. **It was an earthquake!** Knock over some bricks. Let kids toss around the bricks in the area, being careful not to throw them at others.

Seat everybody again, amid the rubble. **When the earthquake was done, Paul and Silas were still there. The jailer was afraid they would try to escape the jail, which would have meant trouble for the jailer. He was so surprised! Paul and Silas were still there and were so calm. Right away the jailer said he wanted to believe in Jesus like them! Then the jailer took Paul and Silas to his home. The jailer's entire family believed in Jesus that night. Then Paul and Silas returned to the Jail and waited to be released.**

Have kids divide into *VeggieConnections Groups.* Reinforce the THINK—LINK—ACT principle by having kids discuss how Paul and Silas used it in their situation. Help kids see how they knew God deserved praise (THINK), how God's Word told people to worship (LINK), and so Paul and Silas sung praises even while in jail (ACT).

Have *VeggieConnections Shepherds* encourage kids to share ways they can worship God, even when they don't feel like it. Then have Shepherds offer a brief prayer for their groups, asking God for a spirit of thankfulness and a desire to worship him in all situations.

B. Activity Connection

Choose from the following activities to help kids explore and remember that God wants us to worship him (approximately 10–15 minutes).

1. High-Powered Game: Worship Wall of Praise

Have kids sit in their *VeggieConnections Groups*. Distribute an index card and marker to each child. **We can worship God and grow closer to him through words of praise. Can anyone give me an example of a praise word, or a word that builds God up?** *(Awesome, almighty, wonderful.)*

Have the kids write one praise word on the card. Distribute paper bag blocks and tape to each group. Have them tape a praise card to each block. If there are more cards than blocks, more praise cards can be added. **It feels good when our friends praise us or tell us what a good job we are doing. God is our friend, and it makes God feel good to hear our praises of him!**

When children are finished, have each group build a tower of their blocks, raising their praises to God. Have kids say each praise out loud as they add it to their tower. Encourage thoughtfulness as the children build. The first team to build a sturdy tower wins the praises of everyone in Snoodleburg!

HIGH-POWERED GAME NEEDS:

- Index cards
- Markers
- Paper bag boulders and bricks from God Connection page 136
- Tape

2. Low-Powered Game: Picture God!

BEFORE YOU START:

Copy the "Names of God" sheet on page 158, one for each *VeggieConnections Group*. Cut the cards out and make a set for each group.

Break the kids into *VeggieConnections Groups,* but have some older kids and younger kids trade places so each group has mixed ages for this game. Provide each group with a set of game cards prepared before the lesson. Let the children take turns choosing a name of God and either acting it out or drawing it. The rest of their group tries to guess the name. Limit them in time to about one minute. If the child chooses to act it out, they may make sounds but no words. If the child chooses to draw, they may not write out letters or words.

Conclude the game when everyone has had a turn. If one name seems too difficult, simply let the player choose another name.

Have children share any other names for God that they know. **All of the names in our game today come from the Bible. These words describe Jesus and God. Maybe you learned a new one! What name means the most to you?** Allow responses. **The more we know about who God is, the easier it is to worship him. By worshiping him, we come near to him. Can anyone say our program verse, James 4:8?** *Come near to God and he will come near to you.*

LOW-POWERED GAME NEEDS:

- Large baskets, boxes, or paper bags
- Paper
- Markers

3. Craft: Worship Chain

Have the children write "praise phrases" with markers on paper strips. *(Love God, Thank You God, Worship the Lord, and so on.)* Form first phrase into a loop and fasten with glue, tape, or staples. Make sure phrase is facing the outside of the loop. Insert the next paper strip into the first, and make it into a connecting loop. Fasten with glue, tape, or staples. Continue until each child has his or her own connecting link of praise phrases.

Explain that worship is a celebration. Encourage the children to make more links at home and use the praise phrases to decorate their rooms or a room in their house. Or the links can all be connected together and used to decorate the classroom.

CRAFT NEEDS:

- Markers
- Construction paper strips, 6" x 1" (five per child)
- Glue, tape, or staples

PART THREE:

Plugging In to My Life

Life application of the lesson to lead kids to THINK–LINK–ACT and build a relationship with God every day

A. Cucumber Connection

CUCUMBER CONNECTION NEEDS:

- Pickle jar
- Pickles artwork from the *VeggieConnections Shepherd* pages (on the *CD-ROM*)
- Green construction paper

Before kids arrive, enlarge and copy the pickles from the *VeggieConnections Shepherd* pages on the CD-ROM included in the *VeggieConnections Elementary Curriculum Kit* onto green construction paper. Cut them out and put into a pickle jar.

Let a volunteer draw a pickle from the Pickle Pot and either the child or a Shepherd should read the dilemma out loud. Each Shepherd should then process the question with his or her small group using the THINK—LINK—ACT phrase.

Your mom complains about your misbehavior in church. What should you do?	At breakfast before going to church, Mary got really angry with her brother. She's still angry when she goes into church. What should Mary do in the prayer time in the worship service?	You just realized that God answered your prayer when you see Jack playing. Jack had been very sick and you had prayed for him. What should you do now?

B. Kid Connection: Snoodle Backpack

KID CONNECTION NEEDS:

- Mural paper
- Crayons or markers
- Tape
- Snoodle backpack (made in *Lesson 1*)
- Pencils
- Scissors
- Yarn (1-foot piece per child)

Have kids form *VeggieConnections Groups* and provide a long piece of mural paper and crayons or markers to each group. Have groups work on their murals at tables or tape the mural paper to the wall at kids' eye level. Ask the kids to think of ways to worship. Spread kids out along the mural paper and allow them to draw their art praises. If kids are having difficulty, suggest one or more of the following ideas: people praying, people praising God with words or song, people reading a Bible, someone helping a friend, giving money in church or to someone in need, painting a picture of Jesus. Be sure everyone contributes to this worship mural. Ask kids to share what they drew. Then say: **Your pictures show fantastic THINKing!**

Now here's the LINK part: We can link our Program Verse: "*Come near to God and he will come near to you*," James 4:8. And to ACT, we worship him, we come near to him. He will come near to us because he loves to hear and see our worship. Remember God is present in worship. We are telling him how great he is.

Part of our Unit Memory Verse says: "*Seek and you will find.*" The best thing to seek is God himself, doing everything you can to know him better. Our Unit Memory Verse says, we will find him. How awesome that is!

Distribute the Snoodle backpacks made in *Lesson 1*. Be sure each child receives his or her backpack. Provide scissors to Shepherds and have them cut out the each child's drawing from the mural. Say: **You have all drawn beautiful ways to worship God!**

Let children roll up their pictures and tie them with a piece of yarn. Have Shepherds help younger children. Then have kids put their rolls in their backpacks. Collect the backpacks for use next week.

C. Christ Connection

CHRIST CONNECTION NEEDS:

- *VeggieConnections Music CD*
- CD player
- *VeggieConnections* take-home newspaper (one per child)

Listen to the *THINK—LINK—ACT* song on the *VeggieConnections Music CD* while kids do the motions. Then have everyone sit in circles with their *VeggieConnections Shepherds*. Ask everyone to think of something to praise or thank God for ("Think"). Next say: **God loves to receive our worship. When we worship we are connected to him** ("Link"). The *VeggieConnections Shepherds* should encourage each child to express specific thanks ("Act") with this prayerstarter: **God, we worship you because you are . . .** (what they appreciate about God). Close with: **Loving Father, thank you for giving us the gift of being able to worship you. In Jesus' name, amen.**

Distribute the take-home newspaper, ***VeggieConnections***.

Connecting to **Communication** through **Paul's Ministry**
Paul explains about the armor of God:
Ephesians 6:10-20

PART ONE:

Plugging In at Snoodleburg

Introduction to the site and lesson focus

LESSON 5:
Connect to God through the Bible.

A. Veggie Connection

Before the lesson, gather up some props to wear as the Mayor. You'll need a bicycle helmet and some protective pads such as elbow and knee pads.

Dressed as the Mayor of Snoodleburg with a helmet and pads, greet the children as they enter Snoodleburg. **I just came from playing our favorite game in Snoodleburg— bicycle soccerhockeyball! I wear this helmet and these pads to keep myself from getting hurt. Have any of you ever been hurt from not wearing a helmet or pads?** Allow responses.

Today's Connection Word of the day is *armor*. Have someone look up *armor* in the *Veggie Bible Dictionary* and read the definition. **My helmet and pads act as armor to protect me from being hurt. Let's have some fun making some armor now!**

Have kids break into *VeggieConnections Groups* and provide groups with construction paper, posterboard, aluminum foil, and other supplies. Have each Shepherd select a volunteer child to stand in the middle of their group. Using the supplies, have the other kids make pieces of armor and attach to the volunteer. If kids get stuck for ideas, suggest using the foil for arm or leg armor and making a shield out of the posterboard. Allow a few minutes for kids to work. Then say: **You've done a great job of making armor! Today we're going to be talking about a different kind of armor and how it can help protect us.**

Have kids remove the armor from their volunteers.

B. Prayer Connection

Say: **We've been learning many ways to connect to God. Today we're going to discover how the Bible helps us connect to God. I want you to think of one way the Bible helps you know God better.**

Lead the group in prayer. Allow the kids a chance to share a way the Bible helps them know God, or to thank God for a favorite verse or for something they've learned about him from the Bible.

THE CHILDREN
will arrive with their *Veggie-Connections Shepherds* from the opening Countertop Connections featuring Bob and Larry. Play the *Veggie-Connections Music CD* as children enter Snoodleburg.

VEGGIE CONNECTION NEEDS:

- *VeggieConnections Music CD*
- CD player
- Bicycle helmet
- Protective pads
- *VeggieConnections Bible Dictionary*
- Construction paper in a variety of colors
- Posterboard
- Aluminum foil
- Scissors
- Glue sticks
- Markers
- Tape

PART TWO:

Plugging In to God's Word

Connecting to God's Word in the Bible and understanding how that can help us to have a better relationship with him

A. God Connection: Paul explains about the armor of God – Ephesians 6:10-20

Gather the children at the base of Mount Ginchez to sit in a circle.

In our Bible verses for today, Paul wrote a letter to his friends at the Ephesian church. Point out Ephesus on the map. **He said, "*Be strong in the Lord and in his mighty power.*"When Paul said that, he didn't mean that he wanted Christians to have big muscles on their arms and legs. He meant that he hoped they would be able to make choices that please God. He wanted them to stay connected to God.**

Think about the last time you wanted to do something you knew was wrong. That's called *temptation.* **Think about when you were worried or afraid or sad. When we face these things, we need to be strong in the Lord. And God gave us something to help us be strong.** Have a volunteer read Ephesians 6:11–13.

Give out copies of the "Armor of God" pictures (on page 159). Ask for a volunteer soldier to come up while you gather the armor props.

Have kids take turns reading verses 14–17, pausing with each phrase to refer to the picture of the armor and give your soldier the appropriate prop.

When Paul said to wear the armor of God, he didn't mean you should put on actual armor like soldiers wear. What do you think these pieces of armor mean? Allow kids to work through defining each piece of armor. After they have tried, allow them to look up the pieces in the *VeggieConnections Bible Dictionary.* As the kids define each piece of armor, allow them to color it on their picture. Write a simple definition for each piece on the flip chart, and leave it posted for the rest of the lesson. Below are some simple definitions that might help the kids.

- **The belt of truth:** *A belt holds clothes close to the body. We have the truth of the Bible close to us to help us know what to believe and do.*
- **The breastplate of righteousness:** *A breastplate protects the heart, and when our heart is right with God, we will live right.*
- **Shoes of the Gospel of peace:** *When we tell others about Jesus, we are wearing the shoes of the Gospel.*
- **The shield of faith:** *A shield protects us from the attacks of unbelievers. Faith in God shields or protects us from these attacks.*
- **The helmet of salvation:** *A helmet protects the head. When we believe in Jesus, we can know God has saved us and will continue to forgive us when we sin.*
- **The sword of the Spirit, which is the Word of God:** *The Bible helps us when we face the battles of living the Christian life.*

That's a lot of armor! What's something that helps us to understand and "put on" all this armor? *(The Bible.)* Draw a large Bible on the flip chart. **Reading the Bible and learning how to do what it says every day will make us strong in the Lord!**

What this means is when you face a difficult situation, you will stop and THINK— what choices do I have? Then you will LINK by remembering that you can use the armor of God to help you. Then you can ACT—do what the Bible tells you, or learn the Bible more so you can do the right thing and keep your connection with God strong.

Ask for a volunteer to read verses 18–20. **After Paul talked about the armor of God, he talked about the importance of prayer. He even asked for prayers himself.**

Have kids divide into their *VeggieConnections Groups* and have *VeggieConnections Shepherds* ask kids for prayer needs and then allow groups to have a brief prayer time.

GOD CONNECTION NEEDS:

- "Armor of God" pictures from page 159
- Armor props
- Bible
- Map of Paul's travels from page 134
- *VeggieConnections Bible Dictionary*
- Flip chart or newsprint pad
- Marker

BEFORE YOU START:

Before the lesson, copy the "Armor of God" pictures on page 159, one for each child. You'll also need armor props: plastic tote lid for a breastplate; bicycle helmet; fat, shiny belt; big snow boots or house shoes; cardboard shield (instructions at High-Powered Game page 141); sword made out of aluminum foil.

B. Activity Connection

Choose from the following activities to help kids explore and remember that the armor of God will keep us connected to God when faced with difficult choices (approximately 10–15 minutes each).

1. High-Powered Game: Temptation Attack!

HIGH-POWERED GAME NEEDS:
- Newspaper or newsprint
- Index cards
- Pencils
- Tape
- Cardboard shields
- Duct tape

Have kids divide into their *VeggieConnections Groups*. Provide newspapers or newsprint, index cards, pencils, and tape. Have groups brainstorm common temptations kids face, and have kids write each temptation on an index card. Instruct kids to wad up newspaper sheets into balls and tape the temptation cards to them. Give one person in each group a shield and have kids stand about ten feet away from the shield-carrying person. Have the kids call out the temptation on the paper balls before launching them toward their group's target. Have the kids with the shields call out: **Strong in the Lord!** or, **Armor of God!** each time they hit away a paper ball. Switch roles often, so everyone has a chance to use the shields.

We used these cardboard shields to bat away paper-ball temptations. In real life we need to use the Bible and our connection with Jesus to help us when we are tempted to do something wrong. Let's all say "I will stay connected to God through the Bible!"

BEFORE YOU START:
Make shields by cutting off a 1-inch wide 1-foot strip from rectangular cardboard pieces. Duct tape the strips in the center of the shield pieces, bowing the strip to make a gripping handle on the back side. You'll need one shield for each *Veggie-Connections Group*.

2. Low-Powered Game: The Armor Game

The goal of the game is to match the physical armor picture to the spiritual armor phrase. Divide kids into as many groups you have card sets for, and give each group a set of cards. Mix up the cards and place them face down on the table in rows and columns. Each child gets to take a turn choosing two cards to see if they match. If they do, the child keeps the pair. If they don't match, the child turns the cards face down and everyone tries to remember where they were. Have the kids play a couple of rounds.

You have all done so well learning about the armor of God. Check to see if they can remember them fairly well by now by saying the physical armor and seeing if anyone can remember the spiritual armor. **Remember, God gives us this important armor so we will be prepared to do his work in the world. Let's remember to put it on every day.**

LOW-POWERED GAME NEEDS:
- "Armor of God" pictures from page 159
- "Armor of God" cards from page 160

BEFORE YOU START:
This game can be played in groups of 2, 3, 4 or larger. Photocopy both "Armor of God" pictures (page 159) and "Armor of God" cards (page 160), and cut out both copies to make card sets. You'll need a set for each game grouping you chose.

3. Craft: Sword of the Spirit

BEFORE YOU START:
Write some Bible verses that show God's help on a piece of paper. Some suggestions: "It is the Sovereign Lord who helps me," Isaiah 50:9; "Come to me, all you who are weary and burdened, and I will give you rest," Matthew 11:28; "The Lord is my helper, I will not be afraid," Hebrews 13:6b. Photocopy sheets for each *VeggieConnections Group* or craft grouping you choose.

Draw a sword shape on card stock, and cut it out for a pattern for kids to cut their own during the craft. Make enough patterns for each group to have one. Then draw a simple blade-shaped book page matching the sword pattern and copy five sheets for each child.

Say: **The sword of the Spirit is given to us by God to help us to LINK to his word in the Bible and ACT to make good choices. Today, you will create your own sword book filled with Bible verses to refer to when you need God's help making choices.**
Divide kids into *VeggieConnections Groups*. Provide groups with scissors and markers. Using the pattern, have kids each cut out two sword patterns on card stock. **Print the words "Sword of the Spirit" on the cover of your book and write your name on the cover as well.** Have *VeggieConnections Shepherds* help younger children. Next, have the children cut out five blade-shaped pages. Insert the pages between the two card-stock pieces, and staple together, forming a book.

Have kids draw each piece of armor with its verse from Ephesians 6:14–17 on the first two pages. **Now, you can choose three Bible verses that you think will help you when you need God's help.** Distribute papers with verses on them. Encourage older children to look up their own verses if they would like, using provided Bibles. Younger kids can draw one picture on each of the remaining three pages to show when they may need God's help, or a time when they received his help.

Sword of the Spirit
Joel

CRAFT NEEDS:
- Prepared Bible verses (one per group)
- Prepared card-stock sword pattern (one per group)
- Copied blade pages (five per child)
- Scissors
- Bibles
- Markers
- Card-stock pieces (two per child)
- Stapler

PART THREE:

Plugging In to My Life

Life application of the lesson to lead kids to THINK-LINK-ACT and build a relationship with God every day

A. Cucumber Connection

CUCUMBER CONNECTION NEEDS:

- Pickle jar
- Pickles artwork from the *VeggieConnections Shepherd* pages (on the CD-ROM)
- Green construction paper

Before kids arrive, enlarge and copy the pickles from the *VeggieConnections Shepherd* pages on the CD-ROM included in the *VeggieConnections Elementary Curriculum Kit* onto green construction paper. Cut them out and put into a pickle jar.

Let a volunteer draw a pickle from the Pickle Pot and either the child or a Shepherd should read the dilemma out loud. Each Shepherd should then process the question with his or her small group using the THINK—LINK—ACT phrase.

| Sandy's friends are teasing her for believing in God. She's beginning to wonder if she is a believer. What armor does she need, and how can that help her? | Timmy can't join a sports team because they practice on a night he has to go to church club. He doesn't want to go to the church club anymore. What armor does he need, and how can that help him? | Stacy wants to tell her friend from another country about the truth of Jesus. But she doesn't want to offend her friend's beliefs. What armor does Stacy need, and how can it help her? |

B. Kid Connection: Snoodle Backpack

KID CONNECTION NEEDS:

- Sets of "Armor of God" pictures and cards (pages 159 and 160)
- Snoodle backpack (made in *Lesson 1*)
- Construction paper
- Glue sticks
- Pencils or markers
- Yarn (1-foot piece per child)

Divide kids into *VeggieConnections Groups* and provide several sets of "Armor of God" pictures and cards (on pages 159 and 160). Have *VeggieConnections Shepherds* review the six armor pieces and their meaning with their kids. Then have kids pick one of the armor pictures or cards that would help them with a difficult situation. For example, a child might say he being made fun of for being a Christian. Possible helps could be the sword of the Spirit for helping him share the truth of the Bible, or the belt of truth to reassure him of his faith.

When kids share a situation, have the group help discuss it using the armor and the THINK—LINK—ACT process. Also talk about the Unit Memory Verse, Matthew 7:7, and how it would help.

Distribute the Snoodle backpacks made in *Lesson 1*. Be sure each child receives his or her backpack. Provide construction paper and glue sticks. Have kids choose the one armor picture or card they used in their situation to glue to their paper. Then have kids write a prayer asking God for help with their situation. Instruct *VeggieConnections Shepherds* to help younger kids. Let children roll up their pictures and tie them with a piece of yarn. Then have kids put their rolls in their backpacks and collect them for use next week.

C. Christ Connection

CHRIST CONNECTION NEEDS:

- *VeggieConnections Music CD*
- CD player
- *VeggieConnections* take-home newspaper (one per child)

Sing the *THINK—LINK—ACT* song with motions.

When done, have everyone sit down in a circle. Ask the kids if they would like to share something they're facing that they'd like some help using the armor of God with. Let volunteers share their situations, and let other kids give ideas of pieces of armor that might help, using THINK—LINK—ACT.

Pray together in *VeggieConnections Groups*. Encourage the kids to pray for each other's situations that they mentioned or to simply ask God to help another child by name put on the armor of God. Have *VeggieConnections Shepherds* pray for everyone's strength in wearing God's armor while out in the world.

Distribute the take-home newspaper, ***VeggieConnections***.

Connecting to **Communication** through **Paul's Ministry**
Paul explains how to live by the Spirit: **Galatians 5:16-26**

Holy Spirit

PART ONE:

Plugging In at Snoodleburg

Introduction to the site and lesson focus

LESSON 6:
Connect to God through the Holy Spirit.

A. Veggie Connection

BEFORE YOU START:
Use masking tape to mark off several paths from the entrance of Snoodleburg to Mt. Ginchez. Make a path for every *Veggie-Connections Group*. Place stickers on index cards (one per card). You can draw a simple happy face or a sad face on the cards if you don't have stickers. In each paper bag, place a card with a happy sticker and a card with a frown sticker. Place bags at various points along each path, five to seven bags per path.

Dressed as the Mayor of Snoodleburg, greet kids at the entrance of the site. Keep the kids near the entrance until you explain the opening activity.

    Everyone, cluster together in your *VeggieConnections Groups*. Have *VeggieConnections Shepherds* line up their groups at the start of the paths. **Kids, you need to walk the path that goes from the Snoodleburg entrance to Mt. Ginchez. Whenever you get to a bag, you should reach in and take out the card. If it has a smiley face, you can move forward to the next bag and stop. If there is a frown face, you move backward to the bag behind you, then stop. Be sure to put the card back in the bag for the next person. Then the next in line gets a turn. Now, Shepherds, before your group members start, you need to tell them how to move— hop, skip, jump, tip toe, walk like a duck, or whatever!**

    Play until everyone reaches Mt. Ginchez.

    Getting from Snoodleburg to Mt. Ginchez wasn't very easy, was it? How did it feel to do that? Allow responses. **You never knew if you were going to get a happy face or a sad face. Only after you looked at the card did you know what direction to go. When we believe in Jesus, we get our directions from the Holy Spirit—that's the Spirit of Jesus living in our hearts. And we don't need to wonder what those directions will be, because God has written his directions in the Bible. The Holy Spirit reminds us of what's in the Bible!** Have a volunteer look up *Holy Spirit* in the *VeggieConnections Bible Dictionary*. **Today were going to explore how we know if the Holy Spirit is living in us.**

B. Prayer Connection

Say: **Let's have another look at our happy and sad cards.** Carry the bags around to the kids, and have each child reach in without looking and pull out a card. Some kids may need to share.

    Have kids turn and face the others in their *VeggieConnections Groups*. **If your card has a smiley face on it, thank God for something good that happened this week. If your card has a frown on it, ask God's help with something that's going on in your life.** Allow time for small groups to pray. Close by asking God to help the kids connect closely with him today.

THE CHILDREN
will arrive with their *Veggie-Connections Shepherds* from the opening Countertop Connections featuring Bob and Larry. Play the *Veggie-Connections Music CD* as children enter Snoodleburg.

VEGGIE CONNECTION NEEDS:
- VeggieConnections Music CD
- CD player
- Masking tape
- Index cards
- Stickers of smile faces and frown faces
- Paper lunch bags (five to seven per *Veggie-Connections Group*)
- *VeggieConnections Bible Dictionary*

PART TWO:

Plugging In to God's Word

Connecting to God's Word in the Bible and understanding how that can help us to have a better relationship with him

A. God Connection: Paul explains how to live by the Spirit – Galatians 5:16-26

GOD CONNECTION NEEDS:

- Bible
- Map of Paul's travels (on page 134)
- Clothing box lid
- Play sand
- *VeggieConnections Bible Dictionary*

Have kids sit at the base of Mt. Ginchez. **In our Bible, there is a letter from Paul to his friends in Galatia.** Point out Galatia on the map. **He wanted to remind them to "live by the Spirit." That means he wanted them to do the things that would please God, with the help of the Holy Spirit.** Have a volunteer read Galatians 5:16–18.

When we talk about the Holy Spirit, we are talking about God. We can't see his Spirit, but when we believe in Jesus, his Spirit comes to live in us. He is called the Holy Spirit because he helps us know right from wrong, he comforts us, helps us, and other things, too.

Bring out the clothing box lid. Pour a cup of play sand in the lid. Smooth the sand with your hand. **Let's imagine we are on a beach. If the sand is smooth like that, do you think anyone's been walking on the beach? No, because there are no footprints in the sand. Now, pretend someone walks on the beach.** Use your fingers to make footprints in the sand. **Even if you leave the beach you can see that someone has been there.**

We can't see the Holy Spirit, but we can see proof that he is working in us. Our behaviors and attitudes show us if we are listening to the Holy Spirit—to God. Paul calls that "living by the Spirit."

Paul names nine parts of the fruit of the Spirit. Read Galatians 5:22–26 aloud. **Now, when we talk about fruit that we eat, where does it come from?** *(From a tree or garden.)* **That's right. The fruit doesn't just grow by itself; it's attached to a tree or vine. What happens if the fruit gets pulled off before it's big and ripe?** *(It stops growing and tastes bitter.)* **Paul used this example because the Holy Spirit works like that with us. When we stay connected to God, like fruit on a tree, we can keep growing in him, becoming like him, and he is like the fruit named here.** Read Galatians 5:22–26 aloud again. **When we choose to act God's way, we show others these behaviors: love, joy, peace, patience, kindness, goodness, faithfulness, gentleness, and self-control.**

Move into *VeggieConnections Groups.* Lead the kids in discussing what these words mean. Let the kids take turns looking up the words in the *VeggieConections Bible Dictionary.* Then invite the kids to talk about this question with their *VeggieConnections Group*: **Why is it important for the Holy Spirit to develop the fruit within us?** *(So we can become like Jesus, so we can do well in life, so we can relate to others well, so we have proof that God's Spirit is living in us.)*

B. Activity Connection

Choose from the following activities to help kids explore and remember that God wants us to stay connected to him through the Holy Spirit (approximately 10–15 minutes each).

1. High-Powered Game: Fruity Responses Relay

BEFORE YOU START:

Write each of the nine fruit of the Spirit qualities from Galatians 5:22–23 on separate index cards. Make duplicate sets so you have one index card for each child. Set up nine chairs in a row at the far end of the playing area. Place the fruit of the Spirit cards on the chairs, with all of the same fruit quality on the same chair.

Form at least two teams. Team members should line up for the relay, forming pairs. Call out a "Think" situation (see suggestions below). The first pair of each team races to the chairs and selects one fruit quality they feel would best be needed for that situation. Pairs race to try to be the first to get the card they want. If that card is missing, they must choose another. They then race back to their teams. The teams must quickly work through Think—Link—Act, using the fruit quality they brought back. Once their *VeggieConnections Shepherd* approves it, they start a pile for their cards and wait for the next situation to be read and the next player to go. Play until all have had a turn, recognizing that there will be fewer and fewer cards available.

HIGH-POWERED GAME NEEDS:

- Prepared index cards (one per every two kids)

Suggested "Think" situations:
- **You studied really hard for this week's spelling test, but you got several words wrong anyway.**
- **Your best friend told you that she doesn't want to be your best friend anymore.**
- **Someone is making fun of one of your friends.**
- **You've had a really bad day.**
- **A younger friend keeps asking you to tie her shoes.**
- **Your teacher punishes you for something you did not do.**
- **One of your parents has been really stressed and busy at work and rarely has time for you lately.**
- **Your mother tells you to share your favorite toy with a cousin who is visiting.**
- **You made a promise that you no longer want to keep.**
- **A bully keeps picking on you at school.**
- **There are yummy cookies at home that your mom told you not to touch.**
- **You can't agree with family members on what to watch on TV.**
- **You really miss a favorite friend who recently moved out of town.**
- **You want to do what your friends in school are doing—writing messages on the playground equipment and walls.**
- **There is a new kid in class whom the teacher has asked everyone to help.**

2. Low-Powered Game: Fruit Bingo

BEFORE YOU START:

Write the nine fruits of the Spirit from Galatians 5:22-23 on nine index cards, one fruit per card. You may use the cards from the Fruity Responses Relay game if you prepared those. Place the color dots on five index cards, one dot per card. Copy the "Fruit Bingo" sheet on page 161, one per every two kids, and cut the game grids out.

Give each child a bingo grid. Give kids dot stickers, five of each color. They should place the dots in every square on their card in any order they choose. This will ensure that each bingo grid is randomly unique. Place the color cards in one bag and the fruit cards in another. On each round, draw a color card from the first bag and a fruit card from the second. Return the cards to the bags after calling. Players who have that color in their fruit column place a bean on that square. Play continues until someone has a row or column completed or a corner to corner diagonal.

After the game, say: **This game was a fun way to hear about the fruit of the Spirit qualities we should have in our lives. How can we show these actions in our real lives?** Allow responses. Then talk about ways kids can live out these fruit of the Spirit qualities, using THINK—LINK—ACT.

LOW-POWERED GAME NEEDS:

- "Fruit Bingo" grids on page 161 (one grid per child)
- Small colored dot stickers in five colors (five of each color per child)
- Two paper bags
- Prepared index cards
- Unpopped popcorn or dried beans
- Fruity snack prizes (optional) (check with parents about food allergies)

3. Craft: Fruit of the Spirit Sand Art

Show kids how to draw a tree with nine branches on card stock, with enough room between the branches to allow for the sand fruit on each branch. Have the children put glue on the branches only. Use paintbrushes to spread glue evenly. Pour sand on the glue. Shake excess sand back into the bowls. Repeat the process with each of the fruits. Encourage the kids to make their pictures colorful. This craft is a reminder that when a relationship with God is developed, it grows and flourishes, just like the fruit on the vine.

CRAFT NEEDS:

- Card stock (one per child)
- Pencils or markers
- Small paint brushes
- Glue
- Colored sand separated in bowls

PART THREE:

Plugging In to My Life

Life application of the lesson to lead kids to THINK–LINK–ACT and build a relationship with God every day

A. Cucumber Connection

CUCUMBER CONNECTION NEEDS:

- Pickle jar
- Pickles artwork from the *VeggieConnections Shepherd* pages (on the *VeggieConnections CD-ROM*)
- Green construction paper

Before kids arrive, enlarge and copy the pickles from the *VeggieConnections Shepherd* pages on the CD-ROM included in the *VeggieConnections Elementary Curriculum Kit* onto green construction paper. Cut them out and put into a pickle jar.

Let a volunteer draw a pickle from the Pickle Pot and either the child or a Shepherd should read the dilemma out loud. Each Shepherd should then process the question with his or her small group using the THINK—LINK—ACT phrase.

Tracy has a bad habit of teasing another girl on her street. She knows it's wrong. What should Tracy do?	Jared is having a hard time sharing his toys. He lets his friend take the toy to play with it, but then wants it back right away. What should Jared do?	Angela has a hard time keeping her promises. What should Angela do?

B. Kid Connection: Snoodle Backpack

KID CONNECTION NEEDS:

- Construction paper in a variety of fruit colors
- Prepared construction paper sheets
- Snoodle backpack
- Snoodle Journal Page on page 156 (one per child)
- Markers or crayons
- Yarn

BEFORE YOU START:

Using nine different construction paper colors, cut out various fruit shapes, one fruit for each color. If you can't find nine colors, repeating colors is fine. Write each fruit of the Spirit from Galatians 5:22–23 on each paper. Copy a Snoodle Journal Page on page 156 for each child.

Divide the group into clusters of four kids. Each cluster should make up a story that requires someone to use THINK—LINK—ACT related to one or more of the fruit of the Spirit. Let the groups use the construction-paper fruit of the Spirit pictures you prepared earlier for reference during their stories. Let the clusters tell their stories to the entire group.

Divide the kids into three groups and the Unit Memory Verse into three parts: 1) "*Ask and it will be given to you*"; 2) "*Seek and you will find*"; 3) "*Knock and the door will be opened to you.*" Each group should act out their part of Matthew 7:7 with pantomime.

Distribute the Snoodle backpacks made in Lesson 1. Be sure each child receives his or her backpack. Give each child a Snoodle Journal page on page 156 and markers or crayons. *VeggieConnections Shepherds* should guide the children in their groups to identify how they need to display the fruits of the Spirit in their daily lives or as they face difficult situations. Encourage kids to color fruit of the Spirit on their papers, and write examples of how they can demonstrate that quality next to the fruit. For example, for *kindness*, kids could write "Be kind to my brother." Have *VeggieConnections Shepherds* help younger children. Let children roll up their pictures and tie them with a piece of yarn. Then have kids put their rolls in their backpacks. Collect the backpacks for use next week.

C. Christ Connection

CHRIST CONNECTION NEEDS:

- *VeggieConnections Music CD*
- CD player
- *VeggieConnections* take-home newspaper (one per child)

Play the *THINK—LINK—ACT* song from the *VeggieConnections Music CD* while kids act out the motions. Have the children sit with their *VeggieConnections Groups*. Before praying, have the children identify the fruit quality that is hardest for them to do. Start the prayer off like this: **God, thank you for sending your Spirit to live in us. We know your power is there for us. Please help us when we have trouble practicing these fruit qualities . . .** Let the kids name any fruits they would like God's help with. **In Jesus' name, amen.**

Distribute the take-home newspaper, *VeggieConnections*.

Connecting to **Communication** through **Paul's Ministry**
Paul sails for Rome: **Acts 27:1–44**

PART ONE:

Plugging In at Snoodleburg

Introduction to the site and lesson focus

LESSON 7:
Connect to God by letting him help me solve my problems.

A. Veggie Connection

Dressed as the Mayor of Snoodleburg, welcome the kids to Snoodleburg and invite them to sit down by Mt. Ginchez. Give each child three feet of yarn. For half a minute, they should tangle up the yarn as much as they can. Each child should pass his or her yarn to someone else to try to untangle. Every thirty seconds, have kids pass the yarn to another person.

These tangles remind me of problems everybody has from time to time, even Veggies! Pass around the Bob and Larry plush toys. Whoever is holding one of them may briefly tell about a problem they remember Larry or Bob having. Kids who don't wish to share may pass the toy along. **How many of you have ever had any of these problems?** Allow for a show of hands. **Often when we have troubles, we can't solve the problem by ourselves. We need help from others.** *Help* is our Connection Word today.

Have a volunteer look up *help* in the *VeggieConnections Bible Dictionary* and read the definition to the group. Show a piece of tangled-up yarn and say: **When we get tangled up with life's problems, we need help. And there's no better place to go for help than God. Today we'll see how Paul had a big problem and needed God's help.**

B. Prayer Connection

Have the kids bow their heads for prayer and pass around the Bob and Larry plush toys. Whoever is holding one of the toys may have a turn to say a sentence prayer naming either one problem they face or a problem that kids in general face. Any child who doesn't wish to pray may simply pass the toy along. Close the prayer time by asking God to lead the kids to connect to him by bringing their problems to him.

THE CHILDREN
will arrive with their *Veggie-Connections Shepherds* from the opening Countertop Connections featuring Bob and Larry. Play the *Veggie-Connections Music CD* as children enter Snoodleburg.

VEGGIE CONNECTION NEEDS:

- *VeggieConnections Music CD*
- CD player
- Yarn (three feet per child)
- Bob and Larry plush toys
- *VeggieConnections Bible Dictionary*

PRAYER CONNECTION NEEDS:

- Bob and Larry plush toys

PART TWO: Plugging In to God's Word

Connecting to God's Word in the Bible and understanding how that can help us to have a better relationship with him

A. God Connection: Paul sails for Rome – Acts 27:1-44

GOD CONNECTION NEEDS:

- Chairs
- Large box fan
- Water mister bottles (one per *Veggie-Connections Group*)
- Map of Paul's travels (on page 134)
- Easel
- Bible

TEACHER TIP:

Younger children may benefit from hearing the story before interacting with it. Explain to kids you'll read the story twice. For the first reading, they should listen very carefully. For the second reading, kids will help tell the story.

Say: **Let's all take chairs and put two side by side, making a long line, like seats in a long boat.**

While the kids are getting chairs arranged, set up a large box fan facing the chairs and give water mist bottles to the *VeggieConnections Shepherds*. Have the kids be seated on the "boat." Place the map on an easel where everyone can see it.

Who remembers something we've learned about Paul? Let volunteers name a few things. Open your Bible and say: **The Bible tells us that Paul was put under arrest for teaching about Jesus. He and some other prisoners were handed over to a soldier named Julius. They sailed for a day and stopped in a city called Sidon.** Point it out on the map. **Paul was allowed to visit some friends, and then he got on a large ship and started on the long voyage to Rome.** Point out Rome on the map, and seat kids in the "boat." **Let's act like we are sailing on the sea.** Have everyone sway from side to side. **They traveled around Cyprus until they reached the city of Myra, where Paul and the others changed ships.** Point out these places on the map.

The wind was getting stronger, which made it hard to sail. Turn the fan on low speed, blowing on the kids. **They sailed along the island of Crete until they reached an area called Fair Havens.** Point it out on the map.

The wind got stronger. Set fan to medium speed and have children sway harder. **God had told Paul that the sailing voyage would be very dangerous. Paul tried to warn the soldier and the ship's captain, but they didn't listen to him. They kept sailing in the bad weather.**

For a while the wind settled down. Turn the fan speed to low, and have children slow their swaying. **But suddenly, the wind became like a hurricane!** Turn fan to high speed and have children sway rapidly. *VeggieConnections Shepherds* should spray mist bottles over the kids' heads. **The crew of the ship were so scared, they threw large boxes of cargo overboard, to lighten the load of the ship.** Have kids pretend to throw boxes overboard.

Have the kids sway gently so they can listen. **Because the storm was so bad, nobody had anything to eat for many days. God spoke to Paul again, to tell him that everyone would be safe, but that the ship would be destroyed. God was helping Paul and the crew to stay alive.**

Some of the sailors tried to escape from the ship by getting the lifeboats ready to sneak away on. But Paul warned them that they needed to stay on the ship to stay alive. He then told everyone to eat some food to get ready for the final part of the trip. Before eating, Paul thanked God, even in the middle of this storm.

Finally, when the captain of the ship saw an island, he sailed the boat toward the beach. The ship hit ground and was broken into pieces! Lead the kids to jump out of their chairs and turn the chairs on their sides, being careful not to hit other kids with the chairs. **The crew held on to pieces of wood from the ship and swam to shore.** Have kids grab their chairs, and pretend to swim with their other hand. **Just as God had told Paul, the ship was destroyed but everyone was safe.**

Ask the kids to return their chairs to the table and be seated.

How did God help Paul with the problem of the big storm? *(He didn't make the storm go away. But he helped Paul and the others get through it. Paul kept talking to God in prayer, and God kept helping Paul know the best things to do.)* **Paul trusted God to help him. God helped Paul to solve the problem of the storm. We can let God help us with our problems, too.**

B. Activity Connection

Choose from the following activities to help kids explore and remember to stay connected to God by letting him help them solve their problems (approximately 10–15 minutes each).

1. High-Powered Game: Safe On the Island

BEFORE YOU START:

Write the letters, H, E, L, P on slips of paper, stacking each letter in a pile and making enough sets for most of the kids in your class. For example, if you have 20 kids, make four slips of each letter. Tape off a circle in the middle of the room large enough to fit the number of kids you have for one of the paper slip's letter. Tape a larger boundary around the circle, to designate the larger playing area.

Assign about a third of the kids to be "Waves" and the rest to be "Sailors." Have the Waves spread out in the larger designated playing area (the ocean), but not on the smaller center circle island. Have the Sailors stand just outside the game area, on any side. Set the four piles of letters anywhere in the ocean but out of reach of any Wave.

The object of the game is for the Sailors to travel through the Waves to pick up the letters that spell *HELP* and then make it to the "island" in the center. The kids who are Waves must plant their feet firmly and not move them, but they wave their hands back and forth and may reach out to touch Sailors as they pass through. Any Sailor who gets touched must go back to the sidelines to begin again. Any Wave who moves, lifts, or shifts his feet must sit out the rest of the round. Once Sailors collect the four letters and reach the island, they get on their knees as if praying.

After reaching the island and "praying," Sailors may move back to the sidelines to watch the others. Play a few times so that everyone has a chance to be a Sailor and a Wave.

What problem did Paul have in our Bible story? *(He was sailing through a storm.)* **How did Paul get help with his problem?** *(He stayed connected to God through prayer; he let God help him solve his problem.)*

2. Low-Powered Game: Help! I'm Shipwrecked!

Divide your class in half. Have one half sit down together in a boat outline made of chairs. Have the other kids form two equal relay teams and line up behind a taped line. Explain the first two kids in line in each team will run to the boat, pick up one child, and carry him or her back to the line. That person joins the next person in line forming a pair, and they run to the boat and pick up another child and bring this person back to the line, where the action repeats. Play until all the people in the boat are rescued (no one left in the boat outline). The winning team is the larger team left at the end of the game (indicating a greater number of boat people rescues).

Play another round, switching boat people and relay team roles. **You helped rescue shipwrecked people in this game. In the Bible story, God rescued the people when they obeyed Paul's instructions from God. And God is always there to help us when we need it.**

3. Craft: Sponge Boat

Distribute the craft supplies to the kids. Show them how to trim their sponges into a boat shape. Have them create a flag out of construction paper to attach to the top of their dowel rods. Then have kids draw a cross on their flags, explaining how the cross is a reminder how Jesus helped Paul. Kids can attach the flag by wrapping it tightly around the top of the dowel and stapling securely in place. This might be done best by *VeggieConnections Shepherds*, especially for younger kids.

Have kids gently twist their dowel rod into the center of their sponge so that the boat will be balanced upon completion. Allow the children to sail their boats in tubs of water, if provided.

Paul went for quite a journey on the sea! Take these boats home as a reminder of how God helped Paul, and to know God will help you with your problems.

HIGH-POWERED GAME NEEDS:

- Prepared slips of paper
- Masking tape

LOW-POWERED GAME NEEDS:

- Masking tape
- Chairs

BEFORE YOU START:
Tape a relay start/finish line at one end of your playing area. Make a boat shaped outline using chairs large enough for half your class to fit in when sitting together.

CRAFT NEEDS:

- New kitchen sponge (one per child)
- Construction paper
- Scissors
- Markers
- Dowel rods, 1/8" x 4" (one per child)
- Staplers
- Optional: large tubs of water to sail finished projects in

Sidebar

CUCUMBER CONNECTION NEEDS:

- Pickle jar
- Pickles artwork from the *VeggieConnections Shepherd* pages (on the *VeggieConnections CD-ROM*)
- Green construction paper

KID CONNECTION NEEDS:

- Prepared Bible verse fans (one for every two *Veggie-Connections Shepherds*)
- Bibles
- *God Helps!* on page 162 (one per *Veggie-Connections Group*)
- Snoodle backpack (from *Lesson 1*)
- Snoodle Journal on page 156 (one per child)
- Pencils or pens
- Yarn

BEFORE YOU START:

Print each Bible verse reference on a separate sheet of paper and fold into a paper fan: James 4:8a; Matthew 7:7; Psalm 5:2; Psalm 18:6; Psalm 25:1–2a; Matthew 28:20b; Matthew 6:33–34; Matthew 11:28. You'll need one set for every two *Veggie-Connections Shepherds*. Copy "God Helps!" page 162, one per *VeggieConnections Group*.

CHRIST CONNECTION NEEDS:

- *VeggieConnections Music CD*
- CD player
- *VeggieConnections* take-home newspaper (one per child)

Main content

PART THREE:

Plugging In to My Life

Life application of the lesson to lead kids to THINK–LINK–ACT and build a relationship with God every day

A. Cucumber Connection

Before kids arrive, enlarge and copy the pickles from the *VeggieConnections Shepherd* pages on the CD-ROM included in the *VeggieConnections Elementary Curriculum Kit* onto green construction paper. Cut them out and put into a pickle jar.

Let a volunteer draw a pickle from the Pickle Pot and either the child or a Shepherd should read the dilemma out loud. Each Shepherd should then process the question with his or her small group using the THINK—LINK—ACT phrase.

Kim is afraid of the dark. What could she do?	Manuel's house is destroyed in a fire. No one was hurt, but he and his family lost everything they owned. What can Manuel do?	Maria doesn't like her new baby sister. She knows she should love her baby sister, but she thinks her parents love the new baby more than her. What should Maria do?

B. Kid Connection: Snoodle Backpack

Have kids from two *VeggieConnections Groups* sit in a circle. If you have an uneven number of groups, put three groups in one circle. Have each *VeggieConnections Shepherd* hold a Bible verse fan and a Bible. These Shepherds may circulate among the groups. Give each circle one set of God Helps! pictures to pass around and look at. For larger circles, provide a second set of pictures. Have the kids pair up and talk together about any one of the pictures they choose, deciding what problem could be represented by that picture. This makes the "Think" part of the activity.

Once pairs have established a problem, they may call on any *VeggieConnections Shepherd* to read a verse from the fan. The pairs then make the "Link" with the scripture and then suggest an "Act" to resolve the problem. When finished, all the pairs should tell their THINK—LINK—ACT story to the rest of the circle.

Distribute the Snoodle backpacks made in *Lesson 1*. Be sure each child receives his or her backpack. Give kids a copy of the Snoodle Journal and pencils or pens. Say: **We've seen today about how God can help us with problems, whether big or small. You may not be facing a shipwreck in a huge storm at sea, but your problems are just as important to God.**

Encourage kids to write down on their journal page a problem they're facing and a prayer asking for God's help. Then give kids yarn and allow them to roll up and tie the journal page, then put it in their packpack. Have *VeggieConnections Shepherds* help younger kids with their journal pages.

C. Christ Connection

Sing the *THINK-LINK-ACT* song together from the *VeggieConnections Music CD* and do the motions.

Gathered with their *VeggieConnections Groups*, encourage kids to share current problems they are facing.

Then encourage the kids within each group to pray for one another. If desired, use this prayer starter: **We thank you, God, that you come close to us when we have problems. You are eager to help us. Today we ask for your help for . . .** Kids say their own prayers. Have *VeggieConnections Shepherds* conclude the prayer.

Distribute the take-home newspaper, ***VeggieConnections***.

150 | Unit 2: The Communication Connection

Connection Word:

preach

PART ONE:

Plugging In at Snoodleburg

Introduction to the site and lesson focus

LESSON 8:
I help others connect with God.

A. Veggie Connection

Dressed as the Mayor of Snoodleburg, welcome back the children as they arrive at Snoodleburg. Ask kids to sit in a circle at the base of Mt. Ginchez.

I've really enjoyed being your host these past few weeks as you've been my guests in our lovely little town of Snoodleburg. I hope you've had as much fun as I've had! Speaking of fun, let's start out today with a game. Get into your *VeggieConnections Groups*, and each group picks one person to be the first "preacher." The preachers stay here with me while the rest of you follow your *VeggieConnections Shepherds* to different spots in Snoodleburg and turn your backs. Give each Shepherd a piece of paper and pencil.

When the groups aren't looking, bring out the covered tray. It's okay if the others hear these instructions. **When I uncover this tray, take a good look at all the things on it. Try to remember as many as you can.** Remove the cloth and allow about thirty seconds for the "preachers" to observe. Then cover the tray again. At your signal, have the "preachers" run to their groups and tell the others what they saw on the tray, seeing how much they can remember. The *VeggieConnections Shepherds* write down what is reported.

Then have each group choose a second "preacher" to come up and do the same activity. Allow thirty seconds for the new "preachers" to observe the tray; then send them back to tell their groups what they saw in addition to what is already written down. If time permits, you may want to do this activity a third time.

Gather everyone back together at Mt. Ginchez. Uncover the tray for all to see, and let the groups compare their lists to the tray.

Think about what you did in this game. Some of you saw something and paid close attention. Then you went and told others what you saw or knew. We could call this sharing or teaching or reporting or witnessing. It's also very similar to our Connection Word today: *preach*. Let a volunteer look it up in the *VeggieConnections Bible Dictionary* and read the definition.

In today's Bible story, someone saw Jesus and paid close attention. Then he went and told others what he knew—that's preaching. We all can learn how to share with others what we know about God.

B. Prayer Connection

To help kids begin thinking about what they know about God, have them take turns praying sentence prayers, praising God for something they like about him or thanking him for something he has done for them.

THE CHILDREN
will arrive with their *Veggie-Connections Shepherds* from the opening Countertop Connections featuring Bob and Larry. Play the *Veggie-Connections Music CD* as children enter Snoodleburg.

VEGGIE CONNECTION NEEDS:

- *VeggieConnections Music CD*
- CD player
- Scrap paper
- Pencils
- Large serving tray
- 20 assorted items to fit on the tray, such as VeggieTales toys or items, vegetables, a candy bar, a ball, a shoe, a book, a feather, a VeggieTales video, and small school supplies and toys
- Cloth (to cover items on tray)
- *VeggieConnections Bible Dictionary*

Plugging In to God's Word

Connecting to God's Word in the Bible and understanding how that can help us to have a better relationship with him

A. God Connection: Paul tells others about God – Acts 9:20-31

Explain that the kids will be helping you tell the story by emphasizing certain points in it. Kids will be assigned one of three roles. Explain how kids will play their story role:

- **Group 1:** When "Paul" or "Saul" is named, these players should extend both arms upward as if preaching dramatically.
- **Group 2:** When the words "preach" or "Jesus" are mentioned, these players should shout: **Preach Jesus!**
- **Group 3:** When the words "followers," "disciples," or "brothers" are used in the story, these players should shout: **Praise God!**

Explain that as you read the Bible story, you will prompt the kids to use their motions at the appropriate time. Explain that the story begins in Damascus, where Saul first believed in Jesus. Remind the group of the first lesson of this unit where Saul met Jesus on the road to Damascus and was blinded. He regained his sight while with the disciples in Damascus. Also explain how Saul was later called Paul. Point out Damascus on the map.

Have the kids playing "Saul" raise their hands as you read Acts 9:20. Then explain: **A synagogue was a meeting place for the Jews to read and study the Scriptures.**

Read verses 21–22, and prompt the kids playing Saul. Then explain: **Saul preached to the Jews, using their own Scriptures, which we call the Old Testament. He showed them that the Scriptures said many years earlier that Jesus would come and that he would be the Messiah or the Christ—that means, the one God sent to be the Savior. The Messiah would make a way for people to connect with God.**

Read verses 23–24, prompting Saul group to respond. Read verse 25 while Group 3 responds.

Then explain: **So Saul went to Jerusalem to see the disciples and the apostles there. Point out Jerusalem on the map. Disciples are people who follow Jesus, just like you and me. Apostles were the leaders over all the Christian churches.**

Read verse 26 and allow Group 3 to respond twice. Then read verses 27–28, prompting Groups 1 and 2 to respond. Read verses 29–30 and allow Group 3 to respond.

Point out Caesarea and Tarsus on the map. Read verse 31 while pointing out Judea, Galilee, and Samaria on the map.

This was the beginning of Paul's preaching ministry. He wanted everyone to know Jesus. He was so excited! He spoke to many people, telling them that Jesus had died on the cross and had come alive again. He told them what he knew about being friends with Jesus and being loved by God.

These past few weeks, we've been learning about Paul's life and ministry. Paul's life example and teachings showed us the importance of prayer, listening to God, worshiping God, and reading the Bible. Paul also taught us how vital the Holy Spirit is for Christians. Last week, near the end of Paul's ministry, we learned how Paul trusted God, especially when he faced tough times, like being shipwrecked.

Paul taught all these things as he preached about Jesus. Because Paul preached and taught about Jesus his whole life, other believers also began to preach the good news about Jesus being the Savior. And so in all the years from then up to today, Christians have wanted to help people connect with God. They tell what they know about Jesus and have experienced with him. We say that they share or witness or report or teach or preach. Those are all words that mean that they help others connect with God. You can help others to connect with God, too!

To help others connect with God, we simply tell what we know about him or tell what our friendship with him is like. Let's give that a try now! Have the kids gather in their *VeggieConnections Group* and each tell something they know about God. It could be an important fact they've learned from the Bible (*God made everything.*) or something they've experienced (*Jesus is my friend.*).

GOD CONNECTION NEEDS:

- Bible
- Map of Paul's travels (on page 134)

TEACHER TIP:

Younger children may benefit from hearing the story before interacting with it. Explain to kids you'll read the story twice. For the first reading, they should listen very carefully. For the second reading, kids will help tell the story.

B. Activity Connection

Choose from the following activities to help kids explore how to help others connect with God (approximately 10–15 minutes each).

1. High-Powered Game: Pass On the Word!

Form teams in lines of eight to ten kids. Give kids Bibles and have them look up the Unit Memory Verse, Matthew 7:7. Have kids review it and say it aloud a few times. When kids think they know the verse, have them put down the Bible.

Give the first player in each line an inflated balloon. That player passes the balloon between his legs to the person behind him and shouts the first word of the verse: **Ask!** The second player passes the balloon overhead to the person behind him or her, and shouts the second word of the verse: **and!** The third player passes it between his legs, and the fourth person overhead, each person saying a word of the verse in order. Continue in this manner until the last person in the lines receives the balloon. Then repeat the game going forward; players shouting the next word in the verse as each person receives the balloon using the over and under pattern above.

Have *VeggieConnections Shepherds* keep track of the verse in their Bibles. Each time a group makes a mistake, have teams start over. After teams can pass the balloon and say the verse all the way through, have kids in that team all shout: **Preach Jesus!**

Have kids try to say the verse faster in additional rounds. Say: **Just as Paul preached the words of Jesus, you can share our Unit Memory Verse with others. Remember we can—say it with me—preach Jesus!**

HIGH POWERED GAME NEEDS:
- Inflated balloons
- Bibles (one per child)

2. Low-Powered Game: Obstacles? Preach Jesus!

BEFORE YOU START:

Print the following cities on index cards, one city per card: 1.) Damascus, 2.) Jerusalem, 3.) Caesarea, 4.) Tarsus. Make one set of cards for every two *VeggieConnections Groups*. Set up two parallel simple obstacle courses, using chairs as obstacles. If you have more than four groups, set up a third course. Place the four cards, in order, equally along each course.

Have two *VeggieConnections Groups* line up behind the first obstacle course and blindfold one person. Repeat with the second pair (and third, if needed) of Groups. On **Go!** start timing kids as they enter the course. Have kids call directions to their group's team member on the course. When a player finds the first card, have them shout out: **Preach Jesus!** Players should leave the cards where they've found them, and proceed to the next card on the course. When the first team reaches the last card and calls out, record their time.

Repeat the game with new players, seeing who can record the fastest time. Before the end of the game time, have kids walk the course and point out the four city cards. Say: **Paul became a Christian near Damascus, and he preached about Jesus in that city. When he went to Jerusalem he preached Jesus there. Everywhere Paul, he preached Jesus to the people, even when he faced many obstacles. Just like Paul, we can tell others about Jesus, too!**

LOW-POWERED GAME NEEDS:
- Prepared index cards
- Chairs
- Blindfolds (one for every two *VeggieConnections Groups*)
- Watch with second hand

3. Craft: Prayer Pillowcase

God wants us to communicate with him every day in order to strengthen our relationship with him. Prayer is one way that we can communicate. Give each child a pillowcase and fabric paint or markers. Have them decorate their pillowcase using words, phrases, or pictures that are related to prayer. *(Pray every day! Now I lay me down to sleep . . . , I can talk to God when I pray, Come near to God and he will come near to you.)*

When building a relationship with God, it is important to communicate with him every day. Prayer is a great way to keep in touch with God, our Father. You can use these pillowcases to hold, lie on, or kneel on while you say your prayers. I challenge you to use your prayer pillow at least once a day!

CRAFT NEEDS:
- One pillowcase per child
- Fabric paint or markers

PART THREE:

Plugging in to My Life

Life application of the lesson to lead kids to THINK–LINK–ACT and build a relationship with God every day.

A. Cucumber Connection

CUCUMBER CONNECTION NEEDS:

- Pickle jar
- Pickles artwork from the *VeggieConnections Shepherd* pages (on the *VeggieConnections CD-ROM*)
- Green construction paper

Before kids arrive, enlarge and copy the pickles from the *VeggieConnections Shepherd* pages on the CD-ROM included in the *VeggieConnections Elementary Curriculum Kit* onto green construction paper. Cut them out and put into a pickle jar.

Let a volunteer draw a pickle from the Pickle Pot and either the child or a Shepherd should read the dilemma out loud. Each Shepherd should then process the question with his or her small group using the THINK—LINK—ACT phrase.

Jean's friend Manuel doesn't have a connection to Jesus. What could Jean do?	Kathy's grandmother recently died. Kathy has a lot of questions about heaven. What should Kathy do?	Bonnie is very shy. She wants to tell others about Jesus, but she is afraid. What should Bonnie do?

B. Kid Connection: Snoodle Backpack

KID CONNECTION NEEDS:

- Snoodle backpack (made in *Lesson 1*)
- Pencils or pens
- Snoodle Journal Page on page 156 (one per child)

Distribute the Snoodle backpacks made in *Lesson 1*. Be sure each child receives his or her backpack. Say: **We've been learning a lot about communicating with God here in Snoodleburg. Just as the Snoodles carry backpacks to keep important things with them, you've been keeping prayers and other important reminders of communicating with God.**

Have kids gather in their *VeggieConnections Groups*. Have kids empty their backpacks and look through the items. Have *VeggieConnections Shepherds* encourage kids to talk about things they've learned while in Snoodleburg. Say: **We've learned a lot about connecting to God through looking at Paul's life. And the most important thing Paul did was tell others about Jesus.**

Shepherds should guide the children in their groups to identify friends who need to hear good news about connecting to God. Encourage kids to write these things down on one of their Journal Pages, reminding them that as they are coming near to God in this way, he is coming near to them. **You created quite a few prayers and reminders as we've been connecting with God through Paul's life and ministry. Take your Snoodle backpacks home with you and look through them when you spend time with God.**

C. Christ Connection

CHRIST CONNECTION NEEDS:

- *VeggieConnections Music CD*
- CD player
- *VeggieConnections* take-home newspaper (one per child)

Sing the *THINK—LINK—ACT* song with motions. Then have everyone say the Unit Memory Verse together, Matthew 7:7.

Have the kids gather in their *VeggieConnections Groups*. Have *VeggieConnections Shepherds* review the unit lessons with this prayerstarter: **God, we know you know us and you want us to know you better. Help us connect to you as we pray to you, listen to you, spend time worshiping you, and reading our Bibles. Thank you for giving us your Holy Spirit to live your way. And thank you for always being ready to help us. We ask now that you help us tell others about you. God, we pray for these people who need to connect to you ...** Kids name friends and family. **In Jesus' name, amen.**

Distribute the take-home newspaper, ***VeggieConnections***.

Lesson 2 – Prayer Types

Rock	**Builder**	**Creator** of Heaven & Earth
Father	**Light** of the World	**Shepherd**
Ruler	**Bread** of Life	**Friend**
Lamb of God	**Holy**	**Morning Star**
King	**Physician** (Doctor)	**Prince** of Peace
Teacher	the **Vine**	the **Door**

Lesson 5 – " Armor of God" pictures

Lesson 5 – "Armor of God" cards

Belt of Truth	**Breastplate of Righteousness**
Shoes of the Gospel of Peace	**Shield of Faith**
Helmet of Salvation	**Sword of the Spirit**

Lesson 6 - Fruit Bingo

Love	Joy and Peace	Patience and Kindness	Goodness and Faithfulness	Gentleness and Self-Control

- -

Love	Joy and Peace	Patience and Kindness	Goodness and Faithfulness	Gentleness and Self-Control

"Come near to God and he will come near to you." James 4:8

WELCOME TO FLIBBER-O-LOO
Connecting to **Love** through **Jesus**

UNIT THREE:

THE LOVE CONNECTION

UNIT VERSE: " 'Love the Lord your God with all your heart and with all your soul and with all your mind.' This is the first and greatest commandment. And the second is like it: 'Love your neighbor as yourself.' "
Matthew 22:37-39

FLIBBER-O-LOO

LESSON FOCUS:

1. God is love: John 3:1-21
2. I have Jesus as my Savior and Counselor: John 16:5-15
3. I have Jesus to teach me how to love: Matthew 5:1-12
4. I have Jesus as my daily source of love: Matthew 14:22-36
5. I have Jesus to show me how to forgive others: Luke 15:11-32
6. I have Jesus to show me how to love my neighbor: Luke 10:25-37
7. I show my love for Jesus because he loves me: John 14:23-31a
8. I show my love to others through service: Matthew 20:20-34

Love Connection Goals

The Love Connection is all about helping kids know and love God. The word *love* is a familiar one, even for kids. They love their families, friends, and pets. And we want kids to know that the best love of all is the joy of receiving God's love and the joy of loving him, too. This is, perhaps, the strongest tool in connecting to a relationship with the Lord.

Each Lesson Focus will take kids on a journey toward various ways we can connect with our Lord in love. The Countertop Connection opening session with Bob and Larry will introduce the concept of having a relationship with God. It will be supported with the Program Verse from James 4:8: "*Come near to God and he will come near to you.*"

When kids are dismissed to Flibber-o-loo, they will have the chance to explore what it means to love God. Kids will be challenged each week to build a relationship with God, grow in their love of Jesus, and share the love that God gives them with others.

The first lesson teaches us that God loves us. Because God loves us, he wants us to love him. This will provide kids with a strong foundation on which to base their relationship.

The next five lessons will focus on a variety of ways Jesus, by his perfect example, shows us how to love God and each other. This will lay the groundwork for many of the biblical principles that young people will use to make all their future choices.

The last two lessons encourage us to take what we've learned and actually begin to share our love with Jesus and others.

Warning: Activities in these lessons may call for foods containing wheat, dairy, or nuts. Please be aware that some children may have medically serious allergic reactions to these foods. Let parents know that their kids will be offered snacks that may include these items, and post a list of ingredients each week for any snacks offered during the lesson. Whenever foods containing wheat, dairy, and nuts are suggested in these lessons, be sure to have safe alternatives on hand.

FLIBBER-O-LOO ———— JIBBERTY-LOT

Welcome to Flibber-o-loo!

One of the VeggieTales® videos that Bob and Larry present to children is called *Are You My Neighbor?* This is the story of the good Samaritan, which comes to life in a delightful adaptation of the parable. Children learn that loving your neighbor means helping those in need—no matter who they are!

The two make-believe towns of Flibber-o-loo and Jibberty-lot are feuding because each town is a little different. Flibbians like to wear shoes on their heads, and Jibberty-lots like to wear pots on their heads. In the end, the citizens of both towns work out their differences because of the loving act of one little asparagus who knows that God wants us to love one another, regardless of our differences.

This provides an excellent backdrop for fun exploration and discovering the joy of connecting with our Creator through love.

In preparation, please watch the video in advance so you'll be familiar with the wonderful world of Flibber-o-loo.

Your Role in Flibber-o-loo: A Flibbian

As the leader of this site, you get to be a Flibbian, citizen of Flibber-o-loo. In this role, you will be hosting a new group of kids as they rotate through Flibber-o-loo for eight class sessions.

To dress for the part, you should wear a Flibbian shoe as a hat. Wear a large shoe or boot upside-down on top of your head, tying the laces beneath your chin. You may need to add another set of shoelaces to extend the length. Or use the clip-art on page 67 to make two enlarged paper copies of a boot or shoe. Attach the paper shoe patterns in an upside-down position onto both sides of a baseball cap. Staple or tape them to the cap. Insert a shoelace on each side of the shoe and tie it beneath your chin. Wear it on your head to look like a real shoe.

How to Build and Prepare the Sites of Flibber-o-loo and Jibberty-lot

OPTION 1:

If you have more time and a permanent space

Set up Flibber-o-loo on one side of the room and Jibberty-lot on the other. Use the transparency art included in the *VeggieConnections Elementary Curriculum Kit* to project the background images onto mural paper or large bedsheets. Hang one background on each town's wall. Use a transparency or enlarge clip art to create life-sized characters to display on the walls about the room. Clip art may be found on page 56. Be sure to

Create a wall mural for Flibber-o-loo using transparency art found on page 56.

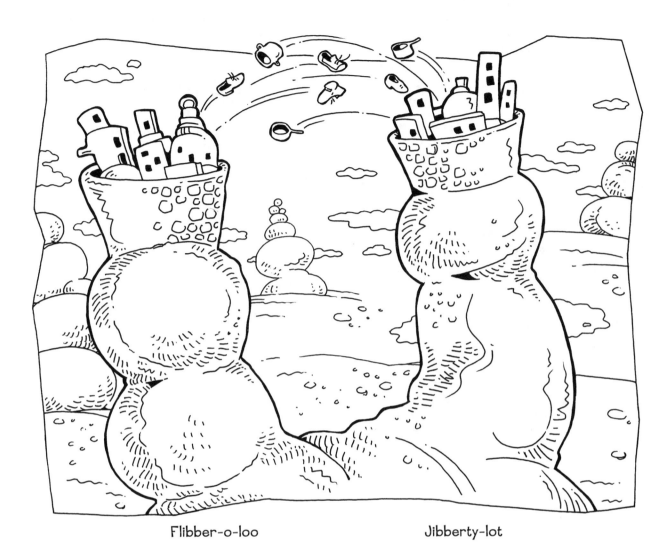

Flibber-o-loo   Jibberty-lot

include the bandits, Flibbian Larry, the mayor, the doctor, and Junior from Jibberty-lot. Highlight these characters as you retell the story. At the entrance to the site, place two large signs labeled "Flibber-o-loo" and "Jibberty-lot," with an arrow on each pointing to their location. Or hang the signs from a coatrack to look like a signpost.

Set up tables in Jibberty-lot to be used for crafts and writing activities. Keep an open floor area in Flibber-o-loo where all the kids can be seated to hear the Bible story. In the "valley" between the towns, keep a large, open space for games.

Set up "rocks" around both towns. These may be drawn on cardboard boxes, made from crumpled paper grocery bags, or be actual large rocks. (Note: If actual rocks are used, they should be too large for children to pick up.)

Fill Jibberty-lot with pots and Flibber-o-loo with shoes. Pots and shoes, the larger the better, will be used in many games and activities. Make sure several of the pots are plastic and lightweight. You can find an assortment of inexpensive shoes and possibly pots at secondhand

stores, yard sales, dollar-type stores, and some mail-order catalogs. You might also ask your congregation for donations of old shoes and pots. Some games also need socks, which can be accumulated from the same sources.

Also fill Flibber-o-loo and Jibberty-lot with flowers and candies. These will be used in many games and activities. They may be real, artificial, or homemade. Artificial flowers and candies may be purchased cheaply at secondhand stores, yard sales, dollar-type stores, and some mail-order catalogs. Instructions for making paper candies and flowers are below. In addition, edible, individually wrapped candies are frequently used in lessons.

In a corner near Flibber-o-loo, set up the Flibbian Hospital. Designate it with a large "Flibbian Hospital" sign. Display medical items, such as bandages, pretend medicine, prescription pad and pencil, crutches, eye chart, a cot, stethoscope, hospital bed, chair, a toy medical kit, and so on. You may wish to enlarge a copy of the clip art of the Flibbian Nurse (on page 67) to display on the wall in this area of the site.

Make a large poster of the Unit Memory Verse, Matthew 22:37–39. This will be used every week in this unit. Decorate the poster with flowers, candies, and Veggie characters. You may use the clip art on pages 62–64. Display the poster where it can be easily seen by all the children when they are gathered together at the beginning of the session.

Designate one bulletin board or other space at the site for the weekly Connection Word. These words will be printed on a construction-paper flower and displayed each week. You may wish to have these eight flowers (kept blank until the lesson) made ahead of time.

Creating large imitation candies: Wrap Styrofoam plates with sheets of colorful cellophane wrapping paper. Twist-tie a ribbon on two ends to secure the wrap around the plate, creating a "wrapped candy" look.

Creating tissue-paper flowers: Stack four sheets of colorful tissue paper together. Fold the papers together accordion style. Twist a chenille wire around the center of the folded papers, securing them to create a flower stem. Carefully separate the papers, pulling them up and toward the center to create a flower.

For mini tissue-paper flowers, simply cut a 4" x 4" square from colored tissue paper, fold it into quarters, grab the center between your fingers, and twist it at the bottom, creating a short stem. The top portion of the tissue will remain flared to look like a flower. These mini flowers are fun for tossing into the air like confetti, and you can make many flowers in a short amount of time for very little cost.

Making a blue lobster: Reproduce the Flibbians' blue lobster from the clip art on page 67 onto blue craft foam. Make the lobster about 12 inches long. Attach the lobster to a windup or pull-back toy car so that it will move about on the floor.

For more ideas, watch the video *Are You My Neighbor?* or find examples among the clip art on page 67.

If you are short on time or do not have a permanent space

Create Flibber-o-loo and Jibberty-lot by projecting the transparency onto mural paper or a white bedsheet. Trace and color the image. Hang onto the wall in your site so that it can be taken down and rolled up each week for easy storage.

Set up the Flibbian Hospital by making a poster with that name on it and displaying a collection of medical supplies, as suggested above, on a small table or shelf. These may be kept in a box during the week.

You will need large numbers or shoes, pots, flowers, and candies, as described above, for use in all lessons.

You can store these in cardboard boxes, paper bags, or plastic laundry baskets during the week. If you do not have access to a bulletin board or wall space for the weekly Connection Word flower, simply omit this one instruction in each lesson.

Life Application Memory Tools

VeggieConnections will teach an important Bible lesson to kids each week. Knowing the Bible is the beginning of a relationship with God. Putting that learning to practice through life application really solidifies a child's relationship with the Lord. It is imperative that we provide kids with the tools they need to carry what they have learned into everyday experiences through life application.

In this curriculum, there are three main ways we will encourage kids to do this:

1. Kids will discover ways to love God throughout each lesson.
2. Kids will learn a catch-phrase that will help them to remember what they should do in real-life experiences.

The catch-phrase we have created is THINK—LINK—ACT. There is a song built on this principle on the *VeggieConnections Music CD* in your kit that will help kids remember this important tool. In addition, each session will focus on various THINK—LINK—ACT activities that help children to walk the walk and talk the talk, hopefully opening doors for the Holy Spirit to enter in and build meaningful relationships that will carry kids through every day of their lives! Here's what it means:

THINK: Stop and think about what God wants you to do.

LINK: Link God's Word and what you've learned to your choices.

ACT: Go and act on what God wants you to do!

Now add some fun hand motions to the catch-phrase!

THINK: Touch head with fingertip two times.

LINK: Left hand out, right hand out.
Clasp your hands together, fingers intertwined.

ACT: Release grip and roll hands three times.
Finish with arms outstretched.

3. Kids will create a weekly life application building tool to help them to remember what each lesson focused on.

Love Shoes

In Flibber-o-loo, kids will decorate shoeboxes to look like shoes. Tell kids since the Flibbians wear shoes on their heads as well as their feet, they have lots of empty shoeboxes lying around. You can use a variety of shoebox sizes. Let kids choose the box they want. Kids will have a choice about what style of shoe to make.

The boxes should be turned upside down. The lid will become the sole of the shoe. On what is now the "top" of the box, have kids use scissors and carefully cut a circular-shaped hole almost to three edges of the box. Have *VeggieConnections Shepherds* help younger kids. If kids want to make high-top shoes or boots, give them 4"-wide strips of lightweight tagboard and have them curl it and fit it inside the hole of their box and use masking tape to. Tape the tagboard to the inside and outside of the box. Make sure the tagboard isn't inserted very far inside the box because kids will need to be able to reach inside the box.

Provide a variety of decorating materials, such as a shiny wrapping paper for dress shoes, construction paper in a variety of colors, bright shoelaces or yarn, sequins, beads, and so on. Allow kids to tape or glue the materials to their boxes. Have kids decorate the box and the lid separately, then attach them together with masking tape taped on the inside of the box. Have Shepherds assist as needed.

The Love Shoes will be utilized every week to hold items made by the children during the Kid Connection portion of the lesson. At the end of the unit, kids will take home their Love Shoes with contents to remind them that God loves them and how they love God.

Suggested Music for Flibber-o-loo

Use these songs from the *VeggieConnections Music CD* in your sessions:
1. *THINK—LINK—ACT* Music motions found on page 48.
2. *Forgiveness Song*

Windup Blue Lobster Reference

Connecting to **Love** through **Jesus**
Jesus and Nicodemus: **John 3:1–21**

love

PART ONE:

**Plugging In
at Flibber-o-loo**

Introduction to the site
and lesson focus

LESSON 1:

God is love.

A. Veggie Connection

BEFORE YOU START:
If not already done in site setup, make a poster with the Unit Memory Verse, Matthew 22:37–39, printed clearly so it can be read easily from across the room. This will be used every week in this unit. Decorate the poster with flowers, candies, and Veggie characters. You may want to laminate the poster for durability.

Dressed as a Flibbian, welcome the kids to Flibber-o-loo and invite them to explore the site. Let kids try shoes and pots on their heads.

Then divide the kids into two groups; send one group to the Flibber-o-loo half of the room and the other group to the Jibberty-lot area of the room. Ask if anyone knows the Veggie-Tales story of Flibber-o-loo, and let volunteers briefly summarize. *(The Flibbians wore shoes on their heads and the people from Jibberty-lot wore pots on their heads. They each thought they were better than the others, so they would throw shoes and pots at each other. Once they plugged in to a relationship with God, they became good friends and threw flowers and candies instead.)*

Invite the kids to have some fun being friends the Flibbian way. At your signal, they will all scramble around their half of the site to pick up any small or lightweight flowers or candies they can find unattached to walls or props and gently lob them over to the other side. The goal is to see which side can give away the most. When more flowers and candies land on their side, the kids may pick them up and toss them back. Remind the kids not to throw hard. Time the kids, and give them up to one minute to throw.

When finished, let all the kids choose one piece of real candy from their side to eat as they sit down. Encourage the kids to eat the candy slowly so they can savor the flavor. Say: **The people from Jibberty-lot and Flibber-o-loo discovered a brand-new flavor. They tasted love, and what a difference it made! Love? Yes, love! Many people have different ideas of what "love" means. So we have something here today to help us figure it out.** Ask a volunteer to look up the word *love* in the *VeggieConnections Bible Dictionary* and read the definition aloud. Print *love* on a construction-paper flower and display it at the site.

Say: **Long ago David gave us a taste challenge when he wrote, "*Taste and see that the Lord is good*" (Psalm 34:8). Much as you tasted your candy now, you can taste the Lord—not with your tongue but inside as you come near to him. When you do that, you discover something wonderful—how much, how very much God loves you! Here is another**

THE CHILDREN
will arrive with their *VeggieConnections Shepherds* from the opening Countertop Connections featuring Bob and Larry. Play the *VeggieConnections Music CD* as children enter Flibber-o-loo.

VEGGIE CONNECTION NEEDS:
- *VeggieConnections Music CD*
- CD player
- Unit Memory Verse poster
- Tissue and artificial flowers (from the site)
- Artificial candies (from site)
- Real, individually wrapped candies (at least one per child)
- Construction-paper flower for Connection Word
- Marker
- *VeggieConnections Bible Dictionary*

wonderful discovery. God wants you to love him, too, and he has told you how you can express your love for him.

Point to the Unit Memory Verse poster and read the verse to the kids. Read it again, phrase by phrase, and have the kids repeat it after you. Say: **In the next few weeks we are going to learn together how to make this love connection.**

B. Prayer Connection

Have each *VeggieConnections Group* move to a different part of the site. This is a good time for *VeggieConnections Shepherds* to get to know the kids and for the kids to get to know one other. Then let each child briefly tell either something good that happened to him or her this week or something hard he or she is dealing with.

Allow time for the kids to pray. They may choose someone in the group and pray for that one, either thanking God for the good thing that happened or asking his help with a problem. If kids do not feel comfortable praying aloud, the Shepherd should lead the group, mentioning each child by name, thanking God for his love for each one.

PART TWO:

Plugging In to God's Word

Connecting to God's Word in the Bible and understanding how that can help us to have a better relationship with him

A. God Connection: Jesus and Nicodemus – John 3:1-21

Have kids gather in the open space of Flibber-o-loo and be seated. Give a question mark card to each child. Explain that in a few minutes you will give those instructions on how to use them. Have a *VeggieConnections Shepherd* ready to dim the lights when you indicate. Show the kids where today's Bible story is found, John 3.

I will tell you the Bible story two times. The first time, you will listen very carefully. Then the second time, I'll give you instructions for something fun you can do.

When Jesus lived on earth, he talked with people about God. News spread that his teaching was different from anything anyone had ever heard. More and more people came to hear him. Their teachers, called Pharisees, told them that God wanted them to follow laws, but Jesus talked about knowing God and loving him. Some of these teachers were jealous of Jesus. They *knew* a lot about God and his Word. Point to your head. **But they didn't know how to *love* him in their hearts.** Point to your heart.

Now, a few of the Pharisees were impressed by Jesus and wanted to learn more from him. But they did not dare let anyone find out, or their other Pharisee friends would get them into trouble. A man named Nicodemus was in that situation. Nicodemus had heard Jesus teach. He had questions he wanted to ask Jesus—big, important questions.

How could he have a chance to talk with Jesus? The other teachers and leaders would laugh at him or get mad at him. So Nicodemus had to be sneaky. One night after dark, Nicodemus set out for the house where Jesus was staying. In Bible times, there weren't any streetlights, and the only house lights were oil lamps. So Nicodemus could walk in the darkness without being recognized.

Ask kids to imagine the scene as Nicodemus came to Jesus with his questions. As you tell what happened, they should listen carefully. The first time, you will simply tell the story. Then the second time, when they hear something that Nicodemus wondered and questioned, they should raise their question card. When they hear Jesus' answer to the question, they should cup their ear and nod their head in understanding. Explain you'll cue the kids to these actions the second time you tell the story. Have a question card and penlight at hand so you can illuminate the card and the script to read in the dim room.

Nicodemus arrived in the dark and may have found Jesus enjoying the cool night breeze on the flat roof of the house where he was staying. Dim lights in the room. **There in the darkness, Jesus welcomed his guest, knowing he had questions he badly wanted to ask.**

Nicodemus started out by wondering. Raise question card. **"Good teacher, we know you have come from God, because no one could do the amazing things you do if God were not with him."** He wanted to know who Jesus really was. All the good teachers could teach *about* God and his laws, but Jesus was different—he *knew* God in a special way that nobody else seemed to understand.

Jesus knew what Nicodemus really wanted to know. Cup hand over your ear. **Jesus said, "I tell you the truth, no one can really know God unless he is born again."**

Nicodemus was puzzled. Raise question card. **He asked, "But how can someone be born again when he is already grown up? He can't go back into his mother's body to be born a second time!"**

So Jesus explained it. Cup hand over your ear. **"I'm not talking about your body being born all over again. I mean that you can't be a part of God's kingdom unless you are reborn on the inside through the God's Spirit."**

Raise question card. **Nicodemus then asked, "How can this happen?"**

Cup hand over your ear. **Jesus said, "You are a teacher who has studied God's Word. You should know these things. So let me tell you the truth. I am the Son of God and the Son of Man. I have lived in heaven and I came from there. Everyone who believes in me will be born of God's Spirit. They'll have eternal life in heaven with me forever."**

Then Jesus said some words that a lot of us have heard. Invite the kids to recite John 3:16 with you if they know it. **Jesus said, "*For God so loved the world that he gave his one and only Son, that whoever believes in him shall not perish but have eternal life.*"**

This was exciting news for Nicodemus—and for all of us. Jesus was telling him about the starting point for a most wonderful God connection. Nicodemus did not have that connection. Jesus took the very first step toward Nicodemus and all of us when he left heaven to come here. Now Jesus was telling how we can be born again by having the brand-new life he came to give all who put their trust in him.

Cup hand over your ear. **Then Jesus explained it again for Nicodemus. "God loves everyone, so he sent me to save the world. I came into the world to be 'light.' Anyone who comes into my light and trusts me will be saved and know God's love. That's how to have a relationship with God."**

Tell the kids that God loves them very much and he wants them to come near to him. Lead the kids in saying the *VeggieConnections* verse, James 4:8.

Discuss these review questions with the kids: **What did Nicodemus want to know so badly that he snuck around in the dark and risked losing his friends?** *(He wanted to know how to have a relationship with God.)* **What did Jesus tell him?** *(That he needed to be born again—to believe in Jesus and be born of God's Spirit.)* **Why does God want us to believe in Jesus and be saved?** *(Because he loves us so much.)*

If this is the start of the *VeggieConnections* program, introduce the kids to the THINK—LINK—ACT concept. If the group already understands this concept, remind them of it here. Tell kids that every time we have to make a decision—big or small, God wants us to THINK—LINK—ACT in ways that express our love for him.

B. Activity Connection

Choose from the following activities to help kids explore and remember that Jesus came to earth to be our Savior because he loved us (approximately 10–15 minutes each).

1. High-Powered Game: Meeting with Jesus

HIGH-POWERED GAME NEEDS:

- Flashlights (one per every two kids)
- Cards with a question mark (one per every two kids)

Divide the kids into two teams. Have them form two large, concentric circles. Pair kids up so that they know who their partner is in the opposite circle. Instruct kids to stand next to their partner but facing opposite directions. The circles will run in opposite directions. The kids on the inner circle are "the words of Jesus." Give them flashlights. The kids on the outer circle are "Nicodemus," and each one holds a question card.

At your signal, the kids start running in the direction of their circle. When you shout: **Get plugged in to God**, turn out the lights and have the kids with flashlights turn them on and shine them on the ceiling. At that point, kids should try to quickly find their partner. Once partners find each other, Nicodemus sits down and says: **I have questions!** The kids playing the words of Jesus sit down and say: **You need God's answers.**

The last pair to find each other and role-play the meeting of Jesus and Nicodemus are eliminated from the game. The game resumes until only one pair remains. Play several rounds, switching game roles and partners each time.

2. Low-Powered Game: Questions in the Dark

BEFORE YOU START:

Prepare cards for each team. Draw a question mark on index cards, and have one card with "Jesus is the answer" written on it. Tape a start line. About 10' away, spread each team's cards face down in a close scattered pattern, about 4'–6' apart from each other.

LOW-POWERED GAME NEEDS:

- Prepared index cards (one per child)
- Masking/painter's tape
- Blindfolds (two per team)

Divide the kids into teams. Have kids line up behind the starting line. Give the first two kids in line blindfolds and have them help each other tie them. Also have *VeggieConnections Shepherds* assist. Explain that kids will crawl to the area where their cards are spread out. When they reach a card, they will pick it up and crawl back to their teams. Kids can shout directions to keep players on course. Once back, the player can remove the blindfold and give it to the next person in line without a blindfold. Unless the first card is the "Jesus" card, play resumes and players will each retrieve a card. Once the "Jesus" card is discovered, the game is over.

Play additional rounds, especially if the "Jesus" card is found quickly in the first round. Have Shepherds mix up the cards for additional rounds.

Nicodemus had lots of questions for Jesus. In this game, you couldn't win unless you found the "Jesus" card. In real life, Jesus is the answer to all our questions.

3. Craft: Plugged In to God Bookmark

CRAFT NEEDS:

- Bible Bookmark on page 168 (one per child)
- Scissors
- Colored markers
- Glue or glue sticks
- 12" pieces of yarn

Give each child a piece of yarn and a bookmark to color and cut out. If they wish, they may add their name on the blank line. Show kids how to fold the bookmark with the yarn inside and glue it closed. Help kids fold and glue the plug to the other end of the string

Encourage kids to tuck this colorful bookmark inside their Bible as a reminder to get plugged in to God's love.

PART THREE:

Plugging In to My Life

Life application of the lesson to lead kids to THINK-LINK-ACT and build a relationship with God every day

A. Cucumber Connection

Before kids arrive, enlarge and copy the pickles from the *VeggieConnections Shepherd* pages on the CD-ROM included in the *VeggieConnections Elementary Curriculum Kit* onto green construction paper. Cut them out and put them in a pickle jar.

Let a volunteer draw a pickle from the Pickle Pot and either the child or a Shepherd should read the dilemma out loud. Each Shepherd should then process the question with their group using the THINK—LINK—ACT phrase.

Whenever you do something wrong, you worry that God will be mad at you and never forgive you. What can you do?	Lately Donovan has been complaining to his parents about going to church because his friends want him to meet them at the park to play catch and shoot baskets. What can he do?	Janelle wants to grow closer to God and know his love better. What can she do?

CUCUMBER CONNECTION NEEDS:

- Pickle jar
- Pickle artwork from the *VeggieConnections Shepherd* pages (on the *VeggieConnections CD-ROM*)
- Green construction paper

B. Kid Connection: Love Shoes

Show kids a variety of shoebox sizes. Let kids choose the box they want. Kids will have a choice about what style of shoe to make.

The boxes should be turned upside down. The lid will become the sole of the shoe. On what is now the "top" of the box, have kids use scissors and carefully cut a circular-shaped hole almost to three edges of the box. Have *VeggieConnections Shepherds* help younger kids. If kids want to make high-top shoes or boots, give them 4"-wide strips of lightweight tagboard and have them curl it and fit it inside the hole of their box and use masking tape to tape the tagboard to the inside and outside of the box. Make sure the tagboard isn't inserted very far inside the box because kids will need to be able to reach inside the box.

Provide a variety of decorating materials, such a shiny wrapping paper for dress shoes, construction paper in a variety of colors, bright shoelaces or yarn, sequins, beads, and so on. Allow kids to tape or glue the materials to their boxes. Have kids decorate the box and the lid separately, then attach them together with masking tape taped on the inside of the box. Have Shepherds assist as needed.

Tell kids they will add reminders of God's love to their shoes each week. Have them write their names on their boxes. Collect the shoes for use in next week's lesson.

KID CONNECTION NEEDS:

- Shoebox with lid (one per child)
- Scissors
- 4"-wide tagboard strips
- Masking tape
- Shiny wrapping paper
- Construction paper
- Colorful shoelaces or yarn
- Tape
- Glue and glue sticks
- Sequins, beads, and other decorative items
- Markers

C. Christ Connection

Ask: **How does God want us to express our love for him?** Refer to the Unit Memory Verse poster and read Matthew 22:37–39 together. Ask kids to think of one way they can show love for God today.

Lead the kids in singing the *THINK—LINK—ACT* song, using the motions. Then recite together the Program Verse, James 4:8.

Remind the kids that prayer is a great way to connect with God. **Being able to pray to God at any time, day or night, is a wonderful gift from him. Jesus wants to hear your prayers. When you talk to him, you are coming near to him.**

Ask the kids to think silently of a time this week when it would help them to remember that God loves them. Then ask them to silently talk to God to finish this prayer in their own words:

Dear God, thank you that you love us so much and that you come near to us. Lord, I really need you to be near to me this week. Please help me remember how much you love me when ... Encourage kids to finish talking to God in their hearts. **Thank you for hearing our prayers and remembering them. In Jesus' name, amen.**

Distribute the take-home newspaper, *VeggieConnections*.

CHRIST CONNECTION NEEDS:

- *VeggieConnections Music CD*
- CD player
- *VeggieConnections* take-home newspaper (one per child)

Dear _____ ,

Because I love you, I'm giving you God's Counselor,
his Holy Spirit. The Spirit will help you know the truth
in God's Word, the Bible. The Counselor will help you
know right from wrong and encourage you to live right.
I, Jesus, have returned to heaven to be with my Father
forever. But the Holy Spirit will live in your heart if
you let him. May the Holy Spirit help you to glorify
God with your life!

Love forever,
Jesus

Connecting to **Love** through **Jesus**
Jesus and the Holy Spirit: **John 16:5–15**

counselor

PART ONE:

Plugging In at Flibber-o-loo

Introduction to the site and lesson focus

LESSON 2:
I have Jesus as my Savior and Counselor.

A. Veggie Connection

BEFORE YOU START:

Arrange for a *VeggieConnections Shepherd* or other adult to dress as a counselor from Jibberty-lot. Give your volunteer a copy of the script to read during the interview. On the Unit Memory Verse poster, attach artificial flowers with tape to cover the words "love." Leave them there for all future lessons.

Dressed as a Flibbian, welcome the children excitedly to Flibber-o-loo. **Today we're having a special guest! And this person is from Jibberty-lot! As you know, things weren't always friendly between us. But now that we're getting to know each other, we're finding out we can learn a lot from one another. In fact, this is such a big event, I'm interviewing our special guest so other Flibbians can hear the advice. Please welcome our guest!**

Have kids applaud as you welcome your guest. Have your guest be seated next to you and bring out your microphone. Hold the microphone in front of your guest when he or she talks.

Teacher: Thank you for coming. I know you are very busy.

Counselor: Oh, yes! Now that people from Flibber-o-loo and Jiberty-lot aren't mean to each other, I've been helping the people from both towns.

Teacher: So you help people. What kind of job is that?

Counselor: I'm a counselor.

Teacher: What else does a counselor do?

Counselor: Sometimes people need help understanding each other, and I help with that. I help people see that everyone is important and worthy of respect.

Teacher: I see. Are there other ways you help people?

THE CHILDREN
will arrive with their *VeggieConnections Shepherds* from the opening Countertop Connections featuring Bob and Larry. Play the *Veggie-Connections Music CD* as children enter Flibber-o-loo.

VEGGIE CONNECTION NEEDS:

- *VeggieConnections Music CD*
- CD player
- Volunteer wearing pot
- Real or fake microphone
- *VeggieConnections Bible Dictionary*
- Construction-paper flower for Connection Word
- Marker
- A balloon (not inflated)
- Tape
- Unit Memory Verse poster (from *Lesson 1*)

Counselor: I also help people handle their problems. Everyone has problems, and sometimes people need some help solving them.

Teacher: What's the most important thing you can do for the people who come to you for help?

Counselor: Oh, that's easy. I get to know the person I'm helping. The more I know about him or her, the better help I can give.

Teacher: Helping people with their problems sounds like a great thing to do. Are you the greatest counselor ever?

Counselor: Oh, no; not at all. The greatest counselor is the one who lives inside us and helps us to know God.

Teacher: What counselor is this?

Counselor: He is called the Holy Spirit.

Teacher: Really? The Holy Spirit. We'll have to learn more about him. Thank you very much for talking with us today. Let's give our guest a hand!

Today we're going to be talking about this very special Counselor who comes from God. Ask a volunteer to look up the word *counselor* in the *VeggieConnections Bible Dictionary* and read the definition aloud. Print *counselor* on a paper flower and display. Then ask the kids to briefly tell what a counselor does.

This counselor from God is also called the Holy Spirit—the Spirit of Jesus. Jesus' Spirit is the perfect counselor who knows everything about you, and he can encourage and help you in every area of your life!

Let's find out a little about what it means to have the Holy Spirit, a gift from Jesus, live inside of you. First, you must put all your trust and love in God and his Son, Jesus. Then Jesus will give you the gift of his Spirit! We can't see the Holy Spirit. It works a little like this. Blow up a balloon and tie it. Ask kids if they can see if the air that went into the balloon. They can't. Explain that that we can't see the Holy Spirit, either. **Just like the air in the filled balloon is there to stay, so is the Holy Spirit we receive from Jesus, who is our Savior. His Spirit fills us, and he stays with us to be our Counselor. The Spirit helps us to come near to God by connecting us with him and filling us with his love.**

Display the Unit Memory Verse poster, and say Matthew 22:37–39 together, including the words that are covered by the flowers.

B. Prayer Connection

In their *VeggieConnections Group*, kids may tell about answers to prayer from the past week and new prayer requests. Have *VeggieConnections Shepherds* lead prayer with prayer starters, pausing to let any kids who wish finish the sentences:

Dear God, thank you for coming near to us! Today we thank you for . . . Let kids express thanks to God.

Lord, thanks for our friends here. Please help these friends . . . Let kids pray about requests mentioned. The *VeggieConnections Shepherds* should pray for any requests that have been overlooked.

Plugging In to God's Word

PART TWO:

Connecting to God's Word in the Bible and understanding how that can help us to have a better relationship with him

A. God Connection: Jesus and the Holy Spirit – John 16:5-15

BEFORE YOU START:
Prepare mural paper for the wall. On the left side print "Savior" and "Counselor" separated by a large space. Down the right-hand side, print phrases as shown below.

Savior	Forgive us
	Understand God's Word
	Die for our sins
	Always there
	Make good choices
Counselor	Alive forever
	Show right from wrong

Read the list with the kids. Explain the list contains the words found in the Bible story. Show where today's Bible story is found, in John 16.

Explain that you'll read through the story once, as kids listen carefully. Then you'll read the Bible story a second time, and kids should raise a hand whenever they hear one of the phrases on the mural read from the story. Have this child come up to the mural and underline the words he or she identified. Continue reading and having kids underline all the words or phrases on the mural.

Jesus talked with his disciples. He knew that he would soon die on the cross. He would <u>die for our sins</u>. But he wouldn't stay dead for long! He would be <u>alive forever</u>. This way he could <u>forgive us</u>. By dying on the cross and coming back to life, Jesus would be the <u>Savior</u>.

Jesus knew his friends would be sad and lonely, so he promised to send them his Spirit to live in them and be <u>always there</u>. He would be their <u>Counselor</u>.

The disciples wondered how the Holy Spirit would counsel them. Jesus explained, "The Holy Spirit will show people their sin—all people have done wrong things and they need to believe in me to be forgiven. And my Spirit living in you will <u>show you right from wrong</u>. You can ask me to forgive you when you do wrong. You can ask me to help you obey.

"The Holy Spirit will give you wisdom when you have tough decisions. He will help you <u>make good choices</u>.

"The Holy Spirit will help you <u>understand God's Word</u>, because his Word is truth. When you read it or listen to it, the Spirit will help you understand what you're learning."

Jesus' friends never forgot his words. We can take his words to heart because Jesus is our Savior, and he has given us the Holy Spirit to be our Counselor.

Once all the words are underlined, ask the kids to figure out which phrases on the right side fit Jesus' role as Savior and which fit his Spirit's work as Counselor. Let one child at a time choose one trait from the right to match the name on the left. If correct, let that child draw a line to connect the two. Some answers can fit either role, but here are some suggested answers: *Savior: die for our sins, alive forever, forgive us; Counselor: always there, show right from wrong, make good choices, understand God's Word.*

Point to the words on the mural as you summarize: **Jesus came to earth to die on a cross** (Die for our sins) **and forgive our sins** (Forgive us) **when we believe in him. God raised him from death** (Alive forever). **Jesus has returned to heaven to be his Father God, but the Holy Spirit stays with believers to counsel us on how to live,** (Always there, show right from wrong, make good choices, understand God's Word). **The Holy Spirit helps us THINK—LINK—ACT so we can connect to a powerful relationship with God.**

You may want to share God's plan of salvation to the kids or share how the Holy Spirit has helped you in your Christian walk.

GOD CONNECTION NEEDS:

- Large sheet of mural paper
- Marker
- Bible

HIGH-POWERED GAME NEEDS:

- Savior and Counselor slips on page 180 (one per *VeggieConnections Group*)
- Masking/painter's tape
- Shoes from the site (one for every two kids)
- Pots from the site (one for every two kids)

BEFORE YOU START:

Copy the Savior and Counselor slips (p. 180), and cut them apart. You need one slip for each child (if groups are larger than eight). Tape a start/finish line and spread out all the slips at the other end of the playing area.

B. Activity Connection

Choose from the following activities to help kids explore and remember that Jesus can be their Savior and Counselor (approximately 10–15 minutes each).

1. High-Powered Game: Neighbors Helping Neighbors

Divide the kids into two equal groups. Have a *VeggieConnections Shepherd* join a group to make them even if needed. Give the kids in each group one shoe each; give the kids in the other group one pot each. Now that the people of Flibber-o-loo and Jibberty-lot are friendly, they need to help each other. Have groups form teams of up to eight by making pairs of kids from each group (taking one Flibber-o-loo child and one Jibberty-lot child to make a pair). Then explain how pairs in each team are to run to the pile of slips, and using only a pot and a shoe, pick up a slip and carefully balance the slip between the shoe and the pot, and return to the start/finish line. Kids can't put slips inside pots!

Once all pairs have returned with a slip, explain the second part of the game. There are eight numbered slips, each with important information about Jesus and his Holy Spirit. Now teams have to carry slips of paper to each other, and go get slips of paper, all in the Flibbian-Jibberty way—using pots and shoes as before. Each team wants all eight slips, so have fun getting them!

Allow teams to play until one team has collected all eight slips. When a team does, have this team read the eight slips. **Flibber-o-loo and Jibberty-lot are make-believe towns, but people in real places need to know Jesus as Savior and his Spirit as Counselor.**

2. Low-Powered Game: Filled with the Spirit

LOW-POWERED GAME NEEDS:

- Pot from the site
- Bag of cotton balls (enough to fill pot plus extras)
- Plastic spoons (one per child)

BEFORE YOU START:

Place a small to medium pot in the center of your play area. Have kids make a circle around the pot. Give each child a plastic spoon and have them put the handle end of the spoon in their mouths. Equally distribute the cotton balls to the kids, but keep a few extras. Hold up a cotton ball in the palm of your hand. **The cotton balls are like the Holy Spirit in this game. You can't see or touch the Spirit, just like I can barely feel this cotton ball in my hand. The Bible talks about being filled with the Spirit. We're going to fill this pot with as many cotton balls as we can. Because we all want to be filled with God's Spirit, let's all work as a large team to fill the pot!**

Have kids place a cotton ball in their spoons, and then crawl to the center and drop the cotton ball in the pot. Kids repeat using up all their cotton balls. Give these kids extra cotton balls while remaining kids are still moving their original supply. Aim to have the game end with everyone finishing about the same time.

Play additional rounds using alternate ways of moving such as walking backward, walking on knees, or scooting across the floor on their bottoms.

CRAFT NEEDS:

- 2" x 2" plain, light-colored ceramic tiles (one per child)
- Stickers
- Fine line permanent or paint markers
- Scrap paper and pencils
- Tacky craft glue or cool glue gun
- Wooden spring-type clothespins (one per child)
- Rubber bands

3. Craft: Homework Helper

Give each child a ceramic tile. Using stickers and/or paint pens, kids should create a symbol on their tile to remind them that Jesus is their Savior and Counselor. They may use common Christian symbols, or they make create their own. Kids may practice drawing their design on paper first. Some Christian symbols are: ICHTHUS (fish symbol), meaning Jesus Christ, God's Son, Savior; a cross; a dove or flame, for the Holy Spirit; a hand, for God our helper; a triangle, for the Trinity.

Help kids glue their tile to the end of a clothespin so that it is even with the bottom of the tile. Use tacky craft glue or a cool-temperature glue gun with adult help. Until the glue dries, place a rubber band around the tile and the side of the clothespin nearest the tile, to keep a firm contact between the clothespin and the tile. The clothespin and tile should be able to stand up when the glue dries.

The kids can use their clip whenever they need a book page held open. When not used in this way they can leave the clip standing to display reminders, such as prayer requests, and Bible verses to memorize.

PART THREE:

Plugging In to My Life

Life application of the lesson to lead kids to THINK-LINK-ACT and build a relationship with God every day

A. Cucumber Connection

Before kids arrive, enlarge and copy the pickles from the *VeggieConnections Shepherd* pages on the CD-ROM included in the *VeggieConnections Elementary Curriculum Kit* onto green construction paper. Cut them out and put them in a pickle jar.

Let a volunteer draw a pickle from the Pickle Pot and either the child or a Shepherd should read the dilemma out loud. Each Shepherd should then process the question with their group using the THINK—LINK—ACT phrase.

A neighbor boy is crying. Matt has always thought this kid was a spoiled brat. Today Matt feels that the boy needs his help. What can Matt do?	Jackie's parents told her to clean her room. She had other things in mind, like talking on the phone with friends. But she feels God is telling her to obey her parents. What should Jackie do?	Shawna loves to come to church. She likes the singing and the fun things to do. But she tunes out when Bible verses are read. Shawna says she does not understand Bible words. Where can she find help?

CUCUMBER CONNECTION NEEDS:
- Pickle jar
- Pickle artwork from the *VeggieConnections Shepherd* pages (on the *VeggieConnections CD-ROM*)
- Green construction paper

B. Kid Connection: Love Shoes

Give each child his or her Love Shoe. Give each child a Holy Spirit letter on page 174. When Jesus returned to heaven, he sent His Counselor, the Holy Spirit to be with us. This letter is a summary of the Bible teaching of the Counselor we learned. Have kids write their name at the beginning of the letter. Then have kids all read the letter aloud in unison.

Give kids glitter pens and markers and allow them to decorate their letters. Then show kids how to roll up both ends of their letters together like a scroll. Have them tie a ribbon or yarn piece to their letter scrolls and put them in their shoes. Collect the shoes for use next week.

KID CONNECTION NEEDS:
- Love Shoes (made in *Lesson 1*)
- Holy Spirit Letter on page 174 (one per child)
- Pens
- Glitter pens
- Markers
- 18" ribbon or yarn (one per child)

C. Christ Connection

Lead the kids in singing the *THINK—LINK—ACT* song, using the motions. Then recite together the Program Verse, James 4:8.

Remind the kids of the opportunity they have to talk with God in prayer at any time. Invite the kids to sit with a partner for this prayer activity. Have them write their name and a prayer request on a slip of paper to give their partner. Begin the prayer for the whole group, and indicate to the kids when they may pray for their partners' request.

Lord, thank you for sending your Holy Spirit so that we could be very close to you. Thank you for promising to help us. Today I ask for . . .

Kids should take the prayer request home to remember to pray for their partner.
Distribute the take-home newspaper, ***VeggieConnections***.

CHRIST CONNECTION NEEDS:
- *VeggieConnections Music CD*
- CD player
- Slips of paper
- Pencils
- *VeggieConnections* take-home newspaper (one per child)

1. Jesus forgives us.

2. Jesus died for our sins.

3. Jesus is alive forever.

4. The Spirit helps us understand God's Word.

5. The Holy Spirit is always there.

6. The Spirit helps us make good choices.

7. The Spirit shows us right from wrong.

8. Jesus is my Savior and Counselor.

Connecting to **Love** through **Jesus**
Jesus teaches the Beatitudes: **Matthew 5:1–12**

teach

PART ONE:

Plugging In at Flibber-o-loo

Introduction to the site and lesson focus

LESSON 3:

I have Jesus to teach me how to love.

A. Veggie Connection

BEFORE YOU START:

Place a posterboard sign at the front of the site. Gather a variety of shoes for kids to try on. On the Unit Memory Verse poster, attach candies over the words "all." ("Love" should still be covered by artificial flowers from last week.)

Dressed as the Flibbian Mayor, welcome the kids to Flibber-o-loo. **I am the Mayor of Flibber-o-loo and I'm told you fine people are interested in becoming citizens of our fine town. Of course you know everyone here wears shoes on their heads, so the first thing you need to learn is how to do this.** Point to the sign and tell them school is in session. Ask for a few volunteers and have kids come to the front. **The first thing to do is to choose a shoe that is a good fit for you.** Have kids try putting a few shoes upside down on their heads. Also have *VeggieConnections Shepherds* help their kids try shoes on their heads while you direct the school session.

Now that you've decided on a shoe, the next step is to try walking around a bit, trying to balance the shoe on your head. You can use your hand to keep the shoe on your head if needed. Allow kids to walk around, encouraging them to balance the shoes without use of their hands.

Since you're just learning how to wear shoes on your head, I'll give you some help. Pass out lengths of yarn and show how to wrap the yarn around the shoe and under the childrens' chins. Tie with a bow knot for easy removal. Have Shepherds fasten shoes to their kids' heads using the yarn.

Well, that's enough to teach you today. If you are a citizen of Flibber-o-loo, it's important to learn what I've just taught you. In your life, there are many things you will be taught. That's what our Connection Word is about.

Ask a volunteer to look up the word *teach* in the *VeggieConnections Bible Dictionary* and read the definition aloud. Print *teach* on a paper flower and display it. **Today, we will look at some teachings of Jesus that will help us to love God and to love others, which is what out Unit Memory Verse is all about.**

Display the Unit Memory Verse poster, and lead the kids in saying Matthew 22:37–39 together. Then have kids remove their shoes.

THE CHILDREN
will arrive with their *VeggieConnections Shepherds* from the opening Countertop Connections featuring Bob and Larry. Play the *Veggie-Connections Music CD* as children enter Flibber-o-loo.

VEGGIE CONNECTION NEEDS:

- *VeggieConnections Music CD*
- CD player
- Large sign: "Shoe Hat School"
- Unit Memory Verse poster (from *Lesson 1*)
- Large candies
- Variety of shoes (from site)
- Yarn
- Scissors
- *VeggieConnections Bible Dictionary*
- Construction-paper flowers
- Tape

B. Prayer Connection

Have kids sit in a circle in their *VeggieConnections Group*. Begin praying with the following sentence. Pause to let kids jump up in any order to say a word or two to complete the sentence. **Dear God, today we want to praise you for being . . . In Jesus' name, amen.**

GOD CONNECTION NEEDS:

- Bible
- eight prepared paper signs

BEFORE YOU START:

Write eight words/phrases, one per sheet of paper:

1. "Really needing God"
2. "Being sad"
3. "Not thinking too highly of yourself"
4. "Hungry to live God's way"
5. "Being kind and forgiving"
6. "Having a clean heart"
7. "Trying to make peace"
8. "Being hurt with words or actions for believing in Jesus"

On the backs of each sheet write, "Blessed." Stack the signs in order.

PART TWO: Plugging In to God's Word

Connecting to God's Word in the Bible and understanding how that can help us to have a better relationship with him

A. God Connection: Jesus teaches the Beatitudes – Matthew 5:1-12

Show in your Bible that today's story comes from Matthew 5.

Jesus went up on a mountain to teach a crowd of people. He starting teaching by telling the people the kinds of attitudes that please God. We're going to look at those attitudes. Jesus starts each attitude with the word *blessed*. If I were to tell you I had a piece of candy for you, would that make you happy? Allow responses. Kids will probably answer yes. **Knowing I would give you candy would give you a happy attitude. Think about having that attitude right now. Now if I told you I don't have the candy, would you still have that happy attitude?** Allow responses. Some kids might still have a happy attitude, while others may not. **If you still have a happy attitude knowing you won't get the candy, you have the happy attitude Jesus is talking about when he says "blessed."**

I will tell you the Bible story two times. The first time, you will listen very carefully. The the second time, I'll give you instructions for something fun you can do. First, read the eight Beatitudes with no interaction from kids. Then have eight volunteers come up to the front. Give each child one paper sign and have them line up in front of the group. Have kids hold their signs in front of them, with the word "Blessed" facing out. As you explain each beatitude, motion the appropriate child to turn over his or her sign.

Turn over sign #1. **Jesus taught blessed or happy is your attitude when you really need God. When you have this attitude, God promises to be in your life. What are some ways you need God?** (*I need God to help me in school.*)

Turn over sign #2. **Jesus taught when you are sad you can know that God will give you comfort. How can God help you when you are sad?** (*He can help me feel better when I lose a pet.*)

Turn over sign #3. **Next, Jesus taught that you will be blessed when you have a humble attitude, which means not thinking too highly of yourself. What ways can you be humble?** (*Giving God the credit when I do well in sports.*)

Turn over sign #4. **Jesus taught when you're hungry to live God's way, God will fill you with his Spirit. How are you hungry for God?** (*I want to do what Jesus taught.*)

Turn over sign #5. **Jesus taught God is kind and forgiving and how we are blessed when are the same toward others. How can you be kind or forgiving to someone?** (*I can forgive my best friend when she hurt me.*)

Turn over sign #6. **Then Jesus taught having a clean heart helps us to see God's love better. How can you have a clean heart?** (*By watching what I say to my friends.*)

Turn over sign #7. **Jesus taught trying to make peace with others will make you feel closer to God. How can you make peace?** (*Choose not to fight when I get angry.*)

Turn over sign #8. **The last blessing Jesus taught is hard. He taught that we should have happy attitudes when others hurt us for being Christians. They could make fun of you, not be your friends, or tell lies against you. But Jesus taught that other believers have been treated badly as well. What are some ways you been treated badly because of your faith in Jesus?** (*Kids at school say mean things; kids make fun of me.*)

Have kids all turn their signs over to "Blessed." **In teaching these blessings, Jesus is saying we should look for our happiness from God. We won't always be happy, but if we look to God to give us a happy attitude, he will give it to us. And this will help us to know how much God loves us.**

B. Activity Connection

Choose from the following activities to help kids explore and remember that God wants us to show our love for him by having attitudes that bring us his blessings (approximately 10–15 minutes each).

1. High-Powered Game: Love Blessings

Jesus taught we are blessed when we have the hearts, attitude, and actions of loving God and others. In this game, you will all go through three game stations, collecting a card at each one.

Divide kids into three teams. Have teams each start at one of the three game stations so you have about an equal number at each station. The goal is for kids to each collect the three cards, so teams aren't competing against each other. Explain the three stations: **Station 1 is an obstacle course. You run in-between the chairs until you reach the game card. Station 2 is a relay you complete by crab-walking to reach the card and to return. In Station 3 you hold on to the yarn as you run the course and return back.**

Once a player finishes one station and collects its card, he or she can choose either of two remaining stations. Have *VeggieConnections Shepherds* help direct the flow of the kids to the stations, so each station has about the same number of kids.

Once kids have all collected the three cards, ask them to discuss which of the three stations was the easiest and hardest station. **Some of the stations were harder than others.** Have kids look at their three cards. **We need to have the right heart, attitude, and actions to love God. Our Unit Memory Verse says a similar thing:** *"Love the Lord your God with all your heart and with all your soul and with all your mind."*

Have kids save their game cards for the Kid Connection later in the lesson.

2. Low-Powered Game: Love in Action Charades

Divide the kids into *VeggieConnections Groups*. Give each *VeggieConnections Shepherd* the game slips. Have kids in each group sit in a semicircle around their Shepherd. Explain this is a charades-type game. Have kids come up in pairs and give them a game slip. Give kids a chance to think how they will act out the loving action. When a child in the group calls out the action, he or she will pick a partner and come get a new slip to act to the group. Play until all the slips are used up.

Jesus taught us to love others. We acted out the second part of our Unit Memory Verse in this game: *"Love your neighbor as yourself."*

3. Craft: Shoes of Love

Have kids select a shoe from the site or choose what they're wearing. Give kids a piece of card stock and have them trace the outline of the shoe. Then have kids add flaps on either side of the outline that can be folded up together. Have *VeggieConnection Shepherds* assist kids in cutting out their shoe patterns.

With gel pens or markers, have kids write, "I will walk with God by showing my love to him and others. Matthew 22:37-39" on the flap of the shoe. Then have kids fold the flaps on top of the shoe. Give kids hole punches and have them punch four shoelace holes on each flap, just like the flaps on real shoes. Give kids eight hole reinforcements and have them color them with markers, then glue then over the shoelace holes. Give kids one shoelace and have them lace the shoe and tie it.

Show kids the photo of the *Compassion International* child that the class sponsors (or display a photo of a child that someone in the class sponsors). **Often children from poorer parts of the world do not have shoes on their feet. One way you can walk with God is to pray for the kids like** (say the child's name) **who may not have shoes. We can send a special monetary gift to** (child's name) **and ask the Compassion staff to buy shoes for him/her if he/she needs a pair.**

HIGH-POWERED GAME NEEDS:
- Love Blessings Game on page 206 (one per child)
- Chairs
- Masking/painter's tape
- Yarn

BEFORE YOU START:
Set up three stations for this game:

1. A zig-zag obstacle course with chairs and taped arrows
2. A relay course with taped start/finish lines
3. A S-shaped course with chairs with yarn attached to each chair

Copy and cut apart the cards. Place a different card at the end of each game station.

LOW-POWERED GAME NEEDS:
- Acts of Love Game on page 207 (one per *VeggieConnections Group*)

BEFORE YOU START:
Copy and cut apart the game slips. Make a set for each *VeggieConnections Group*.

CRAFT NEEDS:
- Card stock pieces (one per child)
- Scissors
- Variety of shoes (from the site)
- Colorful 24" shoelaces (one lace per child)
- Paper reinforcement circles (eight per child)
- Hole punches
- Gel pens
- Glue sticks
- Colored markers
- Picture of a *Compassion International* child that the class or someone from the class sponsors

PART THREE:

Plugging In to My Life

Life application of the lesson to lead kids to THINK–LINK–ACT and build a relationship with God every day

A. Cucumber Connection

CUCUMBER CONNECTION NEEDS:

- Pickle jar
- Pickle artwork from the *VeggieConnections Shepherd* pages (on the *VeggieConnections CD-ROM*)
- Green construction paper

Before kids arrive, enlarge and copy the pickles from the *VeggieConnections Shepherd* pages on the CD-ROM included in the *VeggieConnections Elementary Curriculum Kit* onto green construction paper. Cut them out and put them in a pickle jar.

Let a volunteer draw a pickle from the Pickle Pot and either the child or a Shepherd should read the dilemma out loud. Each Shepherd should then process the question with their group using the THINK—LINK—ACT phrase.

Josh gets in a fight with his little brother over playing a computer game. Josh has only yelled back at his brother, not hit him. But he feels his anger rising. What teaching of Jesus could help Josh?	Jonathan's friend shows off skills on his new skateboard. Everyone is getting tired of it. When the friend falls off and gets hurt, Jonathan is tempted to laugh and say it serves him right. Which of Jesus' teaching should Jonathan remember?	Lindsay wants to follow Jesus. This means that kids at school will see a difference on how she acts and talks. She is afraid they will make fun of her. What can Lindsay learn from Jesus to give her courage?

B. Kid Connection: Love Shoes

KID CONNECTION NEEDS:

- Love Shoes (made in *Lesson 1*)
- Index cards (three per child)
- Scissors
- Game cards from High-Powered game
- Glue sticks
- Colored markers
- Tape

Give each child his or her Love Shoe, three index cards, and scissors. Have kids trim their three game cards to fit on the index cards. Using glue sticks, have kids glue each picture on a separate index card. Then have kids color the pictures with markers. Show kids how to tape the index cards together, forming a trifold booklet.

These booklets remind us to have the heart, attitude, and actions to love God and to love others. Have kids put their booklets inside their Love Shoes. Collect the shoes for use next week.

C. Christ Connection

CHRIST CONNECTION NEEDS:

- *VeggieConnections* take-home newspaper (one per child)

Lead the kids in singing the *THINK—LINK—ACT* song, using the motions. Then recite together the Program Verse, James 4:8.

Remind the kids that showing Jesus' love is a good way to come near him. Sometimes that isn't easy. Ask kids to make tight fists with their hands as they think of someone to whom it is hard for them to show love.

Now invite them open their hands and outstretch them to show they want Jesus to help them to show his love in some way to that person this week. They silently complete this prayer:

Lord, thank you for loving us and promising us blessings as we have attitudes that please you. Please help me show your love to . . . In Jesus' name, amen.

Encourage the kids to follow through with an outward act of loving the person they prayed for. This will help them link to God and others.

Distribute the take-home newspaper, **VeggieConnections**.

Connecting to **Love** through **Jesus**
Peter walks on water: **Matthew 14:22-36**

PART ONE:

Plugging in at Flibber-o-loo

Introduction to the site and lesson focus

LESSON 4:
I have Jesus as my daily source of love.

A. Veggie Connection

BEFORE YOU START:
On the Unit Memory Verse poster, attach artificial flowers over the words "your" and "yourself." (The words "love" and "all" should be covered from previous weeks.) Set up two box fans. Lean the first fan back against a chair, facing the kids, and plugged in. Put the second fan next to its chair, but leave it unplugged. Practice the use of the chairs and two fans to make sure it works right. Wear a lab coat or smock with visor. Include pocket protector, calculator, pencils, ruler, tape measure, compass or protractor, and glasses taped together. Have a dozen or so small tissue-paper flowers in your pocket.

Dressed as a Flibbian inventor, welcome the kids to Flibber-o-loo. **Hello, there! People in Flibber-o-loo call me Flibby the Fantastaventor, because I'm a fantastic inventor. I invent all kinds of wonderful things to help the people of Flibber-o-loo. Maybe you can help me with my latest invention.** Pull out a ruler, tape measure, or similar item and go to the fan leaning against the chair. Pull out a tissue-paper flower. **Now that we throw candy and flowers instead of shoes, people have been asking me to invent something that will make the flowers reach Jibberty-lot. The wind catches these light flowers and they blow away. So I'm inventing a *turbo* flower tosser.** Turn on the fan on high and ask for several volunteers to come up and help you. Give kids flowers, but keep a few. Have kids hold the flower in front of the fan, then release the flower to fly into the group of kids.

After kids have let their flowers fly, get the second chair and place it in front of the fan. Set the fan on the chair, leaning it back. **Now here comes the *turbo* part! Two fans should make the flowers fly all the way to Jibberty-lot!** Turn on the second (unplugged) fan and show disappointment. **I have no power! What happened to the power?**

Have the kids around you look for the fault. When someone discovers the fan isn't plugged in, say: **Aha! The fan wasn't plugged in. Something was missing that reminds me of today's Connection Word.** Turn off the first fan and ask a volunteer to look up the word *source* in the *VeggieConnections Bible Dictionary* and read the definition aloud. Print *source* on a construction-paper flower and display it at the site.

My fan didn't work because it wasn't connected to its power source. Plug in the fan and turn on both fans. Launch a few flowers into the group of kids. Turn off the fans. **Next time I show off one of my fantastic inventions, I'll make sure I have a power source for it. In a few minutes, we'll get to see a power source that is way more amazing than any invention I come up with. It's amazing because the source comes from God!**

Display the Unit Memory Verse poster, and lead the kids in saying Matthew 22:37–39 together, including the words that are covered.

THE CHILDREN
will arrive with their
VeggieConnections Shepherds
from the opening Countertop
Connections featuring Bob
and Larry. Play the *Veggie-
Connections Music CD* as
children enter Flibber-o-loo.

**VEGGIE CONNECTION
NEEDS:**
- *VeggieConnections Music CD*
- CD player
- Unit Memory Verse poster (from *Lesson 1*)
- Two box fans
- Two chairs
- Artificial flowers
- Lab coat or smock
- Visor
- Pocket protector, calculator, pencils, ruler, tape measure, compass, glasses taped together
- Small tissue-paper flowers (from site)
- *VeggieConnections Bible Dictionary*
- Construction-paper flower for Connection Word
- Marker
- Tape

B. Prayer Connection

Encourage kids in their *VeggieConnections Groups* to think about the sources of love in their lives. Invite each child to share what they thought about.

VeggieConnections Shepherds should use these prayer starters to help kids talk to God silently: **God, thank you for this person who loves me . . .** Kids pray.
Help me to show my thanks by . . . Kids think of something.
In Jesus' name, amen.

PART TWO:

Plugging In to God's Word

Connecting to God's Word in the Bible and understanding how that can help us to have a better relationship with him

A. God Connection: Peter walks on water – Matthew 14:22-36

GOD CONNECTION NEEDS:

- Two box fans
- Water-mist bottles with water (one per *Veggie-Connections Group*)
- Bible
- Blue posterboard cut out with wave shape

BEFORE YOU START:

Set the fans to blow on either side of the circle of chairs. Give *Veggie-Connections Shepherds* water-mist bottles and have them spray water during the storm portion of the story. Also have Shepherds operate the fans.

Set up chairs in a circle. For larger groups, arrange concentric circles. Ask the kids to do "the wave" as you tell the story. The kids sit with their hands on their knees. At your signal, the first person stands up, lifts his hands up in the air and back down again in a smooth motion, and sits again. As soon as the first person stands, the second person begins to stand and follows the same motions. Continue until the wave passes around the circle. Say you will hold up a blue wave poster to signal the child seated next to you to begin "the wave." Practice a couple of times. Then show in your Bible that today's story is in Matthew 14.

I will tell you the Bible story two times. The first time, you will listen very carefully. Then the second time, I'll give you instructions for something fun you can do.

Jesus had taught and fed a large crowd of people. Now it was time to send them home. Jesus told his disciples to sail to the other side of the Sea of Galilee while he stayed behind to talk to his Father. Jesus was always closely connected to God, but he wanted special times to pray.

About four in the morning, Jesus saw that the disciples were far from the shore. A violent storm had come up. Turn on the fans. **The wind was blowing hard, and the boat was being hit by huge waves.** Have Shepherds spray water into the circle. Hold up the blue wave poster, and direct the kids to do the "wave."

Jesus stepped out onto the water and began to walk across the lake—on top of the water—and didn't sink! He wasn't afraid of the wind or waves. Hold up the wave poster.

The disciples looked out on the raging sea and were terrified at what they saw. "It's a ghost!" they shrieked. But Jesus called, "Don't be afraid. It's only me." He kept coming.

Peter called out, "Lord, if it's really you, tell me to come to you." He waited breathlessly, watching the big waves. Hold up the wave poster.

Jesus answered, "Come to me." Peter climbed out of the boat and stepped onto the water. He looked at Jesus and walked toward him! Then Peter glanced at the tall waves. Hold up the wave poster.

Suddenly he became afraid and began to sink! He cried out, "Lord! Save me!" Jesus reached out his hand and caught Peter. "Have more faith in me," Jesus said. "You don't need to doubt!"

Peter and Jesus climbed into the boat. What happened to the fierce wind and the huge waves? Hold up the wave poster. Turn off the fans and stop spraying the water. **Suddenly everything was calm and quiet. With hearts full of wonder and love, the disciples worshiped Jesus and said, "Now we really know that you are God's Son."**

Discuss these questions to review: **How did Jesus stay connected to God?** *(He was close to God all the time, but spent special time praying to God.)* **How did Peter show that Jesus was his source of love and power?** *(Peter trusted Jesus and walked out on the water. When he started to sink, he called to Jesus, trusting him to help him.)* **When things are hard or scary for us, what can we do?** *(Trust Jesus to be our source of love and power.)*

Just as he helped Peter, Jesus is available to help us anytime, too. He's always there, ready and waiting to be our source of love so we can stay connected to God. He welcomes us to come close to him so that we can enjoy his love.

B. Activity Connection

Choose from the following activities to help kids explore and remember that Jesus is their source of love (approximately 10–15 minutes each).

1. High-Powered Game: Walking on Water

Tape a start/finish line and an end line about 20 feet away or longer if you have room.

Have kids form two teams and have them line up behind the start/finish line. Station two *VeggieConnections Shepherds* behind the end line and two about halfway between the lines on either side. **Peter walked on the water when he saw Jesus. But he saw the waves and took his eyes off Jesus and then he began to sink. This game may give you an idea of what that might have been like.** Explain how kids will start to walk toward the Shepherds. About a third of the way down the course, the Shepherds will tell kids to start "sinking" by slowly falling to their knees. Then about a third of the way from the end, kids will crawl to the end of the course. When kids reach the end, they should reach out and the Shepherd will pull them up. Kids then shout: **Jesus is my source of faith and love!** and run back to their team, tagging the next player.

When everyone has run the course, say: **You and I will probably never have the chance to walk on water as Peter did. But whenever we start to "sink" in our faith, we can remember Jesus is always there to reach out and pull us to safety. We can be confident that Jesus is our source of love, and he will care for us.**

2. Low-Powered Game: Plugging into the Source

Show kids an extension cord. **We use extension cords so electric things can connect to the power source when they won't reach the power outlet source. Jesus is our source of love. We're going to play human extension cord pieces in this game, and you're going to help each other connect to that source.** Have kids enter the game area and then allow *VeggieConnections Shepherds* to help kids put on blindfolds. Have kids scatter throughout the playing area.

Explain how this game is similar to Marco Polo, except only the "plug" calls out. Choose one child to be the first "plug." The plug is the only one who can call out: **Connect to Jesus!** to help other kids connect by holding hands. Once a child has connected, he or she becomes the new plug and calls out the phrase. Kids can only connect to the child calling out the phrase. Have Shepherds ensure the "cord" keeps moving at all times. When the last child connects, have a Shepherd call out: **Connect to Jesus!** When the cord connects to the Shepherd, the game is over. Play additional rounds if you have time.

Have Shepherds remove blindfolds from kids while they remain connected. **You are all connected in this game. What are some ways you can help each other stay connected to Jesus?** *(Pray for each other, tell a friend about a Bible verse that has helped you, and so on.)*

3. Craft: My Source of Love Spinner

Fold an index card in half, then lay it flat again. On one half of the card place a Jesus sticker. Turn the card around so that the sticker is upside down. On the other half of the card draw a heart that is larger than the sticker. Color the heart. You should now have two pictures on the same side of the card, one of which is upside down.

Fold the card again. Use a hole punch to make holes on the right and left side of the folded card, about midpoint of the sides.

Loop a rubber band through each hole, and secure them by putting one end through the loop of the other end. Pull the rubber bands tight against the punched holes, so that you have a rubber band loop on the right and left sides of the folded card.

To use the spinner, hold the card in front of you. Place the rubber band over several fingers of each hand while your hands are in front of you, palms inward. With the rubber bands on your fingers, wind up the card as much as you can, being careful not to let go of the card. When you have finished winding up, let go and watch the card! As it spins rapidly, it will begin to look like the face of Jesus will be inside the heart. Encourage kids to try using the spinner now.

LOW-POWERED GAME NEEDS:
- Chairs
- Yarn
- Scissors
- Extension cord
- Blindfolds (one per child)

BEFORE YOU START:

Make boundaries for the game using yarn tied to the backs of chairs spread out around the perimeter of the game area.

CRAFT NEEDS:
- Index cards
- 1" Jesus stickers
- Rubber bands (two per child)
- Markers
- Hole punch

OPTIONAL:

If you are unable to obtain Jesus stickers, kids can draw a picture of Jesus, a cross, a fish symbol, or other 1" image. You'll also need scissors and glue.

This is a reminder that Jesus is your source of love! Play with it often and remember the close relationship you can have with Jesus. When you find it hard to love somebody, use the spinner and remember that Jesus is your source of love. He is right there to help you.

PART THREE:

Plugging In to My Life

Life application of the lesson to lead kids to THINK-LINK-ACT and build a relationship with God every day

A. Cucumber Connection

CUCUMBER CONNECTION NEEDS:

• Pickle jar
• Pickle artwork from the *VeggieConnections Shepherd* pages (on the *VeggieConnections* CD-ROM)
• Green construction paper

Before kids arrive, enlarge and copy the pickles from the *VeggieConnections Shepherd* pages on the CD-ROM included in the *VeggieConnections Elementary Curriculum Kit* onto green construction paper. Cut them out and put them in a pickle jar.

Let a volunteer draw a pickle from the Pickle Pot and either the child or a Shepherd should read the dilemma out loud. Each Shepherd should then process the question with their group using the THINK—LINK—ACT phrase.

Josh's parents are arguing again. it really bothers him. it seems to make him both afraid and angry at the same time. Josh is discouraged about it. What can he do to tap into Jesus as his daily source of love?	Someone at school is bullying Chandra. He makes faces at her, knocks her books off her desk, and says things that hurt her feelings. What can Chandra do if Jesus is her daily source of love?	You've been trying hard to get good grades in school. You're doing great in every subject but one. You can't understand that one subject. You've done the homework and you've asked for extra help. How can you keep from getting discouraged?

B. Kid Connection: Love Shoes

KID CONNECTION NEEDS:

• Love Shoes (made in *Lesson 1*)
• Light-switch covers (one per child)
• Blank file-folder label stickers (two per child)
• Fine-tipped permanent markers
• Colored permanent markers
• Veggie clip art

Give each child his or her Love Shoe. Provide a light-switch cover, file-folder label stickers, and fine-tipped permanent markers. Have kids write "Jesus is my source of love," on one sticker and "I will love God and others" on the second sticker. Have kids turn their switch covers side ways and put one sticker near the top edge of the plate, and the second sticker near the bottom edge of the plate. Then have kids decorate the other areas of their plates with Veggie clip art and colored permanent markers. Tell kids to ask a parent to put the light-switch cover on their light-switch in their room, when they take their shoes home at the end of the unit. Have kids put their light-switch covers inside their Love Shoes and collect them for use next week.

C. Christ Connection

CHRIST CONNECTION NEEDS:

• *VeggieConnections* take-home newspaper (one per child)

Lead the kids in singing the *THINK—LINK—ACT* song, using the motions. Then recite together the Program Verse, James 4:8.

Encourage kids to pray often. Remind them that talking with God is a great way to stay connected to him and to know his love. As a reminder, let them use their spinner card made as the craft. Then invite them to bow in prayer and to repeat each line of this prayer after you:

> **Dear Lord, it's awesome that you love me!**
> **You love me SO very, very, very much!**
> **Help me stay close to you every day.**
> **In Jesus' name, amen.**

Distribute the take-home newspaper, **VeggieConnections**.

Connecting to **Love** through **Jesus**
Jesus and the parable of the lost son: **Luke 15:11-32**

PART ONE:

Plugging In at Flibber-o-loo

Introduction to the site and lesson focus

LESSON 5:
I have Jesus to show me how to forgive others.

A. Veggie Connection

BEFORE YOU START:

Ask two *VeggieConnections Shepherds* to prepare the short skit with you. On the Unit Memory Verse poster, attach artificial candies over the words "greatest commandment." Other words should still be covered from previous weeks.

Dressed as the Flibbian and wearing new-looking tennis shoes, warmly greet the kids as they enter Flibber-o-loo. Point out your "new" shoes, commenting on how careful you are to take care of them and keep them clean.

When all the kids have arrived, continue talking about your new shoes. Have a *Veggie-Connections Shepherd* walk by and accidentally spill a box of crayons onto your feet. Show concern over crayon marks on your shoe. Tell the Shepherd you forgive him/her.

Then have the second *VeggieConnections Shepherd* come in and spray canned string on your shoes, laugh, and run off. As you clean off the shoes say: **That wasn't very nice. I'm not so sure I want to forgive him/her. Pause. On second thought, I think I'd better forgive him/her, because forgiveness is what were learning about today.**

Explain that the Shepherds had prepared this skit with you so the kids know the second Shepherd isn't simply mean to help the kids learn about forgiveness.

Let a volunteer look up the word *forgive* in the *VeggieConnections Bible Dictionary* and read the definition aloud. Print *forgive* on a construction paper flower and display it at the site. Explain how forgiveness helps us connect to God, as we learn to love him and others.

Display the Unit Memory Verse poster, and lead the kids in saying Matthew 22:37–39 together, including the words that are covered by the flowers and candies.

B. Prayer Connection

Kids can sit in their *VeggieConnections Groups* "crisscross" in a circle with knees touching. Introduce "whisper prayers." The *VeggieConnections Shepherd* in each group begins by thanking God for hearing and understanding our prayers no matter how softly we say, think, or feel them. Then the kids go around the circle whispering a prayer to God, asking his help with some problem, then tapping the knee of the person next to him or her.

THE CHILDREN

will arrive with their *VeggieConnections Shepherds* from the opening Countertop Connections featuring Bob and Larry. Play the *Veggie-Connections Music CD* as children enter Flibber-o-loo.

VEGGIE CONNECTION NEEDS:

- *VeggieConnections Music CD*
- CD player
- Unit Memory Verse poster (from *Lesson 1*)
- Pair of new-looking tennis shoes
- Box of broken crayons, some with the paper removed
- Spray canned string
- *VeggieConnections Bible Dictionary*
- Construction paper flower
- Marker
- Tape

PART TWO:

Plugging In to God's Word

Connecting to God's word in the Bible and understanding how that can help us to have a better relationship with him

A. God Connection: Jesus and the parable of the lost son – Luke 15:11-32

GOD CONNECTION NEEDS:

- Bible
- Bible-time clothes
- Props: play money, confetti, party noise-makers, cans of soda

BEFORE YOU START:

Copy the script and prepare with *VeggieConnections Shepherds* or older kids to play the parts of Father, Younger Son, Older Son, and Servant. Read the narration yourself.

Show kids in your Bible that today's Bible story comes from Luke 15.

Narrator: Jesus told a story to help people understand the importance of forgiveness. Once there was a man who had two sons. One day the younger son said to his father . . .

Younger Son: Dad, give me my share of what will be mine when you die. I want to go live on my own.

Father: Well, okay, if that's what you think is best. *(Hands him money)*

Narrator: So the father gave his younger son the money, and the boy left town. *(Younger Son walks around.)* When he got to another town, he spent all the money on wild living. *(Younger Son throws confetti, blows noisemaker, drinks soda, throws money in air, whoops and hollers.)*

It wasn't long before the boy was broke. *(Younger son shows empty pockets and sad face.)* He found a job feeding pigs. *(Younger son sits on floor, hunched over in discouragement.)* He was so hungry he wanted to eat the pigs' food. Finally he came to his senses. *(Younger son sits up and hits his head as if realizing something.)*

Younger Son: My father's servants live better than this. I've been wrong. I've sinned against God and my dad. I'm going back to ask if I can work for him as one of his servants.

Narrator: So the boy took off. *(Younger Son walks around.)* When he got near home, he was surprised to see his father looking down the road, almost as if he was expecting him. He didn't know his father had done this day after day.

Father: It's my son! *(Starts to run)*

Narrator: The father ran to meet his son. He hugged the boy. *(The two hug.)*

Younger Son: Dad, listen. I did the wrong thing. I've sinned against you and against God. I shouldn't even be called your son. But could I please come back and live here as your servant?

Father: I forgive you and I love you. You're not a servant—you're my son!

Narrator: The father turned to a servant.

Father: *(Faces Servant, pointing)* Go quickly. Bring the best robe, a pair of sandals, and a family ring for my son's finger. Prepare our best food, because we're going to celebrate! My son was lost and now he is found!

Narrator: The servant did as he was asked, and everyone celebrated the forgiveness of the son. *(Servant throws confetti up in the air, hands party noisemakers and cans of soda to Father and Younger Son and the three make noise and toast one another's cans, and so on. Then the Servant steps aside.)* When the older brother came and heard all the noise, he asked the servant . . .

Older Son: What's going on? Sounds like a party in there.

Servant: You're right. Your brother came home. Everyone is celebrating! *(Throws confetti at Older Son, who stomps away)*

Narrator: The older son wouldn't go inside. He was jealous of the celebration for his brother, who had left home so rudely and wasted his money. When the father heard this, he went to the older son.

Father: *(Walks over and puts his arm around Older Son)* My son, come in and celebrate. Your brother has returned!

Oldest Son: Dad, don't you remember? He went and spent all of his money on wild living. He left our family and sinned against God and you. Why are you celebrating? You've never let me have a celebration like that.

Father: My son, you're always with me. Everything I have is yours. But your brother was like dead to us, and now he is alive again. He was lost, and now he is found. I have forgiven him.

Thank the actors and let them be seated. Explain that God forgives us when we do wrong, just as the father in the story forgave his son. His love never lets us go, no matter what we've done.

Jesus shows us how to forgive others. When we are connected to him, he helps us do this. He wants us to love others the same way he does.

Ask the kids a few questions to be sure they understood the main points: **How did the father treat the younger son?** *(With forgiveness and acceptance; he even threw a party.)* **How did the older son treat his brother?** *(He wouldn't forgive him and wouldn't be glad he had changed his life.)* **How can we forgive people when they do wrong things to us?** *(We can choose not to hold a grudge; we can make sure we don't tell others the bad thing they did; we can be kind.)*

B. Activity Connection

Choose from the following activities to help kids explore and remember that we have Jesus to show us how to forgive (approximately 10–15 minutes each).

1. High-Powered Game: Friends and Forgiveness

Have kids form two teams and stand on opposite sides of the room, lined up side by side. Spread the pots and shoes randomly about, creating obstacles in a large open game area. When you call the command: **Forgive others!** each team hops on one foot across the valley, going around obstacles to get to the other side. If necessary, limit the number of kids who cross at the same time. Have two *VeggieConnections Shepherds* stand on the outskirts of the game area and randomly spray canned string into the playing area, as players cross the game floor. Any time players get sprayed, they must run to the Shepherd and say: **I forgive you!** then go back and continue across. The goal is to be the first team to have all members reach the other side.

2. Low-Powered Game: Storyboard Forgiveness

Have two *VeggieConnections Groups* join together for this review game. If you have an uneven number of groups, have the three smallest groups join together. Have groups sit in a semicircle and give the *VeggieConnections Shepherds* the set of story slips. Explain how this game is like charades, except kids will draw clues instead of act them out. Kids will be given a story slip and they have to draw the part of the Bible story contained on the slip. Kids cannot use the words on the slips. Once the child has drawn the picture, the group guesses the story part. When the guess is made, the child who guesses gets to hold the picture and stand up. Continue with each story slip as above. When the last story part is guessed, have the people holding the pictures come up to the front of the group and arrange themselves in story order, making a picture storyboard. Have some volunteers review telling the story using the storyboard pictures.

Jesus taught this story to show us that God our Father is always ready to forgive us.

3. Craft: Forgiving Love Does Not Let Go

Poke a small hole in the bottom of a paper cup, using a pencil. Tie a metal washer to one end of a 12" elastic cord. Thread the cord through the hole in the cup, pulling the cord so that the washer is lying flat in the bottom of the cup. Place a large heart sticker over the washer to hold it in place in the cup. Tie a bead to the other end of the cord.

HIGH-POWERED GAME NEEDS:
- Pots (from site)
- Shoes (from site)
- Canned spray string

LOW-POWERED GAME NEEDS:
- Lost Son Story Slips on page 208 (one per every two *VeggieConnections Groups*)
- Paper
- Markers

BEFORE YOU START:
Copy, cut apart, and mix up the game story slips. Prepare one set for every two *VeggieConnections Groups.*

CRAFT NEEDS:
- Plain paper cups (one per child)
- Pencils
- Metal washers
- 12" elastic cord (one per child)
- Heart stickers
- Very large beads (one per child)
- Labels that say "Forgiving love does not let go"
- Tape or glue
- Scissors

If cup has a printed pattern, cover with plain colored paper. Decorate the outside of the cup with heart stickers and a prepared label.

Once everyone has completed the craft, have them imitate your actions with their own cups as you summarize the Bible story.

The younger son began with a close, loving connection with his father. Place the bead in the cup. **But the son wanted to go his own way.** Take the bead out of the cup and let it drop. **The father kept on loving his son, even though he had left.** Stretch the cord and let the bead bounce on the cord. **When the son came back, the father forgave him.** Return the bead to the cup. **The father wouldn't let go of his love for his son. This is the same way that God loves us, and it's the same way he wants us to love others and to forgive them.**

PART THREE:

Plugging In to My Life

Life application of the lesson to lead kids to THINK-LINK-ACT and build a relationship with God every day

A. Cucumber Connection

CUCUMBER CONNECTION NEEDS:

- Pickle jar
- Pickle artwork from the *VeggieConnections Shepherd* pages (on the *VeggieConnections CD-ROM*)
- Green construction paper

Before kids arrive, enlarge and copy the pickles from the *VeggieConnections Shepherd* pages on the CD-ROM included in the *VeggieConnections Elementary Curriculum Kit* onto green construction paper. Cut them out and put them in a pickle jar.

Let a volunteer draw a pickle from the Pickle Pot and either the child or a Shepherd should read the dilemma out loud. Each Shepherd should then process the question with their group using the THINK—LINK—ACT phrase.

For the second day, Rachel's good friend doesn't let her join in a game at recess. The friend says, "You can't play. We already have enough for the team." What should Rachel do?	A classmate spilled paint at your table in art class. She says she didn't do it, then later tells the teacher you did it. You end up having to clean up the mess. What can you do to forgive like Jesus?	Javier's big brother Chago did something wrong that hurt the whole family. His parents have worked out a punishment and have forgiven Chago. But Javier feels the punishment wasn't bad enough and is still mad. How can Javier forgive his brother?

B. Kid Connection: Love Shoes

KID CONNECTION NEEDS:

- Love Shoes (made in *Lesson 1*)
- VeggieConnections Music CD
- CD player
- Tagboard
- Black construction paper (one per child)
- White crayons
- Glue

Give each child his or her Love Shoe. Play *Forgiveness Song* from the *VeggieConnections Music CD*. **This song talks about since God has forgiven us, we need to forgive others. Let's make a reminder of God's forgiveness.**

Give kids supplies and help them make small chalkboards by gluing a piece of black construction paper onto a piece of tagboard. **There is a saying "Wipe the slate clean," which means starting fresh. God's forgiveness is like a clean chalkboard of your life.** Have kids write, "God forgives me" using white crayons on their chalkboard.

Have kids put their chalkboards in their Love Shoes, and collect shoes for next week.

C. Christ Connection

CHRIST CONNECTION NEEDS:

- *VeggieConnections* take-home newspaper (one per child)

Because God loves us, he has given us the wonderful gift of forgiveness. He wants us to let his love fill our hearts so that we, too, offer forgiveness to others.

Lead the kids in singing the *THINK—LINK—ACT* song, using the motions. Then recite together the Program Verse, James 4:8.

Have the kids seated in their *VeggieConnections Groups*. They may use their craft to review with a partner that forgiving love does not let go. Then they may take turns saying a sentence prayer, asking God's help in forgiving and loving others. This may be a good opportunity to present God's plan of salvation.

Distribute the take-home newspaper, **VeggieConnections**.

Connecting to **Love** through **Jesus**
Jesus and the parable of the good Samaritan:
Luke 10:25–37

PART ONE:

Plugging in at Flibber-o-loo

Introduction to the site and lesson focus

LESSON 6:
I have Jesus to show me how to love my neighbor.

A. Veggie Connection

BEFORE YOU START:
Copy the Town Tickets (one ticket per child), cut apart and mix together. Set up two tables with a plate of mini donuts and a "Flibber-o-loo" sign on one and a plate of crackers and a "Jibberty-lot" sign on the other. On the Unit Memory Verse poster, attach artificial flowers over the words "neighbor" "Lord," and "God."

Dressed as a Flibbian, welcome the kids as they enter Flibber-o-loo and give each child a ticket. Explain that kids either will either play citizens of Flibber-o-loo or Jibberty-lot, depending on which ticket they received. **Welcome, citizens! For my fellow Flibbian citizens, I have prepared a treat of mini donuts. Please take only one and enjoy! Oh, and for the people from Jibberty-lot, I didn't want to forget you. You may have a cracker.** The kids from Jibberty-lot will probably complain, but insist they can only have the crackers. Allow enough time for Flibbian kids to eat a donut.

Then ask the Jiberty-lot kids: **How did it feel to be left out of having a donut, just because you didn't have the right ticket?** Allow responses. Then ask the Flibbian kids: **What did it feel like to keep all the donuts for yourselves?** Allow responses.

I had you play the citizens of Flibber-o-loo or Jibberty-lot to make a point. The people from Jibberty-lot didn't get a donut, just because they were from Jibberty-lot. So to make up for this, you can now grab two donuts!

Allow Jibberty-lot kids to eat their donuts. Also allow any other kids who want to have a second donut to help themselves. **Sometimes people get left out for reasons that aren't much better than being given the wrong ticket. It happened in Bible times, too. Jesus knew this, and he knew we should show his love to everyone. There's a word Jesus used that we need to understand.**

Have a volunteer look up the word *neighbor* in the *VeggieConnections Bible Dictionary* and read the definition aloud. Print *neighbor* on a construction-paper flower and display it at the site. Explain that the kids will learn more about neighbors in the Bible story.

Display the Unit Memory Verse poster, and lead the kids in saying Matthew 22:37–39 together, including the words that are covered by flowers and candies from previous weeks as well.

Collect the Town Tickets from kids for use later in the lesson.

THE CHILDREN
will arrive with their *VeggieConnections Shepherds* from the opening Countertop Connections featuring Bob and Larry. Play the *Veggie-Connections Music CD* as children enter Flibber-o-loo.

VEGGIE CONNECTION NEEDS:
- *VeggieConnections Music CD*
- CD player
- Town Tickets on page 209
- Mini donut assortment (two per child)
- Saltine crackers (Check with parents about food allergies.)
- Paper plates
- Prepared table signs
- Unit Memory Verse poster (from *Lesson 1*)
- Construction-paper flower for the Connection Word
- *VeggieConnections Bible Dictionary*
- Marker
- Tape

GOD
CONNECTION
NEEDS:

• Bible
• Bible-time clothes
• Props for the Samaritan:
coat, backpack, money,
adhesive bandages

**BEFORE
YOU START:**

Ask six *VeggieConnections Shepherds* or older kids to act out the Bible story as you narrate it. You will need the Jewish man, two robbers, the priest, the Levite, and the Samaritan. Actors can combine roles with a simple costume change if needed.

B. Prayer Connection

Have *VeggieConnections Shepherds* pick up a shoe from the site and stand with their group in a circle or cluster. Let a volunteer begin by holding the shoe and sharing a concern. Then that child hands the shoe to someone else to share a prayer request. Have the Shepherd open prayer time when any child can pray for himself or for another child. Encourage the Shepherds to pray by name for any child who wasn't prayed for.

Plugging In to God's Word

Connecting to God's Word in the Bible and understanding how that can help us to have a better relationship with him

A. God Connection: Jesus and the parable of the good Samaritan – Luke 10:25-37

Gather the kids where all can see the Flibbian Hospital. Show in your Bible where today's story is found, Luke 10.

One day a very important man asked Jesus a question trying to trick him. He asked, "What do I have to do to get to heaven?"

Jesus wouldn't be tricked. He answered, "You know God's Word—what does it say?"

The man answered, "I should love God with all my heart, soul, mind, and strength. And I should love my neighbor as much as I love myself."

"That's right," Jesus answered.

But the man wanted to show how smart he was. So he tried to trick Jesus again. He asked, "But just who is my neighbor?"

To answer that question, Jesus told a story. Motion for Shepherds or older kids to begin acting out the story.

One day a Jewish man was walking from Jerusalem to Jericho. Man walks along. **Suddenly, robbers jumped out and attacked him!** Two robbers jump at him. **They took everything he had.** Grab his coat, pack, and money. **They hurt him badly.** Robbers push the man down. **Then they left him half dead.** Robbers laugh and leave.

A Jewish teacher came down the same road. Priest enters and stops and stares. **He saw the man, but he walked around him on the other side.** Priest walks by holding his nose. **He did not stop to help the man.**

Then a leader of the Jewish people came along. Levite enters and stares, then looks around guiltily. **He wanted nothing to do with the man.** Levite uses his hands to block his view of the man and goes around.

But then a man from Samaria came by. Now the Samaritans and the Jews didn't like each other. But when the Samaritan saw the hurt Jewish man, he came over and knelt down. Samaritan enters and kneels to help. **He felt sorry for the man.** Samaritan gently sticks an adhesive bandage on his arm and head. **Then he took the man to an inn.** Samaritan helps the man walk to the Flibbian Hospital. **He stayed to make sure this stranger was all right. The next day he took coins from his own money and gave them to the innkeeper.** Samaritan pretends to hand money to someone. **He promised the innkeeper he would bring back more money if the hurt man needed it.**

Then Jesus asked, "Who was neighbor to the hurt man?" What do you think the smart man answered? Let the kids respond. **It wasn't the Jewish teacher or the Jewish leader. It was the man from unfriendly Samaria. He didn't really have anything to gain from showing love, yet by going out of his way, he showed what it meant to show God's love.**

Discuss these questions with the kids: **What did Jesus mean when he told us to love our neighbors? Who are our neighbors?** *(Any person we come in contact with is our neighbor, and we can show him God's love.)* **Who are people that you see every day, even people you don't always notice?** *(Kids at school, crossing guards, teachers and coaches, volunteer parents at our activities, store clerks when I'm out shopping with my parents, doctors and dentists and their assistants.)* **What are ways you can show God's love to people you don't know well?** *(Be polite, don't rush them, thank them for helping me, hold a door open, if I see a need point it out to my parents, and so on.)*

B. Activity Connection

Choose from the following activities to help kids explore and remember that we have Jesus to show us how to love others (approximately 10–15 minutes each).

1. High-Powered Game: Good Samaritan Hop

Have kids divide into two teams of at least three kids. Have each team pick a victim to lie down at the end of the playing area, in line with their team's course. Also, place the bandage next to the each victim. In the story Jesus told, the first two people who came upon the hurt man were too busy to help. In this game, the first two people on each team will hop down to the victim and make a circle around him or her before hopping back to your team. But Jesus told how the third person who came upon the hurt man picked him up and cared for him. The third person in each group will hop to the victim, wrap a bandage around his or her head, and help the person up. They then hop together back to the team. The third person then becomes the new victim and the game continues until everyone has played the victim.

Have *VeggieConnections Shepherds* help teams remember their roles in the game (players one and two to round the victim; player three to help).

2. Low-Powered Game: Who's Your Neighbor?

Give each child one of the Town Tickets used in the Veggie Connection and tell kids not to reveal their ticket. Have kids gather in the center of your game area. Have *VeggieConnections Shepherds* available to make even teams of four. **This game has two parts. The first part is to make teams of four. Here's how. If you have a Flibber-o-loo ticket, you'll say, "I wear a shoe on my head." If you have a Jibberty-lot ticket, you'll say, "I wear a pot on my head." Everyone will keep saying that sentence. You want to find another person different from you, and then find another pair of kids, making your team of four. Each team will have two Flibbians and two kids from Jibberty-lot.**

After you have made a team of four go to the start line and read the instructions of how to play the second half of this game.

Have kids follow these instructions printed on the game cards:

1. Line up in pairs. Tell each other who has a Flibber-o-loo ticket and a Jibberty-lot ticket.
2. You will race in pairs. You will balance a balloon between yourself and your partner in the following way:

   - If you are two Flibber-o-loo kids, you balance the balloon between your shoes or ankles, because people from Flibber-o-loo wear shoes on their heads.
   - If you are two Jibberty-lot kids, you balance the balloon between your heads, because people from Jibberty-lot wear pots on their heads.
   - If you and your partner are from different towns, you choose any way except using your hands to balance the balloon between yourselves.

3. After each race, you must pick another partner and race by following Step 2 above.
4. When everyone has raced with a different partner, the game is over.

Have *VeggieConnections Shepherds* help kids with the game as needed. After the game, have kids gather around you. **You had to make teams of neighbors in this game. Then you played the game differently with each neighbor. Jesus taught we are to love our neighbors, even when they are different from us.**

3. Craft: Helping Neighbors Bank

Cut a coin slot in each container lid, using a hobby knife. Give each child a container and lid. Show kids how to cut construction paper and wrap it around their containers. Use craft glue to glue the paper around the container. Set aside to dry.

Give kids magazines and have them cut out pictures of a variety of kids. Using glue sticks, smear glue on the back of pictures and have kids glue them to their containers in a

---

HIGH-POWERED GAME NEEDS:
- Bandages or strips of cloth (one per team)
- Masking/painter's tape

BEFORE YOU START:
Mark start/finish lines for the game.

LOW-POWERED GAME NEEDS:
- Town Tickets from Veggie Connection (one per child)
- Neighbor Game Instructions on page 210 (one for every eight kids)
- Inflated balloons (one for every two kids)
- Masking/painter's tape

BEFORE YOU START:
Mark start/finish lines for the game (or use High-Powered Game lines). Inflate balloons and place them behind the start line. Have Town Tickets mixed up.

CRAFT NEEDS:
- Plastic, cardboard, or tin container with lid (one per child)
- Hobby knife
- Construction paper
- Tacky craft glue
- Magazines with variety of everyday people (especially kids)
- Scissors
- Glue sticks
- Colored markers
- Blank self-adhesive labels

random collage pattern. Have kids write "Helping Neighbors Bank" on blank labels and apply them to the container lid (make sure they don't cover up the coin slot).

The good Samaritan not only helped the hurt man, but he also gave him money for his other needs. Use this bank to put your change in and use it to help a neighbor in need.

If you have a church pantry, explain how kids could save up and give to this ministry.

PART THREE:

Plugging In to My Life

Life application of the lesson to lead kids to THINK–LINK–ACT and build a relationship with God every day

A. Cucumber Connection

CUCUMBER CONNECTION NEEDS:

- Pickle jar
- Pickle artwork from the *VeggieConnections Shepherd* pages (on the *VeggieConnections CD-ROM*)
- Green construction paper

Before kids arrive, enlarge and copy the pickles from the *VeggieConnections Shepherd* pages on the CD-ROM included in the *VeggieConnections Elementary Curriculum Kit* onto green construction paper. Cut them out and put them in a pickle jar.

Let a volunteer draw a pickle from the Pickle Pot and either the child or a Shepherd should read the dilemma out loud. Each Shepherd should then process the question with their group using the THINK—LINK—ACT phrase.

While Dillon is watching TV, his mother comes home from work with a bad headache. He knows he should offer to help her fix dinner, but he really likes the program he is watching. What should Dillon do?	Martina's friend is having a hard time at school and needs extra help. Now he is sick and has to stay home for a few days. Their teacher asks for a volunteer to take his homework home to him. What should Martina do?	Your next-door neighbor's dog died. The woman is very sad. What could you do to show her Jesus' love?

B. Kid Connection: Love Shoes

KID CONNECTION NEEDS:

- Love Shoes (made in *Lesson 1*)
- Elastic bandage roll
- Scissors
- Permanent markers

Give each child his or her Love Shoe. Cut 6-inch lengths of bandage for each child, while reviewing the story. **Jesus told the story of a man who took care of a hurt man. Use these pieces of bandage to remind you how to love your neighbor.** Have kids write on their bandages "I, [name], will love my neighbor," using permanent markers. Then have kids put their bandages in their Love Shoes and collect them for next week.

C. Christ Connection

CHRIST CONNECTION NEEDS:

- Flowers (from site)
- Pencils or markers
- *VeggieConnections* take-home newspaper (one per child)

Lead the kids in singing the *THINK—LINK—ACT* song, using the motions (p. 00). Then recite together the Program Verse, James 4:8a.

Invite each child to pick up a paper flower from the site. Give each child a pencil or marker to write "Love my neighbor" on the flower. Talk to the kids about how the children of the world are neighbors. Show them a picture of the class's *Compassion International* child (or, if the class is not sponsoring a child, ask someone from the class that does sponsor a child to bring the child's photo in) and explain how their prayers for this child and their involvement with children living in poverty is a an act of loving their neighbors. If others in the class have specific children they are helping mention them in a closing prayer. Then invite the kids to place their flowers anywhere in the site to add back into the decorations.

Distribute the take-home newspaper, *VeggieConnections*.

Connecting to **Love** through **Jesus**
Jesus tells us how to show love: **John 14:23–31a**

LESSON 7:
I show my love for Jesus, because he loves me.

PART ONE:

Plugging in at Flibber-o-loo

Introduction to the site and lesson focus

A. Veggie Connection

BEFORE YOU START:

Print one large, bold letter on each of four paper plates to spell out "obey." Wrap a piece of colored plastic wrap around each plate, twisting the two ends to look like candies, then hide the candies around the site. On the Unit Memory Verse poster, attach candies over the words "heart," "soul," "mind," and "first."

THE CHILDREN
will arrive with their *VeggieConnections Shepherds* from the opening Countertop Connections featuring Bob and Larry. Play the *Veggie-Connections Music CD* as children enter Flibber-o-loo.

Dressed as a Flibbian, welcome the children to Flibber-o-loo. Tell them you've misplaced some pieces of candy around the site. Each missing piece has a letter on it. Ask them to find the candies and bring them to you so you can get a significant clue to why the people of Flibber-o-loo and Jibberty-lot stopped hurling shoes and pots at each other and reached out to each other with flowers and candy. Let the kids search the room until they find the four prepared candies.

Have four kids hold up the letters out of order, and ask the rest of the group to figure out what order they should go in. Move the kids around to try different spellings until they find "obey."

Let's do a fun thing with this word. Have everyone stand and form a large circle. Have kids "spell" the word using their bodies "cheerleader" style: O—arms in a circle overhead; B—arms in a circle to one side, one leg drawn up to the side to make sort of a second circle; E—both arms and one leg sticking straight out to the side; Y—stand with feet together, arms up and angled out. Have *VeggieConnections Shepherds* join the circle to spell the last "obey" as needed. For fun, you might want to sing a *YMCA*-style song while kids are forming the letters. **It's one thing to spell *obey* with your bodies, but it's another thing to obey *with* your bodies. Let's look at this Connection Word.**

Ask a volunteer to look up *obey* in the *VeggieConnections Bible Dictionary* and read the definition aloud. Print *obey* on a construction-paper flower and display it at the site. Explain that they will learn more about what it means to obey during the Bible story.

Display the Unit Memory Verse poster, and lead everyone in saying Matthew 22:37–39 together, including the words that are covered by flowers and candies.

VEGGIE CONNECTION NEEDS:

- *VeggieConnections Music CD*
- CD player
- Four large paper plates
- Marker
- Colored plastic wrap
- Tape
- Unit Memory Verse poster (from *Lesson 7*)
- *VeggieConnections Bible Dictionary*
- Construction-paper flower for Connection Word

B. Prayer Connection

Encourage kids to continue expressing themselves with their bodies by praying "action prayers." In *VeggieConnections Groups*, have them stand in a circle. Any child may pray a sentence prayer at any time, even several times. Whenever a child prays thanks or praise to God, he stands with hands raised. Whenever a child prays for help, he kneels with hands folded. *VeggieConnections Shepherds* should open and close the prayer times and be role models in "action prayers."

GOD CONNECTION NEEDS:

- Posterboard on an easel
- Marker
- Bible
- Several stickers for each word: Love, Obey, Father and Teaching

Plugging In to God's Word

Connecting to God's Word in the Bible and understanding how that can help us to have a better relationship with him

A. God Connection: Jesus tells us how to show love – John 14:23-31a

Invite kids to sit where they can see the posterboard. In a column, neatly print the words "Love", "Obey", "Father", and "Teaching". Have the kids read them together with you.

Jesus had been with his disciples three years. During that time he had taught them about his Father in heaven. He had performed wonderful miracles that showed he was truly the Son of God. But Jesus knew that within a few hours he was going to be arrested. Then he would die on the cross.

Jesus met with his disciples one last time. He told them that soon he would leave them. Imagine their sorrow, the worries about what would happen to them, the urge to tell him how much they loved him. Jesus reminded them of some important truths that they needed to remember forever. Show where John 14 is in your Bible.

He began by saying, "*Do not let your hearts be troubled*" (v. 1). Then he urged them to put their full trust in him. He went on tell what he wanted them to keep so tightly in their memories that they would never forget it.

Explain to kids you'll read the story twice. For the first reading, kids should listen carefully. For the second reading, kids will help tell the story.

Read through the story below straight through. Then choose four volunteers to stand by the easel. Give each a set of stickers and assign one of the four words. When they hear their word they should place a sticker next to it.

Tell the rest of the kids that they, too, are to listen for the four words on the posterboard as you tell the Bible story. Here is what they should do when they hear the word —

> *Love:* touch their heart
> *Obey:* walk their fingers down their legs
> *Father:* point up
> *Teaching:* hold hands together, palms up, to indicate an open Bible.

Places to pause for stickers and actions are noted in the text.

Let's listen carefully to what Jesus told his disciples. "If anyone loves me (pause), he will obey (pause) my teaching (pause). My Father (pause) will love him (pause), and we will make our home with him. He who does not love me (pause) will not obey (pause) my teaching (pause). And this truth is from my Father (pause)."

Jesus went on to explain. "Don't worry about being without me! My Father (pause) will send his Spirit to you. And his Spirit will remind you of my teaching (pause). I leave my peace with you. Don't let your hearts be troubled, and don't be afraid."

Jesus encouraged them that his going to the Father (pause) was the right thing to do. He said, "I love (pause) my Father (pause), so I obey (pause) exactly what he told me. You can do this, too."

Ask each of the sticker kids to count how many stickers they put up by their words. **It sounds like showing *love* by *obeying* the Father's teaching is important! But our relationship with the Father all starts when we trust him and believe in Jesus.** Let helpers be seated.

How do we show our love for Jesus? *(By obeying his teaching.)* **What did Jesus promise to help us and to show his love for us?** *(That he and his Father would make their home with us, that he would send his Spirit to remind us of his teaching, that he gives us his peace and we shouldn't be afraid.)* If the kids do not seem to connect with this important truth, reread the passage without the pauses, to help their train of thought.

B. Activity Connection

Choose from the following activities to help kids explore and remember to show their love for Jesus because he first loved them (approximately 10–15 minutes each).

1. High-Powered Game: Tossing Love Candies

Divide the kids into two teams, and have teams gather on either side of the chairs, behind the pot. Give one team one color of sock candies and the other color to the second team. **Jesus taught that if we love him, we will obey him. One way we obey Jesus is to share his love with others. Each time you toss these soft candies, you will shout: I will share Jesus' love!**

Explain the candies are one way to share Jesus' love in the game. Teams will try to give away Jesus' love by tossing their candies into the pot on the other side of the row of chairs. Only half of a team tosses at any given time; assign the other half to be retrievers and pick up missed tosses from their side and give them back to the other team. Both teams toss at the same time, and neither team may block their own pot.

Play until both pots are full and no more candies remain on the floor. Then have kids switch sides and play a second round. If you have extra time, you might want to time the game and see which team can land all their love candies in the other team's pot the fastest.

2. Low-Powered Game: Tic-Tac-Toe: Love to Show

Assign two *VeggieConnections Groups* to each tic-tac-toe grid. Each group plays together as a team. Assign the teams to be either Shoes or Pots. Have kids take turns playing tic-tac-toe using the shoes and pots as Xs and Os. The players on a team take turns choosing where to put their team's pot or shoe on the grid. Each team making three in a row names one way to show love to Jesus. *(Trust him, obey him, love others, learn from him, share, be kind, pray to God, and help those in need.)* Let teams play several times.

3. Craft: Showing My Love Chart

Give kids a piece of paper and have them turn it lengthwise. Have kids write "Showing My Love" along the top edge of the paper. Provide thin-tipped markers and rulers. Show kids how to make six lines across and two down their pages. Each line should be about an inch apart. At the left hand side of the lines, have kids write Monday–Saturday on each line. Then have kids turn over their pages and apply glue stick over their page. Give kids construction-paper sheets and have them glue their pages to the sheets, centering their pages to make a border with the construction paper.

Have kids punch holes in the two top corners and attach a piece of yarn to allow their charts to hang. Provide an assortment of candies and plastic sandwich bags. Allow kids to place six candies in their bags and help kids staple their bags to the charts allowing the bag to be opened and resealed. Then have kids decorate their charts with markers or gel pens. **Jesus wants us to show our love by obeying him. Take these charts home and talk to your parents about ways you can show your love through obedience each day of next week. Write down a chore or task and strive to complete each daily task next week. When you complete a daily task, check it off on your chart and enjoy a treat!**

HIGH-POWERED GAME NEEDS:
- Chairs
- Two large pots (from the site)
- Prepared candy socks (one or two per child)
- Plastic wrap in two colors

BEFORE YOU START:
Make sock candies by balling up a sock, wrapping it in plastic wrap, and twisting the ends of the wrap. Wrap an equal number of socks in two colors of plastic wrap. Set up a long row of chairs to divide the playing area. Set a pot on each side five to eight feet away from the row of chairs.

LOW-POWERED GAME NEEDS:
- Masking/painter's tape
- Pots and shoes (from site)

BEFORE YOU START:
Tape a tic-tac-toe grid on the floor or table for every two *VeggieConnections Groups*.

CRAFT NEEDS:
- Paper
- Colored markers or gel pens
- Thin-tipped markers
- Scissors
- Rulers
- Glue sticks
- Construction paper
- Hole punch
- Yarn
- Individual wrapped fun-size candies (six per child) Check with parents about food allergies.
- Plastic resealable sandwich bags
- Stapler

PART THREE:

Plugging In to My Life

Life application of the lesson to lead kids to THINK-LINK-ACT and build a relationship with God every day

A. Cucumber Connection

CUCUMBER CONNECTION NEEDS:

- Pickle jar
- Pickle artwork from the *VeggieConnections Shepherd* pages (on the *VeggieConnections CD-ROM*)
- Green construction paper

Before kids arrive, enlarge and copy the pickles from the *VeggieConnections Shepherd* pages on the CD-ROM included in the *VeggieConnections Elementary Curriculum Kit* onto green construction paper. Cut them out and put them in a pickle jar.

Let a volunteer draw a pickle from the Pickle Pot and either the child or a Shepherd should read the dilemma out loud. Each Shepherd should then process the question with their group using the THINK—LINK—ACT phrase.

Gage's teacher keeps candy on her desk to give as special rewards. One day he goes back in at recess to get his sweater. He wants some candy and no one is around. Who does Gage need to obey?	Spencer's sister has a new computer game. Every time she plays it, her brother asks if he can try it. He's old enough, but she keeps telling him no. Spencer's sister is not around and he sees the game. How can Spencer obey?	Jolene's parents have told her she can't have friends over unless she checks with them first. Kandra drops by with a new video and wants to watch it with Jolene. Who should Jolene obey?

B. Kid Connection: Love Shoes

KID CONNECTION NEEDS:

- Love Shoes (made in *Lesson 1*)
- White or colored shoelaces (one pair per child)
- Fine-tipped permanent markers

Give each child his or her Love Shoe. Give kids a pair of shoelaces and fine-tipped permanent markers. Have kids write, "[Name] will obey God" near both ends of each shoelace. **When you use these shoelaces, you'll see your written commitment to obey God. How do you think this reminder can help you obey?** Allow responses.

Have kids put their shoelaces inside their Love Shoes, and collect them for next week.

C. Christ Connection

CHRIST CONNECTION NEEDS:

- Light-colored construction paper
- Pencils
- Scissors
- Craft sticks (one per child)
- Glue sticks
- *VeggieConnections* take-home newspaper (one per child)

In their *VeggieConnections Groups*, have kids trace their right hand on construction paper, cut it out, and print his or her name on it. Do one yourself. Glue the hand to a craft stick. While the glue is setting, lead the kids in singing the THINK—LINK—ACT song, using the motions. Then recite together the Program Verse, James 4:8.

When two people make a happy agreement, they give a high-five. Today you can make a happy agreement with Jesus, agreeing to love him and obey him. You can raise your cutout hand to show that you truly love him and want to obey him. He knows, though, that we need help to keep our agreement.

Review ways the Holy Spirit helps us in our relationship with Jesus.

Let's stand in a circle and raise our cutouts as we say thank you to Jesus and tell him we want to love and obey him.

Open a prayer time and let kids take turns praying for help. Allow kids the option of praying silently if they are uncomfortable praying aloud.

There is one other way we get help in keeping our agreement with Jesus—by having others pray for us! Jesus tells us to pray for each other. Let's exchange hand cutouts. Give a high-five with your cutout to indicate you agree to pray for your partner this week.

As we go let's give each other a high-five to show we agree to love and obey Jesus.

Distribute the take-home newspaper, *VeggieConnections.*

Connecting to **Love** through **Jesus**
Jesus and his people: **Matthew 20:20–34**

servant

PART ONE:

Plugging In at Flibber-o-loo

Introduction to the site and lesson focus

LESSON 8:
I show my love to others through service.

A. Veggie Connection

BEFORE YOU START:
Choose four older kids to play Flibbians, and assign each one of these injuries: "I cut my finger and it's bleeding." "My tummy feels awful." "I think I broke my leg." "I fell and hurt my arm real bad." Have two *VeggieConnections Shepherds* dress as Flibbian doctors and wear medical coats or tools, as well as shoes on their heads. Ask one to be a loving servant, the other to be lazy and selfish. Encourage all players to ham it up. On the Unit Memory Verse poster, attach artificial flowers and candies over all the rest of the words that aren't yet covered.

Dressed as a Flibbian, warmly welcome the kids to the Flibbian Hospital area of Flibber-o-loo. **I've had a great time being your host in Flibber-o-loo. We have one more way to learn about Jesus' love. I've asked for some help today, and I want to thank all of you for helping me have fun here in Flibber-o-loo!**

Have the Flibbian guests put on a brief impromptu skit. The injured kids arrive one at a time and tell about their injuries. The doctors should interact with each injured child and treat the patient according to assigned roles.

Being funny is fun, but if you were really hurt, which kind of doctor would you want? Why? *(The one who cared and had a good attitude; the one who wanted to help, and so on.)* **This skit showed that serving is more than just doing the job. It is caring. That is the kind of serving Jesus wants us to do.**

Have a volunteer look up the word *servant* in the *VeggieConnection Bible Dictionary* and read the definition aloud. Print *servant* on a construction-paper flower and display it at the site. Explain that the kids will learn more about what it means to be a servant in the Bible story.

Display the Unit Memory Verse poster, and lead everyone in saying Matthew 22:37–39 together, though all the words are covered.

THE CHILDREN
will arrive with their *VeggieConnections Shepherds* from the opening Countertop Connections featuring Bob and Larry. Play the *Veggie-Connections Music CD* as children enter Flibber-o-loo.

VEGGIE CONNECTION NEEDS:
- *VeggieConnections Music CD*
- CD player
- Two shoes to wear on heads (from site)
- Props from the Flibbian Hospital (see site setup), such as adhesive bandages, fabric bandage wrap, crutches, stethoscope, cot, and so on.
- Two medical lab coats or other "doctor" clothing/tools
- *VeggieConnections Bible Dictionary*
- Construction-paper flower for Connection Word
- Marker
- Unit Memory Verse poster (from *Lesson 7*)
- Tape

B. Prayer Connection

Invite kids to take part in "traveling prayers," to visit different parts of the room to pray silently. For prayers of thanks, the kids should walk to the Flibbian Hospital. For praying for something for themselves, they should go to the Flibber-o-loo side. For praying for someone else, the kids should move to Jibberty-lot.

All the kids will be moving independently and at different times. Have *Veggie-Connections Shepherds* at the locations to pray with any kids who feel more comfortable praying with someone.

PART TWO:

Plugging In to God's Word

Connecting to God's Word in the Bible and understanding how that can help us to have a better relationship with him

A. God Connection: Jesus and his people – Matthew 20:20-34

GOD CONNECTION NEEDS:

- Bible
- Masking/painter's tape
- Unit Bible review props

BEFORE YOU START:
For the Bible review, gather a flashlight, an uninflated balloon, a "Blessed" sign, a filled water-mist bottle, a party hat and whistle, an elastic bandage, and a picture of a heart with "obey" inside it.

Place a long strip of masking/painter's tape on the floor in the center of the site, if possible directly between Flibber-o-loo and Jibberty-lot.

Gather kids around the Bible story area and sit down. Review the unit's lessons by holding up props and asking for kids to share what they remember. **We've been learning about connecting to God's love through the stories of Jesus. Jesus has shown us love in a variety of ways.** Turn on and hold up the flashlight. **Nicodemus came to Jesus at night—and Jesus told him about God's love.** Hold up a balloon, then inflate it. **Jesus taught about being filled with the Holy Spirit. Jesus taught how he is our Savior and his Spirit is our Counselor.** Hold up the "Blessed" sign. **Jesus taught how we are blessed when we show our love for God by living for him, even when others don't and make it hard for us.** Hold up the water-mist bottle and spray it over the kids. **Jesus showed Peter he was his source of love when he reached and grabbed him as he was sinking—*after* Peter walked on the water!**

Next, put on a party hat and blow the whistle. **The father in Jesus' story celebrated when his lost son had come back home. Jesus told the story to show our Father's forgiveness for all of us.** Wrap the elastic bandage around your head. **Jesus told another story about a foreigner who helped a robbed man. He taught us that everybody is our neighbor and we should reach out with Jesus' love to all.** Hold up the picture of the heart. **Last week we learned that to love Jesus means we will obey him.**

Today, you will help me as we learn another way to show our love. Invite the kids to stand along the masking tape line. Show in your Bible that today's story comes from Matthew 20. Say: **I will tell you the Bible story two times. The first time, you will listen very carefully. Then the second time, I'll give you instructions for something fun you can do.**

Read the story one time with no actions. Then, for the second time, say: **Let's play the game "What Do You Think?" I'll tell the Bible story again. At certain points I'll ask you, "What do you think?" You'll need to jump to one side of this line or the other. Let's play!**

Mrs. Zebedee had two sons, James and John, who were Jesus' disciples. She came to Jesus and asked him this favor: "Please make it so that, when you're the king, my sons will have the most important jobs—besides yours!" You see, she thought Jesus would soon become king, and she wanted her sons to be leaders in his government.

What do you think? Did Jesus think she had a good idea? If yes, jump to this side. Indicate which side. **If no, jump to this other side.** Pause while the kids vote. **Let's find what happened. Here's the final word.** Read Matthew 20:22-23. **When Jesus said, "Can you drink this cup?" he was talking about dying on the cross. Mrs. Zebedee certainly did not have a good idea.**

The other disciples overheard this conversation. How did they react? What do you think? If you think they didn't worry about it, jump to this side. Indicate which side. If they were angry about it, jump to that side. Let the kids vote. **Let's get the final word.** Read verse 24. **They were really upset and angry.**

How did Jesus respond to their anger? If you think Jesus just ignored them and went on teaching people, jump to this side. Indicate the side. **If you think he taught them some surprising things, jump to the other side.** Let the kids vote. Read verses 26–28. **So Jesus had something surprising to teach them—to love by serving.**

A ransom is money that is paid to kidnappers to buy back people. The ransom sets people free. When Jesus said that he would give his life as a ransom for many, he meant that he was thinking about what everyone needed. He would die on the cross to take the punishment for all our sins.

When Jesus and his disciples left town, a crowd followed them. Two blind men were sitting by the road. When they heard Jesus was coming, they shouted, "Lord, have mercy on us!" The crowd tried to shut them up, but the men shouted even louder. Jesus stopped and asked them, "What do you want me to do for you?"

Well, what do you think? Did the two men want Jesus to give them some money? If so, move to this side. Indicate the side. **Or did they want Jesus to do something else? If so, move to the other side.** Let the kids vote. Read verse 33.

Finally, did Jesus say they were selfish for asking for help? If you think so, move to this side. Indicate the side. **If Jesus healed them, move to the other side.** Let kids vote. Read verse 34.

Let everyone be seated. Say: **In this Bible story, we saw that Mrs. Zebedee thought selfishly about her own sons. It seems that James and John were also thinking selfishly, because the other disciples became angry with them. Jesus said that anyone who wants to be great needs to be the one to serve other people; they think about other people's needs rather than their own.**

Jesus wanted the disciples to remember to be serve others. How does it feel to serve people who are your friends? How does it feel to serve people who don't treat you well?

The only way we can be servants to people who don't treat us well is to love them the way that Jesus loves. When we are connected to God, his love flows through us.

THINK:
Stop and think about what God wants you to do.

LINK:
Link God's Word and what you've learned to your choices.

ACT:
Go and act on what God wants you to do!

Now add some fun hand motions to the catch-phrase!

THINK: Touch head with fingertip two times.

LINK: Left hand out, right hand out.
Clasp your hands together, fingers intertwined.

ACT: Release grip and roll hands three times.
Finish with arms outstretched.

B. Activity Connection

Choose from the following activities to help kids explore and remember that they can show love to others as Jesus did (approximately 10–15 minutes each).

1. High-Powered Game: Let Me Serve You Relay

Divide kids into two teams. Have everyone remove one shoe and place it in a pile in the center of the room. Then have kids sit in a row on an outer edge of the room on opposite sides. They should sit with their feet out in front of them.

When you shout: **Serve one another,** the first player on each team looks at the shoe worn by the person to his or her left and then runs to the pile to find person's matching shoe. He or she races back to the person and as a servant puts the shoe on the person's other foot. Once that player is wearing matching pair of shoes, that player will do the same for the person on the left. The last person in each line will put a shoe on the first person in the line. If kids return with the wrong shoe, they have to run back to the pile for the correct one.

Once the whole team has been served, they shout: **I show my love to others through service!**

2. Low-Powered Game: Compassion Serving

LOW-POWERED GAME NEEDS:
• World Compassion Puzzle on page 211 (one per *VeggieConnections Group*)
• Tape
• Sandwich bags

BEFORE YOU START:
Copy and cut apart a puzzle (p.211) for each *Veggie-Connections Group*. Put puzzle pieces in a sandwich bag for each group.

Divide kids into *VeggieConnections Groups*. Give each group a bag of puzzle pieces. Say: **Jesus taught that serving others was more important than status. There are lots of way to serve others, but one special way is shown on this puzzle. Put the pieces together to find out what it is!** Have kids gather in a circle and work together on solving the puzzle. When they have pieced together the picture of the world, have *VeggieConnections Shepherds* help kids to carefully tape the puzzle pieces together. Have kids talk about the children shown on the world map, such as what it might be like to live in that part of the world and what needs they might have. Hold up the world map. **This map shows children from all over the world. Many children like this are poor and have many basic needs. One way we can serve is to help children like these.**

If the class is already sponsoring a *Compassion International* child, point out where the child lives and discuss the needs of children who live in poverty in that area. If the class is not yet sponsoring a child, discuss the *Compassion International* program and tell kids how they can become involved. Send the letter about Compassion's ministry home with the children, include child packets if desired.

3. Craft: At Your Service Basket

CRAFT NEEDS:
• Basket frame pattern on page 212 (one per child)
• 3" plastic lids or circle patterns
• Tagboard
• Scissors
• Markers
• Hole punch
• Glue
• Yarn or ribbon (1 1/2 yards per child)
• Paper slips
• Optional: small candies or flowers

BEFORE YOU START:
Copy the basket frame pattern (p. 212) on tagboard.

Hand out supplies and have *VeggieConnections Shepherds* help the kids as needed. Place a plastic lid in the center of the pattern and draw a line around it. This marks the bottom of the basket. Then place the lid on a piece of tagboard and trace around the lid. Cut out the tagboard circle and place aside.

Cut around the outer edge of the pattern and along the lines from the outer edge to the outline made with the plastic lid. Bend each of the eight pie-shaped pieces forward, creating a flower-petal effect. Use scissors to round the top of each petal. Punch two holes toward the top and sides of each petal.

Turn the pattern over and print on it, one or two words on each petal: "I will show my love to others through service," being careful to avoid the punched holes. Glue the tagboard circle in the inner circle on the bottom of the pattern, being sure that the words are on the outer side. Weave yarn or ribbon to weave through the holes to bring the petals together, forming a basket. Decorate the basket with markers.

Fill the basket with slips of paper on which kids will write different ways family members can serve each other. You also might want to provide a few candies or flowers to add to the baskets.

PART THREE:

Plugging In to My Life

Life application of the lesson to lead kids to THINK–LINK–ACT and build a relationship with God every day

A. Cucumber Connection

Before kids arrive, enlarge and copy the pickles from the *VeggieConnections Shepherd* pages on the CD-ROM included in the *VeggieConnections Elementary Curriculum Kit* onto green construction paper. Cut them out and put them in a pickle jar.

Let a volunteer draw a pickle from the Pickle Pot and either the child or a Shepherd should read the dilemma out loud. Each Shepherd should then process the question with their group using the THINK—LINK—ACT phrase.

You're having indoor recess at school because it's raining. All the kids are excited to get games from the teacher's supply. You notice that MacKenzie can't play until she finishes her project. The teacher says that it's okay if anyone wants to help her. What can you do?	For months Haley begged for a pet guinea pig. Now that she's had it for a while, it isn't so exciting. Her dad has started cleaning its cage because she keeps putting it off. What should Haley do?	It's Saturday morning chore time. Leon worked hard at cleaning the bathroom. He's glad to be done. Now he can finally watch cartoons. Then Leon remembers his older sister has plans to go shopping with a friend. She's going to be late because she is still vacuuming. What could Leon do?

B. Kid Connection: Love Shoes

Give each child his or her Love Shoe. Have kids look at their contents. **We've been making reminders of God's love through Jesus. Today, we will make a reminder about being a servant.** Give each child a piece of craft foam. Have *VeggieConnections Shepherds* assist kids in tracing both their hands on the foam using markers. Encourage kids to take these foam sheets home and look for an opportunity to serve. Once they have served, have a parent help them cut out their hands as reminder they are using their hands to serve.

Have kids roll up their foam handprints and place their other reminders back in their Love Shoes to take home.

C. Christ Connection

Lead the kids in singing the *THINK—LINK—ACT* song, using the motions. Then recite together the Program Verse, James 4:8.

Ask kids to pray along in their hearts as you lead this prayer: **Dear God, you are so wonderful to love us so much! Thank you that Jesus taught us how to love and showed us how to serve. Thank you for sending Jesus to be our Savior and Friend. Please help us keep coming near to you and trusting that you will come near to us. We love you! In Jesus' name, amen.**

Distribute the take-home newspaper, ***VeggieConnections***.

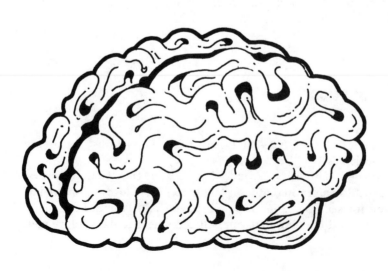

1. Visit a sick person.

2. Help carry in groceries from the car.

3. At lunchtime, sit by a child at school who is alone.

4. Help wash dishes.

5. Comfort someone who is sad.

6. Share your treats with someone else.

7. Help a friend with his homework.

8. Help your parents vacuum.

9. Feed your pet dog.

10. Help a younger child tie his shoes or zip her jacket.

11. Help wash the family car.

12. Help erase and clean a whiteboard at school.

Younger son asks his dad for his money.

Son wastes all his money.

Son is hungry.

Son gets job feeding pigs.

Son decides to go back to his father.

Father hugs son.

Father throws party.

Older son is mad.

Father talks to older son.

Lesson 6 – Town Tickets

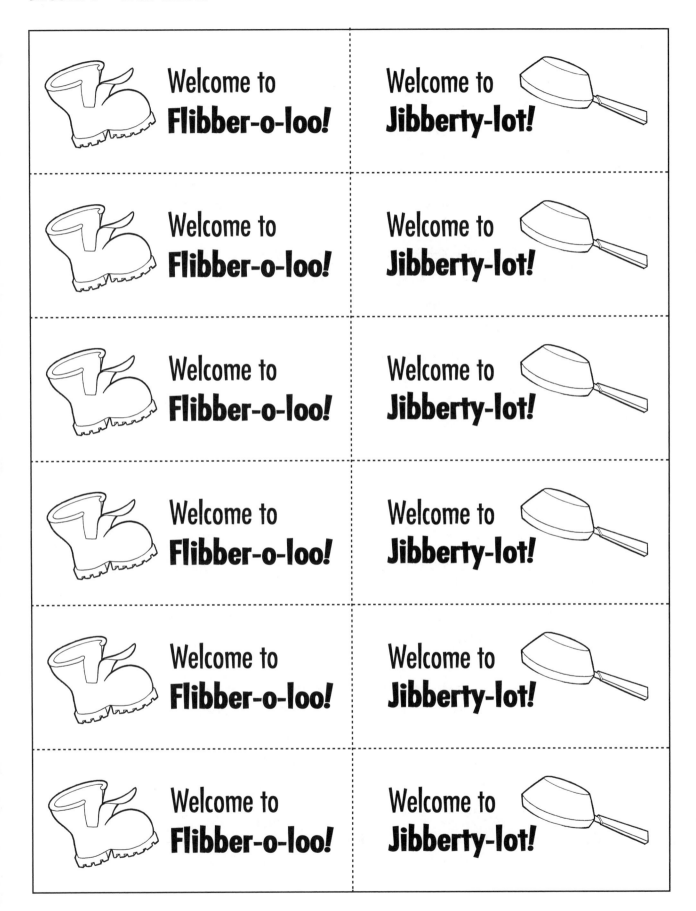

Lesson 6 – Neighbor Game Instructions

1. Line up in pairs. Tell each other who has a Flibber-o-loo ticket and a Jibberty-lot ticket.

2. You will race in pairs. You will balance a balloon between yourself and your partner in the following way:

   - If you are two Flibbero-loo kids, you balance the balloon between your shoes or ankles, because people from Flibber-o-loo wear shoes on their heads.

   - If you are two Jibberty-lot kids, you balance the balloon between your heads, because people from Jibberty-lot wear pots on their heads.

   - If you and your partner are from different towns, you choose any way except using your hands to balance the balloon between yourselves.

3. After each race, you must pick another partner and race by following Step 2 above.

4. When everyone has raced with a different partner, the game is over.

1. Line up in pairs. Tell each other who has a Flibber-o-loo ticket and a Jibberty-lot ticket.

2. You will race in pairs. You will balance a balloon between yourself and your partner in the following way:

   - If you are two Flibbero-loo kids, you balance the balloon between your shoes or ankles, because people from Flibber-o-loo wear shoes on their heads.

   - If you are two Jibberty-lot kids, you balance the balloon between your heads, because people from Jibberty-lot wear pots on their heads.

   - If you and your partner are from different towns, you choose any way except using your hands to balance the balloon between yourselves.

3. After each race, you must pick another partner and race by following Step 2 above.

4. When everyone has raced with a different partner, the game is over.

Lesson 8 - Basket Frame Pattern

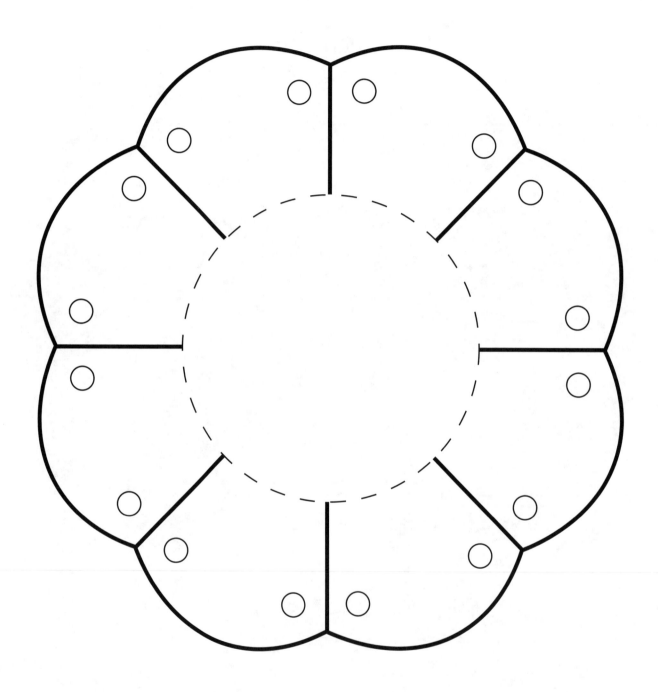

WELCOME TO DODGEBALL CITY

Connecting to **Trust** with life examples from **Joseph**

UNIT FOUR:

THE TRUST CONNECTION

UNIT VERSE: "May the God of hope fill you with all joy and peace as you trust in him so that you may overflow with hope by the power of the Holy Spirit."
Romans 15:13

DODGEBALL CITY

LESSON FOCUS:

1. God knows what's best for me: Genesis 37:1–50:26

2. I will trust God to help me with my problems: Genesis 37:3-36

3. I will show my trust in God by obeying him: Genesis 39:1-20a

4. I will trust God is with me in hard times: Genesis 39:20b-23

5. I will trust God to give me courage: Genesis 40:1-23

6. I will strengthen my trust in God by building my relationship with him: Genesis 41:1-40

7. I will trust in God's plan: Genesis 41:41-45:15

8. I will show my trust in God to others: Genesis 50:15-21

Trust Connection Goals

The Trust Connection is all about helping kids understand what trust is and how to develop a relationship with God. This will develop some new relationships with God for the children, and it will strengthen others.

Each Lesson Focus will take kids on a journey toward various ways they can grow closer to our Lord. The Countertop Connections (opening sessions) with Bob and Larry will introduce the concept of having a relationship with God. It will be supported with the Program Verse from James 4:8: "*Come near to God and he will come near to you.*"

When kids are dismissed to Dodgeball City, they will have the chance to explore what it means to trust in God. Kids will be challenged each week to build a relationship with God, build trust in him and others, and share the trust that God gives them with others.

The first lesson shares that God knows what is best for us by summarizing the story of Joseph from the book of Genesis. The following six lessons will explore Joseph's story and dig deeper into what trust means in their lives.

The final lesson in the Trust unit will encourage the kids to show their trust in God to others.

Warning: Activities in these lessons may call for foods containing wheat, dairy, or nuts. Please be aware that some children may have medically serious allergic reactions to these foods. Let parents know that their kids will be offered snacks that may include these items, and post a list of ingredients each week for any snacks offered during the lesson. Whenever foods containing wheat, dairy, and nuts are suggested in these lessons, be sure to have safe alternatives on hand.

Welcome to Dodgeball City!

Kids will travel to Dodgeball City to explore trust in this unit. One of the VeggieTales® videos that Bob and Larry will present to the children during the Countertop Connection time is called *The Ballad of Little Joe.* In that video, Larry is Little Joe, based on Joseph from the Bible. Dodgeball City is modeled after the name of the same town in the video.

In this fun-filled, Western town, kids will learn about trust as they hear Joseph's story and deepen their relationship with God.

Your Role at Dodgeball City: Deputy Dodge

As Deputy Dodge at Dodgeball City, you will be the host to each group of elementary kids as they rotate through your site every eight weeks.

It is suggested that you appear as a dusty, Western character wearing denim, plaid, bandannas, boots, and even a cowboy hat.

How to Build and Prepare Dodgeball City:

If you have more time and a permanent space

The Dodgeball City site has two main areas: the Town Street (which is "outdoors") and the Rootin' Tootin' Pizza Place. The Town Street needs the silhouettes of the buildings along with cacti, the "porch," and the optional jail.

The Town Street: Use the transparency art in the *VeggieConnections Elementary Curriculum Kit* and clip art on page 57 to project the Dodgeball City town outline onto brown mural paper. Trace the images onto the paper and hang this background on a wall.

Enhance this "outdoor" area with whatever Old West flavor you can find—hay bales, a hitching post (sawhorse), wooden benches, burlap bags, tumbleweeds (crumpled brown paper bags), stick horses, coils of rope, and dodge balls scattered around. If you have a secure way to display a real saddle (so that it doesn't wobble or fall when sat on), the kids would enjoy that as well. If possible, secure a new (unused) pitchfork to a wall or post in a way that it cannot be removed by the kids.

Cacti: Add "cacti" on or near the town street. These may be made of cardboard, foamboard, or green paper and taped to walls. Some may be artificial cacti in individual pots. Do not bring real cacti into the classroom unless they are a type that does not have spines.

Prayer Cactus: Each *VeggieConnections Group* needs a life-sized Prayer Cactus. Cut large cactus shapes from a 4' x 8' sheet of foam insulation (available at home-improvement stores). You may attach these to walls or stick them in a large gardening pot secured with some rocks to hold it in place and some Styrofoam peanuts to keep it lightweight. Cut green chenille stems into thirds; these will be used as cactus spines ("prickles"). The wires sticking out will look like cactus spines.

Create a wall mural for Dodgeball City using transparency art found on page 57.

Dodgeball City Town Street

Porch: You will need a "porch" in front of one of the building silhouettes on which the weekly Bible story is told. Use a wooden pallet or ask a handyman at your church to build a simple platform big enough to hold Deputy Dodge and a chair. Or you could simply lay out a sheet of brown mural paper and draw lines on it for boards so it looks like a wooden porch floor; tape this down to the floor so it doesn't slip when stepped on. Include a wooden chair or simple wood rocking chair on the porch. If you have room, you may include a self-standing lawn canopy, arbor, or gazebo (without sides) to serve as the porch roof.

Jail: You may choose to enhance the outline of the jail building by adding a fake front to it that the kids can enter. Use a large appliance box to stick out from the wall or corner. Cut a door and windows. Use dowels or string for "bars" on the windows.

Rootin' Tootin' Pizza Place (RTPP): Designate a side of the room to be the Rootin' Tootin' Pizza Place, and hang a large banner showing the name. Include tables with red-checked tablecloths or sheets of brown mural paper taped to the tables. Display a dry-erase board or chalkboard with the "Special of the Day" (Connection Word) each week. Have a cowbell handy that Deputy Dodge can use to summon the kids at different points in the lesson. Provide markers and other weekly supplies bundled in twine string or tied up in a bandanna. Display bandannas all over the RTPP (they will be used in many lessons) by tying them to table and chair legs or piling them in a basket. You may decorate the RTPP with root beer bottles, tin cans filled with flowers, cowboy boots, cowboy hats, and lassos.

You may add a long table with stools along one side, topped with pizza boxes, a cash register, and root beer bottles. Here you may also store props and supplies for the lessons.

OPTION 2:

*If you are short on time
or do not have a permanent space*

The Town Street: Use the transparency art in the *VeggieConnections Elementary Curriculum Kit* and clip art on page 57 to project the Dodgeball City town and characters onto brown mural paper. Trace the images onto the paper and hang on a wall in a way that is removable. Loosely roll up the backdrop for weekly storage.

> **Cacti:** Add cacti to the mural.

> **Prayer Cactus:** Each *VeggieConnections Group* needs a life-sized Prayer Cactus. See instructions above to make these. If this option is not workable in your space, make a cactus from paper for each small group to hang on a wall.

All the other Town Street decorations are optional, except that Deputy Dodge needs a rustic wooden chair or rocking chair to designate the "porch."

> **Rootin' Tootin' Pizza Place (RTPP):** Hang a large sign labeled "Rootin' Tootin' Pizza Place" on the opposite side of the room from the Town Street. Put classroom tables here and cover with brown mural paper (taped down). Keep supplies (markers, scissors, bandannas) in baskets. You may still want to have a cowbell. Write "Special of the Day" on a dry-erase board or chalkboard with each week's Connection Word.

Life Application Memory Tool

VeggieConnections will teach an important Bible lesson to kids each week. Knowing the Bible is the beginning of a relationship with God. Putting that learning to practice through life application really solidifies a child's relationship with the Lord. It is imperative that we provide kids with the tools they need to carry what they have learned into everyday experiences through life application.

In this curriculum, there are three main ways we will encourage kids to do this:

1. Kids will discover ways to love God throughout each lesson.

2. Kids will learn a catch-phrase that will help them to remember what they should do in real-life experiences.

The catch-phrase we have created is to THINK—LINK—ACT. There is a song built on this principle on the CD in your kit which will help kids remember this important tool. In addition, each session will focus on various THINK—LINK—ACT activities that help children to walk the walk and talk the talk, hopefully opening doors for the Holy Spirit to enter in and build meaningful relationships that will carry kids through every day of their lives! Here's what it means:

THINK:
Stop and think about what God wants you to do.

LINK:
Link God's Word and what you've learned to your choices.

ACT:
Go and act on what God wants you to do!

Now add some fun hand motions to the catch-phrase!

THINK: Touch head with fingertip two times.

LINK: Left hand out, right hand out.
Clasp your hands together, fingers intertwined.

ACT: Release grip and roll hands three times.
Finish with arms outstretched.

3. Kids will create a weekly life application building tool to help them to remember what each lesson focused on.

At Dodgeball City, kids will create a Big Pocket that will hold trust reminders of how they learned to trust God.

Cut craft foam in half, giving two 9" x 12" pieces. Cut a wide "V" shape at the bottom of the two pocket halves, to resemble a jeans back pocket. Put the two pieces together and fasten with staples along the bottom and two sides of the pocket.

Have kids punch two holes in the back pocket half, one in each top corner, ensuring the holes are ½" down from the top edge of the pocket back. Give kids a length of yarn, and have them tie a hanging loop to the holes. Have each child write "I Will Trust God" on the front of the pocket with gel pens. Kids should also add their names on the front or back of the pockets.

This pocket will be utilized every week to hold items made by the children during the Kid Connection portion of the lesson. At the end of the unit, kids will take home their Big Pocket and it's contents to remind them to trust in God.

Suggested Music for Dodgeball City:

Use these songs from the *VeggieConnections Music CD* in your sessions:

1. *THINK—LINK—ACT*
Music motions found on page 48.

2. *Stop! And Go with Mercy*

Connecting to **Trust** with life examples from **Joseph**
The story of Joseph: **Genesis 37:1–50:26**

Connection Word:

trust

PART ONE:

Plugging In at Dodgeball City

Introduction to the site and lesson focus

LESSON 1:
God knows what's best for me.

A. Veggie Connection

BEFORE YOU START:
Before kids arrive, place all the candy bars in one sack or bag, all the spiders and snakes in a second sack or bag, and all the toys in a third. If you have a large group, make two or three bags of each item. Set the bags where the kids can't see in them. Ask two *VeggieConnections Shepherds* to do the activity with you, assigning each of the three of you one of these roles — someone who likes treats, someone who likes jokes, someone who likes you to try new things.

Dressed as Deputy Dodge, and speaking in a "cowboy" accent (throughout all lessons), warmly greet the kids as they arrive at Dodgeball City. **Howdy, pard'ners! I'm right pleased y'all could make it today. Have yerselves a look-see 'round Dodgeball City, and make yerselves at home. Be sure to stop by the Rootin' Tootin' Pizza Place for a root beer!** Allow a minute for the kids to roam around the area, explore the props, sip some root beer (optional), and look at the scenery.

When it's time to gather the kids together, ring the cowbell (if you chose to include one in the site setup) or give a cowboy whoop such as "Yippee-ki-yay!". Introduce the two *Veggie-Connections Shepherds* who prepared to help. Say: **These here leaders are friends of mine. I like this friend because he loooves treats. And this friend always gives me a chuckle because she loooves jokes! And me, well, one thing I like to do is try out new things and have fun learnin'. And now here's *your* job for this Dodgeball City game. It's called "Who Do You Trust?"**

You and each Shepherd should hold up a prepared bag and spread out. **Each of us has a treat for you—right here in these here bags. But you only get to choose one treat. And you don't get to know ahead of time what it is. You have to choose based on who you trust! Now, we've given you a hint about each of us. You need to decide which Shepherd's surprise you want to try.** Have the kids mill around as they decide, with you and the two leaders making comments to encourage all the kids to choose *their* bag and trust *them*, without giving away what's in the bags.

After giving the kids time to think it over, instruct them to each choose an adult they trust and gather around that person. When everyone has committed to a choice, have the adults hold their bags high enough that the kids can't see in but low enough that they can reach in. Have all the kids raise one hand high in the air, poised to grab. At your signal, all the kids at once must put their hand in the bag and pull out one of whatever is in there. Allow a minute for the kids to react and compare and enjoy the fun. Inform the kids that they may keep whatever they chose.

THE CHILDREN
will arrive with their *Veggie-Connections Shepherds* from the opening Countertop Connections featuring Bob and Larry. Play the *Veggie-Connections Music CD* as children enter Dodgeball City.

VEGGIE CONNECTION NEEDS:
- *VeggieConnections Music CD*
- CD player
- Miniature individually wrapped candies (Check with parents about food allergies)
- Three burlap sacks or large brown-paper grocery bags
- Small plastic spiders and snakes (that the kids may keep)
- Small inexpensive toys, such as yo-yos, brain-teasers, maze puzzles, and so on (may be purchased in bulk from a mail-order catalog or dollar-type store)
- Two *VeggieConnections Shepherds*
- Root beer and mini paper cups (optional)
- *VeggieConnections Bible Dictionary*

Then gather the kids back together to be seated. Ask them what it meant to trust the person whose bag they chose and how that felt. **Here in Dodgeball City, we're going to learn a lot about trust. So we'd better git started figurin' out just what that means.** Teach the group the Dodgeball Dictionary Rhyme, urging the kids to use their best Western accent as they repeat it. They may "clip-clop" their hands on their knees to make the sound of horse hooves on the beats:

> **Look it up, hook it up, what's it all about?**
> **Look it up, hook it up, let's find out!**

Ask a volunteer to look up *trust* in the *VeggieConnections Bible Dictionary* and read the definition aloud. Write *trust* on the "Special of the Day" board (in the Rootin' Tootin' Pizza Place).

B. Prayer Connection

PRAYER CONNECTION NEEDS:

• Prayer Cacti (from site setup)
• Green slips of paper
• Pencils

Have each *VeggieConnections Group* gather around a foam Prayer Cactus made for the site setup. Assign each group its own cactus. Have the *VeggieConnections Shepherds* take a minute to get to know the kids in their group.

First, let each child briefly share something they would like prayer about or something they want to thank God for. Give kids slips of green paper and pencils. Have kids write their brief prayers on the slips and stick them on the cactus spines. Then let each child have a turn to pray and talk to God about what they said.

PART TWO: Plugging In to God's Word

Connecting to God's Word in the Bible and understanding how that can help us to have a better relationship with him

A. God Connection: The story of Joseph – Genesis 37:1–50:26

BEFORE YOU START:

On separate sheets of paper, write these sentences in large print: 1. "Sold as a slave." 2. "Punished for doing the right thing." 3. "Spent years in prison but didn't commit a crime." 4. "Didn't get helped by a friend." 5. "Faced an all-powerful king." 6. "Had to run a country." 7. "Needed to forgive mean brothers." 8. "Had to convince his brothers." On the back of paper #1, print a large T; continue on the backs of #2–5, printing R-U-S-T. On the backs of #6–8, print G-O-D.

GOD CONNECTION NEEDS:

• Eight large sheets of paper in different colors
• Marker
• Bible

Use the cowbell to invite the kids to gather around the porch as you sit in the chair to tell the Bible story.

Did you know that God knows what's best for you? That's what it says right here in God's Word. Hold up a Bible. **But did you know that it's not always easy to *trust* that God knows what's best for you? During our visits here in Dodgeball City, we're going to be learning how to trust God from the example of a young man named Joseph. His story is found in the book of Genesis in the Bible.** Open your Bible to Genesis 37—50 and show the kids.

Say: **I will tell you the Bible story two times. The first time, you will listen very carefully. Then the second time, I'll give you instructions for something fun you can do.** Read the story one time, then add the actions with the signs.

Joseph lived a long life and went through all kinds of hard things. Sometimes he couldn't trust anyone around him, and the only one he could trust to get through it was God. Ask eight volunteers to stand on or by the porch and hold the eight prepared signs in order, with the label "TRUST GOD" facing the group.

Joseph's story starts off with a good old-fashioned family feud—except it wasn't so good for Joseph. Joseph had ten older brothers, and they were all on the same side—but

unfortunately not on the same side as Joseph. And these brothers just couldn't stand him! Now, I'm not going to tell you what happened today because we'll hear this whole exciting story next week. But it ends up with Joseph being sold like a piece of cowhide! Have the child holding the "T" sign turn it over to show the sentence: "Sold as a slave." Read it together. **Joseph had to trust that God knew what was best for him.**

Well, *then* Joseph was working in a faraway country—and doing his best to serve God. But one of the people in charge—I won't tell you who—wanted Joseph to do something wrong. *Really* wrong. But Joseph trusted God and said no. Joseph did the right thing but got the wrong punishment. That person got him kicked off his job! Have the child with the "R" turn it over to reveal: "Punished for doing the right thing." Read it together. **Joseph had to trust that God knew what was best for him.**

Not only did Joseph lose his job, he also got thrown into jail! No one would listen to his side of the story. But he still did his best to serve God while in the prison. But he sure was there a long time—all for doing nothing! Have the child with the "U" turn it over to reveal: "Spent years in prison but didn't commit a crime." Read it together. **Joseph still had to trust that God knew what was best for him.**

While he was there in jail, some friends asked him for help. I won't tell you what their problem was, but it was really strange! And *only* Joseph could help them—no one else! That's because Joseph trusted God. So Joseph decided to help them. Then both of the men got out of jail—one for bad and one for good. And the good friend, who could have helped him in return, forgot all about Joseph. Have the child with the "S" turn it over to reveal: "Didn't get helped by a friend." Read it together. **Joseph had to trust that God knew what was best for him.**

A time came when the powerful king of this great country needed some help—the same kind of help that Joseph's friends had needed. And that friend from jail was working for this king. He remembered how only Joseph had been able to help him. He told the king all about it. So the king called Joseph and commanded him to help. What if Joseph couldn't help this time? What if the king didn't like Joseph's God? You'll have to come back in a few weeks to find out what happens in that part of the story. Have the child with the second "T" turn it over to reveal: "Faced an all-powerful king." Read it together. **Joseph had to trust that God knew what was best for him.**

Joseph always tried to do his best for God no matter what terrible place he found himself in. In an amazing way, one day Joseph found himself in charge of all the food in a big country. He was given a huge job and 14 years to do it. Could he manage something that big? Was he successful? I won't say right now, but I will say that Joseph tackled this job like all his others—by trusting God's plan. Have the child with the "G" turn it over to reveal: "Had to run a country." Read it together. **Joseph had to trust that God knew what was best for him.**

And Joseph's hardest test came at the end of all those hard times. He met up with those mean old brothers of his—the ones who had made sure Joseph was no longer in their family, or even in their country! Why was this test hard? Because he had to decide how to treat them. He finally had the power to get even. Would Joseph trust God and keep doing what was right? Have the child with the "O" turn it over to reveal: "Needed to forgive mean brothers." Read it together. **Joseph had to trust that God knew what was best for him.**

Then Joseph's dad, Jacob, died. Joseph's brothers were worried whether Joseph was still mad at them. Would Joseph finally get even with his brothers? Have the child with the last letter, "D" turn it over to reveal: "Had to convince his brothers." Read it together.

By going through all that, Joseph showed that the best thing we can do is trust God, no matter what. Have all the kids turn their signs over to spell "TRUST GOD." Read it together. **God sees everything that's going to happen in your life along with how it fits into his kingdom. No matter what, you can trust that God knows what's best for you.**

Discuss these questions with the kids: **What are some of the hard times Joseph went through?** Let the kids name what they remember, looking at the signs to help them. **What did Joseph do to help himself through those times?** (*Trusted God, did his best to serve and obey God no matter where he was.*) **What can we trust God for?** (*That he knows what's best for us.*)

Whatever happens to us, we can trust God to be with us. Lead the kids in reading the Unit Memory Verse from Romans 15:13 and ask them to repeat it with you.

B. Activity Connection

Choose from the following activities to help kids explore and remember that God wants us to know him and trust him (approximately 10–15 minutes each).

1. High-Powered Game: Tagging Problems

HIGH-POWERED GAME NEEDS:

- Bandannas of one color for half the class (or wide yellow ribbon)
- Bandannas of a second color for half the class (or wide red ribbon)
- Scissors (if using ribbon)
- Stickers

Show the kids the boundaries of the playing area. Set up a chair on the edge of the playing area. Have one *VeggieConnections Shepherd* hold the stickers and sit on the chair. Identify this as the Trust Station. If you have a large group, you may want to designate more than one Trust Station.

Divide the group into two teams. Give one team the bandannas of one color to tie around their necks or tie a length of yellow ribbon around a wrist of each player. Give the other team the other bandannas or tie a red ribbon around their wrists.

One team begins as the "problems." Their goal is to try to "spread" the problems by tagging players on the other team. When kids are tagged, they should go to the Trust Station. If the tagged kid is able to describe one event in Joseph's life where he showed that he trusted God, the Shepherd puts a sticker on his shirt. If the child is able to identify a time when kids in real life need to trust that God knows what's best, he gets two stickers.

After several minutes, switch the roles of the teams.

2. Low-Powered Game: Trust Croquet

BEFORE YOU START:

Copy and cut apart the eight game cards. For each *VeggieConnections Group*, lay out a game area. Set up additional game areas if groups are larger than eight kids. Put a tape start/finish line about six feet away from the game area. Randomly lay game cards face up on your floor, ensuring cards are out of story order.

LOW-POWERED GAME NEEDS:

- Joseph Story Game cards on page 228 (one per *Veggie-Connections Group*)
- Table-tennis balls (one per group)
- Paper-towel tubes (one per group)
- Masking/painter's tape

Have kids divide into *VeggieConnections Groups* or into groups of up to eight kids and gather around a game area. Give the first child the table-tennis ball and paper-towel mallet. Explain to kids that each card has one part of Joseph story written on it (as used in the Bible story). The first player will look over the cards and determine which is first in the story. Here is the order to reference during the game:

1. Sold as a slave.
2. Punished for doing the right thing.
3. Spent years in prison but didn't commit a crime.
4. Didn't get helped by a friend.
5. Faced an all-powerful king.
6. Had to run a country.
7. Needed to forgive mean brothers.
8. Had to convince his brothers.

The player will them use the mallet to hit the ball so it stops on or rolls over the card. If the player has chosen the correct card, he or she can pick it up and return to the group. If the card is wrong, the player leaves the card there and returns to the group.

The next player will aim for the second story card (unless the first player was wrong), and players continue until the last card is hit and collected (some players may have two rounds). Have kids determine the correct story order and then line up in a semicircle holding the cards in that order, so kids can all see the cards. Say: **Joseph's life story was filled with many years trusting God. Joseph didn't know why some of the things happened to him. But he always trusted God.**

3. Craft: Mini Chalkboard Signs

Explain to the kids that some restaurants have chalkboard signs where they write the "Special of the Day," which is a certain food offered only that day. The Rootin' Tootin' Pizza Place is no different, except that their "specials" are really special—straight from God's Word. The class will enjoy a new "special" each day they come to Dodgeball City.

Give each child a piece of 5" x 7" cardboard. Fold in half so that the cardboard forms a 5" x 3½" shape that can stand up. (If using cereal boxes, put the plain side on the outside.) Kids may write their names on the inside of the fold. Help the kids measure and draw a 3" x 4½" rectangle in the center of one side, leaving a border around the edge so that it looks like an old-fashioned chalkboard slate. Have *VeggieConnections Shepherds* help younger kids.

On the border, help the kids write "Special of the Day." Then the kids paint the rectangle in chalkboard paint. Have the kids spread a little glue around the unpainted border (but not over top of the words). On this glue they drop bits of raffia or hay to give their chalkboard a rustic or "hay bale" look. Tie a length of twine around a small piece of chalk and glue the loose end of the twine to the chalkboard.

Point out today's Connection Word, *trust*, on the large "Special of the Day" board on the wall in the Rootin' Tootin' Pizza Place. While the paint is drying, ask volunteers to tell what it means and how this word can help them connect with God this week.

When the paint is dry, let the kids write "Trust God" on their board, as a reminder of who kids need to put their trust in God!

CRAFT NEEDS:

- 5"x7" piece of cardboard from boxes, back of tablets, or inside of cereal boxes (one per child)
- Permanent markers or pens
- Rulers
- Chalkboard paint (available at craft stores)
- Paintbrushes
- Paint shirts and table coverings (optional)
- Glue
- Raffia or hay
- Twine
- Scissors
- Small pieces of chalk (one per child)

OPTIONAL:

If chalkboard paint is not available, you may use a 3" x 4 ½" piece of black construction paper so that it looks like a chalkboard. Use chalk or white crayon to write "Trust God" on it. Note: this option is not erasable.

THINK:
Stop and think about what God wants you to do.

LINK:
Link God's Word and what you've learned to your choices.

ACT:
Go and act on what God wants you to do!

Now add some fun hand motions to the catch-phrase!

THINK: Touch head with fingertip two times.

LINK: Left hand out, right hand out.
Clasp your hands together, fingers intertwined.

ACT: Release grip and roll hands three times.
Finish with arms outstretched.

PART THREE:

Plugging In to My Life

Life application of the lesson to lead kids to THINK-LINK-ACT and build a relationship with God every day

A. Cucumber Connection

CUCUMBER CONNECTION NEEDS:

- Pickle jar
- Pickles artwork from the *VeggieConnection Shepherd* pages (on the *VeggieConnections CD-ROM*)
- Green construction paper

Before kids arrive, enlarge and copy the pickles from the *VeggieConnections Shepherd* pages on the CD-ROM included in the *VeggieConnections Elementary Curriculum Kit* onto green construction paper. Cut them out and put them in a pickle jar.

Let a volunteer draw a pickle from the Pickle Pot and either the child or a Shepherd should read the dilemma out loud. Each Shepherd should then process the question with their group using the THINK—LINK—ACT phrase.

Danielle's mom and dad don't get along. She often cries in her bedroom when she hears them fighting. She doesn't feel she can trust them. What should Danielle do?	Chuck didn't cheat on a recent test, but his best friend, Jamie, did and told the teacher he and Chuck both cheated. What should he do?	Kara's best friend keeps asking why her dad is not around. Kara doesn't want to tell her that her father is in jail. She doesn't know if she can trust her to keep it a secret. What should she do?

B. Kid Connection: Big Pockets

KID CONNECTION NEEDS:

- Craft foam, 12" x18" (one per child)
- Staplers
- Hole punch
- Yarn
- Gel pens
- Scissors
- *VeggieConnections Music CD*
- CD player

Cut craft foam in half, giving two 9" x 12" pieces. Cut a wide "V" shape at the bottom of the two halves, to resemble a jeans back pocket. Put the two pieces together and fasten with staples along the bottom and two sides of the pocket.

Have kids punch two holes in the back pocket half, one in each top corner, ensuring the holes are 1/2" down from the top edge of the pocket back. Give kids a length of yarn, and have them tie a hanging loop to the holes. Have each child write "I Will Trust God" on the front of the pocket with gel pens. Kids should also add their names on the front or back of the pockets.

Have everyone stand and sing the *THINK—LINK—ACT* song, while doing the motions. Ask the kids to do the THINK motion. **Think about who knows what's best for you.** (*God.*) Do the LINK motion. **Link to Joseph, who trusted God, and God knew what was best for him.** Do the ACT motion. **Trust that God knows what's best for you. What can you do to trust God this week?** Let volunteers suggest ideas. (*I won't get mad when things don't go the way I want. I will pay attention to my parents and to other adults who trust in God. God knows the situation I'm in, and I will trust him because he knows what's best for me.*)

Tell the kids that they will add trust reminders to their pocket each week. Collect the pockets for use in next week's lesson.

C. Christ Connection

CHRIST CONNECTION NEEDS:

- *VeggieConnections* take-home newspaper (one per child)

Help the kids begin to learn the Unit Memory Verse, Romans 15:13, by saying it as an echo. Say one phrase loudly (**"May the God of hope"**), then indicate for the girls to repeat it in normal voice and then for the boys to whisper it. Say each phrase in the verse in the same manner.

Ask kids to name ways they can trust God at school. Include those ways as you lead the closing prayer. **Father, help us to trust you this week at school when we....** (*Have tests, when we are tempted to do something wrong, when things go badly in sports, when we have trouble with friends.*) **Thank you for coming near to us. In Jesus' name, amen.**

Distribute the take-home newspaper, *VeggieConnections*.

Connection Word:

slavery

PART ONE:

Plugging In at Dodgeball City

Introduction to the site and lesson focus

LESSON 2:

I will trust God to help me with my problems.

A. Veggie Connection

Dressed as Deputy Dodge and speaking in your best "cowboy" accent, welcome the kids to Dodgeball City. **Howdy-do, y'all. Usually I'm a' glad to see you'uns, but today I'm a little ashamed. You see, Dodgeball City is jist a mess! It's gonna take a lot of spit 'n' polish to git it all lookin' good agin. I jist wonder if someone might be willing to give me a hand . . .** Make comments like this until the kids start volunteering. Then start giving them "chores":

Have one group of kids head for the Rootin' Tootin' Pizza Place and pretend to clean tables, but rather than really clean, they should use large, slow, back-and-forth motions with their whole arms. Instruct them to keep motioning back and forth over the tables without stopping.

Get a second group to pretend to sweep the Pizza Place floor, again with exaggerated motions. They should clasp both hands together, lean forward, and swing their arms back and forth. Insist that they not stop.

Have a third group join you on the "main street" to push away tumbleweeds. These kids are to get on their knees and push outward with both hands, over and over.

A fourth group can stand by the building silhouettes and pretend to wash windows by waving both hands, back and forth overhead.

By the time you give instructions to a fifth group, the others will start complaining of being tired. Just insist that they not take a break—Dodgeball City needs to be clean! Then instruct the fifth group to brush the horses. They move both hands up and down in front of them as if brushing.

The last group can clean the stalls. Tell them to pretend to hold shovels, scoop something off the floor, and toss it behind their shoulder with a big motion.

Be sure to emphasize to all groups what hard work it is to clean Dodgeball City. Allow a little more time for all the groups to watch one another "work." Walk around and make comments about their needing to work harder and faster and not stop. Then tell the kids that Dodgeball City looks great, and let them be seated.

How did y'all feel havin' to do all that work? Let the kids complain now! **You did work hard, but there wasn't anything in it for you was there? And no breaks, either. That's kind of like working like a slave. For today's Bible story, y'all have to know what slavery is, and this Dodgeball City cleanup jist gave you a taste of it!**

THE CHILDREN
will arrive with their *Veggie-Connections Shepherds* from the opening Countertop Connections featuring Bob and Larry. Play the *Veggie-Connections Music CD* as children enter Dodgeball City.

VEGGIE CONNECTION NEEDS:

- *VeggieConnections Music CD*
- CD player
- *VeggieConnections Bible Dictionary*

Lead the group in reciting the Dodgeball Dictionary Rhyme, urging the kids to use their best Western accent. They may "clip-clop" their hands on their knees to make the sound of horse hooves on the beats:

Look it up, hook it up, what's it all about?
Look it up, hook it up, let's find out!

Ask a volunteer to look up *slavery* in the *VeggieConnections Bible Dictionary* and read the definition aloud. Write "slavery" on the "Special of the Day" board. **Before we head to the Bible story, let's make sure to build our relationship with God a little bit.**

B. Prayer Connection

PRAYER
CONNECTION
NEEDS:

• Prayer Cacti
(from *Lesson 1*)
• Green slips of paper
• Pencils

Have each *VeggieConnections Group* gather by their Prayer Cactus. This week, ask the kids to share with their group about a problem they might be facing. Give kids slips of green paper and have them write prayers on the strips. Then have kids pass their strips to the child sitting on their right, and have this child say a sentence prayer and then stick the slip on the cactus.

VeggieConnections Shepherds may close their group's prayer time, asking God to be with whatever problems they are having.

PART TWO:

Plugging In to God's Word

Connecting to God's Word in the Bible and understanding how that can help us to have a better relationship with him

A. God Connection: Joseph is sold into slavery – Genesis 37:3-36

BEFORE YOU START:
Place cloth, stars, rocks, action figure, and money each in a separate paper bag. Fold over the tops.

GOD
CONNECTION
NEEDS:

• Five large paper
grocery bags
• Pieces of colorful,
rich-looking fabric
• Paper or plastic stars
• Rocks
• Male action-figure toy
• Toy money
• Cowbell
• Bible

Use the cowbell to invite the kids to gather around the porch as you sit in the chair. Divide the kids into five groups and have groups remain seated. Give each group a bag with the items and tell them not to peek. Explain that the items in the bags will help tell the Bible story. When you signal a group, they may open that bag and someone may hold up what's in it. Show the kids in a Bible where today's story is found, Genesis 37. Say: **I will tell you the Bible story two times. The first time, you will listen very carefully. Then the second time, I'll give you instructions for something fun you can do.** Read the story once, then add the following activity with the bags.

Point to the group with the bag containing the fabric. **Fabric is what starts our story. There was a man named Jacob who loved God. He had 12 sons, but he had a favorite—he's the person we learned about last week.** Ask the kids if they remember his name. **Joseph was Jacob's favorite. Because he loved Joseph more than his other sons, Jacob gave Joseph a special gift—a coat woven with many bright colors. Now Joseph was number 11 out of the 12 sons. This beautiful coat gift made Joseph's 10 older brothers angry and jealous.**

Point to the group with the bag of stars. **Then Joseph began having some strange dreams. He dreamed that his brothers were stalks of wheat, and they bowed down to him. He also dreamed that his brothers were stars and his parents were the sun and moon— and they bowed down to him, too! The dreams meant that Joseph's family would bow down to him, like a slave with a master. That made his brothers even madder!**

Point to the group with the bag containing rocks. **The job of the 10 older brothers was to take care of the family sheep. They had to travel very far through rocky desert country-side for weeks and weeks to find enough good grass and water for them. One day, Jacob the dad sent Joseph to check on his brothers. Joseph had to travel a long way, and his brothers saw him coming from a distance. They made an awful plan. They decided to kill him!**

Point to the group with the bag containing the action figure. **But the oldest brother, named Reuben, knew that was wrong. He was a brave man of action. He talked his brothers out of killing Joseph. But when Joseph got there, they were still mean to him. They grabbed him and took his new coat and threw him into a pit. Then Reuben went off to watch the sheep while the others sat down to eat.**

Point to the group with the bag containing money. **While they were eating, a big group of traders came along, with their camels and tents and all sorts of things to buy and sell. They were on their way to the faraway land of Egypt. The brothers said, "He dreams we'll be his slaves! Well, we'll make *him* a slave!" The brothers decided to get rid of Joseph by selling him as a slave. The traders took Joseph to Egypt, where they sold him into slavery.**

Point to the group with the fabric again. **When Reuben came back, he was very upset. And he told his brothers that their dad would be very upset, too! That's when the brothers realized that their dad would probably try to get Joseph back. So they made up a big lie. They took Joseph's coat, tore it up, and put an animal's blood on it. Then they took it back home and showed Jacob. "Joseph must have been eaten by a wild animal!" their dad said. And Jacob cried and cried.**

Now, this part of the story sounds awfully sad, but that's why Joseph had to trust God. Next week, you'll learn how Joseph got along as a slave.

Ask the children in each group to tell what their object had to do with the story. Then discuss these questions: **What were Joseph's problems?** *(His brothers hated him, they sold him as a slave and he got sent to a faraway country, his brothers lied about him so his father couldn't come help him.)* **How did God help Joseph?** *(By giving him at least one loving brother who rescued him from being killed.)*

Explain that though we don't see it in this part of the story, the Bible tells us more. Assure the kids that Joseph would be okay (but don't tell them how yet) and that God would use this in the end to save Joseph's whole family. **What are ways that God helps us?** *(Sending a parent to help us, sending teachers and other trustworthy grown-ups to help us, sometimes sending friends or siblings to help us, giving us the Bible so we know the right things to do, reminding us of Bible stories and verses to make us feel better, and so on.)*

B. Activity Connection

Choose from the following activities to help kids explore and remember that they can trust God to help them with their problems (approximately 10–15 minutes each).

1. High-Powered Game: Brothers Against Brothers Tug of War

BEFORE YOU START:

Tape a masking-tape line about 6' for each *VeggieConnections Group* down the center of the playing area. Tape a sign, "Egypt," on one side of the line.

Joseph was outnumbered by his mostly angry brothers. But one brother, Rueben, tried to save Joseph. Let's see what that might have been like in this game.

Have kids divide into *VeggieConnections Groups* and give each a jump rope or clothesline. Have groups move to the playing area and have groups choose the first Joseph and have this child stand on the side of the line away from Egypt. Choose another child to stand on the other side (choose equal-sized kids for this first round).

Allow the kids to begin the game. If Joseph doesn't get pulled across, add another child to the brother's side and play again. To help Joseph out for the next round, have

HIGH-POWERED GAME NEEDS:

- Masking tape
- "Egypt" sign
- Jump rope or clothesline (one per *Veggie-Connections Group*)

another child join Joseph, while reminding kids how Rueben tried to save Joseph. As long as Joseph continues to hold his or her own, continue to add another brother until Joseph can't avoid being pulled into Egypt. Allow new kids to play Joseph and Rueben.

After several rounds of involving all the kids, say: **At some point in this game, Joseph's brothers were too much for him, and he was pulled over the line into Egypt. In the Bible, Joseph was taken away to Egypt and sold as a slave. He faced big problems. But he kept his trust in God to help with his problems. And we need to trust God with our problems, too.**

2. Low-Powered Game: Knock 'Em Down with Trust in God!

LOW-POWERED GAME NEEDS:

- Long tables (one per group)
- Softball or similar plastic or rubber ball (one per group)
- Plastic bottles, 16 oz– 1-liter size, labels removed (Five per *Veggie- Connections Group*)
- Markers
- Large adhesive labels

Have each *VeggieConnections Group* stand around three sides of a table. One player should stand at one short end of the table with the ball. The kids standing at the far end should set up five bottles for bowling and should be given markers and five labels. Have the *Veggie- Connections Shepherd* stand next to the bowler and offer advice as needed.

Before bowling, the Shepherds ask their groups: **How do you think Joseph felt about the problems he had with his brothers?** *(Angry, confused, hurt, afraid, surprised, disappointed.)* Say: **We have these feelings also when problems come to us.** The kids at the end of the table should write these feelings on each label. If more than five suggestions are made, they may write more than one feeling on the labels. They should attach the labels to the bottles and stand them up on the table across the end.

Say: **We can overcome some bad feelings we have when we have problems, just as Joseph did.** The first bowler should think of one way to handle negative feelings when faced with a problem or a way to build trust in God. The player can ask for help from one other player if he is having trouble coming up with an idea. After saying the suggestion, the player can roll the ball down the table to try to knock over the bottles. You may give each player two chances to roll if he doesn't knock down all the bottles on the first try (but he only needs to give one suggestion).

Kids should then rotate one space, moving another player to the bowling position. The new kids on the end should set up the bottles again. Continue play until all group members have had at least one chance to bowl.

3. Craft: Trust in God Problem Catcher

CRAFT NEEDS:

- Small paper plates
- Scissors
- Hole punch
- Yarn or string
- Beads with large holes
- Feathers
- Twigs
- Transparent tape
- Paper cut into 8½" x 1" strips
- Pencils or pens

Show the kids a completed sample of the craft and explain that this "net" or "web" can remind them that their problems can be "caught" when they pray and ask God's help. Then lead the children through these directions:

Cut out the center of the paper plate to make a ring. Punch holes around the ring, at least eight holes. Weave yarn through the holes, crossing back and forth from one side of the plate to another, until yarn has been looped at least once through every hole. The kids do not have to string the yarn in any particular order. While weaving, beads can be added. Tie the end of the yarn to a hole anywhere on the ring.

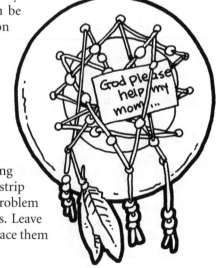

Tie additional small pieces of yarn as desired on the yarns already woven so that they hang down decoratively. Beads, feathers, and small twigs can be tied to these bits of yarn. A small strip of tape can be added to hold items in place. Tie three feathers and beads to the bottom of the ring to hang below the ring.

On a strip of paper, write a brief prayer, asking God to help you with a problem. Weave the strip through some yarns. Say that kids can use this problem catcher to talk to God by writing him prayer notes. Leave the notes up until the prayers are answered, and replace them with notes of thanks as they are answered.

PART THREE:

Plugging In to My Life

Life application of the lesson to lead kids to THINK–LINK–ACT and build a relationship with God every day

A. Cucumber Connection

Before kids arrive, enlarge and copy the pickles from the *VeggieConnections Shepherd* pages on the CD-ROM included in the *VeggieConnections Elementary Curriculum Kit* onto green construction paper. Cut them out and put them in a pickle jar.

Let a volunteer draw a pickle from the Pickle Pot and either the child or a Shepherd should read the dilemma out loud. Each Shepherd should then process the question with their group using the THINK—LINK—ACT phrase.

Erin doesn't usually do well on spelling tests. She studied hard and spelled every word correctly on last week's test. The kid who sits by Erin told the teacher she cheated. What should Erin do?	Joey has a baseball card collection, and his grandpa just gave him a Mickey Mantle card that he had when he was a little boy. His friend Max brought his cards over so that they could compare cards. A couple of days later, Joey noticed that his Mickey Mantle card was missing. What should he do?	Tonight Sandra's teacher gave homework in two subjects, plus she has a dentist appointment after school, then she's supposed to go to a play practice at church, and practice piano at home, and her mom told her she'd have to run some errands with her because she can't stay home alone. Sondra can't handle how big the problem of time has gotten. What can she do?

B. Kid Connection: Big Pockets

Give each child his or her Big Pocket from last week. Provide seven construction-paper strips in a variety of colors. Say: **When Jacob gave Joseph the colorful coat, Joseph's brothers were jealous, and that just added to the bad feelings Joseph's brothers had for him. Joseph's problems really only began when his brother sold him as a slave. We're going to make colorful flip reminders that God will help us with our problems.**

Give kids markers and have them write one word per strip of paper, writing their name first, then "will," "trust," "God," "with," "my," "problems." Then have kids stack the cards in statement order, with their name on top. Have *VeggieConnections Shepherds* help kids use a hole punch to put holes in the two upper corners of their strips, about 1/2" inside both strip edges. Then give kids short lengths of yarn and have them tie a loose loop through the holes in the paper strips. Kids can help each other tie the yarn by inserting two fingers in the loop and tying the yarn snug, then having the child remove his or her fingers.

Have kids all stand and read their flip books in unison. Then have kids put their books in their big pockets and collect them for next week. Then lead kids in singing the *THINK—LINK—ACT* song using motions.

Ask the kids to THINK. **Think about problems you need help with.** Then LINK. **Link to Joseph, who trusted God even when his brothers gave him problems.** Discuss ACT. **Trust God to help you with your problems. What can you do to trust God this week?** *(I can talk my problems over with God or with adults who love God. I can look for the help God sends to me.)*

C. Christ Connection

Help the kids practice the Unit Memory Verse, Romans 15:13, by saying it for them and pausing at various points to let the kids fill in the next word. Do this a few times. Then see how much of the verse the kids can say with you by memory.

Remind the children that God is able to help them with their problems—big or small. Start a prayer and encourage the kids to finish it in their own words as they pray in their hearts to God. **Dear God, thank you for helping us with our problems. We know we can trust you. God, please help me with . . .** Pause to let kids pray. **Thank you for hearing our prayers and caring about us. In Jesus' name, amen.**

Distribute the take-home newspaper, *VeggieConnections*.

CUCUMBER CONNECTION NEEDS:

- Pickle jar
- Pickle artwork from the *VeggieConnections Shepherd* pages (on the *VeggieConnections* CD-ROM)
- Green construction paper

KID CONNECTION NEEDS:

- Big Pockets (made in *Lesson 1*)
- Strips of construction paper
- Small bouncing balls
- Black felt-tipped markers
- *VeggieConnections Music CD*
- CD player

BEFORE YOU START:
Cut 2" strips of construction paper from a variety of colors. You can get six strips from each sheet (using 9" x 12" size). Each child will need seven strips in various colors.

CHRIST CONNECTION NEEDS:

- *VeggieConnections* take-home newspaper (one per child)

Sold as a slave.

Punished for
doing the
right thing.

Spent years in prison
but didn't
commit a crime.

Didn't get helped
by a friend.

Faced an
all-powerful king.

Had to run
a country.

Needed to forgive
mean brothers.

Had to convince
his brothers.

Connecting to **Trust** with life examples from **Joseph**
Joseph is tempted to do wrong: **Genesis 39:1–20a**

Connection Word:

temptation

PART ONE:

Plugging In at Dodgeball City

Introduction to the site and lesson focus

LESSON 3:
I will show my trust in God by obeying him.

A. Veggie Connection

BEFORE YOU START:
Punch holes in each upper corner of the sandwich or snack bags for each child. Cut 2' lengths of yarn for each child. Separate candy into types (chocolate, hard, fruity, tart, and so on) and put each type in a basket. Set them on a table in the front of the porch, along with the bags and yarn. Cover with a tablecloth.

Dressed as Deputy Dodge, welcome the kids back to Dodgeball City. **Howdy, y'all! Why, it's so good to see you'uns that I'm jist happier than a pig takin' a mud bath! That's right! I got somethin' excitin' to give y'all!**

Uncover your treats and have kids choose their favorite treat, but tell them they can't open or eat it yet. Also give them a plastic sandwich bag and a piece of yarn. Have kids divide into their *VeggieConnections Groups* and have kids tie the ends of their yarn to their bags. Have *VeggieConnections Shepherds* help the younger children. Then have kids put their candy in the bag and put the bag around their neck.

I'm guessin' y'all are pleased as a prickled cactus to have the candy. But lemme ask y'all—Do you want to *eat* your piece of candy? Who *really* wants to eat their candy? Have a few kids respond. Then remind kids they still can't eat their candy. **Y'all *not* being able to eat yur candy helps you understand today's Connection Word.**

Lead the group in reciting the Dodgeball Dictionary Rhyme, urging the kids to use their best Western accent:

**Look it up, hook it up, what's it all about?
Look it up, hook it up, let's find out!**

Let a volunteer look up *temptation* in the dictionary and read the definition aloud. Write *temptation* on the "Special of the Day" board. **Sum of y'all are being *tempted* right now to eat the candy hangin' 'round your necks. It's not that big of a temptation. But you and I do face bigger temptations, don't we? What are some of those prickly ol' temptations that kids sometimes find themselves facing?** Let volunteers name temptations or give brief examples. **In jus a few minutes we're going to see how Joseph faced a big-time temptation and see how he trusted God during it.**

Allow kids to eat their candy.

Well, that gits us off to a howdy-do start here in Dodgeball City today. But before we take another step, we ought'er stop and pray!

THE CHILDREN
will arrive with their *Veggie-Connections Shepherds* from the opening Countertop Connections featuring Bob and Larry. Play the *Veggie-Connections Music CD* as children enter Dodgeball City.

VEGGIE CONNECTION NEEDS:
- VeggieConnections Music CD
- CD player
- Hole punch
- Plastic sandwich or snack bags (one per child)
- Yarn (2' piece per child)
- Scissors
- Fun-sized assortment of candy (Check with parents about food allergies.)
- Baskets
- Table and tablecloth
- *VeggieConnections Bible Dictionary*

VeggieConnections | **229**

B. Prayer Connection

PRAYER CONNECTION NEEDS:

• Prayer Cacti
(from *Lesson 1*)

Have each *VeggieConnections Group* gather by their Prayer Cactus. Today ask the kids to speak to God silently in their hearts. Have the *VeggieConnections Shepherds* lead the prayer time for their groups, using a prayer like this, pausing to let the kids think or whisper their prayers.

Dear Lord, thank you for loving us so much. Thanks, too, for these people and things . . . Pause to let kids pray. **And God, you know that I want to trust you. Sometimes it's hard to trust you and obey what I know is right. Please help me to do what's right when these kinds of things happen . . .** Pause to let kids pray. **We love you, Lord. In Jesus' name, amen.**

PART TWO:

Plugging In to God's Word

Connecting to God's Word in the Bible and understanding how that can help us to have a better relationship with him

A. God Connection: Joseph is tempted to do wrong – Genesis 39:1-20a

GOD CONNECTION NEEDS:

• Cowbell
• Bible
• Bag of 10 dodge balls

Use the cowbell to invite the kids to gather around the porch. Keep the bag of dodge balls near your chair. Open your Bible and show the kids where today's story is found, Genesis 39. Ask volunteers to tell what happened to Joseph in last week's Bible story. *(He was sold by his jealous brothers to traders who took him to Egypt and sold him as a slave.)* Say: **I will tell you today's Bible story two times. The first time, you will listen very carefully. Then the second time, I'll give you instructions for something fun you can do.** Tell the story once, and then add the actions with dodge balls.

Joseph was sold as a slave to an important officer of the king of Egypt. The officer, named Potiphar, saw that Joseph was smart and likable, so he gave him work inside the rich, beautiful place where Potiphar lived with his wife and many servants. Joseph always trusted and obeyed God, and God was with him and helped him in everything. Potiphar liked Joseph's work so much that he put Joseph in charge of the whole household! But that's when Joseph's troubles began.

I'm going to continue with the story of Joseph, and whenever I tell about a temptation Joseph needed to dodge, I'm going to toss a dodge ball into where you're sitting. You need to lean away and dodge it! Just let it bounce on the floor and don't touch that temptation.

One day, Potiphar's wife tried to trick Joseph. She wanted him to do something that he shouldn't do. But it was probably very tempting! Toss a dodge ball into the group of children. **That's right, Joseph was tempted, but he dodged that temptation. He showed his trust in God by obeying him, and he said no to Potiphar's wife.**

She was upset, but she didn't give up. The next day, she said to Joseph again, "Come, do this wrong thing. It'll be fun!" Toss another dodge ball into the group, and pause while it bounces to a stop. **But Joseph said, "No, it's wrong. I choose to obey God."**

Potiphar's wife tried again the next day. "Come on! No one will know!" Toss another dodge ball. **But Joseph said, "No! Your husband has trusted me."**

The next day Potiphar's wife tried again. Toss another ball. **Again, Joseph said no.**

The day after that Potiphar's wife tried again. Toss another ball. **Again, Joseph said no.**

The next day Potiphar's wife tried again. Toss another ball. **Again, Joseph said no.**

The day after that Potiphar's wife tried again. Toss another ball. **Again, Joseph said no.**

Finally, one day when no one else was around, not even a servant, Potiphar's wife found Joseph, and she tried to force him to do the wrong thing. Toss another ball. **She grabbed him by the arm and pulled him along!** Toss another ball. **She even pulled off his coat.** Toss the last dodge ball. **But Joseph broke free and went running—out the door without his coat. He was determined to obey God!**

You'd think this would turn out good, with Joseph obeying God and dodging all those temptations. But when Potiphar came home that day, his wife decided to get even with Joseph. She told a big lie. She told her husband that Joseph did the wrong thing after all. She said she caught him, and he was so scared he ran off without his coat. And she held up Joseph's coat to prove it.

Potiphar was so mad that he threw Joseph into prison right away! Joseph didn't even get to tell his side of the story. But even in jail, Joseph showed his trust in God by obeying him.

Let each child who answers one of these questions bring a dodge ball back to the bag: **How did Joseph dodge temptation?** *(He said no over and over, he ran away.)* **Why did Joseph keep dodging temptation?** *(He trusted God and chose to obey him.)* **What are ways you can dodge temptation?** *(Saying no, walking away, not hanging out with people who tempt us to do wrong, not spending time around tempting things, praying for God to make us strong, and so on.)*

B. Activity Connection

Choose from the following activities to help kids explore and remember that they can show their trust in God by obeying him (approximately 10–15 minutes each).

1. High-Powered Game: Temptation Stomp!

Have kids divide into their *VeggieConnections Groups*. Have kids remove their shoes. Give children balloons and have them inflate them and tie them off. Have *VeggieConnections Shepherds* assist younger children. Have Shepherds prompt kids to discuss some temptations they may be facing or general struggles kids face. Give kids markers and have them write a temptation on their balloon.

Have kids move into a central area to play the game. Provide yarn, and have kids tie one end of the yarn securely around the knot in their balloon and tie the other end around their ankles. **When Joseph was tempted by Potiphar's wife, he told her he couldn't sin against God. He chose to stomp out that temptation. In this game, you get to stomp out the temptations written on the balloons. Everyone plays until the last temptation is stomped out (balloons broken). You can't touch anyone during the game; only use your feet to try to stomp another player's balloon.**

Play until everyone's balloon is stomped out. Then have Shepherds cut off the yarn holding the broken balloons. Have kids each give their balloon to another person, saying "God will help you stomp out temptation!"

Just as you helped each other stomp out your balloon temptations, you can help each other stomp out temptation in real life. Keep your balloon as a reminder to help yourself and your friends overcome temptation.

Have kids put their shoes back on before the next activity.

HIGH-POWERED GAME NEEDS:

- Balloons (one per child)
- Yarn (3' pieces per child)
- Black permanent markers
- Scissors

2. Low-Powered Game: Temptation Helpers

LOW-POWERED GAME NEEDS:

- Cotton balls (about 25 per *VeggieConnections Group*)
- Bandanna blindfolds (one per group)

Divide kids into *VeggieConnections Groups* and have groups spread apart so there is about 10 or more feet between groups. If you don't have this much space, combine groups. Provide about 25 cotton balls per group. Have kids sit in a large circle (about 10 feet) equally spaced around the circle. This is the playing area. Have kids in each group brainstorm some common temptations. (*Lying, cheating, stealing, name calling, swearing, hitting or fighting others, cutting in line, disobeying parents.*) After each temptation is listed, have that child toss the cotton ball into the middle of the playing area. Fill the playing area with as many temptations as can be named. Then have *VeggieConnections Shepherds* scatter any remaining cotton balls, saying there are probably at least as many temptations that are unnamed as the ones kids have named.

Temptations are all around us. And if we're honest, we would say that we are often tempted by friends. In this game, each person is going to go out into the world (indicate playing area), **and the rest of us are going to try to help the player avoid temptation. Each player will be blindfolded, and they will very carefully move through the playing field by listening to the advice to help avoid the temptations. Just like in real life, it will be impossible to avoid all the temptations, but we'll see who can be tempted the least by touching the fewest cotton balls.**

Blindfold the first player and have him or her enter the playing field on hands and knees. Keep track of how many cotton balls player touch with their hands only (knees don't count). Allow each player to play about two minutes.

After everyone has played, announce the winning player. Remind kids that to be winners in real life, they can choose friends who will help them avoid temptation and to trust God.

3. Craft: Trust Bandanna

BEFORE YOU START:

Make copies of the Trust Bandanna Pattern (page 234) for each child. Cut the pattern out. Fold bandannas in half, making a triangle. Lay the bandanna on a flat surface, with the folded edge facing away from you. Place the pattern on top of the cloth, lining up the V pattern with the triangle edge of the fabric. Lift the top layer of the triangle-shaped fabric slightly and staple the pattern to the bandanna, where indicated on the pattern. For younger kids, you may want to make the cuts yourself or allow *VeggieConnections Shepherds* to do so during the craft time. If you make the cuts, remove the patterns from the bandannas.

CRAFT NEEDS:

- Trust Bandanna Pattern on page 234
- Stapler
- One bandanna per child
- Scissors to cut fabric
- Staple removers
- Large alphabet beads, can be substituted with plain beads with letters written on them; the beads will spell "I will trust"

Tell the children that they are going to make beaded, bandanna kerchiefs to wear to remind them to trust in God. Pass out bandannas with patterns attached for those needing cuts to each child. Show kids how to carefully cut along the patterns. Then use a staple remover to remove the pattern from the bandanna. Have *VeggieConnections Shepherds* handle the scissors for the younger kids. Place beads on each table. Instruct the children to find the beads that spell "I will trust." Have them thread "I will" on the left side, one bead through each of the five fabric strips that are cut. Have kids refer to the pattern to assist with the bead locations if needed. After each bead is threaded on, tie a knot underneath it to hold it in place. Thread the word "trust" on the right side, and knot below each bead.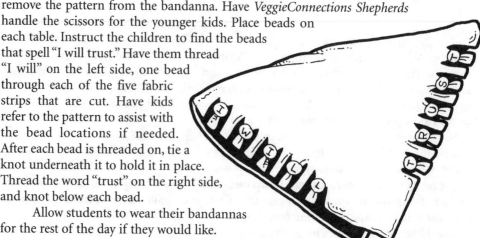

Allow students to wear their bandannas for the rest of the day if they would like.

PART THREE:

Plugging In to My Life

Life application of the lesson to lead kids to THINK–LINK–ACT and build a relationship with God every day

A. Cucumber Connection

Before kids arrive, enlarge and copy the pickles from the *VeggieConnections Shepherd* pages on the CD-ROM included in the *VeggieConnections Elementary Curriculum Kit* onto green construction paper. Cut them out and put them in a pickle jar.

Let a volunteer draw a pickle from the Pickle Pot and either the child or a Shepherd should read the dilemma out loud. Each Shepherd should then process the question with their group using the THINK—LINK—ACT phrase.

Benjamin is at a sleepover with his friends. They rented a movie that Benjamin knows his dad would not allow him to see. But he'd like to watch it anyway. What should Benjamin do?	Jennifer begged her mother to let her take piano lessons. She has taken lessons for six months and doesn't like to practice every day. Jennifer wants to quit, but her mom says she has to stick with the lessons for at least one year.	At school, Collin has a coat hook next to Ian. Ian is always mean to Collin and sometimes knocks Collin's coat on the floor. Collin is tempted to knock Ian's coat on the floor when he isn't around. What should he do?

CUCUMBER CONNECTION NEEDS:
- Pickle jar
- Pickle artwork from the *VeggieConnections Shepherd* pages (on the *VeggieConnections* CD-ROM)
- Green construction paper

B. Kid Connection: Big Pockets

Prior to class, write on one side of tennis balls: "How do you 'dodge' temptation?" Give each child a tennis ball and ask him or her to write on one side of the ball under your question: "I will obey God." Say: **When Joseph was faced with temptations, he refused by choosing to obey God. Let's make a commitment to refuse temptation like Joseph did.**

Give each child his or her Big Pocket from last week. Have kids place their Dodge Temptation balls in their Big Pockets. Collect the pockets for next week's lesson.

Have kids stand and lead them in singing the *THINK—LINK—ACT* song using motions. Ask the kids to do the THINK motion. **Think about times you're tempted to disobey.** Do the LINK motion. **Link to Joseph, who obeyed God when he faced temptation.** Do the ACT motion. **Show your trust in God by obeying him. How can you do that this week?** (*I can obey my parents and teachers as God would want. I can dodge temptation. I can trust in God when it is hard to be obedient.*)

KID CONNECTION NEEDS:
- Big Pockets (made in *Lesson 1*)
- Tennis balls
- Black felt-tipped markers
- *VeggieConnections* Music CD
- CD player

C. Christ Connection

To encourage kids to run from temptations, practice the Unit Memory Verse, Romans 15:13, by running in place. Kids will practice saying the verse together while running. Have kids keep saying the verse until they can say it right. If kids get tired of running, point out it's hard work to run from temptation, but it must be done.

Have the kids form a circle and link arms for prayer. Begin a prayer, and let the kids go around the circle, each praying one word to add to the prayer: **Dear God, thank you for coming near to us. We want to do our best to come near to you and to obey you. We choose to trust you this week because you are . . .** Kids may say words or names of praise, such as *loving, great, our Friend,* and so on.

Distribute the take-home newspaper, ***VeggieConnections***.

CHRIST CONNECTION NEEDS:
- *VeggieConnections* take-home newspaper (one per child)

Lesson 3 - Trust Bandanna Pattern

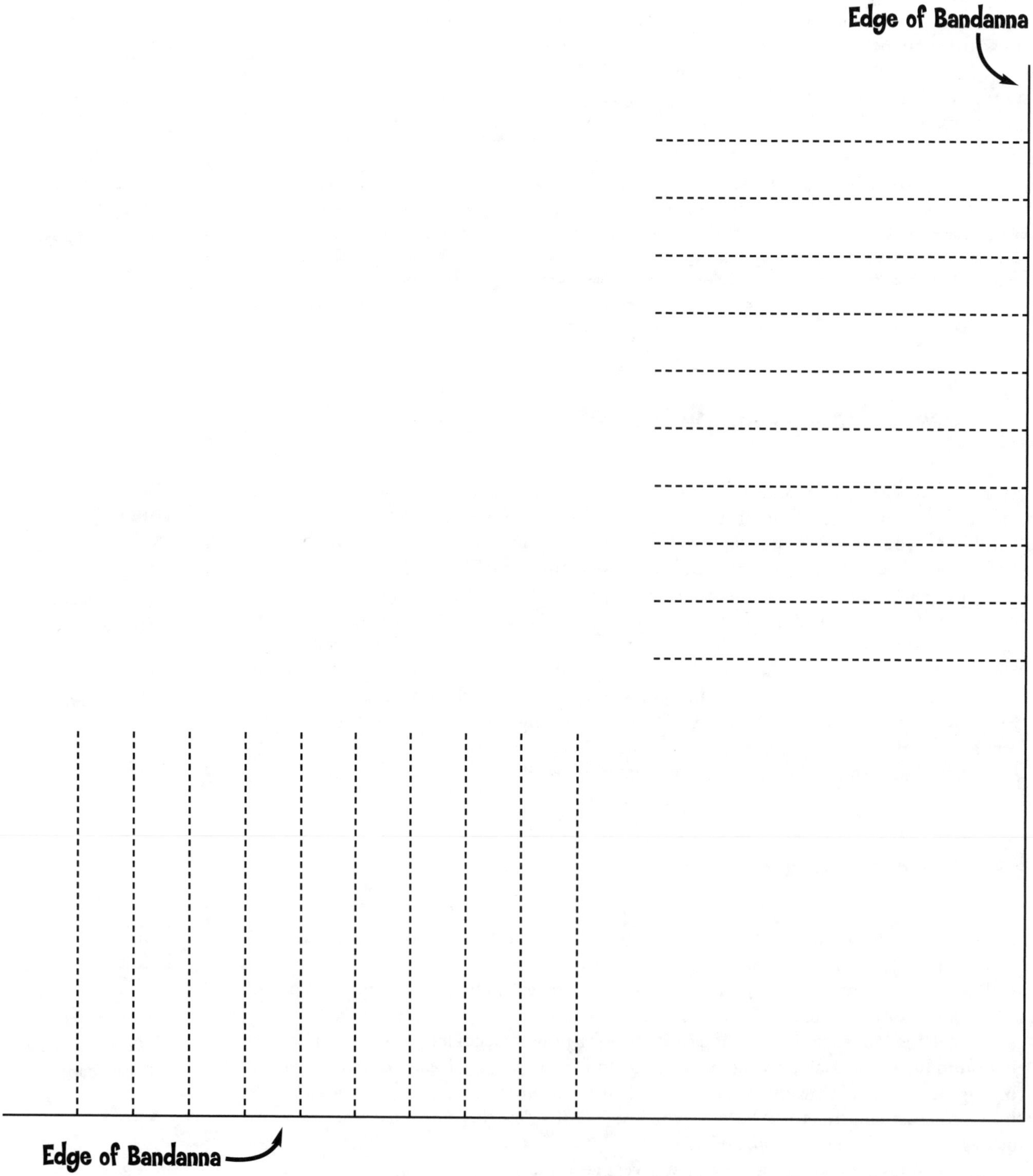
Edge of Bandanna
Edge of Bandanna

Connecting to **Trust** with life examples from **Joseph**
Joseph in prison: **Genesis 39:20b-23**

attitude

PART ONE:

**Plugging In
at Dodgeball City**

Introduction to the site
and lesson focus

LESSON 4:
I will trust God is with me in hard times.

A. Veggie Connection

BEFORE YOU START:

If your site setup does not include a life-sized "Larry-shaped" cactus, make one for this activity: From a large piece of cardboard box or sides of cardboard boxes taped together, make a 4' tall cucumber shape. You could also use foamboard. Apply green tempera paint or glue on green paper. From green, black, and white construction paper, cut out eyes, a nose, and mouth with a tooth in it for Larry. Place one eye and the nose in one area of the site and place the other eye and mouth in another place. You want the two places to be pretty far apart from each other. Recruit two Shepherds to role-play your helpers, each with different attitudes. One should be very positive, and the other should grumble and whine while both help you finish decorating Larry. Show them where their face pieces are and go over the role-play.

THE CHILDREN
will arrive with their *Veggie-Connections Shepherds* from the opening Countertop Connections featuring Bob and Larry. Play the *Veggie-Connections Music CD* as children enter Dodgeball City.

Dressed as Deputy Dodge, warmly greet the kids as they enter Dodgeball City. Gather the kids around the prepared "cactus." Say: **You know, I ben a' thinkin' that this here cactus looks familiar. I'm a'thinking he looks a mite like, well, like our ol' friend Larry the Cucumber! But he's missin' his face, so I was a workin' on that but did't get 'er done. So I got sum helpers.**

Bring out the *VeggieConnections Shepherds* recruited earlier. Walk around and scratch your head and tell the kids you put Larry's face somewhere but forgot where. Have the two Shepherds each go to where their face parts are and bring them to you, each displaying their good or bad attitudes in the process. Take one piece at a time, allowing for some banter between your helpers, to emphasize either the good or bad attitude.

After Larry has a face, have the two helpers comment on how Larry looks. Have the positive helper praise the look of Larry first. Then have the negative helper say something like "Larry is a cucumber—this just looks like a cactus with a face," while shaking his head.

Finally, with a frustrated look on your face, comment about the attitudes of the two helpers by briefly reviewing the attitudes each had during the role-play. **Did y'all notice how one of my helpers was helpful and excited and said nice things about my Larry cactus? And how different my other helper was, complain' and fussin' and sayin' not-too-nice things about ol' Larry here?**

Have both helpers smile and have the "negative" helper apologize and say nice things about Larry. **Now I played a little trick on y'all. I asked each helper to have different attitudes when they helped me.** Point to "positive" person. **I asked this har person to have a real**

VEGGIE CONNECTION NEEDS:

- *VeggieConnections Music CD*
- CD player
- 4'x 1' heavy cardboard or foamboard piece
- Green tempera paint or paper
- Construction paper in green, black, white
- Packing tape
- Glue
- *VeggieConnections Bible Dictionary*

good attitude and this one (point to "negative" person) **to have a real sorry attitude with the fussin' and all. I did this to show you what** *attitude* **looks like. That's our Connection Word for today.** Lead the group in reciting the Dodgeball Dictionary Rhyme, urging the kids to use their best cowpoke accent.

> **Look it up, hook it up, what's it all about?**
> **Look it up, hook it up, let's find out!**

Ask a volunteer to look up *attitude* in the *VeggieConnections Bible Dictionary* and read the definition aloud. Write *attitude* on the "Special of the Day" board. **Today we're going to see what kind of attitudes Joseph had when he faced some hard times.**

B. Prayer Connection

Have each *VeggieConnections Group* gather near their Prayer Cactus. This week, ask the kids to talk about hard times and let volunteers share any specific hard time they might be facing. Others may want to share a hard time they or their family have come through and tell what helped them. Have kids write down these prayers if they wish and stick them to the cactus. Then have the kids hold hands and take turns praying sentence prayers for themselves or another child. They may pray around the circle and squeeze the hand of the person next to them when they are done. Ask *VeggieConnections Shepherds* to be sure to pray for any child who wasn't mentioned aloud.

PRAYER CONNECTION NEEDS:

- Prayer Cacti (from *Lesson 1*)
- Green slips of paper
- Pencils

PART TWO:

Plugging In to God's Word

Connecting to God's Word in the Bible and understanding how that can help us to have a better relationship with him

A. God Connection: Joseph in prison – Genesis 39:20b-23

GOD CONNECTION NEEDS:

- Bible
- Sheriff badge or big star sticker
- Ring of keys

Invite the kids to help you tell today's Bible story by gathering in and around the town jail. Show the kids in a Bible that today's story comes from Genesis 39. Say: **I will tell you the Bible story two times. The first time, you will listen very carefully. Then the second time, I'll give you instructions for something fun you can do.** Read the story one time, and then have the children role-play with you when you read it again. Choose one child to be the warden and wear the badge/star, and choose another child to be Joseph. Explain that all the rest of the kids are prisoners in jail with Joseph and you will give them hints about how to act. Have Joseph and the warden stand away from the jail.

Say: **Now you heard what happened to Joseph last week. What happened?** Let volunteers explain that the officer's wife wanted Joseph to do something wrong, but when he refused, she lied about him and he got sent to jail. **Look! Here comes Joseph now!**

Tell the warden to lead Joseph over to the jail and put him with the other kids. The warden stands with his arms crossed, watching over the prisoners. The prisoners may pretend to do hard work, such as hammering rocks. **Being in prison wasn't a picnic—not even for the warden. He not only had lots of jobs. He had to keep all the prisoners locked up.** Have the warden jingle a ring of keys. **He had to bring the prisoners their food.** Pause to let the warden pretend to hurriedly bring food to serveral kids. **The warden had to help the prisoners when they were sick.** Indicate several kids to pretend to be sick and lie down; the warden rushes from one to another to pretend to give bandages and medicine. **And the warden had to solve any arguments.** Indicate a few different pairs of kids to pretend to argue; the warden frantically tries to calm them down. **He had to keep track of which prisoners were there and why.** Have the warden pretend to write things down on a list on his hand. **And he had to do all these things at the same time.** Let the warden try to do several of these things in succession.

You can see that it was a very hard job! Back then, the warden was allowed to use the good and smart prisoners to help him. They had to be trustworthy and dependable. They had to have a good attitude. So the warden kept an eye out for good prisoners. The warden may walk around looking at prisoners. Indicate that Joseph should get on his knees and pray.

The warden saw that Joseph was different. His good attitude showed. He could have been grumpy about being in jail. But Joseph trusted that God was with him during this hard time.

It was clear that Joseph loved God and obeyed him. Joseph didn't get into fights with the other prisoners. He helped the others without even being asked. So the warden asked Joseph to help with some of his work. Have the warden give Joseph a pat on the back; then Joseph may pretend to serve food to prisoners along with the warden.

Joseph kept trusting that God was with him. He kept a good attitude as he helped the warden. Joseph did such a great job, the warden gave him more important jobs. Indicate a pair of kids to "argue." Have the warden point Joseph to go over to them. Joseph goes over and calms them down.

Joseph kept trusting God and obeying him. God made Joseph smart and likable. Pretty soon, the warden put Joseph in charge of nearly everything! Have the warden sit off to the side and put his/her feet up as if resting. Joseph pretends to keep the counts, help the sick, and so on, but without being frantic. The prisoners all cooperate.

The Lord was with Joseph and gave him success in whatever he did. Even though Joseph was well liked, he was still in prison and it was still a hard time. But Joseph continued to trust in God.

Thank the kids for helping you tell the Bible story. Ask Joseph and the warden to sit with the group, and discuss these questions: **What kind of attitude did Joseph have?** *(He kept a good attitude even though he was in prison because he trusted God.)* **What did Joseph do?** *(He showed his trust in God by obeying him; he helped the prison warden.)* **How can we show our trust in God during hard times?** *(By remembering he is with us, by obeying him, by keeping a good attitude, and so on.)*

B. Activity Connection

Choose from the following activities to help kids explore and remember that they can trust that God is with them in hard times (approximately 10–15 minutes each).

1. High-Powered Game: Catch that Attitude

Have the kids sit in a circle facing each other. Each child will have a bandanna lightly tucked into their back pocket or their collar. Tell the kids in the circle they represent the prisoners that were in jail with Joseph. Choose one child to represent Joseph.

Say: **We all have to go through hard times. But we know that God is with us no matter what we go through. In our game, Joseph has the right attitude and if he comes by and grabs your bandanna, he wants you to "catch" his attitude. You must run around the circle in the opposite direction that Joseph runs. Whoever gets back to your spot first keeps the spot, and the new person gets to be Joseph.** If Joseph doesn't get back to the spot after two tries, he or she gets to pick a new Joseph.

As an option, explain that to make the game harder (just like things seemed to keep getting harder for Joseph) this time when Joseph grabs a bandanna, they must both go around the circle backward, or on their hands and knees, or some other way.

Spend a little time talking about a time when things seemed to keep getting worse for the kids or talk about someone they know who always seem to have the right attitude, even in hard times.

HIGH-POWERED GAME NEEDS:

- Bandannas (one per child)

2. Low-Powered Game: Finding the Right Attitude

LOW-POWERED GAME NEEDS:

- Attitude Words from page 240
- Watch with second hand
- Tape

BEFORE YOU START:

Make two or three copies (depending on the size of your group) of the Attitude Words (p. 240) and cut the words apart, separating the positive and negative words. You'll want to scatter the negative words out in your area, making them easy to find, such as on the floor near chairs or along walls. For the positive words, hide them in more difficult places, like taping under chairs or tables, taping in the site setup areas, and even on your hat!

Say: **Just like in the Old West, people would go searching for gold, we're going to look for another kind of treasure. All around the room little pieces of paper are hidden. Your job is to find them. But you only have one minute.**

Divide the kids into two teams and give them one minute to find the slips. At one minute, call time and have teams join you. Have kids look at their slips. Ask for volunteers to read some of the slips. Most likely, there will be more negative comments. **You didn't have a lot of time to find the paper slips. But what you did find pretty easily were the negative words. How is it easy to have negative attitudes in real life?** Allow responses.

Have kids leave their paper slips before having teams find the remaining paper slips without timing them. Give hints to help kids find them if needed. When the slips are found, have teams join you in the same places they were previously. Have teams count up their *positive* slip total from both rounds. Announce a winner, but tell them they'll get their reward later.

Ask for volunteers to read the slips from each team. Kids should be reading mostly positive words. **It took a little longer to find the positive words. Just like it is easy to quickly find a negative attitude, finding a positive attitudes may take more time, especially when things are hard. Even though Joseph was unfairly put in jail, he chose to have a positive attitude, and things went well for him.**

Encourage kids to keep one or two of the positive attitudes as a reminder and have the winning team collect their reward by gathering all the negative papers and throwing them away (without complaining!).

3. Craft: Good Attitude Flyers

CRAFT NEEDS:

- White paper plates (one per child)
- Feathers
- Glue
- White plastic spoons (two per child)
- Rubber bands
- Duct tape
- Fine-tipped permanent markers
- Scissors

Joseph had a positive attitude and trusted God was with him, even when he was wrongly put in jail. When someone has a good attitude, he may feel like he can "fly" above his problems. These flying birds will help you to remember to have good attitudes when you face hard times, just like Joseph did.

Cut paper plates in half. Also cut one half again for the tail section and set aside. Distribute a paper plate half to each child. Have the kids glue feathers onto one side of their plates. Cut another paper plate in fourths, and give

Give each child a tail-section piece. Show them how to attach the pointed end to the bird's body, forming a tail (see craft illustration).

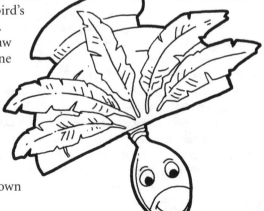

While the glue dries, have kids draw eyes and a beak on the rounded part of one of the spoons. Line up the two spoons together, with rounded edges on the outside, and use a rubber band to fasten the spoons together.

Duct tape the spoons to the bottom of the paper plate with the feathers and spoon face on top. The feathered friends are ready to soar and can be gently flown through the air.

PART THREE:

Plugging In to My Life

Life application of the lesson to lead kids to THINK–LINK–ACT and build a relationship with God every day

A. Cucumber Connection

CUCUMBER CONNECTION NEEDS:

- Pickle jar
- Pickle artwork from the *VeggieConnections Shepherd* pages (on the *VeggieConnections CD-ROM*)
- Green construction paper

Before kids arrive, enlarge and copy the pickles from the *VeggieConnections Shepherd* pages on the CD-ROM included in the *VeggieConnections Elementary Curriculum Kit* onto green construction paper. Cut them out and put them in a pickle jar.

Let a volunteer draw a pickle from the Pickle Pot and either the child or a Shepherd should read the dilemma out loud. Each Shepherd should then process the question with their group using the THINK—LINK—ACT phrase.

Clint's mom just registered him for school, and he found out that he got the strictest teacher in the school. Clint wants his mom to go back and see if they can place him in another class. His mom won't do that, and Clint is upset. What should he do?	Austin has to live with his mom on school days and with his dad on weekends and days off. He can't join a team because he's not in the same place for enough days each week to make enough practices. He thinks it's not fair that he has to keep switching around. But his parents won't change the agreement. What can Austin do?	Samantha just moved in to a new house and she has to go to a new school. She is very shy and is afraid she will not make any new friends. She feels both afraid and mad. What should she do?

B. Kid Connection: Big Pockets

KID CONNECTION NEEDS:

- Big Pockets (made in *Lesson 1*)
- Small paper plates (one per child)
- Yellow paint
- Colored markers
- Raffia or hay
- Scissors
- Glue
- *VeggieConnections Music CD*
- CD player

Give each child his or her Big Pocket from last week and a paper plate. Say: **Joseph chose to trust God and face his hardship with a good attitude. Let's make a reminder for us to do the same.**

Give kids craft supplies and have them paint their paper plate yellow and create a happy face on their plates. On the back side, have kids write: "[Their name] will trust God with a good attitude."

While their plates are drying, have kids stand and sing the *THINK—LINK—ACT* song using motions. Ask the kids to do the THINK motion. **Think about times you need to trust God.** Do the LINK motion. **Link to Joseph, who trusted God was with him even when it was hard.** Do the ACT motion. **Trust that God is with you in hard times. What can you do to trust God this week?** (*I can pray when I'm worried about something or feel too weak to face it. I can look for ways God is with me.*)

Have kids put their plates inside their pockets and collect them for next week.

C. Christ Connection

CHRIST CONNECTION NEEDS:

- *VeggieConnections* take-home newspaper (one per child)

To practice the Unit Memory Verse, Romans 15:13, have the kids form circles with their *VeggieConnections Groups*. Have the kids within each group say the verse one word at a time, "passing" the verse around the circle.

While still in their *VeggieConnections Group* circles, have all the kids put one hand in the middle as if in a huddle. Encourage each child to say a sentence prayer. When finished, *VeggieConnections Shepherds* close by praying: **Father, help us to trust you in hard times.** Then the kids throw their hands in the air and shout: **Trust God!**

Distribute the take-home newspaper, ***VeggieConnections***.

Lesson 4 – Attitude Words

Positive Words:	Negative Words:
Having patience	Being impatient
Sharing with others	Being selfish
Saying kind words	Gossiping
Trying hard	Cheating
Not giving up	Giving up
Helping others	Making excuses
Being friendly	Arguing
Being self-confident	Putting yourself down
Being generous	Swearing
Being joyful	Being grumpy
Looking for good in situations	Seeing the bad in situations
Being a peacemaker	Showing uncontrolled anger
Showing self-control	Disobeying parents
Showing humility	Being prideful
Being thankful	Complaining
Forgiving others	Not forgiving others

Connecting to **Trust** with life examples from **Joseph**
Joseph and the cupbearer and baker:
Genesis 40:1-23

PART ONE:

Plugging In at Dodgeball City

Introduction to the site and lesson focus

LESSON 5:
I will trust God to give me courage.

A. Veggie Connection

Dressed as Deputy Dodge and using a "cowboy" accent, welcome the kids as they arrive at Dodgeball City. You may offer them a sip of root beer at the Rootin' Tootin' Pizza Place. Then gather the kids around you.

Boy howdy, what a week it was! I had the biggest adventure, and I'd like to tell y'all about it. Instruct the kids to imitate your actions as you tell the story.

A few days ago I heard that a little old lady from my church was stuck at home, sick in bed. Hold your head. **And I happen to know that her very fay-vor-rite food in the whole wide world is pizza from the Rootin' Tootin' Pizza Place.** Rub your tummy. **So I made her a promise I'd bring her one.** Cross your heart.

So yesterday morning I set out a' ridin' my old horse, Pepperoni—out across the desert. Slap hands on legs to make clip-clop sound. Continue motion until next action is given. **The wind was really a' blowin'.** Blow air between cupped hands held next to your mouth. **I thought I might just turn back then and there. But did I lose my courage?** All shout **NO!** and punch a fist in the air.

Pepperoni and I could hear a coyote howling nearby. Make coyote howl with hands cupped around mouth. **I thought again about taking that pizza back and eatin' it myself. But did I lose my courage?** All shout **NO!** and punch a fist in the air. **So we hurried on our way.** Slap hands quickly on legs.

After a while, Old Pepperoni was getting tired, so we slowed down. Slow down slapping motion. **It was a long trip and I almost fell asleep.** Snore. **Then suddenly I heard the noise of a rattlesnake with his old rattler a' goin'.** Snap fingers repeatedly. **I told Pepperoni to "giddy up!"** Slap hands quickly on legs. **I almost told him to giddy up going the other way so we could git on home. But did I lose my courage?** All shout **NO!** and punch a fist in the air.

We had just rounded a hill when I spotted a varmint behind a cactus—a pole cat with its tail straight up in the air! Hold nose. **Some of y'all city folk call that a skunk. Phew! That thing stank so bad it was all I could do to keep going! I asked myself, "Am I going to lose my courage?"** All shout **NO!** and punch a fist in the air while still holding your nose with the other hand.

The next thing I knew, there was the little old lady's house. Say: **Whoa** and pull up reins. **She was just as snug as a bug in a rug in her cozy little home. And it looked like she'd**

THE CHILDREN
will arrive with their *Veggie-Connections Shepherds* from the opening Countertop Connections featuring Bob and Larry. Play the *Veggie-Connections Music CD* as children enter Dodgeball City.

VEGGIE CONNECTION NEEDS:
- *VeggieConnections Music CD*
- CD player
- Root beer and mini paper cups (optional)
- *VeggieConnections Bible Dictionary*

had lots of visitors. Peer around with hand over eyes. **Boy howdy, her little house was over-flowin' with flowers and food. But not one sign of a good ol' Rootin' Tootin' pizza! This sweet little lady was so thankful—and hungry! She et that whole pizza!** With fingers make motion of mouth opening and closing.

Then I noticed it was gettin' near dark, and the desert ain't a safe place at night, what with all them wild critters an' all. So I hopped on old Pepperoni, and we raced back to Dodgeball City. Begin slapping hands on knees very rapidly. Quickly repeat each of the previous motions as named. **We raced past the pole cat** (hold nose), **around the rattlesnake** (snap fingers), **right next to the coyote** (howl), **and against the blowin' wind** (blow through cupped hands) **until we got right back here to the Rootin' Tootin' Pizza Place** (give legs a big slap). **Then I had me a root beer, and me and old Pepperoni took a nice, long nap.** Snore.

Now in that story I talked about losin' my "courage." What in the world is that? After the kids offer ideas, lead the group in reciting the Dodgeball Dictionary Rhyme, urging the kids to use their best Western accent:

> **Look it up, hook it up, what's it all about?**
> **Look it up, hook it up, let's find out!**

Let a volunteer look up *courage* and read the definition aloud. Let volunteers share times that kids might need courage. **Today were going to see how Joseph showed courage as he did some unusual things.**

B. Prayer Connection

PRAYER CONNECTION NEEDS:

- Prayer Cacti (from *Lesson 1*)
- Green slip of paper
- Pencils

Have each *VeggieConnections Group* gather around their Prayer Cactus. Give kids slips of paper and pencils. Have them write and stick prayers on the cactus. Then have the kids form a praise huddle. They stand in a tight circle. The *VeggieConnections Shepherd* begins a prayer starter: **Dear God, we are amazed by you! Today we praise you because you are . . .** Kids take turns saying a word they'd like to praise God for, such as *awesome, loving, powerful, listening,* and so on. On each praise, that child sticks his hand into the center of the circle. Once all the kids have both hands in the center, the Shepherd closes the prayer. On **Amen**, all the kids throw their hands up in the air.

PART TWO: Plugging In to God's Word

Connecting to God's Word in the Bible and understanding how that can help us to have a better relationship with him

A. God Connection: Joseph and the cupbearer and baker – Genesis 40:1-23

GOD CONNECTION NEEDS:

- Table
- Sheet
- Piece of colorful cloth
- Large set of keys on a key ring
- Paper or plastic crown
- Bed pillow
- Clear pitcher
- Bagged loaf of bread
- A "Badge of Courage" (made as a sample for the Craft)
- Birthday cupcake with candle (be sure to notify parents about possible food allergies)

BEFORE YOU START:
Make a copy of the Bible story and give to a *VeggieConnections Shepherd* recruited to help with the story. Place a table on its side next to the rocking chair, so kids can't see the Shepherd who will hold up the props while following a copy of the story. Place the props behind the table and cover with a sheet until needed.

Invite the children to gather around the porch (but behind the overturned table) as you tell the Bible story from the wooden chair. Each prop corresponds to a word in the story, all of which are underlined: <u>Joseph</u> = colored cloth; <u>prison</u> = keys; <u>king</u> = crown; <u>dream</u> = pillow; <u>cupbearer</u> = pitcher; <u>baker</u> = loaf of bread; <u>courage</u> = badge; <u>birthday</u> = cupcake with candle. Whenever you read that word, pause to allow the Shepherd to hold up the correct item for a few seconds.

Show the kids in a Bible where today's story is found, Genesis 40. Say: **Last time we talked about how** Joseph **was thrown in** prison **for not doing anything wrong! Some other important people got thrown into** prison**, too. They held important jobs for the Egyptian** king**. One was his chief** baker **who cooked all the** king**'s food. The other person was a** cupbearer**. He had to taste the food and drink for the** king**, to make sure his food was safe. And the only reason the** baker **and** cupbearer **got thrown into** prison **is that the** king **of Egypt got mad at them! While they were there, they got to know** Joseph**.**

One night the baker **and the** cupbearer **each had a** dream**. The next morning,** Joseph **saw that they both were sad and asked, "What's wrong?" They told** Joseph **they were upset by their** dreams**.**

Now in some times and places, people believed that dreams **had meanings. God sometimes spoke to people in the Bible through** dreams**. This was one of those times.**

The men said to Joseph**, "We want someone to tell us what our** dreams **mean."**

Now Joseph **knew that God allowed him to explain the meaning of their** dreams**, but what if the** baker **or** cupbearer **didn't like the meaning of the** dreams**?** Joseph **had to trust God to give him** courage**.**

So Joseph **told them, "All wise things like that belong to God. Only he knows the meaning of your** dreams**. But he will tell me what your** dreams **mean, then I will tell you."**

The cupbearer **agreed and told** Joseph**, "My** dream **had a grapevine with three branches on it. They began to blossom, and soon there were clusters of ripe grapes. I squeezed the juice from the grapes into the** king**'s cup and gave it to him to drink."**

God gave Joseph **the meaning of the** dream**. He said, "The three branches mean that in three days you'll be with the** king **again. Handing him the cup means he is going to give you your** cupbearer **job back!" The** cupbearer **was so happy. But** Joseph **added, "Please, when you're with the** king **again, ask him to help me. I shouldn't be in this** prison**. I shouldn't even be in this country!" The** cupbearer **promised to remember** Joseph**.**

When the baker **heard the good news of the** cupbearer**'s** dream**, he told his** dream **to** Joseph**, too. He said, "My** dream **had three baskets of bread. They were stacked up on my head and birds were eating out of them."**

This time Joseph **knew he needed to trust God for** courage**, because he had bad news for the** baker**. "You will also meet with the** king **in three days,"** Joseph **explained. "But the birds taking the bread away means you will be taken away from the** king**."**

Now, three days later was the king**'s** birthday**. He threw a big** birthday **party. He sent for the** cupbearer **and the** baker **from** prison**. Everything happened just as** Joseph **said. The** baker **was taken away, and the** cupbearer **got his job back.**

After the birthday **party, the** cupbearer **forgot all about** Joseph**. So he didn't ask the** king **to help him. But** Joseph**'s trust in God gave him** courage**.**

Have the Shepherd come out from behind the table.

We all have times when we need courage. We face hard things or scary things. We can pray for help, and God will help us. He doesn't always take away what's going wrong. But our trust in him will give us courage we need to get through it.

Have kids divide into *VeggieConnections Groups* and have them discuss these questions: **How did Joseph get his courage to help these men?** *(He trusted God.)* **What kinds of things do kids face that take courage?** *(Being alone during a scary event, parents' divorce, move to a new town, a relative who is very sick or dying, a lost pet, and so on.)*

B. Activity Connection

Choose from the following activities to help kids explore and remember that they can trust God to give them courage (approximately 10–15 minutes each).

1. High-Powered Game: Courage to Face the Challenge

**HIGH-POWERED
GAME NEEDS:**

- Plastic hoops
  (at least eight)
- Watches with second
  hand (one per Shepherd)

BEFORE YOU START:

This game works best with
a large square area like a
gym. You could play outside
and *VeggieConnections
Shepherds* catch the plastic
hoops.

Divide kids into two teams and have them spread out along both ends of the playing area. Select two kids from each team to be rollers. Have two kids move to one side of the playing area, and the other two on the opposite side. Give these kids an equal number of the plastic hoops. Point out how *VeggieConnections Shepherds* will act as coaches in this game.

Say: **Joseph needed courage as he faced the challenges of prison life. In our game, the hoops represent challenges you face. You will run across the playing area to the other side, trying to avoid being hit by the rolling challenges. Rollers will continue to roll the hoops back and forth to each other. When you are standing on either side, that is the safe zone. You can run at any time, but you can only stay in the safe zone for 10 seconds. Coaches will time you and tell you that you must run and face the challenges after you've been in the safe zone for the 10 second limit.**

Start and stop the game often, allowing new hoop rollers to come from both teams. If kids are finding it easy to avoid being hit by the circles, shorten the boundaries of the game and continue playing.

2. Low-Powered Game: Building Courage

**LOW-POWERED
GAME NEEDS:**

- Paper or foam cups
  (one per every two kids)
- Paper or foam plates
  (one per every two kids)
- Masking/painter's tape

BEFORE YOU START:

Tape a start line, and stack
plates and cups at the far
end of the playing area.

Say: **Joseph needed to build his courage by trusting God to handle the challenges he faced. We're going to "build courage" by trying to build a bigger tower in this game.**

Have kids divide into two teams. If you have more than 20 kids, form another pair of teams. Have teams line up behind the start line and give the first player on both teams a cup and plate. Kids should balance their plate on top of the cup to start. Then have them move to the stack of cups and plates and each place a cup on top of the plates. They must hold their stack with one hand and get the cup or plate with the other hand. Then players will go back to their teams and hand off their stack. Each player will alternately stack plates and cups as high as they can before the stack falls. When the stack falls, the next player will start with the one-plate-cup combination at the beginning of the game and resume play. Have *Veggie-Connections Shepherds* collect fallen cups and plates and restack them.

Play several rounds, counting the number of stacked caps and plates and challenging teams to build higher stacks. After the game, say: **You built plate-and-cup towers in this game. You may have needed more courage as the tower got higher. As you face growing struggles in your life, remember to trust God to help you build courage.**

3. Craft: Badge of Courage

CRAFT NEEDS:

- Small foil pie pans
- Star patterns
  (from cookie cutters,
  cardboard shapes,
  and so on.)
- Markers
- Scissors
- Scrap cardboard squares
- Long, thick nails
- Ribbon or craft pins
  with a cool glue gun
  (optional)

Explain that when people show unusual courage, such as rescuing someone, they are sometimes presented with a medal or a badge. Today's badges represent courage and may even end up looking a lot like the badge of Deputy Dodge!

Instruct children to use a marker to trace the star pattern on the flat part of a pie pan. Help the kids cut out their stars.

Next, the kids place their stars on a piece of cardboard. They use the pointed tip of a nail to punch a design, pattern, or word on the star. The kids may want to brainstorm ideas together. Perhaps a "C" for courage or a simple word like "Try" could be punched into their star.

The kids may want to punch a hole at the top of the badge for a ribbon to thread through so that it can be worn around the neck. Or have an adult use a cool-temperature glue gun to fasten a pin to the back of the badge.

PART THREE:

Plugging In to My Life

Life application of the lesson to lead kids to THINK—LINK—ACT and build a relationship with God every day

A. Cucumber Connection

Before kids arrive, enlarge and copy the pickles from the *VeggieConnections Shepherd* pages on the CD-ROM included in the *VeggieConnections Elementary Curriculum Kit* onto green construction paper. Cut them out and put them in a pickle jar.

Let a volunteer draw a pickle from the Pickle Pot and either the child or a Shepherd should read the dilemma out loud. Each Shepherd should then process the question with their group using the THINK—LINK—ACT phrase.

A friend of yours is having an overnight birthday party in backyard tents. You want to go, but you're afraid of the dark. What can you do?	Nadine is in the school choir, and they've been practicing for a performance in front of the whole school. Nadine loves to sing but is really nervous about being up in front of all those people. She's thinking about pretending to be sick that day. What should Nadine do?	Something really embarrassing happened to Jeremy at school, in front of the whole class. Some of the kids laughed at him, and he felt awful about it. Jeremy thinks he'll never have the courage to go back to school again. What should Jeremy do?

CUCUMBER CONNECTION NEEDS:

- Pickle jar
- Pickle artwork from the *VeggieConnections Shepherd* pages (on the *VeggieConnections CD-ROM*)
- Green construction paper

B. Kid Connection: Big Pockets

Give each child his or her Big Pocket from last week and a copy of the Courage Shield (on p. 246). Let the kids cut out and color their shields. Say: **Joseph trusted God to give him courage. There was another man named Joshua, who took over as leader when Moses had died. Just before he was to lead God's people to the land he had promised them, God encouraged Joshua with these words: "*Be strong and courageous,*" Joshua 1:6a. On your shield, you have a place to write your name and hear God speaking the same words he spoke to Joshua.**

Have kids write their names on their shields. Then have kids put their shields in their pockets and collect the pockets for next week's lesson.

Lead the kids in singing the *THINK—LINK—ACT* song using motions. Ask the kids to do the THINK motion. **Think about turning to God when you need courage.** Do the LINK motion. **Link to Joseph, who trusted God for courage to help the baker and cupbearer.** Do the ACT motion. **Trust God to give you courage. How can you do that this week?** (*I can trust God to give me courage when I am afraid, when someone makes fun of me, when I don't know what is going to happen.*)

KID CONNECTION NEEDS:

- Big Pockets (made in *Lesson 1*)
- Courage Shield on page 246 (one per child)
- Colored markers
- Scissors
- *VeggieConnection* Music CD
- CD player

C. Christ Connection

To practice the Unit Memory Verse, Romans 15:13, have the kids divide into pairs and help each other practice saying the verse.

Then have all the kids hold hands and stand in one long line, "snaked" around the room. Have them close their eyes to pray as the *VeggieConnections Shepherd* begins with: **God, give me courage this week.** He squeezes the hand of the kid next to him, who says: **God, give me courage this week** and then squeezes the next child's hand, and so on down the line. When every child has prayed the sentence, close by thanking God for his promise to come near to us.

Distribute the take-home newspaper, *VeggieConnections*.

CHRIST CONNECTION NEEDS:

- *VeggieConnections* take-home newspaper (one per child)

Connecting to **Trust** with life examples from **Joseph**
Joseph interprets Pharaoh's dreams:
Genesis 41:1–40

PART ONE:

Plugging In at Dodgeball City

Introduction to the site and lesson focus

LESSON 6:
I will strengthen my trust in God by building my relationship with him.

A. Veggie Connection

Dressed as Deputy Dodge, welcome the kids as they enter Dodgeball City. Greet the kids by name, give high-fives, and comment on things you know about individuals. Emphasize the relationships you have with the kids. Then ring the cowbell to get the group's attention.

Howdy, pardner! Here in Dodgeball City, we git to know people by sittin' around at the Rootin' Tootin' Pizza Place a' talkin' and havin' fun. That's how we build our relationships. Sometimes we talk, sometimes we play games, sometimes we watch a favorite VeggieTales video together. Right now how 'bout we build our relationships with each other by playing a game?

Invite the kids over to the Rootin' Tootin' Pizza Place to choose a partner and have a seat. Give each pair some paper and a pencil. Say: **This here's a figurin' out game. One of you is a' gonna give directions to your pardner, and your pardner has to draw exactly what you say.** Explain, or demonstrate with a *VeggieConnections Shepherd* at the board, that the child giving directions may not say what the final picture will be or give any hints. He may tell his partner what to draw only by saying things like, *Start in the middle and draw a line down, then go right, then up, then make a loop, and so on.* Say: **When yer done, you have to interpret what you drew! Interpret—that's what this game's all about. If you wanna *figure out* what *interpret* means, it means to *figure out!* It'll all make sense later.**

Be sure the kids understand the directions. Then ask the *VeggieConnections Shepherds* to go around and whisper a picture to one child in each pair. Good simple pictures to draw would be a cactus, snake, boot, or house. That child starts giving directions. Pairs may work at their own pace. After the drawing is interpreted, the pair should ask a leader for another picture and have the other child in the pair try it.

Play for several minutes. When every child has had at least one turn, point out the "Special of the Day" board and write the word "Interpret." Then lead the kids in reciting the Dodgeball Dictionary Rhyme, with the kids using their best cowpoke accent:

> **Look it up, hook it up, what's it all about?**
> **Look it up, hook it up, let's find out!**

Let a volunteer look up *interpret* and read the definition aloud. Say that the kids will need to know this word to understand the Bible story.

Ask kids how playing a game together helped to build their relationships with each other. Let volunteers talk about other ways to build friendships. Then have the kids move into *VeggieConnections Groups* to build their relationships in yet more ways—through talking, sharing, caring, and praying together.

THE CHILDREN
will arrive with their *Veggie-Connections Shepherds* from the opening Countertop Connections featuring Bob and Larry. Play the *Veggie-Connections Music CD* as children enter Dodgeball City.

VEGGIE CONNECTION NEEDS:

- *VeggieConnections Music CD*
- CD player
- Cowbell
- Paper
- Pencils
- *VeggieConnections Bible Dictionary*

B. Prayer Connection

Have each *VeggieConnections Group* gather around their Prayer Cactus. Ask the *Veggie-Connections Shepherds* to lead prayer for their group, using these prayer starters. Kids may choose to finish the sentences as they speak to God.

> Lord, you are awesome! You've been so good to us. Thank you for . . .
> God, we want to keep coming close to you. Please help us this week to . . .
> Thank you for loving us so much. In Jesus' name, amen.

PART TWO:

Plugging In to God's Word

Connecting to God's Word in the Bible and understanding how that can help us to have a better relationship with him

A. God Connection: Joseph interprets Pharaoh's dreams – Genesis 41:1-40

GOD CONNECTION NEEDS:

• Cowbell
• Bible-time clothes
  for actors
• Crown for Pharaoh
• Bible
• Bed pillow

BEFORE YOU START:

Ask several Shepherds or older kids to play the parts of Joseph, Cupbearer, Wise Men 1–3, and Pharaoh. Either male or female actors can play the parts. You'll play the Narrator. Make copies of the script for your actors.

Use the cowbell to gather the kids around the porch and sit on the floor. Have your volunteers put on the Bible-time clothes. Give Pharaoh the crown to wear.

Ask kids to tell what happened to Joseph in last week's Bible story. (*He was in prison with the king's chief baker and cupbearer; they had dreams and God gave Joseph the meaning; it came true and the cupbearer forgot all about Joseph.*) Show the kids in a Bible where today's story is found, Genesis 41.

Narrator: In last week's story, God allowed Joseph to interpret the dreams of the baker and cupbearer. Today's story picks up two whole years after Joseph helped that cupbearer. For two years Joseph has worked in that prison, still trusting God. One night, the king—called Pharaoh—had some dreams.

Pharaoh: (*Lying down on his pillow snoring then jumps up*) Leapin' pyramids! *That* was a strange dream! (*Lies back down and snores*)

Narrator: And it was! Pharaoh dreamed that he was on the shore of the Nile River. He saw seven big, fat cows come out of the river and start eating grass. Then seven ugly, skinny cows with their bones showing through their skin came up out of the river. The skinny cows ate the fat cows. Then Pharaoh went back to sleep.

Pharaoh: (*Lying down on his pillow snoring then jumps up*) Leapin' pyramids! *That* was another strange dream!

Narrator: And it was! This time Pharaoh dreamed that he was in a farm field. He saw a tall, strong stalk grow with seven healthy heads of grain on it. Then seven more heads of grain grew, and they were shriveled and withered. The bad stalks of grain ate the good stalk!

Pharaoh: (*Gets up and sits on his throne and calls out*) Where are my wise men?

Wise Men 1–3: (*Run up and stand before Pharaoh*) Here we are!

Narrator: So Pharaoh told the wise men his dreams and asked them to interpret them.

Wise Man 1: I dunno.

Wise Man 2: I dunno.

Wise Man 3: I dunno.

Pharaoh: What good are you? Isn't there anyone who can tell me what my dreams mean?

Cupbearer: *(Walks up to Pharaoh)* Uh, excuse me. Uh, I really don't want to *remind* you of when you got, uh, mad at me. It was a loooong time ago—well—two years ago. You put me in prison along with the baker. We both had dreams and this man named Joseph interpreted our dreams. That's why I'm standing here and the baker is, uh, not.

Pharaoh: *(Jumps up from his chair, excited)* Bring Joseph to me! *(Joseph comes in and stands in front of Pharaoh)* I'm told you can interpret dreams.

Joseph: I can't interpret dreams on my own. But God will give the answer to you.

Narrator: So Pharaoh told Joseph his two dreams.

Joseph: Both your dreams mean the same thing. The seven fat cows and strong stalks mean there will be seven years of good crops giving plenty of food. But the seven skinny cows eating the fat cows, and the weak grain eating the strong, mean seven years of famine. No food will grow in the fields and people will starve.

Pharaoh: *(Looking worried)* What should I do?

Joseph: You should give someone a job to store up the food during the seven good years.

Pharaoh: It's clear you are wise and God is with you, so you've got the job!

Narrator: So Joseph was put in charge of the food program. He became a powerful leader in all of Egypt, second only to Pharaoh himself. Joseph continued to trust in God as he ruled in Egypt.

Have the actors take a bow and be seated. Discuss these questions with the kids: **What did Pharaoh's dreams mean?** *(To warn Pharaoh that God was sending seven years with plenty of food followed by seven years of no food.)* **How did Joseph know their interpretation?** *(Joseph kept a growing relationship with God, so he was able to connect with God when he needed the dreams' meaning.)* **What are ways we can build our relationship with God?** *(Praying frequently, trusting God in hard times, reading the Bible, not giving up, remember he is with us whether we're in a good time or a sad time, learning about him at church, and so on.)*

B. Activity Connection

Choose from the following activities to help kids explore and remember that they can strengthen their trust God by building their relationship with him (approximately 10–15 minutes each).

1. High-Powered Game: Grain-Building Race

Divide the kids into two relay teams. Have teams line up next to each other behind the starting line. Give each player a cup. Explain how Joseph had seven years to build buildings to store the grain before the seven years of famine came. In this game, teams will see how high they can build grain towers with their cups. But tell kids they won't have seven years to build their towers—only 70 seconds! (If you have large teams, increase the time to 90 seconds or two minutes).

On **Go**, have kids race to the building line and place their cup (upside down works best) and race back and tag their team member, who repeats the process. Kids will have to think quickly once the building begins, so they don't knock down the cup tower. Play several rounds to see if teams can build bigger towers in the same time. End the game by having everyone build the same tower, without timing them, to see how big the tower can be.

HIGH-POWERED GAME NEEDS:

- Disposable cups, all the same size (one per person)
- Masking tape
- Watch with second hand or stopwatch

BEFORE YOU START:
Tape a starting line and about 10' away, tape a building line.

2. Low-Powered Game: Do You See What I See?

Have the kids sit in a large circle and send one child out of the room with a *Veggie-Connections Shepherd*. If you have more than 20 kids, form two circles and play two games at the same time. The kids should all sit in the same manner, for example with their legs crossed. Pretend the child who left the room is Joseph. Explain to the kids you are going to pick one child to be the Pharaoh and he gets to choose a simple activity such as patting his legs. Everyone else follows and does the same; however, they should try to pick up the change without looking directly at the Pharaoh. The Pharaoh then must quietly change the activity such as patting one leg, then rubbing one arm, rubbing his chin. Practice a bit before Joseph comes back in.

When Joseph re-enters, he or she must try and figure out (interpret) who the Pharaoh is by watching carefully. Say: **Joseph had a tough job to do. He had to figure out what was going on with the Pharaoh. He listened carefully and trusted God to show him what the dreams meant. Let's see if our Joseph can figure out who the Pharaoh in our group is by watching and listening carefully.** Begin the game, and allow as many kids to take turns as you have time for being Joseph and the Pharaoh.

3. Craft: Growing Closer to God Book

CRAFT NEEDS:

- Cardboard pieces 6" x 9" (two per child)
- Tan or beige paper
- Growing Closer to God Book pages 1–2, page 265 (one per child)
- Growing Closer to God Book pages 3–4, page 266 (one per child)
- Glue sticks
- Markers
- Hole punches
- Small 1" notebook circle rings (two per child)

BEFORE YOU START:

Copy the book pages on tan or beige paper, one per child. Also make a few extras for mistakes.

Give kids two pieces of cardboard, tan copies of book pages, and other craft supplies. Say: **All through his life, Joseph trusted God. Even as he faced hard times and difficult challenges, Joseph made his relationship with God the most important thing in his life. We're going to make booklets that will help you build your relationship with God, too!**

Have kids fold each page in half, with the copy facing out, creasing the fold. Have *VeggieConnections Shepherds* help kids to ensure they fold it squarely. Then have kids open the pages and smear glue stick on the inside of the pages and fold it again. Have them use a Bible or other book to flatten the pages. As the children work, encourage them to look at the pages and talk about ways to strengthen their trust in God and build their relationship with him.

Next, have kids use markers to write on one of the cardboard covers: "Growing Closer to God Book." Then have Shepherds help kids punch two holes along the left-hand edge of the cardboard cover, one near the top and one near the bottom. If your hole punches aren't working, have Shepherds use a closed pair of scissors and carefully punch the holes. Line up the back cardboard piece and repeat for it. Have Shepherds help kids line up the pages with the holes punched in the cardboard and mark the holes on the pages with a pencil. Then have kids use the hole punch to make these holes.

Give kids the opened circle rings and have them feed the ring through the cover, pages, and back cover. Have kids feed both rings before closing them to complete the book. Have kids open their books to the first page. Say: **This book has four ways you can grow closer to God. The first page encourages you to read you Bible. On this page you can write favorite Bible stories or Bible verses. Have kids turn to the second page. Page two is for prayers. Here you can write down prayers, like you've been doing on the Prayer Cactus. You can keep track of answered prayers and list people who need prayers, as well as prayers for yourself.**

Have kids turn to page three. **This page is for ways for you to help others. Joseph was willing to help in the prison he was in. You can write down people who need your help or ways you can serve. They don't have to be big things, just things you think God wants you to do.** Have kids turn to last page. **This page is for you to list people you want to tell about Jesus. Bob and Larry remind us that you are special and God loves you very much. What better thing can you tell your friends?**

Take these books home and use them often to help grow your relationship with God!

PART THREE:

Plugging in to My Life

Life application of the lesson to lead kids to THINK–LINK–ACT and build a relationship with God every day

A. Cucumber Connection

Before kids arrive, enlarge and copy the pickles from the *VeggieConnections Shepherd* pages on the CD-ROM included in the *VeggieConnections Elementary Curriculum Kit* onto green construction paper. Cut them out and put them in a pickle jar.

Let a volunteer draw a pickle from the Pickle Pot and either the child or a Shepherd should read the dilemma out loud. Each Shepherd should then process the question with their group using the THINK—LINK—ACT phrase.

Alex hears his friends using swear words all the time. Sometimes he catches himself saying swear words even though he knows he shouldn't. What can he do?	Jordan's parents don't go to Sunday School or church. Jordan has been going to Sunday School with his neighbors. But now he's getting tired of it. His parents don't care if Jordan goes to Sunday School. What should he do?	Your summer camp counselor gave each person in your cabin a list of Bible verses to read each week. You put the verses in the back of your drawer because you didn't have time to read them. Later, you found them and thought about tossing them. What should you do?

CUCUMBER CONNECTION NEEDS:

- Pickle jar
- Pickle artwork from the *VeggieConnections Shepherd* pages (on the *VeggieConnections CD-ROM*)
- Green construction paper

B. Kid Connection: Big Pockets

Give each child his or her Big Pocket from last week and a large craft stick, with a small hole punctured at one end. Provide gel pens and have kids write their name on one side and "will stick to God when . . ." on the other side. Give each child several pieces of thin curling ribbon to thread through the hole and tie off in a knot. Say: **Joseph stuck with God through all he faced. Use these bookmarks as a reminder and a commitment to stick with God no matter what you face.**

Have kids set their sticks aside for the gel pen ink to dry. While drying, have kids sing the *THINK—LINK—ACT* song and do the motions. Ask the kids to do the THINK motion. **Think about why you need to build your relationship with God.** Do the LINK motion. **Link to Joseph, who kept his relationship with God strong.** Do the ACT motion. **Strengthen your trust in God by building your relationship wit him. How can you do that this week?** (*Daily reading the Bible, talking with God throughout the day, attending Sunday School, doing things that are pleasing to him.*)

Allow sticks to dry and have kids wait until the end of the lesson to put bookmarks in their pockets.

KID CONNECTION NEEDS:

- Big Pockets (made in *Lesson 1*)
- Large craft sticks (one per child)
- Gel pens
- Different-colored curling ribbon
- Hole punch
- *VeggieConnections Music CD*
- CD player

C. Christ Connection

To practice the Unit Memory Verse, Romans 15:13, have *VeggieConnections Shepherds* say one word, the students say the next, leaders say the third, and so on until the whole verse has been said. Then switch and have the kids begin the verse.

Have children form a circle and link arms with the persons next to them to make the circle strong. Pray: **God, make my trust in you strong. I want to keep getting closer and closer to you.**

Distribute the take-home newspaper, *VeggieConnections*.

CHRIST CONNECTION NEEDS:

- *VeggieConnections* take-home newspaper (one per child)

Connecting to **Trust** with life examples from **Joseph**
Joseph is in charge of Egypt: **Genesis 41:41–45:15**

plan

PART ONE:

Plugging In at Dodgeball City

Introduction to the site and lesson focus

LESSON 7:
I will trust in God's plan.

A. Veggie Connection

BEFORE YOU START:
Gather as many balls as you can. You'll want as many different kinds from giant beach balls to tennis balls. Inflate balloons and scatter them with the balls all over Dodgeball City.

Dressed as Deputy Dodge and speaking like a cowboy, welcome the kids back to Dodgeball City. When everyone has arrived, explain that you have a problem you'd like the kids' help with.

Y'all know, there're lots of balls round these parts, being that our town is called Dodgeball City. But were not the only town with a ball in our name. No sir-ree. They'res Wiffleball City and Tennisball City, jus to name a couple. And when folks from other cities come to visit, they forget to take their balls back home with them. So now we have a mess. Balls everywhere! Balloons left from Big Balloon City, too! So I need your help. But because this is Dodgeball City, we only use one hand when we throw dodge balls. So you can only use one hand as ya'll figure out how to pick up all these balls and balloons and put them over there. Point to an area. Then indicate the boxes and sheets. **You can use these things here to help y'all, but the rest is up to you. We've gots lots of fun things to do so y'all gotta hurry!**

Allow kids to figure out the quickest way to gather up and move the balloons. Have *VeggieConnections Shepherds* watch to make sure kids only use one hand. If kids don't figure it out, have a Shepherd show kids how to collect the balls on the sheet and have kids carry the sheet (using one hand). When all the balls and balloons are moved, thank the kids for helping. **You know, when you have sumthing to do, it helps to plan how to do it. It was a lot quicker to take a minute and plan the way to move the balls, instead of everyone trying to grab a ball or some other way that wouldn't be very fast.**

It didn't take a lot of planning to figure out how to help me today. But planning is an important part of life, and it's our Special of the Day! Why don't we take a closer look at what it means to plan? Lead the group in reciting the Dodgeball Dictionary Rhyme, urging the kids to use their best Western accent:

**Look it up, hook it up, what's it all about?
Look it up, hook it up, let's find out!**

THE CHILDREN
will arrive with their *Veggie-Connections Shepherds* from the opening Countertop Connections featuring Bob and Larry. Play the *Veggie-Connections Music CD* as children enter Dodgeball City.

VEGGIE CONNECTION NEEDS:

- *VeggieConnections Music CD*
- CD player
- Lots of various balls (two or three per child)
- Balloons (two or three per child)
- Small boxes
- Two or three sheets
- *VeggieConnections Bible Dictionary*

Let a volunteer look up *plan* in the *VeggieConnections Bible Dictionary* and read the definition aloud. Let volunteers share long-term plans that kids are part of. Examples might include specific family plans, plans for improving in a school subject, plans for an upcoming vacation, and so on.

Today we're going to look at a big plan Joseph had for all the people of Egypt and lands beyond. We'll see how Joseph continued to trust God to help him plan.

B. Prayer Connection

**PRAYER
CONNECTION
NEEDS:**

- Prayer Cacti
  (from *Lesson 1*)
- Green slips of paper
- Pencils

Have each *VeggieConnections Group* gather by their Prayer Cactus. Provide green paper slips and pencils and allow kids to write prayers if they wish and stick them on the cactus. Then have the kids pair up. They may share any answers to prayer they've seen or tell about something they'd like God's help with. Then let the kids pray for their partner. Encourage the kids to continue to pray for their partner throughout the week.

PART TWO:

Plugging In to God's Word

Connecting to God's Word in the Bible and understanding how that can help us to have a better relationship with him

A. God Connection: Joseph is in charge of Egypt – Genesis 41:41–45:15

**GOD
CONNECTION
NEEDS:**

- Cowbell
- Royal-looking
  Bible-time clothes
- Bible

**BEFORE
YOU START:**

Recruit a Shepherd to play Joseph. Provide Bible-times clothes and a copy of the script to allow him to act out the motions as you tell the story.

Ring the cowbell to gather the kids around the porch as you sit in the chair and tell the story. Bring your Shepherd out and introduce him as Joseph for today's story.

Begin by showing the kids in a Bible where today's story is found, Genesis 41—45. Ask the kids to tell where you left Joseph last week. *(God made Joseph able to interpret Pharaoh's dreams and Pharaoh put him in charge of the palace and all the people of Egypt so he could save grain before the famine.)*

Joseph trusted God in everything. Joseph kneels to pray. **God used Pharaoh's dreams for a very important plan—to get Joseph in charge of Egypt and to . . . well, you'll see.**

Pharaoh's dream was that there would be seven years with more food growing in the fields than the people could eat. Joseph holds up his hands and elaborately counts off up to seven; invite the kids to count aloud as he does this. **That's right, seven years. Joseph was careful to make a plan.** Joseph taps forehead as if thinking. **He had the Egyptians in every city build huge silos and warehouses to hold all the extra grain. He traveled all over Egypt to save every little bit of extra grain that grew. He kept careful count.** Joseph pretends to make notes on his hand. **But there was so much left over, it was like trying to count the grains of sand on a beach!** Joseph throws up his hands in frustration. **Those were good years, and Joseph kept trusting God.** Joseph kneels to pray again.

Then the second half of Pharaoh's dreams came true. There was a terrible famine, which is a time when no rain falls. Joseph holds his stomach and looks hungry. **The ground dried up, and nothing grew in the fields. Not for seven years.** Joseph again sadly counts off seven on his fingers as the kids count along. **And this famine wasn't just in Egypt; it covered all the countries around Egypt, all the way out to Canaan, where Joseph was from.** Joseph shades his eyes and looks all around.

Joseph was glad that he had trusted God's plan. Joseph raises his arms to praise God. **The people of Egypt were hungry and would have starved to death. But Joseph gave them grain.** Joseph pretends to take food from a bag and hand it out. **Faraway countries were starving, too, and they heard that there was grain in Egypt. So pretty soon, people were traveling to Egypt to buy grain. Guess who traveled there, too?** Joseph shrugs his shoulders.

Joseph's older brothers—all 10 of them! Joseph looks happily surprised. **They came to this powerful leader of Egypt, second only to Pharaoh himself, and bowed down in respect.** Joseph crosses his arms and looks regal and important. **The brothers didn't recognize Joseph after all these years. So Joseph made another plan.** Joseph taps his head, thinking.

Joseph wanted to test his brothers to see if they had changed from being so terribly mean. He also missed his one younger brother, who hadn't come with them. Joseph covers his heart and sighs. **And Joseph really missed his dad, Jacob. So he pretended he didn't know his brothers. He accused them of being spies in Egypt!** Joseph points as if accusing them. **He made them go back to Canaan and bring back his brother and, later, their father.** Joseph points, sending them away. **And Joseph could see that his brothers' hearts had changed.** Joseph puts hands over heart. **They cared about each other and their father. They felt sorry for what they had done to Joseph so many years ago. So Joseph told them who he was. He cried for joy.** Joseph cries happily. **He hugged them all and—a very important part of God's plan—he forgave them for selling him as a slave.** Joseph pretends to hug someone.

Joseph said to them, "You tried to hurt me when you got rid of me. But God used it for good. Now I'm here, in charge of Egypt's grain, and now our family won't starve to death! This was all part of God's plan." Joseph raises hands to praise God.

So Joseph was able to save his whole family because he trusted in God's plan. Joseph kneels to pray.

Thank your actor, and discuss these questions with the kids: **How did Joseph have to trust God?** *(He had to trust that God gave him the right interpretation of Pharaoh's dreams; he had to trust this plan to save the extra grain; he had to trust God when forgiving his brothers.)* **How can we trust God with the big things going on in our lives?** *(That no matter what happens—where we live, who we are, who comes and goes in our lives—God is still with us and has a big plan that we fit into, even if it doesn't make any sense at the time.)*

B. Activity Connection

Choose from the following activities to help kids explore and remember that they can trust God's plan (approximately 10–15 minutes each).

1. High-Powered Game: My Life: God's Plan!

Joseph was put in charge to carry out his plan to save the people from starving. Joseph followed God's plan for his life, from being a slave to a ruler. God has a plan for life, too. In this game you'll be reminded of all the areas of your life that God has a plan for.

Divide kids into *VeggieConnections Group* teams. Give each team a game cube. Explain kids are to roll the cube and the player rolling the cube needs to get the index card with the number on the cube. Have the player run up to the stack of cards and lift the top card. If the number matches, the player runs back with the card. If the card doesn't match, the player puts the card facedown on the bottom of the stack, and runs back to his or her team. Players each take turns rolling the cube and running to the cards. When a team has all four cards, they shout out: **I will trust God's plan for my life!**

The trick in the game is the two possible rolls on the numbers cube. If "Take Card" comes up, this team can take a card from another team. If "Give Card" is rolled, this team must give one of their collected cards away to another team. Teams must select different teams to give cards to or take cards from each time.

Allow teams to play until one team gets all four cards, or all the cards are taken from the piles and teams can't make a complete set of four. Say: **In this game, sometimes other teams took your cards taking away your chance to win. Sometimes in life, people or situations mess up your plans. But you can always remember to trust God and the plans he has for you. His plans are always best.**

2. Low-Powered Game: When Life Gives You Lemons

LOW-POWERED GAME NEEDS:

- Lemons (one per group)
- Lemonade and cups

BEFORE YOU START:

Have lemonade prepared or use boxed lemonade packages. Recruit a Shepherd to have the lemonade set up in another room or outside. Have chairs set up for kids to practice playing. Have the Shepherd review his or her reading role when kids are brought in for losing in the game.

Say: **There's a common saying that many people use, "When life gives you lemons, make lemonade." What does that mean?** *(Lemons are bitter, but lemonade is sweet.)* **When Joseph trusted God's plan for his life, he could endure the hardships that came to him. He told his brothers, "What you used for bad purposes, God used for good." He understood that God was able to use all those problems and reveal what his good plan had been all along.**

Divide kids into small groups. Have each group sit in a circle and explain that they will need to pass the lemon around the circle without using their hands or arms. They should use their feet or legs as best they can. If they can figure out another way (such as standing and passing it under their chin) that's fine, too. When someone drops the lemon, they must leave the room with a Shepherd. Don't tell the kids about the lemonade set up in the other room. Have the *VeggieConnections Shepherds* say to kids when they've taken them out: **Remember how we said sometimes when bad things happen, God uses them for good. Well, in this game when you lose, you win. The people who drop the lemon get lemonade!** Have another circle outside the room where the kids who dropped the lemon can keep playing and practicing! Play until all the kids come out for the lemonade.

3. Craft: Stampin' with Spuds

CRAFT NEEDS:

- Stiff cardboard box pieces (one per child)
- White pieces of fabric (one per child)
- Staplers
- Paper
- Potatoes, cut in half (one per child)
- Markers
- Plastic knives
- Paint shirts (optional)
- Tempera paint, several colors
- Foil pie pans
- Paper
- Paper towels

Ranchers brand their cattle to identify which belong to them. While cattle graze out in the fields, several herds can get mixed up. But when it's time to round them up, ranchers can tell which cattle are theirs by the brand. Their brands are symbols that tell the name of their ranch. For example, a brand of the Double Bar Ranch might be a circle with two bars in the middle.

When we have a relationship with God, we belong to him. He cares for us and we are part of his plan. Let's create brands using the potatoes, making symbols that will remind you that you belong to God. For example, you might make a "JC" that stands for Jesus Christ or your initials linked to a cross. Be creative as you make your own design. After we carve out our symbols, we will dip the stamps in paint and stamp our brands!

Give kids a piece of cardboard and a piece of white fabric, cut larger than the cardboard. Have *VeggieConnections Shepherds* help kids stretch and staple the fabric onto the cardboard, making a canvas.

Kids should design a branding symbol on paper; then carve their symbol with plastic knives onto their potato half, making sure to have the final stamp very distinct from the rest of the potato.

Put several tempera paint colors in the pie pans. Kids should dip their branding stamp into the paint and press it lightly onto paper to take up some excess paint. Practice pressing the brand on a white sheet of paper. When they are happy with their design, then they should press the brand carefully onto their fabric canvas.

Say: **This brand will remind you that you belong to God and that his plan for you is good.**

PART THREE:

Plugging In to My Life

Life application of the lesson to lead kids to THINK—LINK—ACT and build a relationship with God every day

A. Cucumber Connection

Before kids arrive, enlarge and copy the pickles from the *VeggieConnections Shepherd* pages on the CD-ROM included in the *VeggieConnections Elementary Curriculum Kit* onto green construction paper. Cut them out and put them in a pickle jar.

Let a volunteer draw a pickle from the Pickle Pot and either the child or a Shepherd should read the dilemma out loud. Each Shepherd should then process the question with their group using the THINK—LINK—ACT phrase.

Kim's family had planned a trip across the country for nearly a year. About four months ago Kim's father lost his job, and now they can't go on their planned vacation. Kim has been pouting for several weeks because she really wanted to travel the country. What can she do?	Antoine finally had a chance to join the baseball team this summer. Two weeks before the season started, he fell and broke his arm. By the time he gets the cast off, the season will be mostly over. Antoine is "mad at the world." What should he do?	Anna's parents just got divorced. She didn't want them to, and prayed they wouldn't. How can Anna trust God when he didn't seem to answer this prayer?

CUCUMBER CONNECTION NEEDS:

- Pickle jar
- Pickle artwork from the *VeggieConnections Shepherd* pages (on the *VeggieConnections CD-ROM*)
- Green construction paper

B. Kid Connection: Big Pockets

Give each child his or her Big Pocket from last week, a Blueprint Plans page, and a pencil. Say: **Joseph trusted God through all the hard times and knew God's plans for himself were best. And they were big plans! God made Joseph the second-highest ruler in Egypt and used Joseph to save the people during the famine. Joseph built buildings to hold the extra grain during the seven good years. When we build buildings today, we use a blueprint to draw the plans. You each have a blueprint, but the thing that is being built is you. God has plans to build your life. Think about what you might want to do when you grow older.**

Have kids write some plans on their blueprint pages. Then have kids write their names on the first blank line and "his" or "her" on the second blank line in the statement in the corner box of the page. Then have them roll up their blueprint and fasten it with a rubber band. Have kids put their rolls in their pocket and collect them for next week's lesson.

Have kids sing the *THINK—LINK—ACT* song and do the motions. Ask the kids to do the THINK motion. **Think about times you need to trust God's plan.** Do the LINK motion. **Link to Joseph, who trusted God's plan even when it seemed things were going badly.** Do the ACT motion. **Choose to trust God's plan. How can you do that this week?** *(By following his ways even when it seems another way looks better. By trusting that God can see the future and fit me into his big plan. By looking for God's plan and seeing how I fit into it.)*

KID CONNECTION NEEDS:

- Big Pockets (made in *Lesson 1*)
- Blueprint Plans on page 258 (one per child)
- Light blue paper
- Pencils
- Rubber bands (one per child)
- *VeggieConnections Music CD*
- CD player

BEFORE YOU START:

Copy a "Blueprint Plans" page on light blue paper for each child.

C. Christ Connection

Help the kids practice the Unit Memory Verse, Romans 15:13, by asking one *VeggieConnections Group* at a time to recite it for the rest of the class.

Say: **The last thing Joseph did in our story was he forgave his brothers. Rather than get even, he gave them mercy. Mercy is what Jesus gives to us, too. Let's sing a song that will encourage us to give mercy to people when they hurt us.** Have kids stand and sing *Stop! And Go with Mercy* from the *VeggieConnections Music CD*.

Then lead a prayer time, giving the kids an opportunity to pray aloud to finish these prayer sentences: **Dear God, you have been so good to us. Thank you for . . .** Pause to let volunteers pray. **We know you can see the big plan and that you care about us very much. So please help us to trust you with . . .** Pause to let volunteers pray. **And help us always to show mercy to those who hurt us. Thank you for coming near to us. In Jesus' name, amen.**

Distribute the take-home newspaper, *VeggieConnections*.

CHRIST CONNECTION NEEDS:

- *VeggieConnections Music CD*
- CD player
- *VeggieConnections* take-home newspaper (one per child)

GRAIN SILO

_____ will trust in God's

plans for _____ life.

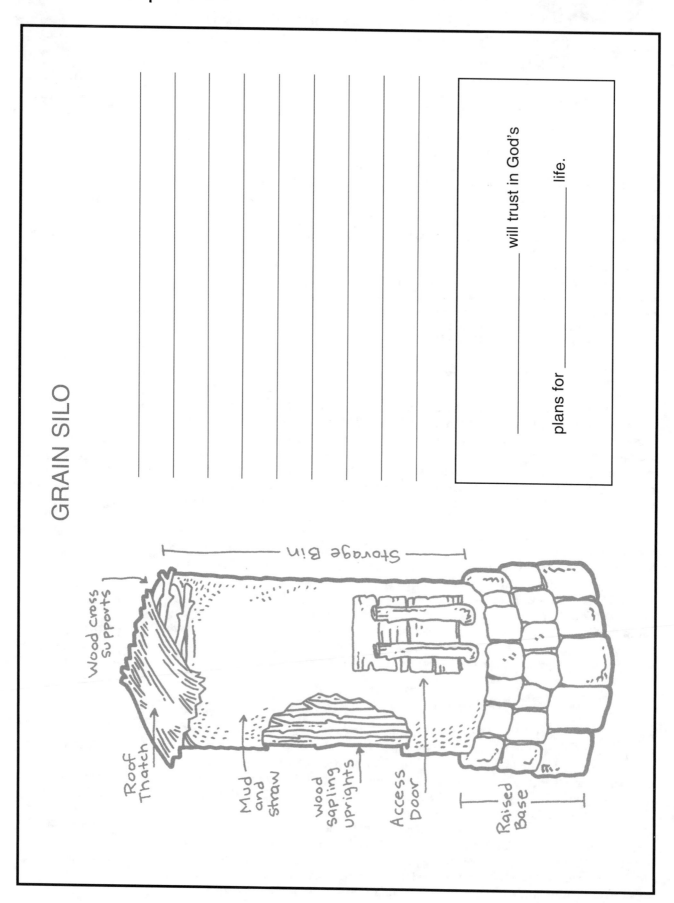

Wood cross supports

Roof Thatch

Mud and straw

Wood sapling uprights

Access Door

Raised Base

Storage Bin

Connecting to **Trust** with life examples from **Joseph**
Joseph reassures his brothers: **Genesis 50:15-21**

PART ONE:

Plugging In at Dodgeball City

Introduction to the site and lesson focus

LESSON 8:
I will show my trust in God to others.

A. Veggie Connection

Dressed as Deputy Dodge and speaking in your best Western accent, welcome the kids back to Dodgeball City for the last time. Invite the kids to be seated. Say: **It's jist been the best havin' y'all here visitin' Dodgeball City. I trust (get it?) you've all had a good ol' time learnin' how to trust God.**

Out here in the Wild West, we do things differ'nt from city folk. Let's all play a game y'all know, but with a Western twist. Have kids stand. **Now this how this little ol' game works. I'll tell y'all to do sum'thin' like, "Put your hands on your head." After I tell y'all what to do, you must call out this here question: "Are you sure?" If I answer, "Yep, I'm sure," then you do what I tell you. If I just say, "Yep," and you do the action, you're out of the game and must sit down.**

Begin calling out things for kids to do, Simon Says-style. Quickly call out things, alternating with your "Yes" and "Yes, I'm sure" answers. Have *VeggieConnections Shepherds* watch for kids who move on "Yes" and motion them to sit down. Play until you have a few kids left who can't be beat. Congratulate those still standing and have them be seated. Thank everyone for playing.

We played this little ol' game to show you what our "Special of the Day" word means. Write "reassure" on the Special board. **You know how I remember what *reassure* means? Look close now. This word has another word right inside of it.** Underline "sure." **That's right. When we say, "Sure," to someone, we're giving them a positive answer to sum'thin'. In our game, you asked "Are you sure?" And If I answered, "Yes, I'm sure," you then did the actions I called out. So to reassure means to make someone feel really sure! But to be sure, let's look it up!**

Lead the group in reciting the Dodgeball Dictionary Rhyme, urging the kids to use their best Western accent:

Look it up, hook it up, what's it all about?
Look it up, hook it up, let's find out!

Let a volunteer look up *reassure* in the *VeggieConnections Bible Dictionary* and read the definition aloud. **Now let's be sure to reassure our relationship with God by spending a little time talkin' with him.**

THE CHILDREN
will arrive with their *Veggie-Connections Shepherds* from the opening Countertop Connections featuring Bob and Larry. Play the *Veggie-Connections Music CD* as children enter Dodgeball City.

VEGGIE CONNECTION NEEDS:

- *VeggieConnections Music CD*
- CD player
- *VeggieConnections Bible Dictionary*

B. Prayer Connection

Have each *VeggieConnections Group* gather near their Prayer Cactus. Have kids look at the prayers on the cactus. Let kids share answers to prayers they've had during the unit. Let them talk about prayers they're still waiting to hear an answer for. They might also talk about disappointment in prayers that weren't answered the way they had hoped and how the kids can still keep trusting God despite that. Have the *VeggieConnections Shepherds* reassure the kids that God still loves them and cares for them, even when they don't see his answers. Then let *VeggieConnections Groups* pray sentence prayers about anything on their minds.

PART TWO:

Plugging In to God's Word

Connecting to God's Word in the Bible and understanding how that can help us to have a better relationship with him

A. God Connection: Joseph reassures his brothers – Genesis 50:15-21

Ring the cowbell to gather the kids around the porch. Have them be seated in a semicircle so that all can see other kids' faces. Say: **We've been learning all about Joseph's life and how he had trusted God through all the things that happened to him. Before we end his story, I want to review his life story.** Explain to kids how you'll pause after summarizing a part of the story, and when you do, have kids shout out: **Trust God!**

Joseph was the favorite son of his father, Jacob, and Joseph's 10 older brothers were jealous of him. They tricked Joseph and sold him as a slave. Pause. **Joseph worked in the household of a ruler named Potiphar. He was tempted by Potiphar's wife and ran away from her. But she lied about Joseph and he was thrown in jail.** Pause. **God was with Joseph and he was given jobs in the jail, helping with a good attitude.** Pause. **Joseph interpreted the dreams of two prisoners, a baker and a cupbearer. But the cupbearer forget about Joseph.** Pause. **Then Pharaoh had strange dreams, and the cupbearer told Pharaoh about Joseph. Joseph interpreted the dreams, and Pharaoh put Joseph in charge.** Pause. **Joseph made a plan to save Egypt. Can anyone tell me about the plan we talked about last week?** *(Joseph saved Egypt's grain for seven years, then made sure people got it during the seven years of famine. Joseph's brothers came from Canaan to buy grain to take back home; Joseph tested them to see if they had changed, and they had. Joseph forgave them, and Joseph's dad and his 11 brothers came to live in Egypt.)*

Now that sounds like a nice, happy ending for the long story of Joseph's life, doesn't it? But there's a little bit more—a little bit that scared Joseph's brothers! Show the kids in a Bible that today's story comes from Genesis 50. Say: **I will tell you the Bible story two times. The first time, you will listen very carefully. Then the second time, I'll give you instructions for something fun you can do.** First, read the story. Then have kids participate by making faces.

As I tell what happened, whenever I talk about how the people were feeling, I'll ask you to try to make a face to show that emotion. You all can look around at each other and see what that feeling looks like.

The Pharaoh gave Joseph's dad and brothers some land of their own in Egypt to live on and raise their sheep. Encourage the kids to put on a surprised face. **You might remember they were shepherds back home in Canaan. They lived in a part of Egypt called Goshen, and Joseph, being busy giving out grain from the big cities, probably didn't get to see them too often. But at least they were nearby for those great family get-togethers, which Jacob, the dad, really loved.** Ask the kids to show big smiles.

Jacob had lived to be very old, as old as a great-grandpa. And the time came when he died. Everyone was very sad. *Encourage the kids to make sad faces.* After the family traveled back to Canaan to bury Jacob and spend some time crying together, they had to get back to their homes and jobs in Egypt. And that's when Joseph's brothers began to worry. *Ask the kids to look worried.*

The brothers got together in secret and said, "Joseph loved our father and wanted us to be one big, happy family. So maybe *that's* why Joseph forgave us. Maybe he just did it for Dad and not because he meant it." *Have the kids look really worried.* One of the brothers said, "Yeah, what if Joseph is still holding a grudge against us? And now that Dad's gone, he's free to pay us back for the rotten things we did to him!" *Ask the kids to make scared faces.* Another brother said, "And he's in charge of practically all of Egypt! Who's going to stop him from getting even with us?!" *Ask the kids to look really scared.*

"We've got to make a plan," they agreed. So they wrote Joseph a letter that said, "Right before he died, Dad told us to tell you that you *really, really* need to forgive us for selling you as a slave so many years ago." Then the brothers sat and waited impatiently for Joseph's reply. *See if the kids can show "waiting" with their faces, such as biting their lips or looking worried again.* Then they threw themselves down at Joseph's feet. "Make us your slaves!" they cried. "Just don't kill us!" *Have the kids put on scared faces again.*

But Joseph reassured them, "What are you talking about? I forgave you." The brothers were so relieved. *Ask the kids to make faces of relief.* Joseph explained why. "What you did to me turned out to be part of God's big plan. I trust in God! And I want you to trust him, too. So I won't change his plan or gripe about it. Don't be afraid. I don't do paybacks." So Joseph reassured them and spoke kindly to them. He told them he would take care of them and their children. *Ask the kids to look very happy.* So Joseph showed his trust in God to his brothers and others.

Discuss these questions with the kids. **What were the brothers afraid of?** *(That after their dad died, Joseph might get even with them.)* **How did Joseph show his trust in God?** *(He reassured his brothers, reminded them of God's big plan, reminded them he forgave them, and didn't get even or hold a grudge.)* **What are ways we can show our trust in God to others?** *(By forgiving others, by not holding grudges or giving paybacks, by reassuring them and being kind.)* *Encourage the kids to brainstorm more ideas.*

B. Activity Connection

Choose from the following activities to help kids explore and remember that they can show their trust in God to others (approximately 10–15 minutes each).

1. High-Powered Game: Trust Sharing Obstacle

BEFORE YOU START:

Set up a large obstacle course using chairs, boxes, tables, and other safe objects. Set the course up to have four to six outside starting points, and have the finish point be the center. Place a "God" sign on the center object. Each leg of the course should have six to eight obstacles. Use masking/painter's tape to make arrows showing the path of the course around and under (for tables).

HIGH-POWERED GAME NEEDS:

- Chairs
- Boxes
- Tables
- "God" paper sign
- Masking/painter's tape
- Bandanna blindfolds

Have kids divide into teams of three. Give a blindfold to one child in each team. Have teams line up at the start areas of the course. Explain the game as follows: **The blindfolded player in each team is someone who needs to trust God. This player will move out on to the course, and when he or she doesn't know which way to go, will call out, "I need to trust God!" Then your two helpers can tell you which way to turn and move to the next obstacle. You can call out for help anytime you need to. Teammates can only call directions when you call out for help.**

Have the first teams begin the course. When kids are about halfway through their leg, send the next set of players through the course. When teams reach the center, have the blindfolded player remove his or her blindfold and shout: **Praise God!**

Have kids in teams switch roles so everyone can negotiate the course. After everyone has completed the course, have kids gather around the center of the course. Say: **You needed to say "I need to trust God!" to get help in this game. That is like people who need to know God. You led blindfolded players to God in this game. That is what people who don't know God need.** Encourage kids to look for ways to share Jesus with their friends.

2. Low-Powered Game: Gold Rush

LOW-POWERED GAME NEEDS:

- Burlap bags or cardboard boxes (one per team)
- Styrofoam packing peanuts or shredded newspaper
- Gold Rush Game on page 264 (one set per team)
- Small-size plastic Easter eggs (seven per team)

BEFORE YOU START:

Fill one bag or box for each team with Styrofoam peanuts or shredded newspaper. Copy and cut apart the seven Bible-story sentences on page 264. Roll up each sentence and place it in its own egg. Hide one set of eggs in each bag/box.

OPTION:

If you don't have plastic eggs, roll up the sentences and wrap small rubber bands around them. Use tan or brown paper to copy the sentences on and use shredded brown grocery bags to fill the boxes with. Alter the instructions to kids to fit the new items.

Have each *VeggieConnections Group* form a team, or divide the kids into groups of up to seven. Explain: **Out here in the Wild West, we sometimes go panning for gold. Here in Dodgeball City, we do it a little differently. Y'all are going to dig for gold nuggets, but our nuggets look a lot like Easter eggs. And they have nuggets of truth hidden inside them! It's your job to find the nuggets and put the sentences from our Bible story in the right order.**

Have the groups spread out, and give each group a prepared burlap bag or box. At your signal, the players take turns digging through their bag/box until they each find an egg. When all seven have been found, the kids open them, read the sentences, and then work together as a team to put them in the right order as they happened in the Bible story. Have *VeggieConnections Shepherds* on hand to help with reading.

3. Craft: "Wanted" Posters

CRAFT NEEDS:

- Brown paper grocery bags (one for every two kids)
- Black markers
- Pencils

Say: **Every Western sheriff has "Wanted" posters hanging in his jail. This "Wanted" poster is of the good variety . . . it's about YOU! God wants you to show your trust in him to others.**

Give children one-half of a brown paper grocery bag each. Have them tear out a large rectangle. They may roll the edges or wrinkle the whole piece to give it an "old" look.

Give each child a black marker to draw a large rectangle in the center. At the top the kids print "God Wants YOU." Beneath the rectangle they print "to show your trust in God to others." Neatly print this on the board for the kids to copy.

Have kids use pencil to draw a picture of themselves in the rectangle. Then they trace their picture in black marker.

As the kids work, talk about people to whom they could show their trust in God and ways to do that. Then brainstorm places they could hang their "Wanted" poster at home to remind them to pray for these people.

PART THREE: Plugging in to My Life

Life application of the lesson to lead kids to THINK—LINK—ACT and build a relationship with God every day

A. Cucumber Connection

Before kids arrive, enlarge and copy the pickles from the *VeggieConnections Shepherd* pages on the CD-ROM included in the *VeggieConnections Elementary Curriculum Kit* onto green construction paper. Cut them out and put them in a pickle jar.

Let a volunteer draw a pickle from the Pickle Pot and either the child or a Shepherd should read the dilemma out loud. Each Shepherd should then process the question with their group using the THINK—LINK—ACT phrase.

Isaiah saw a very bad storm coming, with lots of lightning and thunder. He was very afraid he wouldn't be safe. What can he do?	Dominic forgot to hook the latch on the gate after he played with the family dog, Chip. Dominic's family was very upset with him. What should he do?	Joey had a bad nightmare and is afraid to go back to sleep. What should he do?

CUCUMBER CONNECTION NEEDS:

- Pickle jar
- Pickle artwork from the *VeggieConnections Shepherd* pages (on the *VeggieConnections CD-ROM*)
- Green construction paper

B. Kid Connection: Big Pockets

Lead kids in the *THINK—LINK—ACT* song using motions. Ask the kids to do the THINK motion. **Think about how it would help others to see your trust in God.** Do the LINK motion. **Link to Joseph, who showed he trusted God when he forgave his brothers.** Do the ACT motion. **Show your trust in God to others. How can you do that this week?** *(By praying for my friends and family, by forgiving them when they hurt me, by caring for them, by giving up some things I want to be able to help them.)*

Give each child his or her Big Pocket from last week and a piece of fabric square bandanna. Have kids write their names on their bandannas using permanent markers. Then have kids empty out their Big Pockets. Say: **During your time at Dodgeball City, we've seen how Joseph trusted God through all the things he faced.** Have kids look at their items. **And you've been making reminders that you will trust God. Each reminder has your name on it, which is an important way to say your commitment to trust is** *personal*, **that you own it. This is our last time at Dodgeball City. We are so glad you came. Please take your Big Pocket home to remember all the different ways God can help you when you trust him.**

Have kids place all their items on top of their bandanna, and them wrap them up.

KID CONNECTION NEEDS:

- Big Pockets (made in *Lesson 1*)
- Square Western-print cloth, 18" x 18" (one per child)
- Permanent markers

OPTION:

If you don't have fabric, you could cut large construction paper sheets into 12" x 12" squares and decorate with markers.

C. Christ Connection

Together recite the Unit Memory Verse, Romans 15:13. Congratulate the kids on memorizing such a long verse.

For prayer, pray "popcorn" prayers. Have the kids cluster in one big group and stoop. Instruct the kids that you will begin some sentence prayers. When you pause, they may begin popping up to call out one word to pray, then popping back down again, like popcorn. They may pop up as many times as they wish, and it's okay to overlap.

Dear Lord, we love you! We praise you for being . . . Pause to allow "popping prayers." **We thank you for . . .** Pause to allow "popping prayers." **We want to show our trust in you to these people . . .** Pause to allow "popping prayers." **Thank you for your love for us, which will never end. In Jesus' name, amen.**

Distribute the take-home newspaper, *VeggieConnections*.

CHRIST CONNECTION NEEDS:

- *VeggieConnections* take-home newspaper (one per child)

Joseph's 11 brothers and their dad, Jacob, moved to Egypt.

Jacob died.

Joseph's brothers were scared he would finally get even with them.

The brothers wrote Joseph a letter to ask forgiveness.

Joseph went to visit his brothers.

Joseph reassured his brothers that he forgave them.

Joseph took care of his brothers and their families.

Joseph's 11 brothers and their dad, Jacob, moved to Egypt.

Jacob died.

Joseph's brothers were scared he would finally get even with them.

The brothers wrote Joseph a letter to ask forgiveness.

Joseph went to visit his brothers.

Joseph reassured his brothers that he forgave them.

Joseph took care of his brothers and their families.

Joseph's 11 brothers and their dad, Jacob, moved to Egypt.

Jacob died.

Joseph's brothers were scared he would finally get even with them.

The brothers wrote Joseph a letter to ask forgiveness.

Joseph went to visit his brothers.

Joseph reassured his brothers that he forgave them.

Joseph took care of his brothers and their families.

will grow closer to God

by praying.

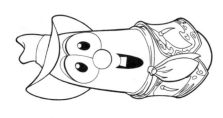

will grow closer to God

by reading my Bible.

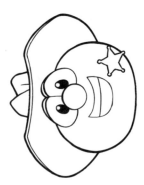

will grow closer to God
by telling others about Jesus.

will grow closer to God
by serving or helping others.

WELCOME TO THE CHOCOLATE FACTORY

Connecting to **Time** through the writings
of the disciple **John**

UNIT FIVE:

THE TIME CONNECTION

UNIT VERSE: "Teach us to number
our days aright, that we may
gain a heart of wisdom."
Psalm 90:12

THE CHOCOLATE FACTORY

LESSON FOCUS:

1. God is eternal: John 1:1-18 and 1 John 5:13

2. God is with me all the time: John 14:15-29

3. I will spend time with God: 1 John 1:5–2:6

4. I will set godly priorities with my time: John 15:1-17

5. I will trust in God's timing: John 11:1-44

6. I will make good use of my time: John 2:1-11 and 4:46–5:17

7. I will look for times to share God's Word with others: John 4:1-39

8. I will use my time to serve others: John 13:1-20

Time Connection Goals

The Time Connection is all about helping kids connect with God and create a desire to spend time with him. The word *time* is a familiar one for all kids. They have family time, play time, school time, and church time. And we want kids to know the best time of all, time with God.

Each Lesson Focus will take kids on a journey toward various ways we can connect with our Lord through our time. The Countertop Connections opening sessions with Bob and Larry will introduce the concept of having a relationship with God. It will be supported with the Program Verse from James 4:8: *"Come near to God and he will come near to you."*

When kids are dismissed to the Chocolate Factory, they will have the chance to actually explore what it means to use their time wisely for God. Kids will be challenged to build a relationship with God, deepen their commitment, and put what they've learned into action in daily life.

The first lesson teaches us that God is eternal. In the second lesson, children learn that God is always with them, wherever they are.

The next four lessons will focus on a variety of ways we can wisely use our time *with* God and *for* God.

The last two lessons encourage us to take what we've learned and actually begin to use our time to share God's Word with others through our service to them.

Warning: Activities in these lessons may call for foods containing wheat, dairy, or nuts. Please be aware that some children may have medically serious allergic reactions to these foods. Let parents know that their kids will be offered snacks that may include these items, and post a list of ingredients each week for any snacks offered during the lesson. Whenever foods containing wheat, dairy, or nuts are suggested in these lessons, be sure to have safe alternatives on hand.

Welcome to the Chocolate Factory!

Kids will travel to the Chocolate Factory to explore how they spend their time. One of the VeggieTales videos that Bob and Larry present to children during the Countertop Connection time is called *Rack, Shack, & Benny*. The Chocolate Factory is modeled somewhat after this.

In the video, the Chocolate Factory president, Nebby K. Nezzer, announces that his workers may eat as many chocolate bunnies as they like. This sounds great until three boys named Rack, Shack, and Benny remember that their parents taught them not to eat too much candy.

Paralleling the biblical story of Shadrach, Meshach, and Abednego and the fiery furnace, this story teaches kids how to resist peer pressure and stand up for what they believe. This provides an excellent backdrop for fun exploration and discovering the beauty of using our time to connect with our Creator.

In preparation for leading this unit, please watch the *Rack, Shack, & Benny* video in advance so you'll be familiar with the wonderful setting of the Chocolate Factory.

Your Role in the Chocolate Factory: Factory Manager

As the Factory Manager, you will be hosting a new group of kids as they rotate through the Chocolate Factory every eight weeks. To dress for the part, you should wear a lab coat, a necktie (whether male or female), and a hardhat or painter's cap. You might also carry a clipboard, wear an employee badge on a lanyard, carry a stopwatch, and have lots of chocolate snacks in your coat pockets. Also carry a chocolate alternative candy for children not allowed to have chocolate.

Then have fun with your role! Remember that you are a proud Factory Manager who wants children to use their time wisely in building a close relationship with God, the Father.

How to Build and Prepare the Chocolate Factory

OPTION 1:

If you have more time and a permanent space

Walls and Decorations: Use the transparency art on page 58 to project the Chocolate Factory interior onto mural paper or flat sheets. Trace the images in permanent markers. Hang these as backdrops on the walls of the room.

Hang a large banner labeled "Chocolate Factory." Hang another smaller sign at the entrance labeled, "Warning: Milk products, nuts, and vegetables may be found in our bunnies," and decorate it with Veggie stickers.

You may further decorate the factory walls by cutting life-sized (4'-5' tall) chocolate bunnies and other familiar chocolate candy shapes from cardboard or mural paper and hanging them up. You may also decorate the site by setting out buckets of real individually wrapped chocolates or candy bars, along with colorful hard candies and lollipops.

Create a wall mural for the Chocolate Factory using transparency art found on page 58.

The Chocolate Factory

Whenever you need to gather the children together or signal for a game to begin, and whenever it's time to bring out the *VeggieConnections Bible Dictionary*, you may want to use an alarm (as from a watch or clock), buzzer, or bell.

Entrance: The entrance to the Chocolate Factory should correspond with your classroom doorway. Make a "time clock" so the kids can "punch in" at the start of each lesson.

To make the time clock, hang a cardboard box in the doorway or place it on a table near the doorway; decorate it with numbers and buttons. You may have the kids pretend to push a button as they enter, or you may attach an actual handle that the kids can turn.

To make employee badges, laminate index cards, punch a hole in each, and pull a ball-chain or ribbon through it so the kids can wear it around their necks. Each time the kids punch in, they should pick up their employee badge; each time they punch out, place Veggie clip art on the badge to reward their attendance.

You may purchase child-sized disposable painters' caps for kids to wear while inside the factory. If you choose to do this, make a sign to hang near the time clock labeled, "Caution: Hats are required beyond this point." The kids may pick up their hats along with the employee badges.

Assembly Line: Set up one side of the Chocolate Factory as the Assembly Line. Place long tables end-to-end where the kids can stand (chairs or stools optional) to form an assembly line and work on crafts or any activity needing a hard surface. Place craft supplies in plastic tubs and store them under the table.

R&D Lab: Leave part of the Chocolate Factory as open space for games and where the kids may be seated on the floor for God Connection. Hang a large sign labeled "R&D Lab" and subtitled "Research and Development, Taste Testing, Lab Work." Beneath that write "Caution: Big imaginations at work." Off to the side in this area you may keep game supplies in plastic tubs. Include an office chair or stool for the Factory Manager to sit in to tell the Bible story.

"Chocomatic" Machine: Design a Chocomatic using a large storage or appliance box. Draw or attach real knobs and dials. Cut two slits on one end of the box. Use a lid or other cardboard piece to create a conveyor belt. Each week before class, place the Connection Word, taped to a candy bar, on this conveyor belt.

Plan a "chocolate dispenser" in the Chocomatic: Cut a hole with a flap near the bottom and place a bowl or tray inside where you can stash chocolate treats for snacks. Or cut a false back in the box so a leader can enter it and hand out treats through a dispenser hole.

Employee Bulletin Board: Label a bulletin board or posterboard "Employee Announcements." Include a picture of Mr. Nezzer and Mr. Lunt (on page 69), and a spot for Employees of the Month. For Employees of the Month, divide the number of kids in your class by eight (for the eight lessons), assign each group to a week, and list their names in big, bold letters in this spot during their week. You could enhance this by taking a picture of each group with an instant-print camera. Also on the bulletin board, provide spots labeled "Weekly Mission Statement" (where you will write the weekly Lesson Focus) and "Today's Connection Word" (where you will write the weekly Connection Word).

If you are short on time or do not have a permanent space

Use the transparencies to make backdrops on mural paper or sheets. These can be taken down, rolled up, and stored between lessons. Set up classroom tables end-to-end to make the Assembly Line. If you don't have room to store a large appliance box, make the Chocomatic from a computer paper box. Make all the signs on construction paper (for convenient storage) as well as cutouts of chocolate bunnies.

Life Application Memory Tools

VeggieConnections will teach an important Bible lesson to kids each week. Knowing the Bible is the beginning of a relationship with God. Putting that learning to practice through Life Application really solidifies a child's relationship with the Lord. It is imperative that we provide kids with the tools they need to carry what they have learned into everyday experiences through life application.

In this curriculum, there are three main ways we will encourage kids to do this:

1. Kids will discover ways to use their time wisely throughout each session.

2. Kids will learn a catch-phrase that will help them to remember what they should do in real life experiences.

The catch-phrase we have created is THINK—LINK—ACT. There is a song built on this principle on the *VeggieConnections Music CD* in your kit that will help children remember this important tool. In addition, each session will focus on various THINK—LINK—ACT situations that help children walk the walk and talk the talk. This will hopefully open doors for the Holy Spirit to enter in and build meaningful relationships that will carry kids through every day of their lives! Here's what it means:

THINK: Stop and think about what God wants you to do.

LINK: Link God's Word and what you've learned to your choices.

ACT: Go and act on what God wants you to do!

3. Kids will also create a weekly life-application memory tool to help them to remember the focus of each lesson.

Time Tracker Journal

In the Chocolate Factory, the kids will create a Time Tracker Journal. Just as a factory has to utilize time effectively to be able to produce a product, kids need to know how God can help them use their time wisely to live productive lives.

Using a variety of construction paper colors, photocopy a Time Tracker Cover on page 313 for each child. Each child will also need one regular paper copy each of the Time Tracker Planner on page 314 and Time Tracker Calendar on page 315.

Show kids how to make a Z-fold book as follows: Fold the Time Tracker Cover in half, forming a front and back cover. Open the cover and using a glue stick, apply glue to the right-hand side of the inside cover. Place the planner page inside the cover (keeping the edge of the paper about ¼" from the crease of the fold), closing the cover and pressing down on it to secure the planner page (the right-hand side of the planning page will be sticking out of the cover). Then tape the calendar page to the edge of the planning page. Next, fold the calendar and planner pages in half, forming a Z shape that nests inside the cover when closed. Fold and refold the creases some to make the pages lie relatively flat when opened.

Provide markers for kids to write their names on the covers and allow them to decorate the covers with markers, glitter glue pens, and other craft supplies.

The Time Tracker Journals will be used each week as kids look at how they are using their time and how they plan to use their time each week. At the end of the unit, kids can take their journals home as a reminder of how they've been helped by God to use their time wisely.

Suggested Music for the Chocolate Factory

Use these songs from the *VeggieConnections Music CD* in your lessons:
1. *THINK—LINK—ACT*
   Music motions on page 48.
2. *You Are the One!*
3. *Stand Up/Stand*

Connecting to **Time** through the writings
of the disciple **John**
John writes about how God became human:
John 1:1-18 and John 5:13

PART ONE:

**Plugging In at
the Chocolate Factory**

Introduction to the site
and lesson focus

LESSON 1:

God is eternal.

A. Veggie Connection

WARNING:
Please be aware of children with dairy and nut allergies. Milk chocolate snacks are often suggested in this unit, and these children may have a medically serious allergic reaction. Be sure to let parents know that their kids will be offered chocolate at the Chocolate Factory. Be sure to have safe alternatives on hand, such as hard candies or taffy.

Dressed as the Factory Manager, warmly greet the kids as they punch in at the Chocolate Factory entrance and receive their badges. See page 269 for explanation of badges and punch cards. Let the kids explore the Chocolate factory for a minute. Then tell the kids that they have 30 seconds to walk around and look for as many different types of candy as they can see and try to remember them. (If you have mostly older kids, you may give paper and pencils and let them write down the candies.) Give a signal to begin.

When time is up, see who found the most. Then ask: **What did you notice about the candy?** *(They're chocolate, taste good, all are sweet, etc.)* Say: **These items are made here at the Chocolate Factory. Can anyone guess what else a lot of these candies have in common?** Encourage them to think outside of the normal. If kids appear to be stuck, ask about the shapes of the candies. Guide the children to see that many of the candy pieces are in the shape of a circle: a Tootsie Pop is a circle, candy buttons are circles, and the bottom of a chocolate kiss is a circle. **What do you know about circles?** *(Circles have no beginning and no end. They go around forever.)* **These circles remind me of something else that goes on forever. Do you know what that might be?** Let the kids guess. **God goes on forever. He was there in the beginning of time—he made the earth and everything in it—and he will be there at the end. Another word for "forever" is "eternal."**

Sound a buzzer or bell. Explain that the buzzer rang because you just said today's Connection Word: *eternal.* Ask a volunteer to go to the Chocomatic and pick up the word on the chocolate bar. Ask for another volunteer to read the definition from the *Veggie-Connections Bible Dictionary.* Tell kids that today they are going to hear a story that explains that God is eternal.

THE CHILDREN
will arrive with their
VeggieConnections Shepherds
from the opening Countertop
Connections featuring Bob
and Larry. Play the *Veggie-
Connections Music CD* as
children enter the Chocolate
Factory.

**VEGGIE CONNECTION
NEEDS:**
- *VeggieConnections
  Music CD*
- CD player
- Many different types and
  sizes of candy around the
  room, real or artificial
  (from site setup, be sure
  and include several round
  varieties)
- Paper and pencils (optional)
- Buzzer or bell
  (from site setup)
- Connection Word taped to
  a candy bar, placed in
  Chocomatic (from site setup)
- *VeggieConnections
  Bible Dictionary*

PRAYER CONNECTION NEEDS:

- Chocomatic dispenser (from site setup)
- Prepared construction paper bunnies
- Paper
- Thin-tipped marker
- Glue
- Scissors

BEFORE YOU START:

Prepare the prayer starters as follows: Copy bunny patterns from page 69 onto brown construction paper and cut out the shapes. Clearly print each of these words on individual slips of paper: *Thank, Others, Praise, Self.* Make the first letter in each word larger and underlined. Glue paper slips onto bunnies, one per bunny. You'll need one bunny for each *VeggieConnections Group*, but make sets of four so you'll have equal chances for each prayer phrase being chosen. Place the bunnies inside the Chocomatic.

GOD CONNECTION NEEDS:

- Bible

B. Prayer Connection

Send one child from each *VeggieConnections Group* (a total of four kids) to the Chocomatic to reach in and pull out a chocolate bunny, and bring it back to their group. Put the cards in the following order: Thanks, Others, Praise, Self. Show kids how it spells TOPS. **When we make prayer a top priority, God is pleased. TOPS can help you remember a way to pray.** Explain the word on the bunny indicates the kind of prayers the kids should focus on. For *Praise*, the kids pray listing reasons they love God or want to praise him. For *Thanks*, the kids spend time thanking God for things they experienced the previous week. For *Self*, the kids may ask God's help for themselves, and for *Others* to ask God to be with those whom they mention. All the groups may take time to share what's going on in their lives before praying. Return the prayer bunnies to the Chocomatic after each prayer time to be used the following week.

Plugging In to God's Word

Connecting to God's Word in the Bible and understanding how that can help us to have a better relationship with him

A. God Connection: John writes about how God became human – John 1:1-18 and 1 John 5:13

Gather the kids in the Research & Development (R&D) Lab. Show the kids in a Bible that today's story is found in John 1 and 1 John 5. Explain how this was written by John, one of Jesus' 12 disciples.

You will read the story through twice. Read it straight through the first time, without pausing for kids' responses. For the second reading, explain there are some important words in the story that you want kids to notice. Ask kids to listen for the name "God" or "Jesus." When they do, they should say: **He is eternal!** Have them practice. Then retell the story, pausing where indicated to let the groups say their phrase.

In the beginning was God (*He is eternal!*). **Not a single thing has been made that God** (*He is eternal!*) **didn't make. Everything God** (*He is eternal!*) **made since the beginning was good. Jesus** (*He is eternal!*) **is also God** (*He is eternal!*). **Many people saw that this was true and believed in him.**

One day, God (*He is eternal!*) **sent a man named John to tell others about Jesus** (*He is eternal!*). **John told everyone that Jesus** (*He is eternal!*) **is God** (*He is eternal!*) **and that God** (*He is eternal!*) **sent him to earth as a human. Only Jesus** (*He is eternal!*) **would be able to save people from their sins. John wanted everyone to believe in Jesus** (*He is eternal!*).

John wanted them to know that Jesus (*He is eternal!*) **had been around since the beginning and would be around forever. He is eternal.**

Jesus (*He is eternal!*), **who was with God** (*He is eternal!*) **in the beginning, became just like you and me—a human. He lived on earth and grew up from a baby to a child to an adult. He had been with God** (*He is eternal!*) **in the beginning, before John was ever born. Jesus** (*He is eternal!*) **was the one John had been talking about before he even came, the one who would save people from their sins.**

When we know Jesus (*He is eternal!*) **and follow him, God** (*He is eternal!*) **promises that we will live forever.**

Thank the kids for helping you tell the story. Then discuss these questions together: **Who did God lead to write down these things about Jesus?** (*John.*) **What do God and Jesus have in common?** (*They are both God, they were both there at the beginning, they are both eternal, everything was created by them.*) **Who else can live forever?** (*People who believe in Jesus are given eternal life—we will live with Jesus in heaven after we die.*)

If the kids have difficulty answering these questions, reread the story without the added phrases from the kids (to help the train of thought). Be sure they understand that Jesus was with God in the beginning of time. God, as Jesus, came to earth as a human. But Jesus, like God, is eternal and will live forever. We can choose to live forever with him, too, when we believe in him.

B. Activity Connection

Choose from the following activities to help kids explore and remember that God wants us to to know that he is eternal (approximately 10–15 minutes each).

1. High-Powered Game: Round and Round

Explain to the kids that this game is all about circles, because a circle reminds us of how God is eternal. He has no beginning and no end. Have the kids stand in a circle and hold hands. Break the circle at one point and let the two players rejoin hands through a plastic hoop. Explain that the goal is to move the plastic hoop around the circle without dropping hands. If more than one *VeggieConnections Group* is playing, you can make it a race. To make it more interesting, add another plastic hoop. (Hint: the child will need to step through the plastic hoop to get it to their other side.) As the hoop goes around, play music from the *VeggieConnections Music CD*. Optional: have the children say the Program Verse as they step through the hoop.

2. Low-Powered Game: Long-term Links

Have *VeggieConnections Groups* gather around the circle. Kids line up relay-style behind the circle line.

Explain that the object of the game is for teams to create the longest link of paper circles. Remind kids that just as John told other people that God is eternal, we need to tell our friends that God is eternal. We can do that by making connections, or linking up with people we know and telling them that God is eternal.

At your signal, a player on each team runs to the center, grabs a strip of paper, makes a loop, and staples it. Have a *VeggieConnections Shepherd* in the circle helping younger kids with their loops. Then the player runs back to their team and hands the loop to the next person. Each player on a team repeats the process, adding more loops to the chain as they go. After everyone has had one turn to make a loop, set a time limit on the game and call out 30-second and 10-second warnings. At the end, see who has created the longest chain.

When you have measured the chains, have all the groups link their chains together into one large circle. Say: **Just like each one of us made one of the links in this circle, we're all connected to each other because we're all connected to God. Do you see how our circle has no beginning and no ending place? It reminds us that God is eternal; he has no beginning or end either!**

3. Craft: Circle String Art

Give each child a prepared foamboard and a copy of the pattern. Have kids cut the circle pattern out and center it on their foamboards. Have *VeggieConnections Shepherds* help younger kids with their pins. Place a map pin at the edge of the circle, next to each number on the pattern. Leave the pins sticking up just a little bit. After all eight pins are on the board, discard the paper pattern.

Give each child a 4'–6' piece of string. Make it a manageable length because they can tie additional string on if necessary. Tie one end of the string onto pin number one and wind around the circle, wrapping the string around each pin, until you go around the entire circle. As the children work, explain the eternity of a circle and the eternity of God's unconditional love for us, his children.

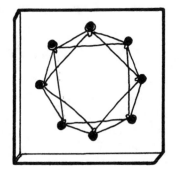

After the kids have gone around the circle, they can continue winding in various directions. One suggestion is to start with pin one and go to each of the odd numbered pins, then go to all of the even numbered pins. Encourage the kids to be creative!

When the children are done with their string art, make a knot at the final pin and cut the excess string.

HIGH-POWERED GAME NEEDS:

- Plastic hoop (one or two per group)
- *VeggieConnections Music CD*
- CD player

LOW-POWERED GAME NEEDS:

- Masking tape
- Strips of 1" x 5" colored paper (three per child)
- Staplers (one per *Veggie-Connections Group*)
- Watch with second hand

BEFORE YOU START:

Use masking tape to make a circle in middle of the game area about 10'–15' in diameter. If you have more than eight groups, form two circles. Place the strips of paper in the middle of the circle. Make sure your staplers are full of staples.

CRAFT NEEDS:

- Foamboards, 9" x 9" (one per child)
- Circle String Art Pattern on page 316 (one per child)
- Scissors
- Eight map pins per child
- Colored string, or embroidery floss

CUCUMBER CONNECTION NEEDS:

- Pickle jar
- Pickles artwork from the *VeggieConnections Shepherd* pages
- Green construction paper

KID CONNECTION NEEDS:

- Time Tracker Cover on page 313 (one per child)
- Construction paper in a variety of colors
- Time Tracker Planner on page 314 (one per child)
- Time Tracker Calendar on page 315 (one per child)
- Glue sticks
- Markers
- Glitter-glue pens
- Other craft supplies

BEFORE YOU START:

Using a variety of construction-paper colors, photocopy a Time Tracker Cover on page 313 for each child. Each child will also need one regular paper copy each of the Time Tracker Planner on page 314 and Time Tracker Calendar on page 315.

OPTIONAL:

You may want to use an easier Bible translation for memorizing the Unit Memory Verse, Psalm 90:12. The NIrV and NLT are good choices.

CHRIST CONNECTION NEEDS:

- *VeggieConnections Music CD*
- CD player
- *VeggieConnections* take-home newspaper (one per child)

PART THREE:

Plugging In to My Life

Life application of the lesson to lead kids to THINK-LINK-ACT and build a relationship with God every day

A. Cucumber Connection

Before kids arrive, enlarge and copy the pickles from the *VeggieConnections Shepherd* pages on the CD-ROM included in the *VeggieConnections Elementary Curriculum Kit* onto green construction paper. Cut them out and put into a pickle jar.

Let a volunteer draw a pickle from the Pickle Pot, and either the child or a Shepherd should read the dilemma out loud. Each Shepherd should then process the question with their group using the THINK—LINK—ACT phrase.

Shauna sees a new girl at the lunch table. Her other friends are ignoring the new girl. Shauna is thinking it might be good for her to spend some time getting to know this new girl, but she doesn't want to miss out time with her friends. What should Shauna do?	Matthew hasn't been to school in a week because he has a virus and fever. He is worried he's never going to get caught up with his schoolwork. What can Matthew do while he is sick?	Mikayla's friend, Sarah, told her that Jesus doesn't last forever. He is only a character in a story that has a beginning and an end. Mikayla learned in church that Jesus is real and is eternal. Mikayla knows this is true. How can Mikayla respond to Sarah?

B. Kid Connection: Time Tracker Journal

Gather the kids at the Assembly Line tables. Say: **The Chocolate Factory works well and makes enough chocolate because they keep track of their progress. They make reports on how well they are doing, kind of like kids getting report cards to track how you're doing in school. The company writes down good things that are going on, plans to improve what they're doing, ideas they would like to try—and they keep track of progress as it's happening.**

As we grow in our relationship with God, it's good to keep track of how we're doing, too. We can see our progress in spending time with him. One way we'll be keeping track of how we're growing in our relationship with him is by writing in a journal called the *Time Tracker: Connecting God & Me*.

Show kids how to make a Z-fold book as follows: Fold the Time Tracker Cover in half, forming a front and back cover. Open the cover and using a glue stick, apply glue to the right-hand side of the inside cover. Place the planner page inside the cover (keeping the edge of the paper about ¼" from the crease of the fold), closing the cover and pressing down on it to secure the planner page (the right-hand side of the planning page will be sticking out of the cover). Then tape the calendar page to the edge of the planning page. Next, fold the calendar and planner pages in half, forming a Z shape that nests inside the cover when closed. Fold and refold the creases some to make the pages lie relatively flat when opened.

Provide markers for kids to write their names on the covers and allow them to decorate the covers with markers, glitter-glue pens, and other craft supplies. Once the kids have finished decorating, set the Time Trackers on the Assembly Line to dry. Explain how the Time Tracker will help kids live out the Unit Memory Verse, Psalm 90:12. Practice saying the verse several times together. The Time Tracker Journals will be used each week as kids look at how they are using their time and how they plan to use their time each week.

C. Christ Connection

Have everyone stand and sing the *THINK—LINK—ACT* song, while doing the motions. When done, have the kids sit in a circle and ask what they would like to pray about (THINK). After each request, focus on God's promise to answer the prayers of those who are connected to him (LINK), as seen in the Program Verse: "*Come near to God and he will come near to you,*" James 4:8. Pray together about the request (ACT). Continue until all kids who have a request have been prayed for.

Distribute the take-home newspaper, *VeggieConnections*.

Connecting to **Time** through the writings
of the disciple **John**
John writes about the Holy Spirit: **John 14:15-29**

Connection Word:
Holy Spirit

PART ONE:

Plugging In at the Chocolate Factory

Introduction to the site
and lesson focus

LESSON 2:
God is with me all the time.

A. Veggie Connection

BEFORE YOU START:
Group the items needed to make bunnies for each *VeggieConnections Group*. However, be sure each group does not have enough of two of the items to complete all of their bunnies.

OPTIONAL:
To introduce this activity, view the opening segment of the *Rack, Shack, & Benny* VeggieTales video, the scene of the Assembly Line of Veggie characters making chocolate bunnies.

Dressed as the Factory Manager, warmly greet the kids as they punch in at the Chocolate Factory entrance and receive their badges.

Invite the kids to your Assembly Line (tables), and divide them into *VeggieConnections Groups*. Place the cutouts of bunnies, eyes, and bow ties, along with glue, on the tables in front of each group. Be sure there are not enough of two of the items in each group to complete their task, but do not let the kids know this. Have each group of kids choose someone to be in charge of each item. *VeggieConnections Shepherds* should stay near their groups but not offer any help.

Inform the kids that their task today is to assemble as many bunnies as they can in two minutes. They need to work together as a team. Hold up a stopwatch, and signal the kids to begin. When they run out of supplies, Shepherds should wait until the kids on their team ask for help, then immediately give the kids what is missing.

When time is up, let the teams count who made the most bunnies. Ask the kids to tell what made their job harder and what made it easier. When they express relief that their Shepherd was nearby to help, say: **It's great to have someone close by to help us when we need it. Your Shepherds helped you with the materials to make the bunnies. Today we're going to be talking about a special helper God has sent to us, the Holy Spirit.** Sound a buzzer or bell. **That's our Connection Word for today.** Ask a volunteer to go to the Choco-matic and pick up the word on the chocolate bar. Ask for another volunteer to read the definition from the *VeggieConnections Bible Dictionary*. **Today we're going to see how the Holy Spirit helps us connect with God.**

If time permits, let the kids further decorate the Chocolate Factory by placing or taping the bunnies around the room. You may let each child take a paper bunny home as well.

THE CHILDREN
will arrive with their *VeggieConnections Shepherds* from the opening Countertop Connections featuring Bob and Larry. Play the *Veggie-Connections Music CD* as children enter the Chocolate Factory.

VEGGIE CONNECTION NEEDS:

- *VeggieConnections Music CD*
- CD player
- Paper cutouts of chocolate bunnies from page 69
- Small paper white circles or "wiggle" eyes
- Small paper bow ties
- Glue
- Stopwatch or watch with a second hand
- Buzzer or bell (from site setup)
- *VeggieConnections Bible Dictionary*

B. Prayer Connection

PRAYER CONNECTION NEEDS:

• Chocomatic with bunnies (from *Lesson 1*)

Be sure the bunnies prepared last week are in the Chocomatic.

Send one child from each *VeggieConnections Group* (a total of four kids) to the Chocomatic to reach in and pull out a bunny and bring it back to their group. The word on the bunny chosen indicates the kind of prayers each group should focus on this week.

For *Thanks*, the kids might pray this sentence: **God, you have been so good to me this week. Thank you especially for . . .**

For *Others*, the kids might pray this sentence: **Lord, someone I know needs your help. Please help ___ with . . .**

For *Praise*, the kids might pray this sentence: **Lord, I love you because you are . . .**

For *Self*, the kids may pray this sentence: **Dear God, this week I've been having a hard time with something. Please help me with . . .**

After praying, return the prayer bunnies to the Chocomatic to be used next week.

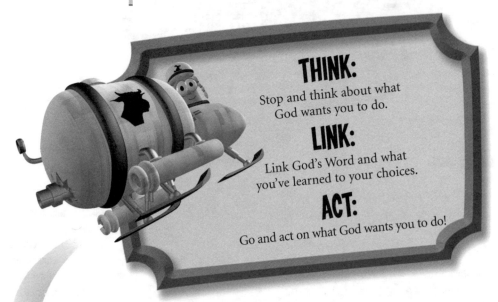

THINK:
Stop and think about what God wants you to do.

LINK:
Link God's Word and what you've learned to your choices.

ACT:
Go and act on what God wants you to do!

Now add some fun hand motions to the catch-phrase!

THINK:
Touch head with fingertip two times.

LINK:
Left hand out, right hand out. Clasp your hands together, fingers intertwined.

ACT:
Release grip and roll hands three times. Finish with arms outstretched.

PART TWO: Plugging In to God's Word

Connecting to God's Word in the Bible and understanding how that can help us to have a better relationship with him

GOD CONNECTION NEEDS:

• Bibles
• 3 cards with Bible verse references on them:
  John 14:15–17;
  John 14:18–24;
  John 14:25–29
• Large box fan or tabletop fan
• Table
• Small clock or alarm clock
• Piece of ribbon
• Foam ball

A. God Connection: John writes about the Holy Spirit – John 14:15-29

Invite the kids to join you in the R&D Lab and be seated on the floor. Set up a table where all can see it. Place the fan on the table, facing away from the kids. Ask for three volunteers who are good readers to help you with the Bible passage today, and give each a card listing the verses and a Bible. Have them find the verses in their Bibles and mark the place with the card.

Turn on the fan. Ask: **How many of you can see the wind that is coming from this fan?** Allow for responses; be sure kids understand the difference between seeing the wind and seeing the effect of the wind. **Can you smell the wind?** Again, kids might confuse the smell of the wind with other things in the room causing scents. **Can you taste the wind?** (*No.*) **Then how do you know any wind is there?** Let the kids try to explain; the only way they can know is to feel it blowing or to see its effects. **As long as we're in the Research and Development Lab, we're going to perform a test to show that the wind is truly there even though we can't see it.**

Show the alarm clock, piece of ribbon, and foam ball. Let the kids make guesses about what they think would happen if these things were placed in the wind of the fan. After guessing, turn the fan to blow across the table, and place the clock in front of it. Invite the kids to watch carefully. **Nothing happened to the clock. Does that mean that the wind doesn't exist? Why not?** *(The clock was too heavy, but the wind still exists.)* Next, place the foam ball in front of the fan; the wind will push the ball away. Then hold the ribbon in front of the fan; it will flutter. If you let go it will blow away. **Now is it obvious that the wind exists? Why?** *(Because we can see what it does.)* **Sometimes it is easier to believe that something is real when we can see it or we can see what it does.**

Explain that John wrote about something that exists but can't be seen. It's the Holy Spirit. Ask the child with the card labeled John 14:15–17 to read that passage from their Bible now. **Who did Jesus promise would come to be with his followers?** *(v. 17, the Spirit of truth or the Holy Spirit.)* **How will the world respond to the Holy Spirit? Why?** *(v. 17, they won't be able to see the Holy Spirit so they won't believe he's there or understand what he's doing.)* **Where will God's Spirit live?** *(v. 17b, with us and in us.)* **Jesus encouraged his followers by telling them that though they can't see the Holy Spirit, they would know he was there because they see what he does or how he works—like the wind.** Turn the fan to blow gently on the kids. **And the kinds of things that we can see the Holy Spirit doing are things like helping us know right from wrong, helping us understand the Bible, and giving us encouragement. How has the Holy Spirit done this for you?** Have kids and *VeggieConnections Shepherds* share their own experiences.

Ask the next volunteer to read John 14:18–24. **To be able to connect to a growing relationship with Jesus, what do we have to do?** *(vss. 21 and 23, love Jesus and show that love by obeying him.)* **Jesus did not ask the disciples—or us—to do this on our own. How did Jesus say he would help us and be with us?** *(vss. 18 and 20, by sending the Spirit to be in us and make his home with us.)*

Have the next volunteer read John 14:25–29. **Why did Jesus send the Holy Spirit?** *(v. 26, to teach and remind the disciples—and us—of everything Jesus had taught and to assure us of Jesus' love.)* Give real-life examples. **How long will the Holy Spirit stay with us?** *(v. 28, until Jesus comes back again.)*

Explain to the kids that when we have a relationship with God through Jesus, Jesus promises that he will send the Holy Spirit to live in us and be our helper. We won't be able to see him with our eyes, but we'll be able to tell he's there by what he does, just like the wind from the fan. This is a promise we have from Jesus when we connect to a relationship with him.

B. Activity Connection

Choose from the following activities to help kids explore and remember that God is with them all the time (approximately 10–15 minutes each).

1. High-Powered Game: Stuck-Together Relay

Designate the starting line. Divide the kids into two teams. Say: **We know that Jesus sent the Holy Spirit to be with us. When we have a relationship with Jesus, the Holy Spirit is with us all the time. It's like he's stuck together with us like superglue. Now you can be glued to someone and help.**

Have the kids within each team pair up with a partner and use 3-foot strips of cloth to loosely tie together one ankle of each partner. Set two bunnies at the opposite end of the game area. Explain that the goal of the game is for two pairs to be the first to grab their bunny. Allow each pair a moment to decide how they want to get to the bunny—hop, crawl, roll—whatever crazy way they want to get there.

Allow everyone to call: **Ready, set, go!** The first pair that grabs the bunny must call out: **God is with me all the time!** before racing back to their team with it. Continue to play until all of the pairs have had a turn.

Let the kids sit down, and briefly discuss with them: **How would having God's Spirit with you be a help to you?** *(The Spirit could help me know right from wrong when I face a temptation; he could give me peace when I'm afraid; he could help me understand what I'm learning from the Bible; and so on.)*

2. Low-Powered Game: Time and Place Connection Game

LOW-POWERED GAME NEEDS:

- Copies of the Here and Now Chart on page 280
- Scissors
- Hard candies, various colors and shapes in pairs (optional)
- Chalkboard or large blank paper

Gather the kids in the R&D Lab to play. Mix up the strips, and give one to each child. If you have an uneven number of children, let a *VeggieConnections Shepherd* play. Allow a moment for kids to read their strips; let Shepherds help as needed.

At your signal, the kids are to find another child (with the opposite color strip) whose "Here" makes sense with their "Now" situation or vice versa. Kids may need to talk with a number of other kids before finding a good match. (Younger kids who do not read well will be able to find their pairs by the candies attached, or with help from Shepherds.) As soon as pairs match, they should throw their arms up in the air and shout: **Connection!**

Once the pairs are connected, they should move over to the board and read the question: **How can the Holy Spirit help you here and now?** (referring to the situation on their matched pair). Pairs should discuss ideas and should remember the answers they come up with. Have a *VeggieConnections Shepherd* available to help as needed. Once a pair has thought of an answer, they give each other a high-five and wait for the other pairs to finish.

At the end, come together in a large group and let each pair share their situations and answers with everyone.

3. Craft: "All the Time" Clock

CRAFT NEEDS:

- Circles of wood 4" x 3/4" (one per child)
- Letter stickers, 1/2" tall, to spell "God is with me!"
- 1 1/2" arrows cut from craft foam (one per child)
- 1" arrows cut from craft foam (one per child)
- 3/4" brads (nails) (one per child)
- Hammers
- 1/8" bit and drill (optional)

Set out the letter stickers and craft foam arrows in the middle of the Assembly Line tables. Give each child a wooden "clock." Explain that instead of adding the 12 numbers to the clock, they are going to add the letters that spell, "God is with me!" in the spots where the numbers go. Allow kids to choose their own letters and colors for the phrase. Have the kids place the letters on their clocks; help as needed.

Give each child a brad and have *VeggieConnections Shepherds* help the kids poke a hole in the end of both arrows and thread the arrows onto the brad. Then help the kids find the premade hole in their clock. With help from Shepherds, the kids take turns hammering their brad into the hole. They should leave the brad sticking up a little (not hammered down tight) so that the foam arrows can be turned.

Ask the kids questions about how they spend their day. **What time do you get up in the morning?** Have them set their clock for the various times. **What time does school end? What are you usually doing at 4:30?** Talk briefly about how God is with them throughout the day. **Is there any time that God takes off and is not with you?** (*No! God even watches over us while we sleep.*)

PART THREE:

Plugging In to My Life

Life application of the lesson to lead kids to THINK-LINK-ACT and build a relationship with God every day

A. Cucumber Connection

Before kids arrive, enlarge and copy the pickles from the *VeggieConnections Shepherd* pages on the CD-ROM included in the *VeggieConnections Elementary Curriculum Kit* onto green construction paper. Cut them out and put into a pickle jar.

Let a volunteer draw a pickle from the Pickle Pot, and either the child or a Shepherd should read the dilemma out loud. Each Shepherd should then process the question with their group using the THINK—LINK—ACT phrase.

Jasmine gets to spend two weeks with her cousins on vacation. Her parents aren't going. Jasmine worries she won't want to stay the entire trip, because her cousins aren't Christians. How can Jasmine know that God is always with her?	Noah has to walk home from school because his bike was stolen. He knows there is a bully on the route to his house, who has been picking on him lately. He wants God to keep him safe. What can Noah do?	Sydney has trouble remembering her math facts. Her mom helped her practice for her math test but Sydney thinks she can't get a good grade because it's a timed test. Sydney's mom has told her God will be with her. What can Sydney do?

CUCUMBER CONNECTION NEEDS:

- Pickle jar
- Pickle artwork from the *VeggieConnections Shepherd* pages
- Green construction paper

B. Kid Connection: Time Tracker Journal

Have the kids pick up their Time Tracker Journals from the Assembly Line. Read together the Unit Memory Verse, Psalm 90:12, on the back cover of their journals. Then ask: **What does it mean to "number our days"?** Let the kids speculate. **It's not so much that we count our days—that's what we do when we celebrate birthdays! Rather, it means that we think about what we're doing during our days—how we spend them and if we're using our days for important things. We notice whether or not we are keeping a close connection with God.**

Have the kids open their Time Tracker to the calendar page. **This blank calendar reminds us to do what our Unit Memory Verse says. This page represents all the months of our lives.** Instruct kids to write "God is with me all the time" at the bottom of the calendar page. On the blank page 1 next to the calendar, encourage kids to write or draw one time coming up this week that they want to remember that God is with them.

KID CONNECTION NEEDS:

- Time Tracker Journals (from *Lesson 1*)
- Pencils
- Colored markers

OPTIONAL:

You may want to use an easier Bible translation for memorizing the Unit Memory Verse, Psalm 90:12. The NIrV and NLT are good choices.

C. Christ Connection

Have everyone stand and sing the *THINK—LINK—ACT* song using motions.

Close by asking the kids to pair up with a partner. They may share what they wrote or drew in their Time Tracker Journals. Then have kids pray for each other, asking God to help them remember that he is with them all the time. Lead a closing prayer: **Father God, thank you for being with each one of us all the time. Thank you for giving us your Holy Spirit to guide our lives. Help us to follow your Spirit and use our time wisely. In Jesus name, amen.**

Distribute the take-home newspaper, *VeggieConnections*.

CHRIST CONNECTION NEEDS:

- *VeggieConnections* Music CD
- CD player
- *VeggieConnections* take-home newspaper (one per child)

Lesson 2 – Here and Now Chart

HERE	NOW
Alone in bed at night	You've had nightmares.
In front of the chore list at home	You don't feel like doing your chores.
In the family room	You don't want to share videos with your brothers or sisters.
At the school playground	A mean kid wants to play where you are.
In class at school	You're taking a test.
At your best friend's home	You tell your best friend about a problem.
On the school bus	There are always arguments about where to sit.
At the mall	You feel like taking something without paying for it.
On the ball field	You didn't get to play the position you wanted.
At church	You're having trouble understanding what a Bible verse means.
In the hospital	You're getting ready for surgery.
At your desk at home	You're having trouble with your homework.
In the car	You always fight with brothers and sisters about where to sit.
On the basketball court	Your friends are acting very unsportsmanlike, and they want you to join in.
At the dining table with your parents on their payday	You get your allowance.

Connecting to **Time** through the writings
of the disciple **John**
John writes about walking in the light: **1 John 1:5–2:6**

PART ONE:

Plugging In at the Chocolate Factory

Introduction to the site
and lesson focus

LESSON 3:
I will spend time with God.

A. Veggie Connection

BEFORE YOU START:

Make 2–3 chocolate bunnies with defects, such as the bow tie attached to one ear, an eye in the middle of the bunny, and so on. You'll need to darken the Chocolate Factory as much as possible. Make copies of the Job Opening Survey on page 286 for each *VeggieConnections Shepherd*.

Dressed as the Factory Manager, warmly greet the kids as they punch in at the Chocolate Factory entrance and receive their badges. Give each *VeggieConnections Shepherd* a flashlight and a copy of the Job Opening Survey, and have groups sit together. Say: **We have a little problem at the factory. We lost one of our most loyal employees, the plant light manager. The manager's job was to make sure we had enough light for the employees to make the chocolate bunnies. When it's too dark in here, this is what happens!** Show kids the defective bunnies by shining your flashlight on them. **Mr. Nezzer needs your help to choose the right person for the job. He wants each of you to answer interview questions to find out if someone here would be the right person.**

Have Shepherds ask their kids the questions. Ask a few volunteers to share responses. Then have a leader turn on the lights or brighten the room. Say: **I'm sure all of you could be hired by Mr. Nezzer! After all, it not too hard to make sure the lights stay on in the factory. But today we're going to be talking about a different kind of light.** Sound buzzer or bell. **That type of *light* is our Connection Word for today.** Ask a volunteer to go to the Chocomatic and pick up the word on the chocolate bar. Ask for another volunteer to read the definition from the *VeggieConnections Bible Dictionary*. Explain how living God's way is "walking in the light," the topic of the Bible story for today.

THE CHILDREN
will arrive with their *VeggieConnections Shepherds* from the opening Countertop Connections featuring Bob and Larry. Play the *Veggie-Connections Music CD* as children enter the Chocolate Factory.

VEGGIE CONNECTION NEEDS:

- *VeggieConnections Music CD*
- CD player
- Flashlights (one per group plus extras)
- Job Opening Survey on page 286 (one per *Veggie-Connections Group*)
- Prepared paper chocolate bunnies
- Buzzer or bell
- *VeggieConnections Bible Dictionary*

B. Prayer Connection

PRAYER CONNECTION NEEDS:

• Chocomatic with bunnies (from *Lesson 1*)

Be sure the bunnies from *Lesson 1* are in the Chocomatic.

Send one kid from each *VeggieConnections Group* to the Chocomatic to reach in and pull out a bunny and bring it back to their group. The word on the bunny chosen indicates the kind of prayers each group should focus on this week.

For *Thanks*, the kids might pray this sentence: **God, you have been so good to me this week. Thank you especially for . . .**

For *Others*, the kids might pray this sentence: **Lord, someone I know needs your help. Please help ___ with . . .**

For *Praise*, the kids might pray this sentence: **Lord, I love you because you are . . .**

For *Self*, the kids may pray this sentence: **Dear God, this week I've been having a hard time with something. Please help me with . . .**

After praying, return the prayer bunnies to the Chocomatic to be used next week.

Plugging In to God's Word

Connecting to God's Word in the Bible and understanding how that can help us to have a better relationship with him

A. God Connection: John writes about walking in the light – 1 John 1:5–2:6

GOD CONNECTION NEEDS:

• Prepared posterboard signs
• Glow-in-the-dark paint (available at craft and hardware stores)
• White shirt
• Black light
• Bible
• Flashlight

BEFORE YOU START:

Use glow-in-the-dark paint to write these phrases in large letters on pieces of posterboard: *walk in darkness; walk in the light; what Jesus did; obey his commands; I will spend time with God.*

Find a way to completely darken the Chocolate Factory or plan to have Bible Connection in another location that can be completely without light; you could call it "The Top, Top Secret Lab" as you lead the kids there. If you are not already wearing a white shirt in your role as the Factory Manager, be sure to put one on before starting the Bible story. You may need to use a flashlight to read from this page during the Bible story.

Invite the kids to be seated in the R&D Lab (or wherever you've planned). Ask if anyone is afraid of the dark and allow for a show of hands. **Some people are afraid of the dark. Other people like the dark. They like it because then they can do cool things with special kinds of light.** Say that you like to play with black lights and do cool things with light and dark. Turn off the room lights and turn on the black light. Your white shirt will glow. Have kids look at their own clothes. What do they see? Ask: **What are some fun things we can do in the dark?** *(Star gaze, watch fireworks, flashlight walks, enjoy candlelight, black-light painting, sleeping, and so on.)*

Some animals like the dark. They're called nocturnal, which means night. What are some animals that only come out at night? *(Bats, raccoons, owls, and so on.)* **They like the dark because it's easier to catch their food or to not get caught.**

Some people like to live in the dark, too, but that's not because they're nocturnal. It's because they do bad things and don't want to get caught. It's easier to hide in the dark. That's the kind of darkness our Bible story talks about today.

Turn on the room lights. Show the kids that today's Bible story is found in 1 John chapters 1 and 2. Explain that the kids are going to learn about what it means to walk in the light, not live in darkness.

Turn out the room lights again, leaving the black light on. Hold up the posterboard labeled "walk in darkness." **John wrote that some people "walk in darkness." What do you think he meant?** Let the kids speculate. **John is using darkness to describe sin. Sin is what we say, do, and think that is not God's way; it's any kind of wrongdoing. People who walk in this kind of darkness choose to do things that God doesn't like, things that are against his rules.** Ask kids for examples of things that are sin.

Hold up the next posterboard, labeled "walk in the light." **John wrote that we should try to walk in the light. What could that mean?** Let the kids speculate. **Having a relationship with Jesus, being plugged into him, helps us to know the way Jesus wants us to live. The more time we spend with Jesus, the more we will know what he wants us to do.** Ask for examples of things God wants us to do, things that please him.

Hold up third posterboard, labeled "what Jesus did." **Jesus did something that only he could do—he gave up his life so that we can be clean of our sin. He took the punishment for the things that we did wrong, even though he never did anything wrong. Jesus never sinned or disobeyed God.**

Hold up the fourth posterboard, labeled "obey his commands." **John wrote how we can know we are walking in the light. What is it?** *(By obeying God's commands.)* Tell kids that as they learn the Bible they learn God's commands—all the things God says are best for us to do. We have a choice to obey those things. When Jesus lives inside us, he helps us obey. That's a way we know we are walking in the light.

Hold up the final posterboard, labeled "I will spend time with God." **What does it mean to spend time with God?** *(To learn the Bible, pray, think about what God wants, and so on.)* **Spending time with God will help us obey his teachings—and then we'll be walking in the light.**

Turn the lights back on, and discuss these questions with the kids: **What does the Bible mean by "walking in darkness"?** *(Choosing to sin, to do wrong things—that's outside of God's light.)* **What does the Bible mean by "walking in the light"?** *(Obeying Jesus' teachings, staying close to him so we can be strong to obey.)* **How can we be wise and strong enough to walk in the light?** *(By spending time with God.)*

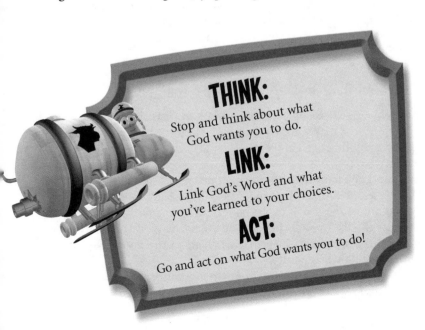

THINK:
Stop and think about what God wants you to do.

LINK:
Link God's Word and what you've learned to your choices.

ACT:
Go and act on what God wants you to do!

Now add some fun hand motions to the catch-phrase!

THINK:
Touch head with fingertip two times.

LINK:
Left hand out, right hand out. Clasp your hands together, fingers intertwined.

ACT:
Release grip and roll hands three times. Finish with arms outstretched.

B. Activity Connection

Choose from the following activities to help kids explore and remember to spend time with God (approximately 10–15 minutes each).

1. High-Powered Game: Walking in the Light Relay

BEFORE YOU START:
You'll need as dark a room as possible for this game. Place penlights in the middle of your playing area, covering them with a box. Using the box as a center hub, place masking tapes start lines equally distant from the hub, forming a circle outline with the lines. Make the line distance about 10' from the box if you have room. You'll need one line for each *VeggieConnections Group* team.

HIGH-POWERED GAME NEEDS:
- Penlights (one per child)
- Box
- Masking tape

Say: **We've been talking about "walking in the light." If we are walking in the light, others will be illuminated from our glow.** Turn on your penlight and turn off the lights. Divide kids into *VeggieConnections Groups* or equally distribute kids in teams around the taped start lines. Kids should line up relay-style. Kids will crab-walk to the box in the center, get a penlight from under the box, turn it on, placing it on their stomachs, balancing it as they walk, and crab-walk back to their team. Once kids have retrieved a light, they should leave it on.

As more kids complete the course, the room will get brighter and brighter. Allow all the groups to finish, then have teams sit down where they are. Turn on your penlight and ask kids to turn off theirs. **God wants us to walk in the light.** Have kids, one at a time, turn on their lights. **Remember to allow your light to shine around you so others will be attracted to Jesus' light!**

2. Low-Powered Game: Lights, Camera, Action!

BEFORE YOU START:
Write one word or phrase each on slips of paper: *flashlight, light bulb, Christmas tree lights, lamp, sun, star, lightning, lighthouse, street light, lantern, campfire, firefly, match, car headlights, torch, candle, camera flash.*

LOW-POWERED GAME NEEDS:
- Prepared paper slips
- Chalkboard or easel with large paper for drawing
- Chalk or markers

Divide the kids into two teams. Have one member of Team 1 pick a word and draw it on the easel or board. Give Team 1 one minute to call out the correct name of the item. If Team 1 hasn't guessed correctly, allow Team 2 one minute to guess. When a team guesses correctly, they must also call out a way they can "walk in the light." Award one point to the team with a correct guess. Have the teams switch back and forth taking turns guessing and calling out ways to walk in the light.

After the game, announce the winning team and say: **It may have been pretty easy to call out the types of light in this game. But walking in God's light may not be as easy. Whenever you see these different kinds of light used in our game, let it remind you to look to Jesus' light as you walk with God.**

3. Craft: Glow-in-the-Dark Heart Hangers

CRAFT NEEDS:
- 2"–3" wooden hearts (one per child)
- Small paintbrushes
- Glow-in-the-dark paint
- Craft foam doorknob hangers (one per child)
- Permanent markers
- Glue
- Paint shirts or smocks (optional)

Gather kids at the Assembly Line. Pass out a wooden heart to each child. Instruct kids to paint one side with glow-in-the-dark paints. Explain to the kids the glow paint can remind them that God's love shines brightly, even in the dark. Set the hearts aside on the Assembly Line to dry.

Give kids a foam doorknob hanger and permanent markers. Have kids write, "Jesus is the Light!" near the top of the hanger (leaving enough room for the hearts to be glued on the lower half of the hanger and not cover up the words). Kids could also use the markers to decorate the hanger.

After the hearts are dry, show kids how to glue them to the door hangers. Set aside on the Assembly Line to dry.

Say: **You can put these on the door of your room as a reminder that Jesus is the Light; and God's love can encourage you, even when you face dark times in your life.**

PART THREE:

Plugging in to My Life

Life application of the lesson to lead kids to THINK–LINK–ACT and build a relationship with God every day.

A. Cucumber Connection

Before kids arrive, enlarge and copy the pickles from the *VeggieConnections Shepherd* pages on the CD-ROM included in the *VeggieConnections Elementary Curriculum Kit* onto green construction paper. Cut them out and put into a pickle jar.

Let a volunteer draw a pickle from the Pickle Pot, and either the child or a Shepherd should read the dilemma out loud. Each Shepherd should then process the question with their group using the THINK—LINK—ACT phrase.

Emma's mom told her not to watch TV when she gets home from school. But Emma has been watching TV anyway and denying it when her mom asks. What should Emma do?	It's Sunday morning and Colin wants to hang out with his friend at the park. His mom told him that he had to go to church. Colin would rather play with his friend. What should he do?	Chandra went to church and was challenged to memorize a Bible verse. She thinks it will be easy to memorize the verse. Unfortunately, the week goes by and she never works on it. What should Chandra do?

CUCUMBER CONNECTION NEEDS:

- Pickle jar
- Pickle artwork from the *VeggieConnections Shepherd* pages
- Green construction paper

B. Kid Connection: Time Tracker Journal

Have the kids pick up their Time Tracker Journals from the Assembly Line. Cut black construction paper in half, and give a half sheet to each child. Using glue sticks, have kids glue the sheet to the inside cover of their book. Give kids gel pens and have them write "I will walk in Jesus' Light!" on the black page.

Say: **We can all do things to grow closer in our walk with God. One way we can do this is to remember God's Word.** Have kids look at the calendar page in their books. Give them pencils and have them write, "I will spend time with God," at the top of their calendar page. Then referring to the Unit Memory Verse printed on the back cover of their books, have kids write a word of the verse in each "day" box, leaving a blank box between words. **Seeing our Unit Memory Verse on a calendar page reminds us to plan to walk in God's light every day of our lives.** Have kids return their journals to the Assembly Line for use next lesson.

KID CONNECTION NEEDS:

- Time Tracker Journals
- Black construction paper (one piece per every two kids)
- Scissors
- Gel pens in various colors
- Glue sticks
- Pencils

OPTION:

You may want to use an easier Bible translation for memorizing the Unit Memory Verse, Psalm 90:12. The NIrV and NLT are good choices.

C. Christ Connection

Have everyone stand and do the motions for the *THINK—LINK—ACT* song.

Gather in *VeggieConnections Groups*. Say: **God does not forget his promises, and he does not forget our prayers either.** Pray together for the children's concerns, and be sure to thank God for how he will answer.

Distribute the take-home newspaper, **VeggieConnections**.

CHRIST CONNECTION NEEDS:

- *VeggieConnections Music CD*
- CD player
- *VeggieConnections* take-home newspaper (one per child)

The Chocolate Factory

JOB OPENING SURVEY

1. How much light do we need in the Chocolate Factory?

2. Why is light important to the Chocolate Factory?

3. What are your favorite things to do when it's light?

4. What do you do when there is no light?

Connecting to **Time** through the writings
of the disciple **John**
John writes about Jesus' teachings: **John 15:1-17**

PART ONE:

Plugging In at the Chocolate Factory

Introduction to the site
and lesson focus

LESSON 4:
I will set godly priorities
with my time.

A. Veggie Connection

Dressed as the Factory Manager, warmly greet the kids as they punch in at the Chocolate Factory entrance and receive their employee badges. Explain that just before the kids arrived, you received an urgent memo to pass on to them. Read the following:

> To: All workers in the Chocolate Factory
> From: Mr. Lunt
> Date: Today
>
> **It has come to our attention that the locks on the doors need to be changed. Too many people have been getting into the Chocolate Factory when they aren't allowed. Since everyone is working today, the doors will be closed all day until dinner. No one comes in. No one goes out. You have five minutes to decide if you want anything before the doors close. You may choose five items from this list to have with you. Oh, and by the way, the cafeteria is closed today.**

Have the kids divide into *VeggieConnections Groups*. Give each group a copy of the Chocolate Factory Survival List (page 292), and instruct them to decide together which items would be most important to survive the day. Give groups about two minutes to decide on their items.

When finished, allow the groups to tell the others which items they chose and why. Ask: **How did you know that some of these things were better ideas than others?** (*Because some we need to stay strong throughout the day; the others are just for fun or we could live without.*)

Say: **Choosing things that are more important is called setting priorities. You had to choose certain items to be a priority over the others.** Ring the buzzer or bell. Say: **It looks like I said our Connection Word!** Choose a volunteer to pick up the word from the Chocomatic and another volunteer to read the definition in the *VeggieConnections Bible Dictionary*. **One of our priorities here at *VeggieConnections* is prayer, so let's do that before we continue.**

THE CHILDREN
will arrive with their *VeggieConnections Shepherds* from the opening Countertop Connections featuring Bob and Larry. Play the *Veggie-Connections Music CD* as children enter the Chocolate Factory.

VEGGIE CONNECTION NEEDS:

- *VeggieConnections Music CD*
- CD player
- Chocolate Factory Survival List on page 292 (one per *Veggie-Connections Group*)
- Pencils
- Buzzer or bell
- *VeggieConnections Bible Dictionary*

B. Prayer Connection

PRAYER CONNECTION NEEDS:

- Chocomatic with bunnies (from *Lesson 1*)

Send one child from each *VeggieConnections Group* to the Chocomatic (a total of four kids) to reach in and pull out a bunny and bring it back to their group. The word on the bunny chosen indicates the kind of prayers each group should focus on this week: *Thanks, Others, Praise,* or *Self.* Let the kids share their thoughts or requests and then spend some time praying.

Return the prayer bunnies to the Chocomatic after Prayer Connection to be used next week.

PART TWO:

Plugging In to God's Word

Connecting to God's Word in the Bible and understanding how that can help us to have a better relationship with him

A. God Connection: John writes about Jesus' teachings – John 15:1-17

GOD CONNECTION NEEDS:

- Gardener's hat
- Real or artificial potted plant
- Various lengths of rope or yarn (one per child)
- Bible

Put on the gardener's hat, and invite the kids to join you in the R&D Lab and be seated. Hold up the potted plant and use it to illustrate the points you will make. Tell the kids that one of the things you like to do during your time away from the Chocolate Factory is to take care of your garden. Explain how tending the plants relaxes you after a long day of work. You enjoy the digging, watering, and weeding. Explain that sometimes the plants that you are caring for need to be trimmed. They have wilting leaves, so you have to cut them off. It's called pruning and helps the plant grow even better.

Have the kids stand up in their *VeggieConnections Groups* and make a circle around their *VeggieConnections Shepherd*. Explain that the Shepherds are going to be the "vine" of the plant, which is like the stem or trunk. Give each child a length of rope. Instruct a few of the kids in each group to hand one end of the rope to their Shepherd while they hold on to the other end. These kids are the branches. Then have the other kids choose someone to give their end of the rope to hang on to. These are parts of the branches, such as twigs and leaves.

Say: **While you're connected to the vine, you're healthy. But let's pretend that some of your leaves start to wither.** Ask the kids to close their eyes. Walk around the room and tap different "leaves" (kids) on the shoulder. Then have the kids open their eyes. Instruct them that if they were tapped, they should slowly start falling to the ground while pulling on the rope. This will have the effect of pulling down the branches and even leaning the vine. **This is similar to what happens to a plant when a part starts to wither or doesn't bear fruit. It affects the rest of the vine.** Walk around and "prune" the wilted leaves by taking away their rope. Ask: **Can the parts that are pruned go off on their own and produce any fruit or leaves? Why not?** (*No, because they need to be attached to the vine; they can't grow on their own.*) **Branches, twigs, leaves—all parts of a plant—must be connected to the vine or trunk in order to live. Then they can bear fruit—that means to grow fruit or flowers or more leaves or just grow bigger and stronger.**

Pass out the ropes again. This time explain that the Shepherds represent Jesus, and the kids are Christians who are connected to Jesus. Say: **This is like our relationship with God. Our Bible story comes from the Gospel of John in the New Testament. John wrote that Jesus was using this same example with his disciples. Jesus told them that he is the vine, and we are the branches. And we can choose to form a strong connection with him. We do that by making him a priority, by putting him first.**

As you name each of the following things, point to or tap a "leaf" (child) to have the whole branch grow healthier (taller and more tightly gripping the rope). **We make God a priority by doing things like talking with him, learning the Bible, loving him and others, and obeying his teachings. These things make the whole branch stronger. Then we "bear fruit"—that means we grow stronger in our faith and we become more like Jesus.**

But if we don't use our time wisely, and make God a low priority, our leaves start to wither. As you name each of these things, tap other "leaves" (kids). **If you don't take any time to pray or read the Bible, if you don't want to learn about God, if you know you have a choice to do the right thing but you choose to do wrong—those kinds of priorities can make you wither and wilt.** Have those leaves start pulling down on the branches. **They will drag down your relationship with God.**

This is what Jesus said in our Bible reading for today. Open your Bible and read John 15:5–8. **We can work together with God, the gardener, to prune or cut off the wrong priorities we set. We can work together with God to "water" and encourage the good priorities that help us grow stronger on the vine, Jesus. We need to set godly priorities with our time. And God can help us do that.**

Collect the ropes and ask the kids to be seated.

Discuss these questions with the kids: **What does Jesus mean when he says that he is the vine and we are the branches?** *(That he is the part that gives life, and we have to be connected to him to have life.)* **What kinds of priorities will drag down our relationship with God?** *(Not taking time to learn about him or be with him or obey him, and so on.)* **How do we set godly priorities to keep growing in Jesus?** *(By taking time to pray, read the Bible, learn about him, love others, obey his teachings, and so on.)*

B. Activity Connection

Choose from the following activities to help kids explore and remember that God wants us to set godly priorities with our time (approximately 10–15 minutes each).

1. High-Powered Game: Vine and Branches Connect

Divide the kids into two teams. Have one team tie red ribbons around their wrists and the second team tie blue ribbons on their wrists. Have *VeggieConnections Shepherds* help kids. Station a Shepherd in the center of your playing area. Have one person in each pair blindfold his or her partner. Give one piece of the shorter lengths of rope or yarn to every pair of kids on both teams. Have a Shepherd join a team to make a pair if needed.

Have pairs each hold one end of their rope. With pairs holding their ropes, have them scatter throughout the playing area, mixing red and blue pairs. Say: **We've been seeing that when a branch is connected to the vine, it stays healthy. Each pair is a "branch" in this game.** Point to the Shepherd in the center. The Shepherd is our "vine."

HIGH-POWERED GAME NEEDS:
- 1' pieces of red ribbon for half the class
- 1' pieces of blue ribbon for half the class
- Blindfolds (one per every two kids)
- Rope or yarn from God Connection activity

Explain how pairs will be guided by the seeing partner to find other pairs. When a pair touches another pair, they connect and search for other pairs or larger groups. When all the branches are connected, they move together to touch the vine. The first team that connects everyone and reaches the vine wins. If time permits play a few rounds, having pairs switch seeing roles.

After the game, say: **In this game, you had some obstacles to overcome to reach the vine. In real life, what are some obstacles that keep you from being connected to our vine, Jesus?** Allow responses.

2. Low-Powered Game: Priorities on the Move

LOW-POWERED GAME NEEDS:

- Priority Cards on page 317
- Six containers for the cards
- Basket of bite-sized chocolate bars or wrapped candies (one per child)
- Green construction paper
- Scissors
- Tape

BEFORE YOU START:

Make two copies of the Priority Cards (p. 317), and cut them apart. Mix up the cards and divide them among six containers, being sure that the ones naming locations do not end up at the location named on them. If the six locations do not already exist at your site, hang up signs designating them for this game: *Chocomatic, Delivery Truck, Factory Entrance, Assembly Line, R&D Lab, Employee Bulletin Board.* Place a container of cards at each location. Cut out leaf shapes out of green construction paper and tape them to the candy. Place the basket of candy somewhere in the center of the room.

WARNING:

Please be aware of children with dairy and nut allergies. Milk chocolate snacks are often suggested in this unit, and these children may have a medically serious allergic reaction. Be sure to let parents know that their kids will be offered chocolate at the Chocolate Factory. Be sure to have safe alternatives on hand, such as hard candies or taffy.

Divide the kids into teams of three to four kids each. Assign each team to start at one of the six locations. (If you have more than six teams, some may start at the same spot.) Tell the teams that their goal is to collect a piece of candy for each team member, but do to so they must travel around the Chocolate Factory, following the directions on the Priority Cards.

As they reach each location, they draw one card from the container. Some priorities on the cards are good, and the team will be told to move forward (to a designated spot). Some priorities are bad and will send a team back to their previous spot. Some priorities are just silly, and the team has to stay at the same spot until another team comes and has a turn; then they may draw another card and move on. Kids may take a piece of candy only if their card tells them to. Kids should return a Priority Card back to its container after reading it. When their team has collected one piece of candy for each player, they are done and should move to an empty spot in the room to watch and wait for the others, while enjoying their candy.

Have *VeggieConnections Shepherds* stationed where they can help the kids read the Priority Cards. At your signal, each team chooses one card from the container at their starting spot and follows its directions. The teams will be heading to different spots at different times, and have different results. Play until all the teams have collected enough candy for their whole team. Say: **When you picked good choices in this game, you got the candy attached to the leaf. When a leaf is attached to a branch, it is strong. And as we stay attached to Jesus by choosing good priorities, we'll stay strong, too!**

3. Craft: God's Word Is Like a Seed...

CRAFT NEEDS:

- Natural sponge (one per child)
- Water
- Fast-growing seeds
- Two ribbons per child

Wet the sponges and squeeze out any extra water so that the sponges are damp. Put a variety of seeds carefully into each of the sponge's holes. Tie one ribbon around the sponge and knot it at the top. Loop the second ribbon through the first, and create a hanging project. Instruct the children to hang their sponges in a sunny window and keep it moist at all times. Enjoy the plants! Remind the children that God's Word is like a seed. It produces life and is powerful, even though we can't always see it.

PART THREE:

Plugging In to My Life

Life application of the lesson to lead kids to THINK-LINK-ACT and build a relationship with God every day

A. Cucumber Connection

Before kids arrive, enlarge and copy the pickles from the *VeggieConnections Shepherd* pages on the CD-ROM included in the *VeggieConnections Elementary Curriculum Kit* onto green construction paper. Cut them out and put into a pickle jar.

Let a volunteer draw a pickle from the Pickle Pot, and either the child or a Shepherd should read the dilemma out loud. Each Shepherd should then process the question with their group using the THINK—LINK—ACT phrase.

Brandon wants to see the latest superhero movie. Opening day is the same day his family volunteered to help with a church service project for their community. Brandon would rather spend his time seeing the movie than helping. What should Brandon do?	Selah is spending more and more time with her best friend, Kylie. But Selah's other friends are feeling hurt and left out. What should Selah do?	Bryant wants to read the Bible more but can't seem to figure out when to do it. He wakes up late in the morning, watches TV after school, and plays with his friends until he has to do his homework. What should Bryant do?

B. Kid Connection: Time Tracker Journal

Have the kids pick up their Time Tracker Journals from the Assembly Line. Ask the kids to open their books to the planner page. Have kids look at their planners to assist in responding to the next two questions: **We've been learning how to set godly priorities with our time. What are some things you do with your time?** *(Go to school, eat, get dressed, go to practices, play with friends, do chores and homework, watch TV, spend time with family, and so on.)* **Which of those things do you think are godly priorities?** Allow for responses. Be sure kids understand that it's good to have relaxing time as long as it's not what they spend most of their day doing.

Explain to kids that one way to set priorities is to number their choices. Have kids turn over their foldout pages to blank page 2. Ask the kids to number 1-5 on this page and list five godly priorities that they can do with their time. Then let them decorate the page with stamps or drawings that will help them to remember to set godly priorities with their time. When done, have kids return their journals to the Assembly Line for use next lesson.

C. Christ Connection

Have everyone stand and sing the *THINK—LINK—ACT* song using motions.

Lead the group in praying the Unit Memory Verse, Psalm 90:12, back to God. Have the kids stand in a circle, close their eyes, and pray: **Dear Lord, teach us to number our days aright, that we may gain a heart of wisdom.** (They may need to repeat phrases after you.) Then close by praying: **God, help us to set godly priorities with our time this week. Thank you for coming near to us. In Jesus' name, amen.**

Distribute the take-home newspaper, *VeggieConnections*.

CUCUMBER CONNECTION NEEDS:

- Pickle jar
- Pickle artwork from the *VeggieConnections Shepherd* pages
- Green construction paper

KID CONNECTION NEEDS:

- Time Tracker Journals
- Pencils
- Colored markers
- Stamps in shapes of bunnies, clock, watches
- Stamp pads in various colors

CHRIST CONNECTION NEEDS:

- *VeggieConnections Music CD*
- CD player
- *VeggieConnections* take-home newspaper (one per child)

OPTIONAL:

You may want to use an easier Bible translation for memorizing the Unit Memory Verse, Psalm 90:12. The NIrV and the NLT are good choices.

The Chocolate Factory

To: All workers in the Chocolate Factory
From: Mr. Lunt
Date: Today

It has come to our attention that the locks on the doors need to be changed. Too many people have been getting into the Chocolate Factory when they aren't allowed. Since everyone is working today, the doors will be closed all day until dinner. No one comes in. No one goes out. You have five minutes to decide if you want anything before the doors close. You may choose five items from this list to have with you. Oh, and by the way, the cafeteria is closed today.

——— CHOCOLATE FACTORY SURVIVAL LIST ———

☐ Chocolate bunnies   ☐ Chocolate cake   ☐ Chocolate chip cookies

☐ Bottle of milk   ☐ Water bottles   ☐ *Rack, Shack, & Benny* movie

☐ Sandwiches   ☐ Basketball   ☐ Apples

☐ *VeggieBeat* magazine ☐ Carrot sticks   ☐ Trampoline

☐ Radio   ☐ Dog food   ☐ Backpack

☐ Cheese curls   ☐ Soda   ☐ Ice

☐ Rope   ☐ Flashlight   ☐ Batteries

Connecting to **Time** through the writings
of the disciple **John**
John writes about Lazarus: **John 11:1–44**

Connection Word:

patience

PART ONE:

Plugging In at the Chocolate Factory

Introduction to the site
and lesson focus

THE CHOCOLATE FACTORY

LESSON 5:
I will trust in God's timing.

A. Veggie Connection

BEFORE YOU START:
Set out the ingredients and supplies for making the chocolate pudding on the Assembly Line tables.

Dressed as the Factory Manager, warmly greet the kids as they punch in at the Chocolate Factory entrance and receive their badges. **Today is your lucky day! Today you get to make something chocolaty!**

Lead the kids over to the Assembly Line. Ask the kids to gather into groups of four. Explain that while they get to make the chocolate pudding, it actually takes a while before they'll be able to enjoy it.

Have the kids choose who in their group will open the box, pour the mix into the bowl, measure the milk, and pour the milk into the bowl (so each child has one task). Then let the kids begin, following the directions on the box. Each child in the foursome will get to stir for 30 seconds. Have *VeggieConnections Shepherds* circulate to help as needed. When finished, ask the Shepherds to gather up the bowls and place them in the refrigerator or cooler.

Ask: **How many of you would like to eat the pudding right now?** Pause for a show of hands. **How many of you couldn't wait and snuck a taste before the pudding was ready?** See if anyone admits to this! **It sure is hard to wait, isn't it? But it's important that we learn patience.** Ring the buzzer or bell. **It looks like we found our Connection Word!** Choose a volunteer to pick up the connection word from the Chocomatic and another to read the definition for *patience* from the *VeggieConnections Bible Dictionary*.

When we're waiting for someone or we want something to happen, that's when we need patience. It can be hard to be patient, and learning to have more patience is even harder! Today we're going to hear about two women who had to wait for something to happen to someone they loved very much.

THE CHILDREN
will arrive with their
VeggieConnections Shepherds
from the opening Countertop
Connections featuring Bob
and Larry. Play the *Veggie-
Connections Music CD* as
children enter the Chocolate
Factory.

VEGGIE CONNECTION NEEDS:
- *VeggieConnections Music CD*
- CD player
- Boxes of instant chocolate pudding (one per four kids)
- Small mixing bowls (one per four kids)
- One-cup measuring cup (several to share)
- Milk (check about possible food allergies)
- Large spoon (one per four kids)
- Access to refrigerator (or cooler with ice if no refrigerator)
- Buzzer or bell
- *VeggieConnections Bible Dictionary*

B. Prayer Connection

PRAYER CONNECTION NEEDS:

- Chocomatic with bunnies (from *Lesson 1*)

Send one child from each *VeggieConnections Group* to the Chocomatic (a total of four kids) to reach in and pull out a bunny and bring it back to their group. The word on the bunny chosen indicates the kind of prayers each group should focus on this week: *Thanks, Others, Praise,* or *Self.* Let the kids share their thoughts or requests and then spend some time praying.

Return the prayer bunnies to the Chocomatic after Prayer Connection to be used next week.

PART TWO:

Plugging In to God's Word

Connecting to God's Word in the Bible and understanding how that can help us to have a better relationship with him

A. God Connection: John writes about Lazarus – John 11:1-44

GOD CONNECTION NEEDS:

- Large name signs labeled *Mary, Martha, Lazarus, Jesus*
- Bible

TEACHER TIP:
Younger children may benefit from hearing the story before interacting with it. Explain to kids you'll read the story twice. For the first reading, they should listen carefully. For the second reading, kids will help tell the story.

Gather the kids in the R&D Lab and have them be seated where all can see the skit. Choose four volunteers to help you tell this story—two girls and two boys—and give each a name sign. Show the kids in a Bible where today's story is found, John 11. Have Mary, Martha, and Lazarus stand on one half of the "stage" and Jesus on the other half.

Once there was a family that had two sisters and one brother. They were named Mary, Martha, and Lazarus. They loved each other very much. Indicate that the three should put their arms around each other. **They also had a good friend. His name was Jesus.** Have Jesus wave at the family as they wave back.

One day, something sad happened to the family. Lazarus became very sick. Lazarus lies down. **His sisters, Mary and Martha, were scared. They didn't want their brother to die.** Sisters hold up hands like they don't know what to do. **Mary and Martha decided they would ask Jesus to help them. They knew Jesus had done many miracles—amazing things that only God could do. They asked a messenger to run and tell Jesus to come to them as fast as he could.**

Jesus got the message from the sisters. Have Jesus pretend to read a letter on a scroll. **He loved Lazarus very much. But he also knew that these friends—and many people who followed him—needed to learn something important. So he waited.** Have Jesus sit down and pretend to do other things. **Jesus didn't go to help Lazarus. He kept on waiting. In fact, while he was waiting, his friend Lazarus died.** Have Lazarus pretend to be dead on the floor.

The sisters were very sad. The sisters sit by Lazarus and cry. **And they were surprised and discouraged. They had thought that Jesus would come and make Lazarus better. After all, Jesus had healed lots of other people. But he didn't come. Jesus waited four days.** Have Jesus hold up a hand and count off four fingers. **Then Jesus went to Mary and Martha.** Jesus begins to walk toward them.

When Martha saw Jesus coming, she ran to him and cried, "Why didn't you help my brother?" Martha moves toward Jesus, motioning between Lazarus and Jesus. **She was sad her brother died. Jesus felt sad for her, too.** Jesus cries. **But Jesus knew something that Mary and Martha didn't know.** Have Jesus look up toward heaven. **He was waiting for God's timing.**

But Martha trusted Jesus. So he told her that Lazarus would live again! Jesus holds up his hands toward heaven. **Martha thought Jesus meant that Lazarus would be alive in heaven. Then Jesus wanted to know if Martha believed in him.** Jesus points to himself and then to heaven. **She said yes.** Martha shakes her head yes. **She believed that Jesus was God's very own Son. But she still didn't understand what Jesus was really talking about.**

Then she went and got her sister Mary. Martha brings Mary to Jesus. **Mary was also sad. She told Jesus that if he had been there, Lazarus wouldn't have died. Jesus felt bad for Mary and Martha. He asked where they had put Lazarus.** Jesus holds up hands as if questioning. **Mary and Martha took Jesus to the tomb—which was like a cave—where they had buried their brother.** All three walk toward Lazarus.

There were lots of people there, crying about Lazarus. Jesus told Martha to have the stone that blocked the opening removed. Martha wasn't so sure. Martha shakes her head no and pinches her nose. **Lazarus had been dead for four days, she explained, and he would stink! Jesus told her to do it anyway.** Jesus points in a command.

The stone was rolled away. Then Jesus called out to the dead Lazarus. Jesus told him to wake up! Jesus beckons. **And Lazarus came back to life!** Lazarus stands up and walks toward the three. **Jesus had waited on God's timing. Jesus had not healed Lazarus when he was sick so that Jesus could bring Lazarus back to life after he had died.**

Thank the volunteers and have them sit down. **It's hard to be patient, especially when something doesn't seem to be happening as we think it should. Mary and Martha thought that Jesus should have come right away to save Lazarus from dying. But he didn't. He had a different plan. Mary and Martha needed to learn to trust God's timing.**

Ask the kids to gather into their *VeggieConnections Groups* and discuss the following. First have the kids share how they would have felt if they were the sisters—first when Jesus didn't come to heal Lazarus and then after he was raised from the dead. Next discuss: **Why did Jesus wait to help Lazarus?** After the kids explain in their own words, be sure they understand: **Because Jesus waited, more people came to know him as God's own Son. Mary and Martha learned to trust God's timing.** Then, ask the kids: **What is an area in your life where you need to learn to trust God's timing?** *(Learning a subject or skill, waiting for something I want, watching parents' relationship problems, and so on.)*

B. Activity Connection

Choose from the following activities to help kids explore and remember that God wants us to trust in his timing (approximately 10–15 minutes each).

1. High-Powered Game: Lazarus Tag

Divide kids into teams of four to six kids. Have teams gather at one end of the playing area. Each team picks a child to play "Lazarus," who then lies down. Team members will each grab a hand or foot and lift Lazarus. At your signal, teams will carry their Lazarus to the opposite end of the playing area. Once there, teams will lay Lazarus on the ground. At that point, Lazarus is alive again and has to chase his or her team members until a new Lazarus is tagged. When the new Lazarus is tagged, kids will go back to the starting area and carry their new Lazarus while the game continues.

Once the game begins, kids will need to watch out for any other teams' Lazarus being carried across the game area. Play until every person who wants to play Lazarus can. If a child doesn't want to be carried, another child may substitute playing the dead Lazarus part (being carried), and then the original Lazarus can still try to tag his or her team members.

HIGH-POWERED GAME NEEDS:

- Masking/painter's tape

BEFORE YOU START:
Tape off a playing area for this tag game.

2. Low-Powered Game: Yes, No, Wait

- Newsprint
- Scissors
- Cardboard
- Hole punch
- Brad fastener
- Yes, No, Wait Game Cards on page 298 (one per *Veggie-Connections Group*)
- Playing pieces, such as buttons or rocks (one per child)

BEFORE YOU START:
For each *VeggieConnections Group*: Draw a gameboard grid on newsprint, 15 rows and a column for each child. Make a spinner, cutting a circle and pointer from cardboard. Mark three equal sections on the circle for "Yes—Move one space forward," "No—Stay put," and "Wait—Pick a card and follow its directions." Cut out a pointer, punch a hole in the center, and fasten it to the center of the circle with a brad fastener, ensuring the pointer spins freely.

OPTIONAL:
Instead of a newsprint game board, have kids play as human game pieces. Use paper sheets spaced out on the floor for game spaces.

Have each *VeggieConnections Group* lay their gameboard on the floor or a table and gather around it. Have players put their game markers on the bottom row. Each group shuffles their cards. Say: **We should always pray for all of our needs and concerns. We can trust God to answer in the best way and time to answer. He may say yes, no, or wait.**

Then explain the game directions: **Let's imagine you have asked God to do something. Spin the arrow on the spinner to see what God's answer might be. It could be yes, and he acts right away; then you move forward one square. If the answer is no, you don't move. If it is wait, draw a card to see what your reaction could be, and move according to the card's instructions.**

Keep taking turns playing until one player reaches the end of the board. Then say: **This game didn't give a choice of how to respond. Some of the cards gave good ways to handle the situation, but others did not. In real life, you have choices of how you will handle waiting on God's timing. Let's choose the good ways!**

Allow volunteers within groups to share prayers that they are waiting for God to answer, or times in the past when God has answered prayers in various ways. *Veggie-Connections Shepherds* should encourage kids to keep praying, trusting that God's answers and his timing are best.

3. Craft: Patience Placard

CRAFT NEEDS:
- Cardboard pieces
- Wax paper
- Air-dry clay in different colors
- Masking tape
- Rolling pins
- Plastic knives
- Pencils
- Ribbon, yarn, or string
- Plastic bags

OPTIONAL:
If you want to prepare your own salt clay, follow these instructions: mix 1 1/2 cups of white flour, 1 1/2 cups salt, 1 Tablespoon of oil, and about 1/2 cup of water. Mix until soft and smooth. Store in plastic in refrigerator until ready to use. You'll want to paint the placards if you use this option.

Remind the kids of their Connection Word, *patience*, and what it means. Explain that they will make a Patience Placard to take home that will remind them to be patient and accept things in God's time.

Give each child a piece of cardboard, length of wax paper, and a lump of clay. Have kids cover their cardboard with the wax paper and secure it with masking tape. Then have kids roll out their clay with the rolling pin until it is about 1/4 inch thick. Use the plastic knife to cut the clay into a rectangle, long enough to fit the word *patience* on it. Place the clay on the cardboard.

Have the children take smaller balls of clay and roll them into strips with their hands to make a border. They can also use the knives to create a pattern on their border. Use the hand-rolling technique to roll out the letters that spell "Patience." It would be helpful to display the word on the table for kids to copy. Help kids place their letters on the clay placard. They can also use clay to make other decorations (flowers, hearts, balls).

Poke two holes in the top corners with the bottom of a pencil. Tie string, ribbon, or yarn through the holes so that the placard can hang. Let the project dry completely, and send it home in a plastic bag. If the craft isn't dry before you send it home with the kids, tell kids to take it out of the bag when they get home and to be patient while it dries fully.

PART THREE:

Plugging In to My Life

Life application of the lesson to lead kids to THINK–LINK–ACT and build a relationship with God every day

A. Cucumber Connection

Before kids arrive, enlarge and copy the pickles from the *VeggieConnections Shepherd* pages on the CD-ROM included in the *VeggieConnections Elementary Curriculum Kit* onto green construction paper. Cut them out and put into a pickle jar.

Let a volunteer draw a pickle from the Pickle Pot, and either the child or a Shepherd should read the dilemma out loud. Each Shepherd should then process the question with their group using the THINK—LINK—ACT phrase.

Devon wants a new bike. Unfortunately, his dad has been out of work for a while. There's no spare money. Devon thinks he'll never get a new bike. What should Devon do?	Sharise's dad is in the army and stationed overseas. She misses him very much. She knows that he is serving the country, but she's getting mad that he's not home. What can she do?	Georgianne's mom is talking on the phone and she wants to ask her a question. Georgianne has a hard time waiting for her mom to be done. She gets in trouble for not being patient with her mom when she's busy. What can Georgianne do to learn patience?

CUCUMBER CONNECTION NEEDS:

- Pickle jar
- Pickle artwork from the *VeggieConnections Shepherd* pages
- Green construction paper

B. Kid Connection: Time Tracker Journal

Have the kids pick up their Time Tracker Journals from the Assembly Line. Ask the kids to open their Time Trackers to the calendar page. Say: **We need patience to trust God's timing. Think about something you want in your life.**

Remind the kids that we need patience to trust God's timing. Have kids turn over their pages to blank page 3. Then have them draw a picture of a situation where they are waiting for God's timing. Then encourage the kids to each write a prayer to God asking for his help in this situation.

KID CONNECTION NEEDS:

- Time Tracker Journals
- Pencils
- Colored pencils or markers

C. Christ Connection

CAUTION:
Please be aware of children with dairy and nut allergies. Milk chocolate snacks are often suggested in this unit, and these children may have a medically serious allergic reaction. Be sure to let parents know that their kids will be offered chocolate at the Chocolate Factory. Be sure to have safe alternatives on hand, such as hard candies or taffy.

The kids may be wondering about the pudding they made earlier. Tell them that they are going to be able to enjoy the chocolate pudding now because they waited so patiently for it. Pass out the pudding in small bowls with spoons. Say: **This pudding can remind you to wait on God's timing. We made this pudding in the beginning of our time together in the Chocolate Factory today. But it took some time for the pudding to be ready to eat. In the same way, there may be things in our life we are waiting on God. Only God knows the best way to answer us. Sometimes we may not like God's answer, but we need to remember that he loves us and will only do what is best for us.**

Close in prayer, thanking God for his timing and asking for his help in trusting him. Distribute the take-home newspaper, *VeggieConnections*.

CHRIST CONNECTION NEEDS:

- Pudding made in Veggie Connection
- Disposable bowls
- Serving spoon
- Plastic spoons
- Napkins or moist towlettes
- *VeggieConnections* take-home newspaper (one per child)

**Trust God patiently.
Move forward 2.**

**Pray that God will
help you be patient.
Move forward 1.**

**Get angry because you
did not get the answer
you wanted right away.
Move back 2.**

**Pick a fight with a
friend because you are
angry about God's
answer. Move back 2**

**Complain about not
getting what you wanted.
Move back 1.**

**Ask your parents to
pray for you because
patience is hard.
Move forward 1.**

**Think that God
knows best.
Move forward 1.**

**Thank God for
teaching you patience
in a hard situation.
Move forward 2.**

Connecting to **Time** through the writings
of the disciple **John**
John writes about what Jesus does in Cana and
Jerusalem: **John 2:1–11 and John 4:46–5:17**

PART ONE:

Plugging In at the Chocolate Factory

Introduction to the site
and lesson focus

LESSON 6:

I will make good use of my time.

A. Veggie Connection

BEFORE YOU START:

Make several copies of the Bob and Larry puzzle (p. 304), about one copy for every four or five kids. Attach one copy to an empty puzzle box. Cut apart the other puzzles, and mix up the pieces. Spread the pieces along the Assembly Line.

Dressed as the Factory Manager, warmly greet the kids as they punch in at the Chocolate Factory entrance and receive their badges. Try to rush them along and look frantic. **There's no time to lose. You have to get to work right away! I have a job for you!**

Explain that as you were coming to the Chocolate Factory, boxes of puzzles were knocked out of your hands and fell all over the floor. They're all mixed up. You need the kids to put them back together.

Have the kids move to the Assembly Line tables. Tell them that they need to work together and work their hardest to put the puzzles all back together—quickly. Hold up the "puzzle box" to show the kids what the puzzle is supposed to look like. Then urge the kids to get started. Walk around, checking your watch and making worried comments like, **We'll never get this done on time!** Different kids will react differently to this activity; just encourage all of them to keep trying their best.

When the puzzles are just being finished up, announce that time is up. **Good job! You gave it your best shot getting those puzzles back together! I really appreciate your effort.** Sound the bell or buzzer. **I must have said our Connection Word!** Choose someone to walk to the Chocomatic and pick up the word "effort." Let another volunteer read the definition of *effort* from the *VeggieConnections Bible Dictionary*.

Say: **It's important that when we're given something to do, we give it our best effort. Sometimes we need to try something we've never done before. Other times we need to make the best use of our time. Today we're going to hear a story about how Jesus gave his best effort. He made good use of the time he was on earth.**

THE CHILDREN
will arrive with their
VeggieConnections Shepherds
from the opening Countertop
Connections featuring Bob
and Larry. Play the *Veggie-
Connections Music CD* as
children enter the Chocolate
Factory.

**VEGGIE
CONNECTION
NEEDS:**

- *VeggieConnections Music CD*
- CD player
- Bob and Larry puzzle on page 304 (one per every four kids)
- Buzzer or bell
- *VeggieConnections Bible Dictionary*

B. Prayer Connection

Send one child from each *VeggieConnections Group* to the Chocomatic (a total of four kids) to reach in and pull out a bunny and bring it back to their group. The word on the bunny chosen indicates the kind of prayers each group should focus on this week: *Thanks, Others, Praise,* or *Self.* Let the kids share their thoughts or requests and then spend some time praying.

Return the prayer bunnies to the Chocomatic after Prayer Connection to be used next week.

PART TWO:

Plugging In to God's Word

Connecting to God's Word in the Bible and understanding how that can help us to have a better relationship with him

A. God Connection: John writes about what Jesus does in Cana and Jerusalem – John 2:1–11 and John 4:46–5:17

GOD CONNECTION NEEDS:

• Paper (three per child)
• Pencils (one per child)
• Bible
• Newsprint pad on easel
• Markers or crayons

BEFORE YOU START:

Place an easel with paper at front of your Bible story area. Or move the Bible story area to have access to a whiteboard and markers.

Gather the kids to hear the Bible story. You may have them sit on the floor or at tables. Pass out three sheets of paper and a pencil for each child. Tell the group that you are going to read three stories of how Jesus made the best use of his time. After each story is read, kids will draw a picture of it. Encourage kids to "use their time wisely" and to listen carefully to each story, so they may draw it well.

When you're finished with each story and the kids are done with their drawings, choose one person to draw the story for the whole group. Encourage kids to be creative but not to worry about how well they draw. Ask simply for their best effort.

Read John 2:1–11, about the wedding in Cana. When done, allow another minute for kids to finish their drawings. Then ask for a volunteer to redraw their picture on the newsprint. While the volunteer is drawing, discuss these questions with the group:

1. **Why was Jesus at the wedding?** (*He had been invited as a guest.*)
2. **What happened to the drink?** (*It ran out.*)
3. **What did Jesus do?** (*He helped the person in charge by turning plain water into the best wedding drink at that time—wine.*)
4. **How did Jesus make good use of his time?** (*He cared about others' problems and helped them; he didn't get up and do anything but sent someone else with instructions of what to do.*)

Admire the picture that was drawn by the volunteer, and let him be seated.

Read John 4:46–54. Let the kids draw on the next sheet of paper as you read. Ask for a volunteer to redraw their picture on the newsprint. As they draw, discuss:

1. **How did Jesus respond to the officer's question?** (*He told the officer to leave because Jesus had healed his son.*)
2. **Did the officer believe Jesus? How do you know?** (*Yes, because it says, "he took Jesus at his word," and he left to go see.*)
3. **What happened because of the officer's decision to believe Jesus?** (*The officer's whole household believed in Jesus.*)
4. **How did Jesus make good use of his time?** (*He didn't take time to go to the officer's home but healed the boy from a distance; he still cared and acted.*)

Admire the new picture drawn by the volunteer.

Read John 5:1–17. Have kids draw on the third sheet of paper. Continue to encourage kids to make good use of their time and draw while the story is being read. While the third volunteer draws on the newsprint, discuss:

1. **What was the rule about the Sabbath?** *(People couldn't "work" or even pick up their mat or walk any distance.)*
2. **What did Jesus tell the man to do?** *(Pick up his mat and carry it.)*
3. **What happened to the man?** *(He was suddenly able to walk.)*
4. **How did Jesus make good use of his time?** *(He healed/helped someone on a day when it wasn't allowed.)*

Admire the final drawing.

Explain that not everyone agreed with how Jesus used his time. Some people wanted him to drop everything and come. Some people wanted him to wait for another time. But Jesus knew how to make good use of his time. He knew where to put his effort and when to send others.

Ask the kids to turn their papers over. Ask: **What are some things you do with your time? Write down the things that take up most of your time.** Allow time for kids to write or draw pictures of what they do with their time. **If you think these are a good use of your time, put a "G" for "good" by those things. If you think you should probably try to put effort into something else, put an "E" for "effort" by those things.**

Explain to the kids that we need time for lots of different things each day, and playing and relaxing are very important, too. We just have to look at how much time we spend doing them.

Lead the kids in saying the Unit Memory Verse, Psalm 90:12. **This verse reminds us to do the same thing. How do we number our days aright?** *(By making good use of our time.)* **What will be the result?** *(We'll gain a heart of wisdom, or learn to use our time and effort wisely.)*

OPTIONAL:
You may want to use an easier Bible translation for memorizing the Unit Memory Verse, Psalm 90:12. The NIrV and the NLT are good choices.

B. Activity Connection

Choose from the following activities to help kids explore and remember that God wants us to get to know him (approximately 10–15 minutes each).

1. High-Powered Game: Jump Time

Ask kids to choose a partner. Explain that in this game, the kids will give their best "effort" to jump rope and learn a time rhyme. The age and experience of the kids will determine how they jump.

Younger kids will have enough effort just taking turns jumping individually. Older kids or kids who regularly jump rope should be challenged to jump in ways that require more effort. For pairs-jumping, have the kids stand side by side. One holds one end of the rope and one holds the other.

No matter which way they jump, help the kids learn this rhyme to jump in rhythm to:

HIGH-POWERED GAME NEEDS:
- Jump ropes (one per pair)

> **God is good**
> **He helps me grow**
> **When I'm connected**
> **I will know**
> **How to make**
> **Good use of my**
> **Time – t-i-m-e - time**
> **Count it!**
> **1, 2, 3 . . .** *(continue counting until they miss)*

2. Low-Powered Game: Memory Motion Circle

Have the kids stand or sit in a circle with eight to ten kids in each circle. Ask the kids to think about things they do during a week that are a good use of their time. They might think of anything from playing a sport to learning a certain school subject to doing chores. Then ask the kids to think of a motion or action that represents that thing.

Choose one child to begin. He says: **I make good use of my time by . . .** and does a motion, (for example, sweeping the floor). Have the child, and all following children repeat the same motion until the game is over. The next child says the same phrase, repeats the first child's motion, and then adds his own (for example, sleeping). The third child says the phrase, then sweeps, sleeps, and adds his own (for example, riding a bike). Continue this way around the circle, seeing how long the kids can keep the actions going before someone forgets. At that point, begin with the child who forgot to start over.

3. Craft: Block Calendars

BEFORE YOU START:

From page 63, duplicate smiling Bob clip art on red tagboard, one per child. Duplicate smiling Larry clip art on tagboard, one per child.

CRAFT NEEDS:

- 1" wooden blocks (two per child)
- Index cards (one per child)
- Scissors
- White and green craft foam
- Craft glue
- Permanent markers
- Smiling Bob and Larry clip art

Explain to the kids how calendars are one way to track time. Distribute wooden blocks and permanent markers to the kids. Have them write the following numbers on each cube: Cube #1, write numbers 1, 2, 3, 4, 5, 6. Cube #2, write numbers 7, 8, 9, 0, 1, 2 Then make the cube holder out of an 3" x 5" index card as follows: Fold the card lengthwise and open it to form a 90-degree fold. Along the fold line, cut both ends of the card, slightly more than 1" and fold flaps at the end of the cut line (making the card look like a square shape). Bring the two end flaps together and tape together on both ends of the card, forming the cube holder.

Have each child cut out a green craft foam rectangle to go behind the cube box. Then, cut out a white craft foam rectangle just a little bit smaller to go in front of the green rectangle. Glue the white to the green. At the top of the white foam, in small to medium print, use a permanent marker to write: "Teach us to number our days aright." Psalm 90:12.

Have kids cut out their Larry and Bob characters and glue them to the back of the cube box. Affix the foam sheets to the Larry and Bob characters firmly with glue. Allow to dry. Tell the kids that they can change the date every day by moving the wooden cubes to say what the current date is. Remind the kids that while calendars keep the time for us, the time that matters most is God's time and what he does with it.

PART THREE:

Plugging In to My Life

Life application of the lesson to lead kids to THINK—LINK—ACT and build a relationship with God every day

A. Cucumber Connection

CUCUMBER CONNECTION NEEDS:

- Pickle jar
- Pickle artwork from the *VeggieConnections Shepherd* pages
- Green construction paper

Before kids arrive, enlarge and copy the pickles from the *VeggieConnections Shepherd* pages on the CD-ROM included in the *VeggieConnections Elementary Curriculum Kit* onto green construction paper. Cut them out and put into a pickle jar.

Let a volunteer draw a pickle from the Pickle Pot, and either the child or a Shepherd should read the dilemma out loud. Each Shepherd should then process the question with their group using the THINK—LINK—ACT phrase.

Miguel likes to watch cartoons every day after school. Sometimes he even watches them until supper. Then he rushes to get his homework done right before he goes to bed. What can Miguel do to make better choices with his time?	Crystal loves to read. She also likes to help people. In her class, she has seen that Sarah isn't that good at reading. How can Crystal use her time to help Sarah?	Josh really wants a new skateboard. He daydreams about it so much that he's not paying attention in school. He received a poor grade because he didn't know about a homework assignment. What should Josh do?

B. Kid Connection: Time Tracker Journal

KID CONNECTION NEEDS:

- Time Tracker Journals
- Index cards (one per child)
- Pencils

Have the kids pick up their Time Tracker Journals from the Assembly Line. Ask the kids to open their Time Tracker Journals to the planner page. Provide index cards and pencils. Have kids write "I will make the best use of my time" at the top of their cards. Say: **Look at the things you wrote down on your planner two weeks ago. Today we've been talking about putting forth good effort when using your time. Go down your list and write an "E" next to the things that you need to put more of an effort into doing. Then write those things on your index card as a reminder to work on those things this week.** For kids who missed *Lesson 4*, have them write down the things they do during the day and continue as above.

God wants us to make good use of our time. We need to be like Jesus. He made sure that he knew what God wanted him to do—and he always put forth his best effort doing those things. Take your cards home as an encouragement to put forth your best effort this week.

C. Christ Connection

CHRIST CONNECTION NEEDS:

- *VeggieConnections Music CD*
- CD player
- *VeggieConnections* take-home newspaper (one per child)

Have everyone stand and sing the *THINK—LINK—ACT* song using motions.

Encourage all the kids to take part in praying by giving them a chance to finish these prayer starter sentences in their own words:

Dear Jesus, you were so kind to the people in today's Bible story. We praise you for being so ... (*let kids offer words to complete the sentence*).

And Lord, we want to learn to do our best and use our time wisely. Please help us make good use of our time when we are ... (*let kids fill in their own choice of places and times.*)

Thank you for letting us come near to you and for coming near to us. In Jesus' name, amen.

Distribute the take-home newspaper, *VeggieConnections*.

Connecting to **Time** through the writings
of the disciple **John**
John writes about the woman at the well: **John 4:1-39**

living water

PART ONE:

**Plugging In at
the Chocolate Factory**

Introduction to the site
and lesson focus

LESSON 7:
I will look for times to
share God's Word
with others.

A. Veggie Connection

Dressed as the Factory Manager, warmly greet the kids as they punch in at the Chocolate Factory entrance and receive their badges. Announce you have a message from Mr. Nezzer. **Mr. Nezzer has been reading about how exercise helps make better employees. So, effective immediately, there will be a 15-minute exercise period in each workday.**

Have kids spread out and lead them in doing jumping jacks, running in place, sit-ups, and other exercises that will have kids working up a sweat! After few minutes, stop the exercising and say: **I bet you are thirsty. How about some chocolate?**

If kids don't say they want water, point out how water is what you would use to quench thirst, not chocolate. **You *can* live without chocolate (*sorry*, Mr. Nezzer!), but you can't live without water.** Sound a buzzer or bell to indicate the Connection Word has been said. **In fact water is part of our Connection Word today. But this is a special type of water that only Jesus can give us. Let's see what I mean.** Let a volunteer pick up the Connection Word, "living water," from the Chocomatic. Choose another volunteer to read the definition in the *VeggieConnections Bible Dictionary*. Tell kids that people receive living water when they hear God's good news and start a friendship with him. **When we've received the living water by believing in Jesus, we need to share that living water with others. Today we'll discover when Jesus took the time to share God's Word with a woman who was growing in her relationship with God.**

B. Prayer Connection

Send one child from each *VeggieConnections Group* to the Chocomatic (a total of four kids) to reach in and pull out a bunny and bring it back to their group. The word on the bunny chosen indicates the kind of prayers each group should focus on this week: *Thanks, Others, Praise,* or *Self.* Let the kids share their thoughts or requests and then spend some time praying.

Return the prayer bunnies to the Chocomatic after Prayer Connection to be used next week.

THE CHILDREN
will arrive with their *VeggieConnections Shepherds* from the opening Countertop Connections featuring Bob and Larry. Play the *Veggie-Connections Music CD* as children enter the Chocolate Factory.

**VEGGIE
CONNECTION
NEEDS:**

- *VeggieConnections Music CD*
- CD player
- Pitchers of water
- Cups (one per child)
- Buzzer or bell
- *VeggieConnections Bible Dictionary*

**PRAYER
CONNECTION
NEEDS:**

- Chocomatic with bunnies (from *Lesson 1*)

PART TWO:

Plugging In to God's Word

Connecting to God's Word in the Bible and understanding how that can help us to have a better relationship with him

A. God Connection: John writes about the woman at the well – John 4:1-39

GOD CONNECTION NEEDS:

- Bible
- Bible-time clothes
- microphone, real or made

BEFORE YOU START:

Ask a *VeggieConnections Shepherd* to prepare the Bible story skit with you, with one of you playing the Woman and the other playing the Reporter, both wearing Bible-time clothes. The reporter will need a microphone, real or made from a cardboard tube and Styrofoam ball glued to the top, painted black or silver.

Have all the kids be seated where they can see the skit. Show the kids in a Bible where today's story is found, John 4. Before starting the skit, explain: **Jesus and his disciples were traveling through an area called Samaria. Now, people from Israel—where Jesus was from—had nothing to do with people from Samaria. They wouldn't even talk to each other if they ran into each other. Also, during the times of Jesus, it was not usual for a man to speak with a woman.**

Tell the kids that there is more to the story. In order to get the best understanding of what happened, they are going to travel to Samaria and go live on location to meet with the woman at the well.

Reporter: *(Holds microphone.)* Welcome to Samaria! I am Ace Reporter, here live, with a Samaritan woman at the town well. *(Turns to woman.)* What can you tell me about what just happened to you? You were with Jesus, right?

Woman: Yes, I was.

Reporter: How did you meet Jesus?

Woman: Every day I come to this well to draw water. I don't like to come when the other women are here. I like to come alone.

Reporter: You come alone because you don't want to meet up with anyone else? Why don't you want to see anyone?

Woman: Well, I've made some bad choices in my life. People don't like to be around me.

Reporter: Were you surprised, then, when you walked up to the well and saw someone sitting there?

Woman: Very surprised. What surprised me even more was when this man asked me for a drink.

Reporter: You were surprised he was thirsty?

Woman: No, I was surprised he was willing to talk with me.

Reporter: What did he say then?

Woman: It was odd. He said that if I knew who I was talking to, I'd ask him to offer me a drink.

Reporter: Did he have a bucket or anything to use to give you a drink?

Woman: No. He said that if I asked, he would give me water so I would never thirst again. He said that his water would give me eternal life. He talked as if he knew me. In fact, he knew all about the bad choices I had made.

Reporter: How did you find out who he was?

Woman: Rumors have been going around about the man they called Jesus. They said that the Messiah was coming.

Reporter: What did he say next?

Woman: He told me that he was the promised Messiah.

Reporter: There we have it, folks. This Samaritan woman met the coming Messiah. Right here at the town well. *(Looks around.)* And now I have to tell you that the crowds are coming. People have heard that Jesus was here. After this woman met Jesus, she dropped everything and took the time to share God's Word with others. Looks like another group of lives are being connected to a powerful relationship with God. Remember the **VeggieConnections** Program Verse reminds us to "*Come near to God and he will come near to us!*" Thanks for tuning in.

Take a bow with the other actor. Then discuss with the kids: **How did Jesus share God's Word with others?** *(He took time to talk with the lonely woman at the well.)* **What did Jesus tell her?** *(That he is the Messiah and he could give her eternal life.)* **How did the woman share God's Word with others?** *(She went back to her town and told everyone about Jesus.)* **What are ways we can share God's Word with others?** *(Telling a friend what I learned in Sunday School or sharing the take-home paper, inviting a friend over to watch a Christian video or listen to a Christian CD, inviting a friend to church, and so on.)*

B. Activity Connection

Choose from the following activities to help kids explore and remember that God wants us to share God's Word with others (approximately 10–15 minutes each).

1. High-Powered Game: Well Water Relay

BEFORE YOU START:
Hole-punch two opposite sides of two cups near the top. Tie a piece of yarn in the middle to the end of a pencil. Then tie the ends of the yarn to the 2 holes in a cup, forming a small pail. For each team, fill a bucket half full of water, and put it behind a chair, with a towel underneath. Place the other bucket near the team.

This would be a fun game to play outside, if the weather is nice. Line the kids up into two teams. Explain to kids how this game will give them an idea of what is was like to get water in Bible times. Give both teams a pencil pail. The first person in each team will run with the pail to the chair, kneel on it, and drop their pail into the bucket "well." Kids will need to be patient for the pail to fill with water. Once it does, kids will carefully bring their pail back to the second bucket, where they can use their hands to dump the water. Players will give the pail to the next person in line, and kids play until the second bucket is as full as possible.

Remind the kids that it used to be a lot of work to gather water in Jesus' time. But he knew just when and where to find the woman he wanted to meet that day. Ask four kids to get the buckets. **Remember how Jesus said the living water that he would give the woman would bring her eternal life? Well in this game, our first bucket is like that living water Jesus gives to us. And just like the woman at the well we can share that gift by telling others about Jesus. Our second bucket is what we took from the well to share. Let's remember we can give people living water when we share Jesus with them!**

2. Low-Powered Game: Woman at the Well Revisited

Divide kids into *VeggieConnections Groups*. Each group should sit in a circle around a bucket placed in the center. Have kids go up and get one card from the bucket. If you have more than eight kids, have some kids pair up. If you have fewer than eight kids, have kids get extra cards. Have kids read cards aloud, one at a time. Then have kids line up in story order, as best they can remember. While standing in this order, give kids Bibles and have them check and move as needed to establish the correct order.

After kids have the story in order, say: **Jesus talked to the Samaritan woman, when Jews and Samaritans didn't talk to each other. And because he did, the woman told people in her town and many believed in Jesus. Our willingness to talk to anybody about Jesus, could lead to many people believing in him. Let's all remember to share Jesus with everyone we can!**

3. Craft: Good News Well

Tell the kids that today they are going to make a well similar to the one in the Bible story.

Have kids gather at the Assembly Line tables. Provide a can to each child and spread out craft supplies. Have *VeggieConnections Shepherds* help younger kids with this craft. Cut pieces of paper grocery bags slightly larger than the outside and inside surfaces of the can. Include a circle for the inside bottom of the can. Crumple the paper pieces and them spread them out.

HIGH-POWERED GAME NEEDS:
- Two chairs
- Four buckets
- Four absorbent towels
- Two disposable plastic cups
- Hole punch
- Two pencils
- Yarn

LOW-POWERED GAME NEEDS:
- Woman at the Well Cards on page 318 (one per *VeggieConnections Group*)
- Bucket (one per group)
- Bibles (several per group)

BEFORE YOU START:
Copy and cut apart the game cards. Mix them up and place in a bucket. You'll need one filled bucket for every two *VeggieConnections Groups*.

CRAFT NEEDS:
- Small soup can (one per child)
- Scissors
- Paper grocery bags
- Craft glue
- Earth-tones marbled paper
- New pencils (three per child)
- Strips of paper (one per child)
- Markers
- Small rubber bands (one per child)

This will give the paper a rocky texture. Smear craft clue on the can and paper surfaces and glue the paper to the can.

Tear small pieces of earth-toned paper into rock stapes and glue them randomly on the can. While cans are drying, talk about how the woman at the well went into her town and told all the people about Jesus. Give kids three new pencils and small strips of paper. Have kids write "Jesus loves you" on the strips of paper and wrap the paper around the pencils, securing with a small rubber band. **Just as the woman at the well went and told her town about Jesus, you can share Jesus with people by giving away these pencil-holder wells.**

CUCUMBER CONNECTION NEEDS:

- Pickle jar
- Pickle artwork from the *VeggieConnections Shepherd* pages
- Green construction paper

KID CONNECTION NEEDS:

- Time Tracker Journals
- Pencils
- Colored markers

CHRIST CONNECTION NEEDS:

- *VeggieConnections* take-home newspaper (one per child)

OPTIONAL:

You may want to use an easier Bible translation for memorizing the Unit Memory Verse, Psalm 90:12. The NIrV and the NLT are good choices.

PART THREE:

Plugging In to My Life

Life application of the lesson to lead kids to THINK–LINK–ACT and build a relationship with God every day

A. Cucumber Connection

Before kids arrive, enlarge and copy the pickles from the *VeggieConnections Shepherd* pages on the CD-ROM included in the *VeggieConnections Elementary Curriculum Kit* onto green construction paper. Cut them out and put into a pickle jar.

Let a volunteer draw a pickle from the Pickle Pot, and either the child or a Shepherd should read the dilemma out loud. Each Shepherd should then process the question with their group using the THINK—LINK—ACT phrase.

Dana loves ballet. She spends a lot of time with other girls at ballet class. Dana knows many of the girls don't have a connection with Jesus. What can she do?	Ian's mom goes to visit her grandmother in a nursing home. Ian sits by himself watching TV. He's noticed an older man watching TV, too. Ian wonders if the man knows Jesus. What can Ian do?	Mirta is being made fun of by another girl at school. Mirta wants to get back at this girl, but she thinks the girl is lonely and is trying to attract attention by being mean to her. What can Mirta do?

B. Kid Connection: Time Tracker Journal

Have the kids pick up their Time Tracker Journals from the Assembly Line. Ask the kids to fold open their Time Trackers to a blank page.

Tell the kids that in order to find times they can share God's Word with others, they need to be on the lookout—or keep their eyes open. Have the kids draw a large face on the page. Encourage them to add all the features. They should title the page, "I will look for times to share God's Word with others." When finished, ask the kids to write by the ears a way they can use listening to share God's Word with others. Repeat this for their eyes, mouth, and brain. Then let the kids share their answers with the others.

C. Christ Connection

To help the kids continue to practice the Unit Memory Verse, Psalm 90:12, have them stand with their *VeggieConnections Groups*. Have the kids in each group say the Unit Memory Verse alone, one immediately after another.

Then close by leading the group in prayer. **Dear God, thank you that we can tell other people about you. Help us to find time to do that. Thank you for your example of the woman at the well who shared your Word with others. Give us strength to follow her example of sharing our faith with others. In Jesus's name, amen.**

Distribute the take-home newspaper, ***VeggieConnections***.

Connecting to **Time** through the writings
of the disciple **John**
John writes about Jesus washing the disciples' feet:
John 13:1-20

serve

PART ONE:

Plugging In at the Chocolate Factory

Introduction to the site
and lesson focus

LESSON 8:
I will use my time to serve others.

A. Veggie Connection

BEFORE YOU START:
On single slips of paper write names of jobs that serve people: *doctor, fire fighter, police officer, teacher, mayor, principal, dentist, coach, pilot.*

Dressed as the Factory Manager, warmly greet the kids as they punch in at the Chocolate Factory entrance and receive their badges. Tell them you've had a great time being their Manager and they've been great employees for the Chocolate Factory.

Invite kids to the R&D Lab for an experiment. Tell them that the experiment is a guessing game. Some kids will have a turn to act out a type of person. The rest will see if they can figure out who that person is or what type of job that person has.

Begin by going first. Choose a slip of paper. Act out the profession that is on the paper. Ask kids to guess what it is. The person who guesses can have the next turn. Play until all the slips are used up.

Tell the kids that the next part of the experiment is to figure out what all the people acted out have in common. *(These jobs all help people.)*

Say: **Another word that describes helping someone else is *serving*.** Sound a buzzer or bell to indicate the Connection Word. Choose a volunteer to pick up the word from the Chocomatic. Ask a different volunteer to read the definition of *serve* from the *Veggie-Connections Bible Dictionary*.

Ask: **What is one job you'd never want to do for someone else? Why not?** Allow for discussion. **Even though you say you wouldn't want this job, what might make you change your mind and do it?** Let volunteers explain. **Some jobs involve serving others, even when it's not the most fun job in the world. That's what happens in our Bible story today, and you may be surprised who's doing the serving!**

B. Prayer Connection

Send one child from each *VeggieConnections Group* to the Chocomatic (a total of four kids) to reach in and pull out a bunny and bring it back to their group. The word on the bunny chosen indicates the kind of prayers each group should focus on this week: *Thanks, Others, Praise,* or *Self.* Let the kids share their thoughts or requests and then spend some time praying.

Return the prayer bunnies to the Chocomatic after Prayer Connection.

THE CHILDREN
will arrive with their *VeggieConnections Shepherds* from the opening Countertop Connections featuring Bob and Larry. Play the *Veggie-Connections Music CD* as children enter the Chocolate Factory.

VEGGIE CONNECTION NEEDS:
- *VeggieConnections Music CD*
- CD player
- Prepared slips of paper
- Buzzer or bell
- *VeggieConnections Bible Dictionary*

PRAYER CONNECTION NEEDS:
- Chocomatic with bunnies (from *Lesson 1*)

PART TWO:

Plugging In to God's Word

Connecting to God's Word in the Bible and understanding how that can help us to have a better relationship with him

A. God Connection: John writes about Jesus washing the disciples' feet – John 13:1-20

GOD CONNECTION NEEDS:

- Props for Time Connection review
- Basin of clean play sand mixed with sidewalk chalk dust
- Bible
- Very low table or box cut to be a low table
- Floor pillows
- Basin of clean water
- Towel

BEFORE YOU START:

Gather a paper circle, a wristwatch, a flashlight, a potted plant or branch, a stopwatch, a clear glass of water, and a *Time Tracker* booklet.

Gather the kids in the R&D Lab to be seated. Use the following props to review the Time Connection unit by holding up each item and asking kids to share what they remember.

Say: **We've been learning about our time connection to God while in the Chocolate Factory. I've brought some items that will help you remember what we've learned in past weeks.** Hold up your circle. **The circle represents how God is eternal—he has no beginning or end.** Hold up a clock. **My wristwatch is with me all the time and it reminds us how God is always with us.** Hold up a flashlight. **We learned from the Apostle John to walk in God's light and use our time wisely.** Hold up a plant or branch. **We learned how Jesus is the vine and that we need to stay connected to him by making time for God.** Hold up a stopwatch. **You use a stopwatch to time things. We learned in the story of Jesus raising Lazerus from death, that we need to trust God's timing in our lives.**

We've been using this each week. Hold up a Time Tracker Journal. **Jesus made good use of his time when he helped people and performed many miracles. Your Time Trackers are helping you remember to do the same. You'll be taking them home with you to help you plan your time.**

Who can tell me what we learned last week? Hold up a clear glass of water. *(Jesus gave the woman at the well living water and she told her town about Jesus. We can use our time to share Jesus with others.)*

Today, were going to be looking at how we can use our time to serve others. In today's story, feet play an important part. Explain that in Bible times, most people had to walk to get around. There weren't any cars or buses to help people get around. Because it was usually hot there, people wore sandals. So feet would get dirty and stinky. Ask for a volunteer who would like to get his or her feet dirty. (You may choose two or three, if you wish.) Let the volunteer put his feet in the basin and move them around to get sand and sidewalk chalk dust all over them.

In Jesus' day, people liked to have visitors and dinner guests. And in those times, the dining tables were very low to the ground, and people often "sat" at the table by lounging on a pillow on one elbow. Have the volunteer do this with your low table and floor pillow. **Look at the feet! And think about how they must have smelled! Would you want to eat dinner looking at and smelling that? Of course not. So what do you think people back then did?** Let the kids speculate or tell what they know. Then explain that the host would often have a servant or slave who would tie a towel around his waist and bring a basin of water. Then the servant would kneel down and wash the guests' feet. But everyone knew what a gross job that was. Only the lowest person in the household would do it.

We're going to leave our friend with dirty feet while we read about a dinner that Jesus and his disciples had. Read John 13:1–5. Ask: **How do you think Jesus' disciples felt about Jesus washing their feet?** *(That Jesus was too important to do such a yucky job.)*

Bring the basin of clean water to your volunteer(s). Place a towel on your lap, caringly rinse off his feet, and dry them.

Say: **The disciples were shocked at what Jesus was doing. Peter even said that he wouldn't let Jesus wash his feet! But Jesus told him that unless Peter allowed Jesus to serve him by washing his feet, he would never understand what Jesus was calling his disciples to do. Then Jesus explained it. He came to serve others. And if he—the King of the universe—would serve others, then we, his followers, should, too.**

Thank your volunteer, and have him put his shoes and socks back on. Then discuss these questions: **How did Jesus use his time?** *(Serving others.)* **Why did Jesus wash his** disciples' feet? *(To be an example that they—and we—should follow.)* **Should we go around washing feet? Why not?** *(No, because in our time and place, that's not a useful way to serve.)* **What are ways that we can use our time to serve others?** *(Doing chores, helping a younger sibling with something that's hard for them, giving up recess to help a classmate with a project or a teacher with some preparation, and so on.)*

B. Activity Connection

Choose from the following activities to help kids explore and remember that God wants us to use our time to serve others (approximately 10–15 minutes each).

1. High-Powered Game: Serving Tag

Pair up the kids. Have one child from each pair stand on one side of the game area. The others stand on the opposite side. Designate one group as the Servers. Explain that when we serve others, we are putting their needs first or looking out for them.

Choose someone to be "It." Have "It" stand in the middle of the game area. The Servers must run to serve their partner by trying to hand them candy before "It" tags them. If the Servers help their partners (give them the candy), together they run back to the Server's side. If they are caught, they must serve "It" by helping catch other kids.

HIGH-POWERED GAME NEEDS:
- Wrapped hard candies or lollipops

2. Low-Powered Game: Serving Shoes

Divide kids into teams, and have teams sit in circles. Have kids remove their shoes and put them in a pile in the middle of their circle. Have the child whose birthday is closest to today's date begin the game as the first "servant." The servant goes to the pile of shoes and picks a pair of shoes not his or her own. The owner of the pair will tell the servant and he or she will put the shoes on the child (tying laces if applicable). Then this child becomes the new servant and goes the circle and repeats the above actions. When the last person in the circle has his or her shoes on, the game is over.

After kids have finished, say: **Jesus washed the feet of his disciples, taking the role of a servant. You each took the role of a servant in our game. If you have younger brothers or sisters, you might serve them in this way. But there are lots of other ways you can serve each other. Let's remember to follow Jesus' example in serving others.**

3. Craft: Gift Box of Service

Tell the kids that they are going to make a gift box of service pictures to give to someone. Give out tissue boxes, and let the kids each wrap one, leaving the hole open. Let *Veggie-Connections Shepherds* help as needed. As the kids work, encourage them to think about who they would like to give a gift of service to. They might choose a parent, a sibling, a friend, or a teacher/coach. Have the kids write the reference Psalm 90:12 on the box. Use this opportunity to see if the kids can say the Unit Memory Verse by heart.

Ask the kids to think about the kinds of serving they could do for the person they chose. Then pass out copies of the Service Pictures. Ask the kids to choose a few that match the ways they want to offer to serve. The kids should color those and cut them out. If the kids have other ideas that are not included on the Service Pictures, let them look through other pictures to find their ideas and cut them out. The kids should place all the pictures of ways they're offering to serve inside their gift box.

Give each child a piece of index card. Have them write "To:" and "From:" and add the appropriate names. The kids tape this gift tag to their box.

Encourage the kids to plan a time to give their Gift Box of Service to the person they chose. Whenever that person needs the serving, they take that picture from the box and give it to the child. Then the child must perform that act of service.

CRAFT NEEDS:
- Tissue boxes (one per child)
- Gift wrap paper (unrelated to holidays or birthdays)
- Transparent tape
- Scissors
- Markers
- Service Pictures on page 319 (one per child)
- Pictures from magazines
- Colorful index cards cut in half

PART THREE:

Plugging In to My Life

Life application of the lesson to lead kids to THINK–LINK–ACT and build a relationship with God every da.

A. Cucumber Connection

CUCUMBER CONNECTION NEEDS:

- Pickle jar
- Pickle artwork from the *VeggieConnections Shepherd* pages
- Green construction paper

Before kids arrive, enlarge and copy the pickles from the *VeggieConnections Shepherd* pages on the CD-ROM included in the *VeggieConnections Elementary Curriculum Kit* onto green construction paper. Cut them out and put into a pickle jar.

Let a volunteer draw a pickle from the Pickle Pot, and either the child or a Shepherd should read the dilemma out loud. Each Shepherd should then process the question with their group using the THINK—LINK—ACT phrase.

Sonia's mom wants her to come and help in the pantry at church. Sonia would rather visit her friends. What can Sonia do?	Jerome's little sister is always asking him to help her with her homework. Jerome knows he should help but he doesn't think he has the time. What could Jerome do?	Jason and his younger brother have a lot of toys and like to play with them. But they often forget to put them away. Jason's mom keeps busy with work and volunteering at church and school. She has told Jason he needs to be more responsible. What can Jason do?

B. Kid Connection: Time Tracker Journal

KID CONNECTION NEEDS:

- Time Tracker Journals
- Muslin cloth scraps
- Glue or stapler
- Pencils

Have the kids pick up their Time Tracker Journals from the Assembly Line. Ask the kids to fold open their Time Trackers to a blank page.

Tell the kids that one way to learn to be a servant is to ask God to give them opportunities to serve. Remind kids Jesus used a towel to serve. Give kids small pieces of cloth. Have kids glue or staple the cloth to an empty page in the Time Tracker. Then let them write the names of people they could serve around the cloth. Kids can also jot down ways to serve them. Encourage the kids to use their Time Tracker to remind them of people to pray for and serve. Say: **Take your booklets home with you and use them to help you use your time wisely, and include God in your daily priorities.**

C. Christ Connection

CHRIST CONNECTION NEEDS:

- *VeggieConnections Music CD*
- CD player
- Time Tracker Journals
- *VeggieConnections* take-home newspaper (one per child)

OPTIONAL:
You may want to use an easier Bible translation for memorizing the Unit Memory Verse, Psalm 90:12. The NIrV and the NLT are good choices.

Have everyone stand and sing the *THINK—LINK—ACT* song with motions.

Have the kids get into their *VeggieConnections Groups*, bringing their Time Tracker Journals with them. Let them look through what they learned during their time at the Chocolate Factory. They may tell some favorite things they learned that they are thankful for and also some areas that they'd like to keep working on and want God's help with. Then have *VeggieConnections Shepherds* open a prayer time where the kids can thank God for what they have learned and pray for one another. Then have kids pray the Unit Memory Verse Psalm 90:12, aloud together. Conclude with this prayer: **Father God, thank you for the time we've had together learning how to use our time for you. Help us make time for you in our busy lives. Help us to share your love with others. And just as Jesus washed dirty feet, help us to serve others with good attitudes. Thank you for everything we've learned at the Chocolate Factory. In Jesus' name we pray, amen.**

Distribute the take-home newspaper, *VeggieConnections*.

Time Tracker: Connecting God & Me

"Teach us to number our days aright, that we may gain a heart of wisdom."

Psalm 90:12

All lessons – Time Tracker Planner

Week Planner

Monday

Tuesday

Wednesday

Thursday

Friday

Saturday

Sunday

Day Planner

6 am

9 am

12 pm

3 pm

6 pm

9 pm

Sunday	Monday	Tuesday	Wednesday	Thursday	Friday	Saturday

Lesson 1 - Circle String Art Pattern

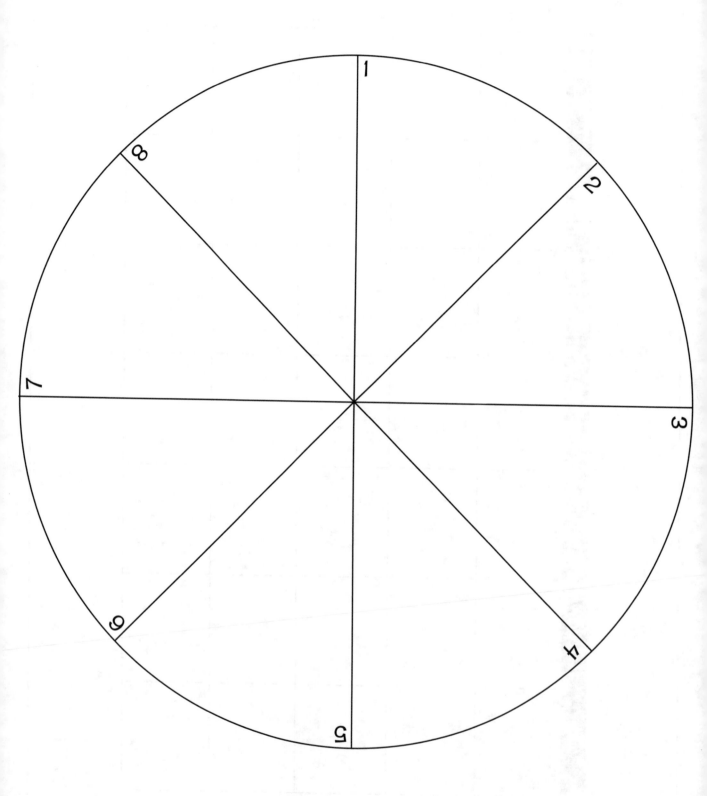

You went to Sunday School, even though you woke up tired.

GOOD PRIORITY!

Move to the Chocomatic.
Take one candy

You told a lie to get yourself out of trouble.

BAD PRIORITY

Go back to your last spot.

You read a Bible story with your sister.

—**GOOD PRIORITY!**—

Move to the Delivery Truck.
Take one candy

You played video games instead of doing your homework.

BAD PRIORITY

Go back to your last spot.

You didn't cheat even though you had a chance to.

—**GOOD PRIORITY!**—

Move to the Factory Entrance.
Take one candy

You spent *all day* Saturday watching TV.

BAD PRIORITY

Go back to your last spot.

You took time to pray at bedtime.

—**GOOD PRIORITY!**—

Move to the Assembly Line.
Take one candy

You, Bob, and Larry sang *VeggieTales* silly songs for four hours.

TOO SILLY!

Stay put until another team comes.

You did all your homework before you went out to play.

—**GOOD PRIORITY!**—

Move to the R&D Lab.
Take one candy

Your dog took himself for a walk.

TOO SILLY!

Stay put until another team comes.

Today you thought about ways to stay connected to God.

GOOD PRIORITY!

Move to the Employee Bulletin Board.
Take one candy

You did cartwheels down the sidewalk.

TOO SILLY!

Stay put until another team comes.

Jesus asks a
Samaritan woman
to give him a drink.

"I know the
Messiah (called Christ)
is coming."

"You are a Jew
and I am a
Samaritan woman."

"I who speak
to you am He."

"Whoever drinks
the water I give
will never thirst."

"Come, see a man who
told me everything
I ever did. Could this
be the Christ?"

"Give me this
water so I won't
get thirsty."

Many of the Samaritans
from that town believed
in Jesus because of
the woman's testimony.

WELCOME TO MADAME BLUEBERRY'S TREE HOUSE

Connecting to **Joy** by looking at **David's Life**

UNIT SIX:

THE **JOY** CONNECTION

UNIT VERSE: "You have made known to me the path of life; you will fill me with joy in your presence, with eternal pleasures at your right hand." Psalm 16:11

MADAME BLUEBERRY'S TREE HOUSE

LESSON FOCUS:

1. God is my source of joy: Psalms 24, 103, 104

2. I find joy in whom God created me to be: 1 Samuel 16:1-13

3. I can find joy even in times of trial: 1 Samuel 17:1-50

4. I find joy in being content: 1 Samuel 26:1-25

5. I find joy in being thankful: 2 Samuel 7:18-29; Psalm 100

6. I find joy in being kind: 2 Samuel 9:1-13

7. I find joy in walking with God: 2 Samuel 22

8. I want to share my joy in the Lord with others: Psalm 145

Joy Connection Goals

The Joy Connection is all about helping elementary-school kids experience and share the joy in having a relationship with God. They easily connect to the feeling of being happy or joyful. This unit will help them identify the difference between being happy about the circumstances and things of this world and the joy they can experience in trusting, loving, and praising God.

Each Lesson Focus will take the kids on a journey toward various ways we can connect with God in joy. The Countertop Connections opening sessions with Bob and Larry will introduce the concept of having a relationship with God. It will be supported with the Program Verse from James 4:8: *"Come near to God and he will come near to you."*

When kids are dismissed to Madame Blueberry's Tree House, they will have the chance to explore what it means to find joy in a relationship with God.

The first lesson shares that God is our source of joy. The remaining seven lessons will explore David's life, and challenge kids to find joy in how God made them, facing trials, and being content, and in other ways. The final lesson in joy will encourage kids to share the joy of the Lord with others.

Warning: Activities in these lessons may call for foods containing wheat, dairy, or nuts. Please be aware that some children may have medically serious allergic reactions to these foods. Let parents know that their kids will be offered snacks that may include these items, and post a list of ingredients each week for any snacks offered during the lesson. Whenever foods containing wheat, dairy, and nuts are suggested in these lessons, be sure to have safe alternatives on hand.

Welcome to the Tree House!

Kids will enjoy their time at Madame Blueberry's Tree House during this unit. One of the VeggieTales videos that Bob and Larry will present to the children during the Countertop Connections time is called *A Lesson in Thankfulness.* In that video, Madame Blueberry is consumed with wanting more stuff, because she believes that material things will bring her joy. Throughout the video, she learns that true joy comes from having a relationship with God.

In this site, the kids will grow their relationship with God as they are guided through their lessons by a deliveryperson from StuffMart, the superstore where Madame Blueberry gets all her stuff. The deliveryperson will help kids see that real joy can come only from a relationship with God.

Your Role at the Tree House: A Deliveryperson (Delivery Dan or Darlene)

As the leader of this site, you are the hard-working Delivery Dan/Darlene, an employee of StuffMart who often delivers items to Madame Blueberry. You will host a new group of elementary-aged kids as they rotate through the Tree House every eight lessons. Wear any clothing that a deliveryperson or warehouse worker might wear; an element of silliness is always welcome.

This clothing might include matching pants/shorts and a work shirt, a baseball cap, a stock person's apron, work boots, work gloves, and a back support wrap. Keep a cloth in your pocket for wiping your brow and carry a clipboard that you use to keep track of deliveries, signatures, or even attendance! You work for StuffMart, so if you can label your hat or shirt, that would be appropriate. Watch the video to prepare yourself for the look of the role.

The Deliveryperson should often have a box under his or her arm and several boxes nearby for props and games. Because you often eat your lunch near the Tree House, carry a lunch pail and a picnic blanket you can spread out if appropriate.

How to Build and Prepare the Tree House

OPTION 1:

If you have more time and a permanent space

Utilize the transparency to project the overall Tree House site onto mural paper or a sheet. Use colorful permanent markers to trace the pictures to fit your walls.

Forest: To add three-dimensional trees, roll up brown paper (somewhat crumpled to look like bark) to make tree trunks on the wall. Make high spreading branches along the tops of the walls and the ceiling. You could also check with carpet stores for the long, round cores at the center of carpet rolls. They will usually give them away. You can build stands for the tubes with 1" x 4" scraps found at building stores. Wrapping paper tubes or rolled brown paper can then be used for branches.

If possible, create an overhead canopy of green "leaves" on the ceiling, or at least along the ceiling edges. To do this, cut green paper circles and tape them to the

Create a wall mural for the Tree House using transparency art found on page 59.

Madame Blueberry's Tree House

branches. Make clusters or strings of leaves by tying paper leaves to green yarn and hanging them.

Add colorful butterflies to the trees and flowers to the ground, either store-bought or made from paper. (Paper butterflies will be needed to write on by the kids in a later lesson.) If possible, include real or artificial plants, especially large potted plants and trees.

Tree House: To build the Tree House, first decide what perspective you would like it to have. If you have a lot of room and want a large Tree House, use a cardboard appliance box and cut it so that the Tree House stands out from the wall. Plan on putting it in "a tree" low enough for children to touch but high enough that they can't try to climb into. Decorate the box using paper and paint for the windows, columns, door, and so on. Carpet cores can hold up the box; you may need something sturdy such as L-brackets to secure it to the wall. Have plush toys of Larry and Bob looking out the windows.

If you'd like a Tree House that kids can enter, recruit woodworkers at your church to safely build a raised platform and put a molded plastic playhouse on it. The walls/roof should be tall enough to give the impression it is up in the trees. You can attach a large picture of Madame Blueberry to a wall.

Make a Connection Word sign to look like an elevator sign. Write "Connection Word Elevator" across the top of a posterboard sign. One left side, draw "up" and "down" triangle arrows and color with green and red markers. Number one through eight down the edge of the posterboard. Make the numbers look like elevator buttons by putting a circle around each number. Each week, the number can be colored in with a yellow highlighter, when the word is written on the poster.

StuffMart: Label one corner of the room "StuffMart" with a sign pointing off into the distance. You could also attach a "billboard" to the wall in this spot, picturing all the "stuff" that StuffMart has for sale. Include slogans such as "You want it!" and "Big stuff!"

In this corner, have a shopping cart, wagon, or a big box with wheels drawn on it. Fill it to overflowing with "stuff"—a variety of things that will be used during the lessons plus any other appealing items. Include any sorts of clothes, toys, sports gear, equipment, and other items that are safe for kids to play with.

More Site Elements: Make a path on the floor through the "forest," leading past the Tree House and all the portions of the site. You could make the path using a roll of paper and drawing steppingstones on it. Be sure any path is taped securely so it doesn't slip out from under the kids' feet. Because the Unit Memory Verse, Psalm 16:11, talks about "the path of life," you could print this verse on the steppingstones.

Use picnic tables in place of classroom tables. If they are too rough for a smooth writing surface, use colorful plastic tablecloths. You may set up benches in various spots for small groups to sit on when they meet, or use green blankets or carpet squares to represent grassy patches on the floor. You should also have a corner of the site setup with boxes of all sizes.

OPTION 2:

*If you are short on time
or do not have a permanent space*

Utilize the transparency art on page 59 to project the overall Tree House site onto mural paper or a sheet. Use colorful permanent markers to trace the pictures to fit your walls. These can be taken down and rolled up for storage during the week. Include a Tree House painted on paper and a sign for StuffMart in opposite corners.

Include a wagon or large shopping bags filled with "stuff," which can also be used during the lessons. Include items such as clothing, toys, and sports gear. Keep the stuff in the wagon or bags, and place it in a storage closet during the week.

Make a floor "steppingstone" path in a few long sheets, which can also be removed and rolled up. Have several empty boxes of different sizes stacked in one corner.

Make a Connection Word poster (see Option 1 above). Use mural or butcher paper instead of a posterboard if you need to be able to roll it up after each lesson.

Life Application Memory Tools

VeggieConnections will teach an important Bible lesson to kids each week. Knowing the Bible is the beginning of a relationship with God. Putting that learning to practice through life application really solidifies a child's relationship with the Lord. It is imperative that we provide kids with the tools they need to carry what they have learned into everyday experiences through life application.

In this curriculum, there are three main ways we will encourage kids to do this:

1. Kids will discover ways to express joy in God throughout each session.

2. Kids will learn a catch-phrase that will help them to remember what they should do in real life experiences.

The catch-phrase we have created is THINK—LINK—ACT. There is a song built on this principle on the *VeggieConnections Music CD* in your kit that will help kids remember this important tool. In addition,

each session will focus on various THINK—LINK—ACT activities that help children to walk the walk, and talk the talk, hopefully opening doors for the Holy Spirit to enter in and build meaningful relationships that will carry kids through every day of their lives! Here's what it means:

THINK:	Stop and think about what God wants you to do.
LINK:	Link God's Word and what you've learned to your choices.
ACT:	Go and act on what God wants you to do!

3. Kids will create a weekly life application-building tool to help them to remember what each lesson focused on.

Joy Bags:

At the Tree House, kids will create a Joy Bag that will hold items made each week to remind the children of each Lesson Focus.

Each child will need a plain paper gift or shopping bag with handles, about one foot tall. Have kids write their names on the bags with markers. Kids will decorate one side of the bag, and will save the other side for decorating during *Lesson 8* (to show Madame Blueberry's joyful transformation).

Give kids a copy of the Joy Harp on page 364. Provide scissors and have kids cut out the harp shape. Have kids fold their bags flat and, using a glue stick, apply glue to bag and back of the harp picture. Then have kids glue the harp onto their bags.

Give kids gold, silver, or other glitter-glue pens to decorate the frame of the harp. Then give kids lengths of various colored yarn and have them cut the yarn to make strings to glue onto their harp pictures. Have *VeggieConnections Shepherds* help kids spread thin lines of glue along the harp string lines of the harp picture. Let the glue set a few minutes and then have kids stretch each yarn piece onto the glue lines, making colorful harp strings. Set bags aside to dry.

Each week, during the Kid Connection, the children will make a new item to be added to their bag. At the end of the unit, the kids can take home their Joy Bag and its contents to remind them that God is our source of joy.

Suggested Music for the Tree House

Use these songs from the *VeggieConnections Music CD:*

1. *THINK—LINK—ACT*
   Music motions found on page 48.
2. *God Connection*
3. *Thankfulness Song*
4. *Down in My Heart*

Connection Word:

joy

PART ONE:

Plugging In at the Tree House

Introduction to the site and lesson focus

LESSON 1:
God is my source of joy.

A. Veggie Connection

Dressed as the Deliveryperson and calling yourself Delivery Dan or Delivery Darlene, greet the kids as they enter the Tree House site. Invite them to walk around and explore. Then have them gather around you on the "grass" carpets, blankets, or benches (two or three chairs next to each other). **Hello, everyone! Welcome to the Tree House. I'm the Deliveryperson here, and I'm looking forward to spending some time with you over the next several weeks. I work for that big store off in the distance called StuffMart. Does anyone know what a deliveryperson does?** (*Loads trucks, delivers items, picks up returns, drives a truck, keeps track of orders, and so on.*) **That's right! Well, today I'm delivering items to Madame Blueberry's Tree House. Usually, I like to stop and take my lunch break right here under this tree. I'm sure glad to have some company today.** Lay out a blanket for you to sit on and set out a lunch pail. **Madame Blueberry sure has been ordering a lot of things lately. She told some people at StuffMart that she's been feeling kind of down, and she's hoping some of this stuff will make her feel better.**

Talk with the kids briefly about where the boxes came from. **Do you know what makes me happy? Bringing people packages from all over the world and knowing it will make people happy to get them. Let's play a game to see what makes you happy.** Ask the kids to think about some things that make them really happy. Let volunteers stand and do the motions for any activity that they really enjoy and have others guess what it is. Kids might pantomime bike riding, an outdoor sport, playing a musical instrument, or playing with a specific indoor toy or pet.

Wow, there are lots of things that make you happy! But there is a special happiness that comes from God—it's called joy. Every time we get together here at the Tree House, we'll be doing happy things and learning about the joy we can have with God!

Ask a volunteer to look up *joy* in the *VeggieConnections Bible Dictionary* and read the definition aloud. Then pick up a box and shake it. **I don't think you can get love or peace from what's in this box. Joy in God is something you get in your heart.** Have another volunteer go to the Connection Word sign, color in the number 1 with the yellow highlighter, and write "joy" next to the number on the poster.

Another way to look at joy is to remember our Program Verse. Lead the kids in reciting James 4:8. **As we come near to God, he will come near to us. Joy comes from knowing God and knowing he is with us in our hearts. That just seems to fill up any empty places we may be feeling in our hearts.** Hold up an item from one of the boxes. **Madame Blueberry seems like she might have an empty place in her heart these days.**

THE CHILDREN

will arrive with their *VeggieConnections Shepherds* from the opening Countertop Connections featuring Bob and Larry. Play the *Veggie-Connections Music CD* as children enter the Tree House.

VEGGIE CONNECTION NEEDS:

- *VeggieConnections Music CD*
- CD player
- Blankets or "grass" carpets
- Lunch pail
- Three or four different size boxes
- *VeggieConnections Bible Dictionary*
- Yellow highlighter
- Black marker

BEFORE YOU START:

Make several paper labels, "Made in China," "Made in Taiwan," "Made in the USA," and glue then to boxes.

Some of this stuff might make her happy for a little while, but it won't bring her joy like we can find in having a relationship with God.

B. Prayer Connection

Have kids divide into their *VeggieConnections Groups*. **Let's start today by thanking God for all the happy things you acted out.** Let the kids take turns saying thanks to God for something that makes them happy. Let anyone who wishes have a turn to "deliver" a sentence prayer. **Thank you, God, for all the things that you created to bring us happiness. Our greatest joy though is in knowing you. Help us to grow in the joy of knowing you more. In Jesus' name, amen.**

PART TWO:

Plugging In to God's Word

Connecting to God's Word in the Bible and understanding how that can help us to have a better relationship with him

A. God Connection: David shares his joy in the Lord – Psalms 24, 103, 104

Gather the kids together on the "grass" blankets, carpet squares, or on benches for the Bible story. Open your Bible to Psalms to show children where the lesson is from.

The Bible tells us about a young man named David. When he was a boy and a teenager, his job in the family was to be a shepherd. He took care of the family sheep. He was the youngest of many kids. Back in Bible times, shepherds spent night and day with their sheep. Shepherds would sleep out under the stars and walk long ways every day with their flocks to find them food and water.

Shepherds also spent a lot of time alone or with a few other shepherd helpers. During all those hours watching the sheep, one thing David did was write songs. David loved music. He had a little harplike instrument that he carried with him, and he made up lots of songs. They were songs that showed his close connection to God. They were songs full of joy! David's songs of joy are called "psalms."

Lay out long sheets of mural paper on the floor or tables and have kids gather around the sheets. Provide a supply of markers for groups of kids. **Take a few minutes and write or draw things that come from God and give you joy.** Allow kids a few minutes to work on their murals. Then have a few kids share what they wrote or drew. **David knew everything comes from God. It gave David great joy to see God giving him the food he needed, along with peace and comfort, and all kinds of good things. These things gave David joy, and he praised God with the songs he wrote.**

As I read some verses from some of David's psalms, I want you to write or draw the things that God made that give you joy.

Read Psalm 24:1–2 and pause for kids to work. Then read Psalm 103:1–5 and pause for kids to work. Next read Psalm 104:2-6 and pause for kids work. Then read verses 19–25, 27–28, pausing to allow kids to work. Ask kids to share what they recorded on their murals. Some of the things God is the source of include the earth (Psalm 24), forgiveness, healing, love, compassion, good things (Psalm 103), and the heavens, clouds, wind, oceans, days and nights, creation of animals, and providing food for them (Psalm 104).

All these things give us reasons to be joyful. God giving us a beautiful earth, and everything in it is a reason to be joyful. And most importantly, we can be joyful for the forgiveness and promise of heaven God offers us.

We looked at parts of only three psalms that David wrote. But David was so full of joy for God that he wrote over 70 psalms! David began and ended many of his psalms with the words, "praise the Lord." Let's joyfully do the same. Lead the kids in shouting **Praise the Lord!** three times, with increasing excitement.

GOD CONNECTION NEEDS:

- Bible
- Long pieces of mural paper
- Markers
- Tape

TEACHER TIP:

Younger children may benefit from hearing the story before interacting with it. Explain to kids you'll read the story twice. For the first reading, they should listen carefully. For the second reading, kids will help tell the story.

B. Activity Connection

Choose from the following activities to help kids explore and remember that God is their source of joy (approximately 10–15 minutes each).

1. High-Powered Game: Catch the Joy! Tag

Choose one person to be the Joy Giver. Give this person the stack of yellow happy-face circles. Randomly give the blue sad-face circles to kids. Have everyone move out to the game area. Place the Joy Giver in the middle. Designate *VeggieConnections Shepherds* as coaches for the game. Say: **The Joy Giver will run and try to tag someone. When you are tagged, you will stop and receive a stack of yellow happy faces, and you both will run and tag more people. Each time a Joy Giver tags someone, this person will stop and get some yellow happy faces. You must have a happy face to give someone if you tag him (plus always hold your own). If you run out, you need to go to another Joy Giver and get some more.**

Madame Blueberry was sad and blue in her Tree House. If you have blue sad faces, you will need more encouragement to be happy. It will take three attempts by any Joy Givers to make you happy. For the first and second times you are tagged, hold up your blue sad face and say, "I'm so blue!" You also must be tagged by a different person each time. But on the third time you can take a happy face. The game is over when everyone has a yellow happy face.

Have kids play several rounds, choosing new kids to be "blue" each time. After the game talk about how quickly the joy spread and how even the "blue" players were added with just a little extra effort. Encourage kids to always look to the joy that comes from God.

Collect the happy face circles for use later in the lesson.

2. Low-Powered Game: Can't Make Me Laugh

If your group is large, divide into smaller groups to play. Have all the kids sit in a row facing the front. Tell them they have lost their joy. They should each silently think of a reason they sometimes feel grumpy. (*I hate getting up in the morning; my little brother annoys me; my dog knocked over what I was building; I got too much homework.*). Their job is not to laugh, giggle, or even smile at all.

Choose one child to be the grumpy actor, and have that child stand in front of the others. His goal is to get the seated kids to crack a smile. He does this by acting grumpy— as funny as he can—and saying one thing that takes away his joy or puts him in a bad mood. The grumpy actor should ham it up as much as possible, using any voice or actions to make it funnier. Any kids who laugh or smile have to call out: **God is my source of joy!** Once several kids have laughed, choose from among any of the kids who didn't smile to have a turn to make a grumpy statement.

Sometimes things happen in our day that make us grumpy. Maybe you can remember this game and how you were able to smile even when you were thinking grumpy thoughts. God can be our source of joy even when we are feeling down.

3. Craft: Praise Instruments

To make a hummer, wrap colored paper around a cardboard tube and secure with tape. Decorate with stickers. Cut a square of wax paper larger than the end of the tube. Place over the end of tube and secure with a rubber band. Hum into the opposite end.

To make a tom-tom, remove the lid from a cylindrical container. Decorate the outside with colored paper and stickers. Replace the lid. Use the eraser end of unsharpened pencils to tap out a rhythm.

To make streamers, cut 2' lengths of various colors of ribbon. Fold each ribbon in half, laying the looped end under one edge of the ring. Bring ribbon ends up and through the looped end so that it catches the ring, and pull tight. Continue with three more strands of ribbon. Wear a ring and wave hands around to make the ribbons fly.

HIGH-POWERED GAME NEEDS:

- Yellow construction paper
- Blue construction paper
- Markers
- Scissors
- Masking/painter's tape

BEFORE YOU START:

Make yellow happy-face circles for each child. Make blue sad-face circles for 1/3 of the class. Mark a tape boundary for the tag area.

CRAFT NEEDS:

Hummer:
- Toilet-tissue tubes
- Wax paper
- Rubber bands
- Colored paper
- Stickers

Tom-Tom:
- Cylindrical cardboard container with lid (from oatmeal, bread crumbs, and so on.)
- Colored paper
- Tape
- Stickers
- Unsharpened pencils

Praise Streamers:
- Ribbon in several colors
- Plastic or metal rings (1" diameter)
- Scissors

CUCUMBER CONNECTION NEEDS:

- Pickle jar
- Pickles artwork from the *VeggieConnections Shepherd* pages (on the *VeggieConnections CD-ROM*)
- Green construction paper

KID CONNECTION NEEDS:

- Plain paper shopping/gift bag with handles (1 per child)
- Joy Harp on page 364 (1 per child)
- Scissors
- Glue and glue sticks
- Glitter pens
- Yarn
- Markers

CHRIST CONNECTION NEEDS:

- *VeggieConnections* take-home newspaper (one per child)

Plugging In to My Life

Life application of the lesson to lead kids to THINK–LINK–ACT and build a relationship with God every day

A. Cucumber Connection

Before kids arrive, enlarge and copy the pickles from the *VeggieConnections Shepherd* pages on the CD-ROM included in the *VeggieConnections Elementary Curriculum Kit* onto green construction paper. Cut them out and put in a pickle jar.

Let a volunteer draw a pickle from the Pickle Pot, and either the child or a Shepherd should read the dilemma out loud. Each Shepherd should then process the question with their group using the THINK—LINK—ACT phrase.

Jon was planning on flying his just-finished model airplane on Saturday. When Saturday arrives, it's raining and windy. Jon's joy was taken away by the weather. What can he do?	Karen made plans with a friend to come to her house after school. Her friend tells her that she can't come, and Karen later finds out that her friend is going to someone else's house. Karen is sad because this happened. What can she do?	It's time for Dolan to do his chores. He doesn't like his assigned chores this month. They put him in a bad mood. What can he do?

B. Kid Connection: Joy Bags

In the Joy Unit, the kids are going to fill a special shopping bag with reminders that true joy comes from God. Tell the children that the StuffMart has lots of interesting stuff. Some people find joy in stuff, but while we're at the Tree House, we will learn that God is our source of joy.

Give each child a plain paper gift or shopping bag with handles, about one foot tall. Have kids write their names on the bags with markers. Kids will decorate one side of the bag, and will save the other side for decorating during *Lesson 8* (to show Madame Blueberry's joyful transformation).

Give kids a copy of the Joy Harp on page 364. Provide scissors and have kids cut out the harp shape. Have kids fold their bags flat, and using a glue stick, apply glue to bag and back of the harp picture. Then have kids glue the harp onto their bags.

Give kids gold, silver, or other glitter pens to decorate the frame of the harp. Then give kids lengths of various colored yarn and have them cut the yarn to make strings to glue onto their harp pictures. Have *VeggieConnections Shepherds* help kids spread thin lines of glue along the harp string lines of the harp picture. Let the glue set a few minutes and then have kids stretch each yarn piece onto the glue lines, making colorful harp strings. Set bags aside to dry.

Give kids the happy-face circles from the Catch the Joy! game. Let kids write one way they found joy in God in today's lesson. Have kids put their happy-face circles in their bags. Once bags are dry, collect them for use next week.

C. Christ Connection

Lead the kids in saying the Unit Memory Verse, Psalm 16:11, having them repeat it after you phrase by phrase.

Have the kids divide into *VeggieConnections Groups* for a prayer time. Lead the kids in a prayer starter like this, letting the kids take turns filling in their own answers: **Dear God, thanks for drawing near to us. Thank you for giving us joy. Help us to find your joy this week as we face these things . . .** Kids pray. **In Jesus' name, amen.**

Distribute the take-home newspaper, ***VeggieConnections***.

Connecting to **Joy** by looking at **David's Life**
Samuel anoints David: **1 Samuel 16:1-13**

PART ONE:

Plugging In at the Tree House

Introduction to the site and lesson focus

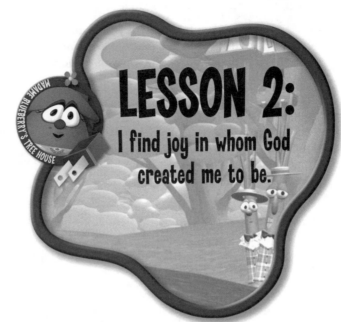

LESSON 2:
I find joy in whom God created me to be.

A. Veggie Connection

BEFORE YOU START:
Arrange for helpers to play a recording of screechy sounds when you roll your hand truck. Or have several helpers off to the side make screechy sounds for you. Practice before class to get the timing right. Put the can of oil in your pocket.

Dressed as the Deliveryperson, wheel in a hand truck loaded with boxes, bobbing your head and showing a huge smile on your face. While moving the hand truck, have your chosen method of screeching sounds commence. Pretend not to notice the screechy sound, and enthusiastically read portions of the company letter each time you stop moving.

Show kids the letter and say: **I'm sooo excited today! I've been awarded the employee of the week from StuffMart! And as big as StuffMart is, that is no easy task. There are hundreds of people working here!** Move your hand truck to the opposite side of the stage. **Let me read you what it says. "As president of StuffMart, I am pleased to award you the employee of the week. You have shown an amazing ability to solve problems on the spot.** Move your hand truck to the other side. **I was especially impressed how you delivered not only your packages, but** *two* **other deliverypersons' packages because they called in sick. And** *you* **did it in one day! Congratulations!"**

Move the hand truck to the middle of your storytelling area. **You know, I'm really happy to help serve people the way I do. I'm filled with joy to know God made me the way I am. Today were all going to learn about finding joy in whom God created each of us to be. Were going to do that by looking at the story of David's life in the Bible.** Move the hand truck a little, and this time wince at the screeching sound. **I can fix that!** Pull out your can of oil and motion oiling the wheels on the hand truck. Roll it back and forth and smile with the silence.

I used this oil to fix those noisy wheels. But oil was used for other things in Bible times. That brings us to our Connection Word for today.

Have a volunteer look up *anoint* in the *VeggieConnections Bible Dictionary* and read the definition. Explain that in Bible times, a person chosen for a special job would be anointed by having a little oil poured over his head. Have another volunteer go to the Connection Word sign, color in the number 2 with the yellow highlighter, and write "anoint" next to the number on the poster.

THE CHILDREN
will arrive with their *VeggieConnections Shepherds* from the opening Countertop Connections featuring Bob and Larry. Play the *Veggie-Connections Music CD* as children enter the Tree House.

VEGGIE CONNECTION NEEDS:

* *VeggieConnections Music CD*
* CD player
* Hand truck with boxes loaded on it
* Typed letter
* Recording of screechy, squeaky wheel sound (optional)
* Small, flat can of oil
* *VeggieConnections Bible Dictionary*
* Yellow highlighter
* Marker

B. Prayer Connection

Divide into groups according to age or height or some other easily definable feature. Have a *VeggieConnections Shepherd* join each group. The Shepherds can begin each of these prayer sentences and pause to let the kids fill in their own answers:

> Thank you, God, that you made us all like this . . .
> Thank you, too, that not everyone is like us. Thanks also for kids like this . . .
> Thank you for the way you made me, because I like this about myself . . .
> Help us to learn to find joy in whom you created us to be. In Jesus' name, amen.

PART TWO:

Plugging In to God's Word

Connecting to God's Word in the Bible and understanding how that can help us to have a better relationship with him

A. God Connection: Samuel anoints David – 1 Samuel 16:1-13

GOD CONNECTION NEEDS:

- Bible
- Prepared signs (see below)
- Small bowl or ram's horn

BEFORE YOU START:

Prepare signs for the roles in the story: Samuel, Town Leader 1, Town Leader 2, Jesse, Eliab, Abinadab, Shammah, Other Son 4, 5, 6, 7, David. Combine Other Sons if you have fewer kids (and combine the script roles).

TEACHER TIP:

Younger children may benefit from hearing the story before interacting with it. Explain to kids you'll read the story twice. For the first reading, they should listen carefully. For the second reading, kids will help tell the story.

Have the kids gather around the Tree House for the Bible story. Show kids a Bible open to 1 Samuel 16, and explain that is where today's story comes from. **Last week, we learned David took care of sheep and wrote songs that are called psalms in the Bible.** Show kids the book of Psalms. **Today we are going to begin with the long story of David's life. God had created David for a special purpose. To find out what that purpose was, I need some help telling the story today.**

Ask for volunteers to play the parts in the story. They can be male or female, but make sure Eliab is a mature boy or man and David a smaller boy. Have *VeggieConnections Shepherds* play additional roles if you have a smaller group of kids. Give actors their signs, and have everyone except Samuel move offstage.

God told the prophet Samuel that it was time for a new king to lead God's people, the Israelites. God said, "Go to Bethlehem, to the family of Jesse. I have chosen one of his sons to be king." *(Have Samuel show a worried face)*

But Samuel was afraid that Saul, the current king, would be mad if Samuel helped replace him. Samuel told God that he was scared. *(Samuel kneels and prays)*

God told him, "Tell everyone that you're going to Bethlehem to make a special sacrifice to me. Then I'll show you the one you should anoint to be king." *(Samuel gets up)* **Samuel did what the Lord told him.** *(Town Leaders walk up to Samuel)* **When he got to Bethlehem, the town leaders were scared because sometimes a prophet would come with bad news.** *(Town Leaders look worried)*

But Samuel told them, "I'm here with good news." The leaders were relieved! *(Leaders smile)* **Samuel explained, "First, we'll worship God with a sacrifice." Samuel made sure he invited Jesse and his sons. And he was keeping an eye out for whom God would pick to be the next king.** *(Jesse and Eliab enter)*

When Jesse's family arrived, Samuel saw the oldest son, Eliab. He was tall and strong. Samuel thought, "He'd make a good king. This must be whom God has picked." But God told Samuel, "Not this one! Don't just look at how strong he is on the outside. Look at the inside—his heart." *(Eliab leaves and Abinadab enters)*

Then Samuel looked at the next oldest son, Abinidab. He looked like he would make a good king, too. But God told Samuel that he was not the one. *(Abinidab leaves and Shammah enters)*

So Samuel looked at the third oldest son. But he said, "God has not chosen this one either." *(Shammah leaves and Other Son 4 enters)*

Jesse called another of his sons to meet Samuel. But Samuel said, "God has not chosen this one." *(Other Son 4 leaves and Sons 5–7 enter and pass by Samuel one by one)*

So he asked Jesse, "Are these all the sons you have?" Jesse told Samuel, "There is still my youngest son, but he's out in the fields taking care of the sheep." Samuel told Jesse to send for him.

So Jesse sent for his youngest son, named David. *(David enters)* When Samuel saw him, God said, "Go and anoint him. He is the one I've chosen to be the next king." God knew that David loved him with all his heart. So Samuel anointed David to be the next king of Israel. *(Samuel "pours" oil from a bowl or horn onto David's bowed head)*

David didn't become king right away. He kept being a shepherd and later a soldier. But this was whom God created David to be, and David found joy in God.

Thank your actors and have them sit down with the other kids. **David found joy in whom God made him. God made each of you. And you can find joy in how special you are. As we grow closer to him and make our relationship strong, he will help us figure out and grow into being exactly whom he created us to be!** Have the kids give high-fives to the kids sitting near them.

Briefly review by discussing these questions: **What was Samuel looking for in a king?** *(Someone who looked strong and good on the outside.)* **What was God looking for in a king?** *(Someone who loved him and wanted to obey him.)* **What did David find joy in and what can you find joy in?** *(In whom God created us to be.)*

B. Activity Connection

Choose from the following activities to help kids explore and remember to find joy in whom God created them to be (approximately 10–15 minutes each).

1. High-Powered Game: Cupfuls of Joy!

Have kids into teams of about 10 kids, and give each child a cup. Have teams line up behind the start line. **Samuel anointed David because God had a special purpose for him. We may not know what purpose God has for you, but we can be joyful about whom God has created you to be! To do that, we are going to anoint each other. But instead of using oil poured from a ram's horn, we are going to anoint one another by filling your empty cups with packing peanuts.**

Explain that the first child on each team will run to the bucket (or box) of peanuts and scoop peanuts into his or her cup. Players will then run back to the next person in line and carefully empty their cups into the next player's cup. But before this second person can run to the peanuts, he must pour his peanuts in the third person's cup. He then runs and fills his cup, pouring his peanuts in the third person's cup, who has just poured his peanuts in the fourth person's cup. This assembly line "pouring" will end with the last person pouring his peanuts in the first person's cup.

Play additional rounds, and for fun, try more difficult ways to hold the cup, such as holding the cup between their knees while moving.

Everyone has had a cup full of joy for being created by God in his special way. Remember, that is a joy no one can every take away from you!

2. Low-Powered Game: Joyful Jelly Beans

Have kids gather in a circle. If you have more than 20 kids, form two circles. Set a bowl of jelly beans in the center of the circle. Explain to kids that you'll call out characteristics, and if the item called matches them, they are to go grab a jelly bean out of the bowl and return to the circle.

Call out characteristics that make the kids unique. Try to choose some characteristics that apply to lots of the kids and some that will be unique to a particular child. **If you're a girl, get a joyful jelly bean! If you have a brother . . . , If you have a pet . . . , If you've been to Florida . . . , If you were born in July . . . , If you're good at spelling . . . , If you play a musical instrument . . . , If you told someone you love them today . . . , If you have blue eyes . . . , If you wear size 4 shoes . . . , If you play soccer . . . , If your name is Rachel . . . , If your parents are Tom and Linda . . . ,** and so on.

HIGH-POWERED GAME NEEDS:

- Paper or foam cups (one per child)
- Masking/painter's tape
- Large bucket or box
- Packing peanuts

BEFORE YOU START:

Fill a box or large bucket with packing peanuts. You'll need enough for each child to have a cupful, plus spilled peanuts. Put the box at one end of your play area. Mark start/finish lines at the opposite end of the playing area.

LOW-POWERED GAME NEEDS:

- Bowl of jelly beans

Play until all players have been called two or three times. Make up more of your own and have other *VeggieConnections Shepherds* make sure all the kids are getting jelly beans. Give out a handful of jelly beans to each player at the end.

Wow, God sure created lots of special kids here today. Isn't it great how some things we share with our friends and some things are special just for us? God made you the way you are for a reason. That's why you can find joy in whom God created you to be!

3. Craft: Joy Acrostic Banner

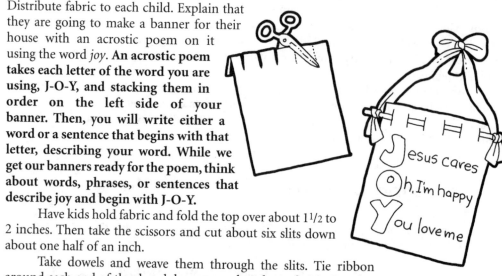

CRAFT NEEDS:

- 9" x 12" fabric segments (one per child)
- Scissors to cut fabric
- 12" long wooden dowels (one per child)
- Colored ribbon
- Fabric paint, fabric markers, or permanent markers

Distribute fabric to each child. Explain that they are going to make a banner for their house with an acrostic poem on it using the word *joy.* **An acrostic poem takes each letter of the word you are using, J-O-Y, and stacking them in order on the left side of your banner. Then, you will write either a word or a sentence that begins with that letter, describing your word. While we get our banners ready for the poem, think about words, phrases, or sentences that describe joy and begin with J-O-Y.**

Have kids hold fabric and fold the top over about 1½ to 2 inches. Then take the scissors and cut about six slits down about one half of an inch.

Take dowels and weave them through the slits. Tie ribbon around each end of the dowel, long enough to hang finished project. The kids may also tie a few ribbons on the end of the dowels for decoration.

Pass out writing utensils to kids and have them make a large J, O, and Y in a vertical line, on the left side of the banner, with J on top. Then have the kids write out their descriptive words of joy to fill in each line. Remind the kids that these words do not have to rhyme. The first word of each line should start with the letter that is already printed.

God created us, and we can find great joy in that! To remind us of joy in our lives, we have created these banners to hang in our homes. The closer that we get to God, the stronger our relationship with him is, the more joy we will feel in our lives.

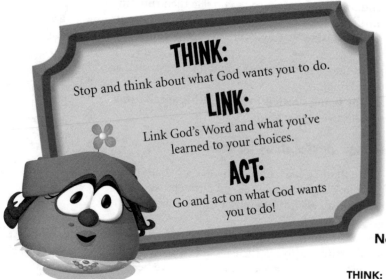

THINK:
Stop and think about what God wants you to do.

LINK:
Link God's Word and what you've learned to your choices.

ACT:
Go and act on what God wants you to do!

Now add some fun hand motions to the catch-phrase!

THINK: Touch head with fingertip two times.

LINK: Left hand out, right hand out.
Clasp your hands together, fingers intertwined.

ACT: Release grip and roll hands three times.
Finish with arms outstretched.

PART THREE:

Plugging In to My Life

Life application of the lesson to lead kids to THINK–LINK–ACT and build a relationship with God every day

A. Cucumber Connection

Before kids arrive, enlarge and copy the pickles from the *VeggieConnections Shepherd* pages on the CD-ROM included in the *VeggieConnections Elementary Curriculum Kit* onto green construction paper. Cut them out and put in a pickle jar.

Let a volunteer draw a pickle from the Pickle Pot, and either the child or a Shepherd should read the dilemma out loud. Each Shepherd should then process the question with their group using the THINK—LINK—ACT phrase.

Kelsey tried out for the school choir but was told she needed to get better first. She tried to join an after-school playground T-ball game but didn't get picked by either team. And her report card came home with no A's on it. She's discouraged about all the things she's not good at. What can Kelsey do?

Sterling loves to get up in front of people and always volunteers to be in plays or give reports. But his brother teases him and tells him he looks weird and says silly things. His feelings are hurt. What can Sterling do?

Justin knows that God created him and loves him very much. Sometimes Justin doesn't like the way that he looks and doesn't understand why God created him to be that way. As Justin's friend, what can you say to him about this?

B. Kid Connection: Joy Bags

BEFORE YOU START:

Arrange for kids to bring in photos or have an instant-print camera and film. If you have access to a photo printer, you could use a digital camera. If you can't get the pictures, you can still make the frames for kids to use when they take their bags home.

Give kids their Joy Bags from last week. Take pictures of kids who don't have one and print them if needed. **We've learned that God created you, and I want you to find joy in that! We're going to take these pictures of your fabulous selves, and we're going to put a frame around them. These frames will be made out of some other things that God created to remind you that you were made by God with a purpose.**

Distribute cardboard a few inches bigger around than each picture, pictures, and glue to each child. Have them glue their picture in the center of the rectangle. Give each table natural materials to work with. Encourage the children to glue down all of the sticks first and then glue down nuts, shells, and other items last. Set the frames aside to dry.

As you grow in your relationship with him, THINK about why he made you the way you are, LINK to David and his special purpose, and ACT in a way that would make God proud.

When frames are dry, have kids put them in the their Joy Bags and collect them for next week.

C. Christ Connection

Have kids gather with their *VeggieConnections Groups*. First, go around the circle and let each child say thank you to God for making them who they are, naming specific traits. Then encourage *VeggieConnections Shepherds* to thank God for each child by name, adding more qualities that define each one. Close by praying: **Help each kid here to walk on the path of life, find joy in your presence, and find joy in whom you made them to be.** Close the prayer by having the group pray the Unit Memory Verse, Psalm 16:11. **In Jesus' name, amen.**

Distribute the take-home newspaper, *VeggieConnections*.

CUCUMBER CONNECTION NEEDS:

- Pickle jar
- Pickles artwork from the *VeggieConnections Shepherd* pages (on the *VeggieConnections CD-ROM*)
- Green construction paper

KID CONNECTION NEEDS:

- Photograph of each child
- Joy Bags (made in *Lesson 1*)
- Cardboard rectangles
- Scissors
- Glue
- Pile of small twigs
- Acorns, nuts, small seashells or other natural items

CHRIST CONNECTION NEEDS:

- *VeggieConnections* take-home newspaper (one per child)

Your computer crashed and you lost your homework assignment.	A bully knocked you down and stole your lunch money.	You told only your best friend a secret and now others know it.
You lost out to another player for the last spot on the team.	You got really sick and missed a friend's birthday party.	Your sister told a lie about you to your mom and now you're grounded.
Your pet has gotten real sick and your vet isn't sure if your pet will live.	You broke your finger and can't play for a big piano recital.	Your family vacation was cancelled because your dad lost his job.
You are feeling really down lately.	You just found out you're moving to another state.	Your parents told you they are getting divorced.

Connecting to **Joy** by looking at **David's Life**
David fights both criticism from others and a big giant: **1 Samuel 17:1–50**

Connection Word:

trial

PART ONE:

Plugging In at the Tree House

Introduction to the site and lesson focus

LESSON 3:
I can find joy even in times of trial.

A. Veggie Connection

Dressed as the Deliveryperson, greet the kids calling out several of their names if you can. Tell them you've been waiting for them because it's been such a slow day. Even though Madame Blueberry continues to buy and buy and buy from StuffMart, some of the other customers have started visiting a new store that opened. **Believe it or not kids, I'm already done with my deliveries for the day. You see, a new store opened this week. I mean this store is a giant! It's called Stuff Superstore. It's taking over a lot of StuffMart's business. If we lose too many customers, I might lose my job!**

Write down "job" on an index card and tape it to the boxes that have been stacked one on top of the other. Ask the kids if any one has something big they're worried about. If the kids are quiet, ask some of the following questions: **Does anyone have a friend or family member in the hospital or sick?** Write down "illness" on an index card. **Is anyone having trouble with a class in school?** Write down "school." Ask about family, friends, moving, and so on. Tape the index cards randomly onto the boxes.

These are all big problems. Another word for a problem is a *trial*. Let's look up that word in our *VeggieConnections Bible Dictionary*. Let a volunteer look it up and read the definition aloud. Have another volunteer go to the Connection Word sign, color in the number 3 with the yellow highlighter, and write "trial" next to the number on the poster.

The trials we're talking about are the tests and hardships or problems we all face. Everyone goes through trials, but we know someone who is bigger than our trials don't we? *(Yes. God or Jesus.)* **When we're connected to God, we can still find joy in times of trial. Later, we'll see what our Bible story teaches us about giants in our lives.**

B. Prayer Connection

Take a few minutes for *VeggieConnections Groups* to meet together and pray about some of the trials they may be facing. *VeggieConnections Shepherds* can ask about any answers to prayer the kids may have experienced, along with any prayer concerns. Then allow several minutes for groups to pray. Encourage the kids to pray for one another, even if it's just a sentence.

THE CHILDREN
will arrive with their *VeggieConnections Shepherds* from the opening Countertop Connections featuring Bob and Larry. Play the *VeggieConnections Music CD* as children enter the Tree House.

VEGGIE CONNECTION NEEDS:
- *VeggieConnections Music CD*
- CD player
- Three cardboard boxes, medium-sized
- Index cards
- Marker
- Tape
- *VeggieConnections Bible Dictionary*
- Yellow highlighter

Plugging In to God's Word

Connecting to God's Word in the Bible and understanding how that can help us to have a better relationship with him

GOD CONNECTION NEEDS:

- Bible
- Adult or teen volunteers, one to be David and four others to play various parts as you tell the story.
- Goliath prop
- Bible-time clothes and props (optional)

BEFORE YOU START:

Recruit your volunteer actors ahead of time and give them a copy of this story so that their actions flow smoothly. Create a Goliath prop (recruit church artists) out of heavy cardboard nailed or stapled to a long, tall stick, 1' x 4" or 2' x 2". Draw a huge giant on the cardboard, 9' tall (or as tall as will fit in your room). Use a circle for a large shield and wrap foil around a 1 x4 for Goliath's sword. Have the Goliath actor stand behind the prop and hold the sword in one hand and the shield in the other.

OPTION:

A portable option for Goliath is to draw the giant on mural paper and fold over and tape the top of the mural to a push broom, using the handle to hold up the mural. The Goliath actor won't have use of his arms with this option.

A. God Connection: David fights both criticism from others and a big giant – 1 Samuel 17:1-50

What person from the Bible have we been talking about here at the Tree House? *(David.)* Have David wave to the kids. **David went through a lot of trials during his life. Trials are hard things—they can make us scared or sad. David faced a huge trial that is told in the book of 1 Samuel in the Bible.** Open your Bible and show the passage to the kids. **We have some helpers to help you see how huge David's trial was!**

David's job was to take care of his family's sheep. *(David tends to four sheep)* **He spent days and nights out there, leading the sheep to good food and water and protecting them from wild animals. Then it happened—WAR!** *(All five actors make serious faces)* **The Philistines, Israel's enemies, came to attack Israel. David's older brothers went to join the army.** *(Four soldiers march around)* **David was too young to go.** *(David looks disappointed)* **So he had to stay home and keep taking care of the sheep.** *(David tends to four sheep)*

Time passed, and there was no news about the battle. So Jesse, David's father, sent David with some food and supplies for his brothers. *(David skips off with a basket of goodies.)* Three actors are now soldiers (one will be Goliath with his props). **When he arrived, he saw a giant from the Philistines named Goliath. This fierce soldier was over nine feet tall!** *(Goliath looks intimidating)* **Goliath came out to the battle line and roared threats at the Israelite soldiers, calling them dogs!** *(Angry Goliath)* **David couldn't believe his ears! This enemy of God thought that he could defeat God's people. David looked around to see who was going to stand up to Goliath.** *(Soldiers cower away)* **But no one stepped forward, no one wanted to fight him. In fact, God's people were afraid!** *(Scared soldiers)*

David wasn't afraid. *(Brave David)* **So he went to his brothers and asked them when *they* were going to fight Goliath.** *(David goes to three brothers)* **They got so mad at him!** *(Angry brothers)* **They said, "What do *you* know about fighting? You're just a little kid! Go home and watch your useless ol' sheep and leave us alone!"** *(Brothers shake fingers at David)*

But David trusted God. *(David prays)* **He went to King Saul, who was the not-so-great king of the Israelites, and told him that he would fight Goliath.** One actor is now the king. *(David goes to him to speak)* **David was not afraid of the giant because he knew that God was bigger and stronger.** *(David points upward and pantomimes "bigger" and "stronger")* **David trusted God so he could be joyful, even in the trial.** *(David looks content)*

Now remember, David was no more than a teenager, and huge Goliath had been trained as a fighting soldier, so King Saul wasn't so sure about letting David go. *(King scratches his chin and thinks)* **King Saul tried to talk him out of it, but David reminded Saul that he had some training, too. In the fields, while he was watching the sheep, David had to fight off lions and bears.** *(David mock fights off animals)* **David said, "The Lord who protected me from the paw of the lion and bear will protect me from the hand of this Philistine."** *(David points toward Goliath)*

So, with King Saul's permission, David went to a creek and picked out five smooth stones. *(David gets five stones from a creek)* **These, along with his sling and his shepherd's staff, would be his only weapons. The next day, when Goliath came to the battle line to challenge the army of Israel, David stepped forward.** *(David and Goliath face off)* **Goliath looked at David and laughed, "Am I a dog, that you come at me with sticks? Come closer and I'll make sure you end up dead!"** *(Goliath laughs and bellows at David)*

David said to Goliath, "You come at me with your big size and your big weapons. But I come at you with the Lord's name. You insulted God! So now God will help me beat you, and you're the one who's going to die. Then the whole world will know that the God of Israel is the one true God." *(David is yelling at Goliath)*

As the giant moved closer to attack, (*Goliath approaches David*) **David reached into his bag, took out a stone, and put it in his sling.** (*David now follows all remaining actions*) **He whirled the sling round and round. Then at just the right split-second and with careful aim, he slung it at Goliath. It hit him on the forehead and Goliath fell facedown on the ground, dead.** (*Goliath falls to the ground and David takes his sword*) **The Philistine army ran away scared!** (*Remaining soldiers run away*) **So the Lord helped David win this battle over the Philistines because David trusted God, even in this trial.** (*David stands in victory*)

Thank actors and review the story. **What trials did David face?** (*Brothers who made fun of him, a king who didn't believe he could fight the giant, facing the giant Goliath.*) **We probably won't have to face giants, but we can face whatever trials come our way with God's help. How can we be joyful when we endure trials and hardships?** Allow responses.

B. Activity Connection

Choose from the following activities to help kids explore and remember that they can find joy even in times of trial (approximately 10–15 minutes each).

1. High-Powered Game: Balloon Trials

Have kids form pairs, and let them tie one leg to each other with a strip of cloth or piece of rope/twine. Have a *VeggieConnections Shepherd* match up with a older child to make a pair if needed. Give one kitchen trash bag to each pair. Show kids the balloons and say: **You face trials or problems with a variety of people or things. These balloons represent those trials.** Show kids each balloon and have kids give an example of a trial in that area. For example: kids might mention facing bullies for "Others."

Scatter the balloons throughout the area but away from a taped circle. Explain how kids are to collect one of each five trial balloons by pushing or kicking them into the circle. Once a balloon is in the circle, one child will pick up the balloon and put it in the bag that is held open by his or her partner. Then pairs will search out remaining balloons and repeat the process.

Point out the circle. **This is called the Joy Circle. It represents having joy even when you face trials. That is why you must only bag your trial balloons in this circle.**

Begin the game and have *VeggieConnections Shepherds* watching to see that pairs collect all five different balloons. Replace any broken balloons with spares (be sure to write the correct trial on the new balloon). When everyone is done, scatter the balloons out and have pairs switch bagging and collecting roles. If you have more time, have kids form new partners and play again.

We will all face trials in our life. But just as David looked to God when he faced trials, we can, too. And even as we face the trial, we can find joy in God!

2. Low-Powered Game: Trials Table Game

Have *VeggieConnections Groups* gather around long tables. Give kids time to look at the trials written on the cards. Give the two table-tennis balls to two kids and have them draw a happy face on the balls. Select two different kids to stand on either end of the table and give them each a ball. Tell kids they will roll their balls down the table and try to knock over the paper cards that have trials written on them. Kids will both roll their balls at the same time. Have other kids retrieve balls that roll off the table.

For the first round, give kids one roll each. After everyone has one roll, play a second round, giving kids two rolls each. For the third round, give kids three tries. Kids will probably knock over more trial cards with each round. After the third round, say: **Each round of this game gave you more tries to knock down the trial cards.** Show kids the happy face on the ball. **The ball represented having God's joy as you faced trials. The more joy you had from God, the more you were able to knock over the trials. Real trials will be harder to face, but having God's joy will make it easier to handle the trials in life.**

HIGH-POWERED GAME NEEDS:

- Strips of cloth or length of rope/twine
- Kitchen plastic trash bags (one for every two kids)
- Balloons (five per child)
- Black permanent markers
- Masking/painter's tape

BEFORE YOU START:

Tape a circle area about 10' for up to four *Veggie-Connections Groups*. Make the circle larger if you have more groups. Inflate balloons and write one word on each: Family, Friends, School, Others, Hobbies. You'll need a set of five marked balloons for every pair of kids.

LOW-POWERED GAME NEEDS:

- Trial Game Cards on page 334
- Long tables (one per group)
- Table-tennis balls (two per group)
- Markers

BEFORE YOU START:

Photocopy and cut apart the game cards. Fold the bottom edge of each card so they will stand up. Set up long tables and stand up the 12 cards in the middle of the table, six facing toward one end, six facing the other end.

3. Craft: Cross Paperweight

CRAFT NEEDS:

- 4" nails (one per child)
- 3" nails (one per child)
- 19-gauge craft wire (two feet per child)
- Beads (one per child)
- Air-dry clay (4 oz. per child)
- Wax paper

Give each child one four-inch and one three-inch nail, two feet of 19-gauge craft wire, and one bead. Show the kids how to form a cross with the nails and secure into place with the wire. Have the kids continue to wrap wire around the cross. Before the last couple of wraps, the kids may insert a bead to hang at the center of the cross.

Give kids wax paper sheets and put some clay on the sheet for each child. Have kids work the clay and mold it into a dome shape, 2" around at the base, and about 1" high at the center. Then have kids stick their cross into the center of the clay dome and leave it to dry.

Jesus faced the greatest trial of all—dying for our sins so that we could be forgiven. Use this paperweight cross as a reminder that God will help us face our trials.

PART THREE:

Plugging In to My Life

Life application of the lesson to lead kids to THINK-LINK-ACT and build a relationship with God every day

A. Cucumber Connection

CUCUMBER CONNECTION NEEDS:

- Pickle jar
- Pickles artwork from the *VeggieConnections Shepherd* pages (on the *VeggieConnections CD-ROM*)
- Green construction paper

Before kids arrive, enlarge and copy the pickles from the *VeggieConnections Shepherd* pages on the CD-ROM included in the *VeggieConnections Elementary Curriculum Kit* onto green construction paper. Cut them out and put in a pickle jar.

Let a volunteer draw a pickle from the Pickle Pot, and either the child or a Shepherd should read the dilemma out loud. Each Shepherd should then process the question with their group using the THINK—LINK—ACT phrase.

Evan is in the hospital. He may have to be there awhile. Evan is discouraged handling this trial. What can he do?	Tiesha moved to a new town and now is in a new school. She doesn't know anyone and is nervous about her first day. How can Tiesha find joy in God during this trial?	in your class, you are assigned to sit next to an annoying kid. You've talked to the teacher and you can't get out of this seating arrangement until the end of the month, when seats change. What can you do to get through this trial?

B. Kid Connection: Joy Bags

KID CONNECTION NEEDS:

- Joy Bags (made in *Lesson 1*)
- 8–9" paper plates
- Yarn
- Scissors
- Glue
- Gel pens
- Markers

Give each child his or her Joy Bag and a paper plate. Provide yarn, scissors, glue, gel pens and markers. **David faced the giant Goliath. Just as David joyfully faced the giants in his life, you can, too. Create giant heads on these plates to remind yourselves how God will help you overcome the trials, even the giant ones, in your life!**

Have kids use the supplies to create their giant heads. On the back of their plates, have kids write simple phrases such as: "My joy comes from God!" and "God will help me face my trials."

After kids have completed their giant heads, have them put them in their bags. Collect bags for use next week.

C. Christ Connection

Have kids stand and lead them in singing *THINK—LINK—ACT* song with motions. Say: **Facing trials is probably the last thing we want to do. And facing them with joy may seem even harder. But the words of our Unit Memory Verse can encourage us.** Say several words of the unit verse, Psalm 16:11, pausing to allow kids to say them before saying the next phrase. Repeat the verse a few times.

Have kids divide into their *VeggieConnections Groups*. Have *VeggieConnections Shepherds* ask kids to share trials they are facing and have Shepherds pray for their kids.

Distribute the take-home newspaper, **VeggieConnections**.

Connection Word:

content

PART ONE:

Plugging In at the Tree House

Introduction to the site and lesson focus

LESSON 4:

I find joy in being content.

A. Veggie Connection

Dressed as the Deliveryperson, enthusiastically welcome the kids back to the Tree House. Announce to the kids that you are really happy to see them today. Explain you're doing a little experiment and you need their help. **Every day when I pack my lunch, I like to put a little snack in it. Animal crackers are my favorite snack. The problem is I just don't know how many to put in. It never seems to be quite enough. I want you to help me figure out the right number.**

Give each child a paper cup and have kids line up behind the taped line. Explain that you're not going to look. They can go about getting the crackers as often as they want, but they can only get one at a time. Then they must cross back over the taped line. However, when you turn around, anyone who is not behind the line has to sit down with only the crackers he or she has.

Wait about 10 seconds, then turn around. Have the "caught" kids sit down. Repeat several times varying the time from about five to 10 seconds. Then have all the kids sit down with their cups. **I see some of you ended up with just a few treats, and some of you were lucky enough to get lots of crackers.** Ask the kids with only a few crackers if they are happy with their amount of crackers. Then ask kids who got increasingly larger number of crackers the same question. **In this game you had no way of knowing when you would be out. Most of you who got called out early probably weren't too happy with the numbers of crackers you got. We played this game to help you understand today's Connection Word, _content_.**

Let a volunteer look up _content_ in the _VeggieConnections Bible Dictionary_ and read the definition. Then let the kids try to describe _contentment_ in their own words. Explain to the kids that you wanted them to see how many crackers it would take to make them content. Have another volunteer go to the Connection Word sign, color in the number 4 with the yellow highlighter, and write "content" next to the number on the poster. **Things may not always seem fair. There may be other people who have more than we do, but God wants us to trust him and be thankful for what he decides is enough for us. The most important thing we have is a relationship with God. He loves us and cares about each one of us so much and it pleases him when we don't try to get too much stuff. We can find joy in being content with everything God brings us.**

THE CHILDREN
will arrive with their _VeggieConnections Shepherds_ from the opening Countertop Connections featuring Bob and Larry. Play the _Veggie-Connections Music CD_ as children enter the Tree House.

VEGGIE CONNECTION NEEDS:
- _VeggieConnections Music CD_
- CD player
- Paper cups (one per child)
- Masking/painter's tape
- Bowl of animal crackers (check about possible food allergies)
- _VeggieConnections Bible Dictionary_
- Yellow highlighter
- Marker

BEFORE YOU START:
Put a bowl of crackers on a table or chair, and tape a long line about six feet away from the bowl.

B. Prayer Connection

Break into *VeggieConnections Groups* and have *VeggieConnections Shepherds* encourage the kids to think of things they've had to wait for that ended up being great. Have kids take turns saying sentence prayers to thank God for those things. Also, let kids thank God for anything good they did or received this past week.

PART TWO:

Plugging in to God's Word

Connecting to God's Word in the Bible and understanding how that can help us to have a better relationship with him

A. God Connection: David waits to be king in God's time – 1 Samuel 26:1-25

GOD CONNECTION NEEDS:

- Bible
- David and Saul Script on page 365 (one per child)
- Crown on page 344 (one per child)
- Goldenrod or yellow paper (one per child)
- Scissors
- Tape

BEFORE YOU START:

Copy a David and Saul Script for each child. Copy crown onto goldenrod or yellow paper and cut apart on the zig-zag line. Tape the two ends together.

TEACHER TIP:

Younger children may benefit from hearing the story before interacting with it. Explain to kids you'll read the story twice. For the first reading, they should listen very carefully. For the second reading, kids will help tell the story.

The last few weeks we have been talking about David. What has David been going through in the last three lessons? (*He was a shepherd who wrote praise songs to God, he was chosen to be the next king of Israel, he fought with Goliath by trusting God and won.*)

Open your Bible to 1 Samuel 26 and explain this is where in the Bible today's story comes from. **The leader of Israel was named King Saul. He didn't obey God very well, so God told the prophet Samuel to choose David to be the next king. But God never said when that would happen!**

King Saul found out that God was replacing him. He didn't like it, and he wasn't going to obey it. What should David do? He decided he would be content as he waited for God to work things out. But King Saul was very jealous of David and grew to hate him. King Saul even started trying to have David killed. Wouldn't it be better if David just went ahead and made himself king? What should he do? Let's find out what David did.

Explain you'll read the part of David, and kids will read the parts of King Saul. Give kids a copy of the script and the gold crown. Distribute tape and have *VeggieConnections Shepherds* assist kids taping the crowns so they fit around their heads.

David: King Saul had tried to kill me so often that I had to run into the rocky, hilly desert to hide and live. But I had lots of good, fighting men with me. We managed to survive. I often wondered, "When would the Lord keep his promise to let me be king?"

Saul: Kill David! My kingdom will not be safe until I get rid of him! I must kill David!

David: We know Saul's army has been following us, but we are keeping our distance by staying in desert."

Saul: I heard that David was in the desert, so my 3,000 soldiers and I have set up camp here, near David. But now we need to rest."

David: I sent men to discover where Saul was and they gave me a good report. So I asked for a volunteer, and Abishai and I went down to Saul's camp and found him sleeping. I came up to Saul, and Abishai wanted to kill Saul. But I told him Saul was God's king and he couldn't kill him. So I grabbed his spear and water jug and we left his camp. Then I stood a distance from the king and called out to him.

Saul: Is that you, David?"

David: King Saul, why are you trying to kill me? I have done you no wrong. I took your spear but did not kill you with it as I could have.

Saul: I have sinned. Because you saved my life I will not try to hurt you again. I have been a fool!

David: Here is your spear. Have one of your men come and get it. The Lord rewards those living for him. I would not kill you, and I ask the Lord to bless me.

Saul: May the Lord bless you, David. You will be a great man, and God will give you victory in your life!

Set aside the props and discuss these questions with the children: **What had David been promised by God?** (*To be the next king of Israel.*) **Why do you think it would have been hard for David to be content to wait?** (*Because God had already promised he would become king, because Saul was so bad to him, because he had a chance to get rid of Saul and speed up his kingship.*) **How did David actually feel about waiting—what did he do (or not do) to show it?** (*David was content to be king in God's time, he didn't kill Saul when he had the chance.*) **How did David show he was finding joy in being content?** (*By not killing Saul, by trusting God to put him on the throne in his timing, by making good promises.*)

Just like David, we can learn to find joy in being content, whether we're waiting for something or being happy with what we have.

B. Activity Connection

Choose from the following activities to help kids explore and remember that they can find joy in being content (approximately 10–15 minutes each).

1. High-Powered Game: Pile it On

BEFORE YOU START:
Set the piles of stuff at the start line. Halfway across the room, tape a line. Set the balls on it. At the other end of the game area, tape an open box goal on its side. Plan on having *VeggieConnections Shepherds* retrieve balls and replace them on the midpoint line as needed.

Explain to the kids that having lots of stuff can be a real burden. Divide the kids into two even teams. Add a Shepherd to make teams even if needed. At your signal, the first player picks up all the "stuff" (he may "wear" some), runs to the midpoint, and kicks the ball toward the goal. Without dropping anything, the player tries to score a goal. If players drop anything, they must stop and pick it up before continuing to kick or run.

When the player runs back to the team, he or she drops the team's "stuff" and shouts: **I'll find joy in being content.** Then the next player has a turn. The first team to run the course, try kicking a goal, and return with all the stuff is the winner.

When finished, ask the kids: **What was it like to run with all that stuff?** (*Hard, frustrating, it slowed us down.*) **What are some things that get in our way of finding contentment in God?** (*Toys and other stuff we own, too many activities, things that entertain us, impatience, wanting more stuff, and so on.*)

It's easy to think that having lots of stuff will bring us joy. The truth is, lots of stuff just gets in the way. Our Unit Memory Verse, Psalm 16:11, says, *"You have made known to me the path of life; you will fill me with joy in your presence..."* We can find joy when we learn to be content with what that God has given us.

HIGH-POWERED GAME NEEDS:

- A pile of "stuff" for each team (coats and hats, stuffed animals, toys, sports gear, and so on.)
- Soccer or playground balls
- Masking/painter's tape to mark lines
- Box (one per team)

2. Low-Powered Game: The "I" Game

- A bag of beads or marbles
- Small cups

Have kids form circles and stand. If you have more than 15 kids, form two circles. Hand each child three to five beads or marbles and a cup. The goal of the game is to try to collect the beads of the other players. You collect beads by asking questions that encourage the other players to say the word "I."

Sometimes the reason we don't feel content is because we're thinking more about ourselves than other people. "I" want, "I" need, and so on. In this game, using the word "I" will put you out of the game. Explain that you get to ask people questions. If they use the word "I" when they answer, they must give you their beads and sit down. Give them examples of questions: What do you want for your birthday? Tell me three things you did last week. What was your favorite vacation and why? The game is over when only one person is standing or after a specific time limit.

3. Craft: Contentment Bulletin Boards

BEFORE YOU START:

Cut foamboard sheets into 10" squares with a utility knife and a ruler (six squares for a standard 20" x30" sheet from art/craft store.)

CRAFT NEEDS:

- 10" x10" foamboard (one per child)
- Construction paper
- Scissors
- Glue sticks
- Markers
- Several short map pins in small bags (one bag per child)
- Craft-pattern scissors (optional)

David wasn't willing to kill King Saul. He knew God was going to make him king, but he was willing to be content and wait until God was ready to do it. We all have things that we are trying to be content with. We're going to make bulletin boards that will help us to be content while waiting on God.

Give each child a foamboard square, construction paper, and other supplies. Have kids cut one-inch strips of construction paper for borders. If you have craft-pattern scissors, have kids use them to cut patterns for their paper border strips. Have kids use glue sticks to glue their borders around the edges of the foamboard. Then have kids write "I will be content with God" on the top border with markers. Give kids small bags filled with several short map pins.

THINK:
Stop and think about what God wants you to do.

LINK:
Link God's Word and what you've learned to your choices.

ACT:
Go and act on what God wants you to do!

Now add some fun hand motions to the catch-phrase!

THINK: Touch head with fingertip two times.

LINK: Left hand out, right hand out.
Clasp your hands together, fingers intertwined.

ACT: Release grip and roll hands three times.
Finish with arms outstretched.

PART THREE:

Plugging In to My Life

Life application of the lesson to lead kids to THINK-LINK-ACT and build a relationship with God every day

A. Cucumber Connection

Before kids arrive, enlarge and copy the pickles from the *VeggieConnections Shepherd* pages on the CD-ROM included in the *VeggieConnections Elementary Curriculum Kit* onto green construction paper. Cut them out and put in a pickle jar.

    Let a volunteer draw a pickle from the Pickle Pot, and either the child or a Shepherd should read the dilemma out loud. Each Shepherd should then process the question with their group using the THINK—LINK—ACT phrase.

It's three days until Christmas and there are presents under the tree with your name on them. You'd really like to open one carefully when no one's looking. What should you do?	Manuel has a toy that he really likes to play with, and it's based on his favorite movie. He saw an ad for the same toy that now comes with lights and sound effects. It looks like lots more fun. What should he do?	Julia is the smallest kid in her class. She feels that because she is small she doesn't fit in. Sometimes she's embarrassed about being the shortest. How can Julia be content with the way she is?

CUCUMBER CONNECTION NEEDS:

- Pickle jar
- Pickles artwork from the *VeggieConnections Shepherd* pages (on the *VeggieConnections CD-ROM*)
- Green construction paper

B. Kid Connection: Joy Bags

Give kids their Joy Bags. Give each child a key ring and enough bead string to hold the letters C-O-N-T-E-N-T plus some extra for fun beads. The kids should tie one end of the string to the ring and thread the beads onto the rest of the string. Suggest a few decorative beads, followed by the word CONTENT, and then more decorative beads. After all beads are on the string, have the kids do an overhand knot to secure them. Then have kids clip their key chain to their Joy Bags.

    Have kids stand and sing the *THINK—LINK—ACT* song with motions. **David was content with waiting to act as king on God's time. David had the opportunity to take out his enemy, King Saul, but he chose not to. He chose to wait for the time that God chose to step up and be king. Keep these key chains clipped to your bag as a reminder to remain content with things. THINK about what you want that you don't have. LINK to David who wanted to be king and knew he would be when the time was right. ACT the way that would make God smile.**

    Collect the Joy Bags for next week's lesson.

KID CONNECTION NEEDS:

- Joy Bags (from *Lesson 1*)
- Key rings (one per child)
- Letter beads to spell "CONTENT"
- Fun beads to decorate with
- Bead string
- *VeggieConnections Music CD*
- CD player

C. Christ Connection

Divide kids into three groups and have a *VeggieConnections Shepherd* join each group. Give each Shepherd one of the three Unit Memory Verse papers. Have each group say their portion of the verse as a Shepherd holds the words for kids to see. Say it several times.

    Then have the kids sit in their *VeggieConnections Groups* and pray one-word prayers. The *VeggieConnections Shepherds* begin the prayer, and the kids pray around the circle, saying one word to complete the sentence. Kids may pray around the circle as many times as they wish.

    Dear God, thank you for giving me these wonderful gifts: Kids pray.
    And help me to be content with: Kids pray.
    Help us to find joy in staying connected to you, Lord. In Jesus' name, amen.
    Distribute the take-home newspaper, *VeggieConnections*.

CHRIST CONNECTION NEEDS:

- *VeggieConnections* take-home newspaper (one per child)

BEFORE YOU START:
Write each of the three phrases of the Unit Memory Verse, Psalm 16:11, on separate sheets of paper.

Connecting to **Joy** by looking at **David's Life**
David's prayer of thanksgiving: **2 Samuel 7:18-29** and
Psalm 100

PART ONE:

Plugging In at the Tree House

Introduction to the site
and lesson focus

LESSON 5:
I find joy in being thankful.

A. Veggie Connection

Dressed as the Deliveryperson, welcome the kids warmly as they arrive at the Tree House. Tell them Madame Blueberry said to tell them all hello. **I have had a pretty easy day today. Madame Blueberry didn't have an order today. In fact, today I was picking up a few items she decided to return because she really didn't need them. Before I left, she told me she appreciated the work I do for her. Then she said asked me If I wanted to play a fun little word game. I did and it was fun, so I've decided to play it with you!**

Before reading the story, call out the categories (named on the blanks) and let kids offer words that fit that category. Have *VeggieConnections Shepherds* assist kids as needed. When you ask for a "thing," examples could be a book, a snowball, a school, or any "thing" the kids can think of. Write down the chosen answer in every blank of that description. For example, if "book" is the chosen "thing," write "book" on every blank labeled "thing." Don't tell the kids ahead of time anything about the story. Once all the blanks are filled in, read the story aloud and let the kids laugh!

Once upon a time, there was a boy named _____, and he had a(n)
(boy's name)

_____, _____, _____ that he was very thankful for.
(adjective)   _(color)_   _(thing)_

The reason that he loved his _____ so much was because it reminded him of
(same thing)

a(n) _____ _____. One day, while he was playing, a(n)
(adjective)   _(noun)_

_____ walked right up to him and said, "Three words that are hard to say
(animal)

together." Well, the boy was so surprised that he got up and ran to_____.
(place)

He had never been there before and he quickly got lost.

But suddenly he met a girl named _____, who was lost also.
(girl's name)

They were afraid but soon found _____ to help them.
(famous person)

THE CHILDREN
will arrive with their
VeggieConnections Shepherds
from the opening Countertop
Connections featuring Bob
and Larry. Play the *Veggie-Connections Music CD* as
children enter the Tree House.

VEGGIE CONNECTION NEEDS:

- *VeggieConnections Bible Dictionary*
- Pencil
- *VeggieConnections Music CD*
- CD player
- Yellow highlighter
- Marker

_____ told them to find their way home they must
(same famous person)

_____, then _____, then _____
(verb)   *(verb)*   *(adverb)*

_____. They were so thankful for the help that they gave
(verb)

_____ a _____.
(same famous person)   *(thing)*

The two kids promised never to wander that far from home again. To show their

parents they were serious and that they were glad they didn't get in trouble, they thanked

them by _____ and _____ around the entire house!
                 (verbing)   *(verbing)*

That was a silly story, but did you notice what the story featured? *(It was about being thankful).* **Let's look up the word *thankfulness* in our *VeggieConnections Bible Dictionary*?** Let a volunteer look it up and read the definition aloud. **The kids in our silly story were full of gladness and appreciation for getting home. Thankfulness is an attitude that pleases God. It helps our joy to grow. All good things come from God, and thanking God for those things makes us joyful. Today were going to see how David was thankful for God's promise to him.** Ask a child to highlight the numbers button and write "thankfulness" on the Connection Word sign.

B. Prayer Connection

Let the large group pray "popcorn" prayers. Begin a prayer time with **Thank you, God,** and then let kids pop up out of their seats in any order and call out one word of something they're thankful for; then they pop back down. Kids may pop up repeatedly and may even overlap, just like popcorn. When the "popping" starts winding down, close the prayer time by thanking the Lord for *VeggieConnections* and asking his help in learning about joy today.

PART TWO:

Plugging In to God's Word

Connecting to God's Word in the Bible and understanding how that can help us to have a better relationship with him

A. God Connection: David's prayer of thanksgiving –
2 Samuel 7:18-29 and Psalm 100

Gather the kids together on their benches or "grass" carpet squares. Ask the kids to name some things that have been happening to David in the last four lessons. *(He was a shepherd boy who wrote praise songs; he was chosen to be the next king of Israel; he fought the giant Goliath and won; he hid from King Saul, who was trying to kill him; he waited with contentment for God to keep his promise to make David king.)*

GOD CONNECTION NEEDS:
- Bible

TEACHERS TIP:
Younger children may benefit from hearing the story before interacting with it. Explain to kids you'll read the story twice. For the first reading, they should listen very carefully. For the second reading, kids will help tell the story.

Divide the kids into three groups (they may remain seated). Assign the first group the idea of "time"—whenever you signal them during the Bible story, they roll their arms in front of them to show time passing. Assign the second group "king"—they hold their hands on their heads in the shape of a crown. The third group is "thanks" and "praise"—they lift their arms up to God. Have the kids practice a few times as you point to each group. Then show the kids where in the Bible today's story is found: 2 Samuel 7. Read the following summary, and point to each group as indicated.

David had been waiting a long time *(Time).* **God had promised he would be the next king** *(King).* **But years and years** *(Time)* **were passing. When would David become the ruler** *(King)* **of the Israelites? But all this time** *(Time),* **David chose to be content and thankful** *(Thanks)* **to God.**

Finally, about 20 years *(Time)* **after he was chosen to be the next king** *(King),* **the old king** *(King)* **died. Finally, David could sit on the throne** *(King)* **and lead God's people as promised! And one of God's prophets named Nathan also promised David that his son and grandsons over the years** *(Time)* **would also be kings** *(King)* **after him.**

David was SO thankful! *(Thanks)* **He prayed with joy to God** *(Thanks).* **He said, "God, why are you being so good to me? You've made me the king!** *(King)* **And for years to come** *(Time)* **my family will be kings,** *(King)* **too. Thank you so much!** *(Thanks)* **You are so great!** *(Thanks)* **There is no one like you** *(Thanks),* **and there is no God but you!** *(Thanks)* **May your name be praised** *(Thanks)* **forever!** *(Time)* **Thank you!** *(Thanks)***"**

Thank the kids for helping you tell the story. Show them Psalm 100 in the Bible. **Even after David became king he was still full of thanks and still liked to write songs. Psalm 100 is one of his songs of thanksgiving. He wrote it to express his joy.** Read Psalm 100 to the kids.

Then discuss these questions: **What was David thankful for and joyful about?** *(That he finally became king, that God had made good promises about his son/grandsons being king, simply that God is Lord, and so on.)* **How did David show his thankfulness?** *(He prayed, he wrote songs.)* **What are ways you can show thankfulness to God?** *(Praying, singing, clapping hands, obeying, telling others about him, and so on.)*

B. Activity Connection

Choose from the following activities to help kids explore and remember that they can find joy in being thankful (approximately 10–15 minutes each).

1. High-Powered Game: Thankfulness Toss

BEFORE YOU START:

Tape a 10' line. Pile an equal number of toss-able items at both ends of the line. Place two large boxes about 12'–15' away about 10' apart.

HIGH-POWERED GAME NEEDS:

- Masking/painter's tape
- Balls, stuffed toys, clothes, shoes, empty boxes (anything that can be tossed without damage)
- Two large same-sized open boxes
- Two watches with second hand or stopwatches

Have kids divide into *VeggieConnections Groups*. Pairs of *VeggieConnections Groups* will play against each other in this game. If you have a leftover group, have them play against the winner of the last *VeggieConnections Group* pair. Have *VeggieConnections Shepherds* time their groups during the game. **David had to wait 20 years after his anointing to be the next king. David praised God during those years, writing prayers and praises in the psalms. God made David king, and David praised God with a prayer of thanksgiving.**

In this game, we borrowed lots of stuff from StuffMart. We all own some of the items in these piles and we should be thankful for everything God gives us. You will offer prayers of thanks by tossing these items in the box in front of you. Each team will be timed to see how many items you can land in the box in the fastest time. Let's see who can land the most prayers and record the fastest time.

Count the items in the pile, and equally divide the number each player should toss on a team. On your signal, have teams begin the game. When both teams have finished tossing, have Shepherds record the times and then count the items landed in the boxes and bring the items back to the starting line. Give one point for every item landed in the box and one point for every five seconds faster a team is than the other.

Have two new teams play a round of the game. Then have winning teams play against each other, until you have a team with highest score. **You all tossed a lot of items quickly in this game and that represented saying a lot of prayers of thankfulness. Remember, just as David did, we can never thank God too much for all he has given us!**

2. Low-Powered Game: Give me a T!

BEFORE YOU START:
Cut six paper sheets in half. Spell out "THANKFULNESS" 1 letter per sheet. Make two sets (for 30 kids). Make additional sets for larger classes. Also cut 10 blank sheets in half. Tape a line down the middle of your game area. Scatter one set of letters facedown and 10 blanks on both sides of the line.

LOW-POWERED GAME NEEDS:
- Paper or construction paper in one light color
- Thin-tipped black marker
- Scissors
- Masking/painter's tape

Have kids form two teams and have each form a circle around one of the game areas with paper sheets spread out. Each team will start at one point in the circle and have the kids take turns pointing to pages. Have *VeggieConnections Shepherds* turn over the pages. Kids must uncover the letters in order. This means they are looking for a "T" first. Players will take turns flipping over paper and showing the rest of the group which letter they picked. When a child picks up a letter, they must also name something that begins with that letter that they are thankful for. For example, if a player flips over a T, that's the first letter and they should say something like **I'm thankful for tangerines** and then set the letter below the line on the floor. This is the area for spelling out the word.

If a child picks an "L" first, they must say **I'm thankful for l_____**, and put the letter back. The other kids should pay attention so they know where the letters are for their future turns. If any player draws a blank, they should shout out: **I thank God for Jesus!** The game may have slow start while they learn where all the letters are, then it will go very quickly.

You sure are creative with all the things you can thank God for. Just as David was thankful to God for making him king, we can be thankful for all the good things God brings into our life!

3. Craft: Thankful Basket

CRAFT NEEDS:
- Medium-sized inflated balloon (one per child)
- Yarn and ribbon
- Bowls
- White glue
- Hair dryer
- Tagboard strips
- Stapler
- Scissors

Give each child a balloon. Pour glue into bowls and have several at each table. Have the children dip yarn and ribbons in glue, fully coating the yarn and ribbons. Position the balloon with the tied end up. Wrap glue coated pieces around the balloon (mostly around the lower half), in a variety of directions. Set balloons aside to dry. Use a hair dryer to speed up the drying process.

While balloons are drying, make stands by bending one inch tagboard strips in a four-inch circle and stapling it. Glue ribbon or yarn to the strip for added decoration. Allow the glue to dry.

You may have to wait to the end of the lesson if the glued strips on the balloons aren't dry. Once they are, pop the balloon and peel away the balloon pieces. Cut away the top part of the wrapping, forming a basket with the lower half. Place baskets on stands. If crafts aren't fully dry by the end of the lesson, keep them until next week.

PART THREE:

Plugging In to My Life

Life application of the lesson to lead kids to THINK–LINK–ACT and build a relationship with God every day

A. Cucumber Connection

Before kids arrive, enlarge and copy the pickles from the *VeggieConnections Shepherd* pages on the CD-ROM included in the *VeggieConnections Elementary Curriculum Kit* onto green construction paper. Cut them out and put in a pickle jar.

Let a volunteer draw a pickle from the Pickle Pot, and either the child or a Shepherd should read the dilemma out loud. Each Shepherd should then process the question with their group using the THINK—LINK—ACT phrase.

Life has been sailing along pretty smoothly lately. Your family is getting along, school's not so bad, and you're doing great in your hobbies. Do you take this for granted, or can you find a way to show thankfulness to God? How?	Leah is annoyed this evening. She says there's nothing to do and nobody to play with. She flops down on the sofa and crosses her arms. What should Leah do?	Cody had a great birthday, and he got lots of gifts at his party. But he felt a little sad that evening. No one gave him the toy he really wanted, and he doesn't have enough money to get it. How can Cody be joyful without this favorite toy?

CUCUMBER CONNECTION NEEDS:
- Pickle jar
- Pickles artwork from the *VeggieConnections Shepherd* pages (on the *VeggieConnections CD-ROM*)
- Green construction paper

B. Kid Connection: Joy Bags

Give each child his or her Joy Bag and a copy of the Horn of Plenty page 350. Have kids carefully cut out the horn-shaped outline. Give each child a paper grocery bag. Have *VeggieConnections Shepherds* assist younger kids. Show kids how to cut down on one side of the bag and cut off the bag bottom. Then have them lay out their bag, printed side down. Show them how to measure and trace pencil lines for cutting the paper 12" x 18". Have kids fold their papers to a 12" high by 9" wide size, with the fold on the left (like a book).

Hold up a picture of the horn of plenty. **This picture shows fruit inside a horn-shaped basket. It represents being thankful for the food we have. We are using it to say we joyfully thank God for everything!** Have kids color their horn pictures with markers. Then have them use glue sticks to glue the picture in the center of their paper book covers. **When you take your bags home, you can fold and tape these covers over your Bible.** Have kids put their covers in their Joy Bags and collect them for next week's use.

KID CONNECTION NEEDS:
- Joy Bags (from *Lesson 1*)
- Horn of Plenty on page 350 (one per child)
- Paper grocery bags (one per child)
- Scissors
- Rulers
- Pencils
- Markers
- Glue sticks

C. Christ Connection

Have the kids recite the Unit Memory Verse together, Psalm 16:11. Explain that our greatest joy is not in the things we have but in spending time with God. Ask: **Which part of this verse talks about being with God?** (*"You fill me with joy in your presence."*) **One of the ways we can do that is to thank him for everything!**

Play the *Thankfulness Song* and ask kids to listen to the words as if they were words of a prayer. Then divide into *VeggieConnections Groups*, and encourage the kids to make up a responsive prayer or psalm, like David's Psalm 100. A responsive prayer has a repeated line, such as "Thank you, Lord, for you are good," after each sentence of individual thanks. If you have time, let all the groups have a turn to lead in prayer by reciting their prayers for the other groups to pray along with.

Distribute the take-home newspaper, *VeggieConnections*.

CHRIST CONNECTION NEEDS:
- *VeggieConnections* take-home newspaper (one per child)

I will joyfully thank God for everything!

Connecting to **Joy** by looking at **David's Life**
David shows kindness to Mephibosheth:
2 Samuel 9:1-13

PART ONE:

Plugging In at the Tree House

Introduction to the site and lesson focus

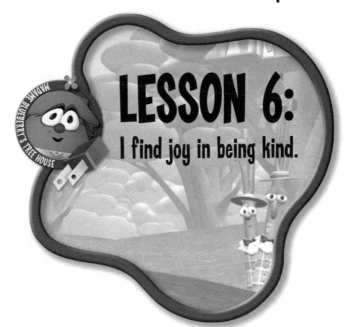

LESSON 6:
I find joy in being kind.

A. Veggie Connection

BEFORE YOU START:
Have several glasses, pieces of bubble wrap, and boxes set out in front of the Tree House.

Dressed as the Deliveryperson, welcome the kids back to the Tree House. Pack up the glasses as you explain: **Madame Blueberry is going through her extra stuff. She said that she used to think buying a lot of stuff from StuffMart would make her happy, but now she's just been thinking how she can make other people happy. She's donating lots of her stuff to help those who need them. Here are some extra glasses she doesn't need so she's asked me to help her pack up these things so they don't get broken when they are shipped away.**

Madame Blueberry is showing concern for others by giving stuff away, and I'm doing the same to make sure nothing gets broken. Demonstrate dropping a well-wrapped glass from a few feet. **That should be enough to keep it safe.**

You know, wanting to be kind to someone is what today's Connection Word is about. Ask a volunteer to look up *compassion* in the *VeggieConnections Bible Dictionary* and read the definition. Then explain that one reason God's people show kindness is that they care about others. Have a child highlight the number 6 button and write "compassion" on the Connection Word sign.

Have the kids sit in a circle and ask them if they've been kind to anyone this week. Pass a piece of bubble wrap around the circle, and have kids pop a bubble as they describe opportunities they've had to show kindness.

It feels good to show kindness and help others in need. That's compassion! Today, were going to see King David have a chance to show compassion to someone. Let's see what David will do.

B. Prayer Connection

Invite the kids to pray sentence prayers to thank God for any kind thing they've experienced. You may wish to divide into *VeggieConnections Groups* for this time.

THE CHILDREN
will arrive with their *VeggieConnections Shepherds* from the opening Countertop Connections featuring Bob and Larry. Play the *Veggie-Connections Music CD* as children enter the Tree House.

VEGGIE CONNECTION NEEDS:
- *VeggieConnections Music CD*
- CD player
- Several glass glasses or other breakable items
- Several pieces of bubble wrap
- Several small boxes
- Packing tape
- *VeggieConnections Bible Dictionary*
- Yellow highlighter
- Marker

GOD CONNECTION NEEDS:

• Bible

OPTION:

Photocopy the rap for each *VeggieConnections Group*. Have groups spread out and make up their own rap rhythm.

PART TWO:

Plugging In to God's Word

Connecting to God's Word in the Bible and understanding how that can help us to have a better relationship with him

A. God Connection: David shows kindness to Mephibosheth – 2 Samuel 9:1-13

Gather the kids on their "grass" blankets or carpet squares. Ask volunteers to tell what your group has been learning about King David in the past five weeks.

Now that David was finally king, would he still love and obey God? Would he still be fair and kind? The old king—King Saul—had been so mean to David. Would David try to get even with anyone from old King Saul's family?

Show the kids where today's Bible story is found, in 2 Samuel 9. Then ask them to listen carefully to the story, told as a rap, about King Saul's grandson named Mephibosheth. Have the kids clap the rhythm as the rap is spoken.

> There was a boy in days of old
> Who grew up in a royal household.
> His days were filled with joy and fun
> He was, after all, the king's grandson!
>
> His feet were formed in such a way
> He could not walk or run or play.
> Then came days of dark and fear,
> For it was then that war came near.
>
> And here is how the story's told—
> The day was dark and sad and cold,
> For out upon the battlefield
> The boy's family all were killed.
>
> A new king then began to reign;
> Good King David was his name.
> Now it was custom in his day
> To drive the old king's family away.
>
> Mephibosheth (the grandson's name)
> Knew that he was done with fame.
> His royal rights all now were gone
> Would he even have a home?
>
> But David to the rescue came
> Gave him a home, restored his name!
> Compassion—that was David's way
> To help others every day.
>
> That is why the people sing,
> "Long live David; he's our king!"

Discuss the following questions. **When David became king, what could have happened to King Saul's grandson, Mephibosheth?** *(He could have been killed, he could have lost his home.)* **How was David kind to Mephibosheth?** *(He gave him a place to live, he took care of him.)*

Encourage the kids to think carefully about this before answering these questions: **Why do you think David was so kind when he didn't have to be?** *(Because David loved God and found joy in God; because David wanted to show God's compassion.)*

B. Activity Connection

Choose from the following activities to help kids explore and remember that they can find joy in being kind (approximately 10–15 minutes each).

1. High-Powered Game: King David's Kindness Race

Divide the kids into three teams and have them line up. Give each team a box. Players on each team will race in groups of three. Explain that since Mephibosheth in the Bible story had a handicap and could not walk, one player in each trio will sit or kneel in the box while the other two push the box. Ask three *VeggieConnections Shepherds* to play "David" and share a ball/beanbag. The goal is for each trio to reach the "David" with the ball/beanbag and return to their team, so that the next trio can race to "David" and return back, and so on until every player on the team has had a turn racing in the box. If you have more than 30 kids, form additional teams and add Davids.

The trick is that the "David" goal keeps moving and changing. Only one of the three Shepherds holds the ball or beanbag at a time, and that is the only adult who is "David." At any point in the game, that Shepherd may toss the ball/beanbag to another one, who then becomes "David." So if a trio is on the way to the first David, they have to switch directions if the ball is tossed away. (Instruct the Shepherds not to change "David" very often so that the kids don't get frustrated; but remaining David for very long would make the game too easy.) Whenever any trio reaches David, that Shepherd calls out **I find joy in being kind!** before they can race back to their team.

If any trios are having a hard time making progress pushing, any *VeggieConnections Shepherd* can pitch in and help push. In fact, this would be an act of kindness.

When finished, let the kids relax while you discuss this question: **David showed kindness to Mephibosheth. Why should you be kind to others?** *(Because God loves us and wants us to be like him—he is kind to us, because we are filled with God's joy when we are kind to others.)*

HIGH-POWERED GAME NEEDS:

- Large cardboard boxes (computer paper boxes or larger) (one per team)
- Packing tape
- Soft ball or beanbag
- Heavy-duty trash bags (optional)

BEFORE YOU START:

This game is best played on a smooth or slippery floor, such as tile rather than carpet. If you play on carpet, wrap the boxes in a heavy-duty trash bags so they'll slide easier. Reinforce the boxes with packing tape.

2. Low-Powered Game: Helping Hands

BEFORE YOU START:
Copy and cut apart the hands, one hand per two kids. Write one helping action on the back of each hand, such as: baking cookies, washing dishes, washing the car, cleaning the floor, dusting, mowing the lawn, picking up toys, visiting an elderly person, babysitting, walking someone's dog, reading to a younger sibling, helping a friend with homework. Tape hands up (front side facing out) around the Tree House site.

Divide kids into *VeggieConnections Groups*. Then have kids in each group form pairs or trios. Have one pair from each group go find a hand and bring it back to the group. Then have pairs act out the helping action printed on the back of the hand while the rest of the group guesses the action. Continue to have pairs get new hands and mime the actions out until everyone in the group has done an action. If you have more hands left, have kids continue to play.

This game showed some good ways we can show kindness this week. It's also fun to remember that inviting a friend to come along and help is a great way to spread the joy around. God can use each of us to show his love and kindness to others. When we do, he blesses us with the joy of helping!

LOW-POWERED GAME NEEDS:

- Helping Hand pattern on page 366 (one hand for every two kids)
- Tape

3. Craft: Compassion Coupons

The Bible tells us that it is very important to be kind to others. David was kind, even when others felt that he didn't have to be. That made God very happy. As we grow in our relationship with God, we can find joy in being kind to others. Today, you are going to make Compassion Coupons. Your job is to "catch" people being kind to others and give them a Compassion Coupon.

Distribute coupon pages and have kids spend a few minutes coloring the coupons. Then have them cut apart the coupons. Give kids sheets of construction paper and have them cut a front and back cover, a little bit larger than their coupons. Have *VeggieConnections Shepherds* assist kids in putting the coupons inside the front and back covers and stapling the far left side of the new booklet. Encourage the kids to be on the lookout for people being kind in their family, school, or neighborhood.

CRAFT NEEDS:

- Compassion Coupons on page 367 (one per child)
- Markers
- Scissors
- Construction paper
- Stapler

CUCUMBER CONNECTION NEEDS:

• Pickle jar
• Pickles artwork from the *VeggieConnections Shepherd* pages (on the *VeggieConnections* CD-ROM)
• Green construction paper

PART THREE:

Plugging in to My Life

Life application of the lesson to lead kids to THINK-LINK-ACT and build a relationship with God every day

A. Cucumber Connection

Before kids arrive, enlarge and copy the pickles from the *VeggieConnections Shepherd* pages on the CD-ROM included in the *VeggieConnections Elementary Curriculum Kit* onto green construction paper. Cut them out and put in a pickle jar.

Let a volunteer draw a pickle from the Pickle Pot, and either the child or a Shepherd should read the dilemma out loud. Each Shepherd should then process the question with their group using the THINK—LINK—ACT phrase.

> All Cassandra's friends run out to the playground. One of them falls and scrapes up her knees. The other kids run off. Cassandra wonders about stopping and helping, but that means she'll be last to play. What can Cassandra do?

> Your next-door neighbor is an old man who is always cranky. He doesn't want to be friends with your parents, and he always yells at you to get off his yard, even when you're on the sidewalk. Now his grandson, who is your age, is visiting. You see him playing alone outside. What could you do?

> Jaray sees a sign that says, "Coats for Kids." His family has a coat for every occasion. Jaray thinks his parents would encourage him to get involved. What could he do?

> It's important for kids to be kind, even to those who are mean to them. But be sure the children do not misunderstand being "kind" in dangerous situations. If they are being bullied or abused, it is not unkind to tell someone, turn someone in, or to get help.

B. Kid Connection: Joy Bags

KID CONNECTION NEEDS:

• CD player
• *VeggieConnections Music CD*
• Joy Bags (made in *Lesson 1*)
• Red and white construction paper
• Magazines with pictures of poor children
• Scissors
• Markers
• Glue sticks

Have kids stand and gather around the CD player. Show kids how to make a heart shape with their hands over their heads, with fingers touching the top of their heads. Have kids make this motion during the lines "I've got the joy, joy, joy, joy . . ." On the line, " . . . Down in my heart. Where? Down in my heart," kids will point to their heart. Play the song, "Down in My Heart" from the *VeggieConnections Music CD* leading kids in the motions. Then explain the next song will help kids to know how to show compassion. Play *THINK—LINK—ACT* and have kids do the motions.

Have kids return to their seats. **We've been singing about having the love of God in our hearts. David also had the love of God in his heart, and it caused him to act kindly to Mephibosheth. We have an opportunity to show kindness to a poor child who needs our help. Let's make a reminder of this kindness.**

Give kids their Joy Bags, construction paper, *National Geographic* or other magazines showing Third-World poor children, scissors, and glue sticks. Have kids cut or tear out pictures of kids and create a collage on their paper sheets. Then have kids cut their collages into a heart shape that will fit in their bags.

Have kids write on the back of their hearts, "God wants me to joyfully show kindness to others." Then encourage kids to write someone they can show kindness to, or a prayer asking for God's help to be kind. Then have kids place their hearts into their Joy Bags and collect the bags for next week.

C. Christ Connection

CHRIST CONNECTION NEEDS:

• *VeggieConnections* take-home newspaper (one per child)

Divide kids into *VeggieConnections Groups*. Have kids pick a partner. Ask them to share one kind deed they commit to do this week. Remind them to use THINK—LINK—ACT. If you have mostly older kids, ask them to be specific (what they will do, for whom, when, and how). Then encourage the kids to pray for one another for God to fill them with joy so they can keep their commitment. Close by having a *VeggieConnections Shepherd* pray the Unit Memory Verse, Psalm 16:11, as a thank-you to God.

Distribute the take-home newspaper, ***VeggieConnections.***

Connecting to **Joy** by looking at **David's Life**
David's song of praise: **2 Samuel 22:1-51**

praise

PART ONE:

Plugging In at the Tree House

Introduction to the site and lesson focus

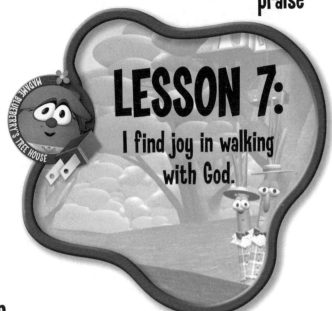

MADAME BLUEBERRY'S TREE HOUSE

LESSON 7:
I find joy in walking with God.

A. Veggie Connection

Dressed as the Deliveryperson, greet the kids as they arrive. **Welcome back to the beautiful Tree House! I just came from Madame Butterfly's Tree House. She was listening to that wonderful song about having a thankful heart. Her heart sure has changed from wanting stuff to being joy filled.** Explain that when you woke up this morning and looked around at the beautiful forest and all the wonderful creation God had made, you were filled with joy. Then when you sat down to read your Bible, you were filled with more joy. Then you paused to pray, and you had so much to praise God for that you just couldn't name it all.

Ask the kids if they could help you name things to praise God for. They will do this through a butterfly hunt. Explain that butterflies go through a beautiful change just like Madame Blueberry has been going through.

Give each child a marker or crayon, and send them off to "catch" a butterfly. When they find one (one per child), they may carefully remove it from where it is so they write one thing they praise God for. They may write it in one word or sketch a picture. Encourage the kids to think of all the wonderful things they think are so awesome about God and what he has made. After they write or draw, have kids carefully tape or place their butterfly back where they found it (leave these up for use in *Lesson 8*).

Then gather the kids back together. **All the things that you wrote or drew are praises to God. What does it mean to praise? Let's find out for sure.** Let a volunteer read the definition for *praise* from the *VeggieConnections Bible Dictionary*. Ask a child to highlight the number 7 button and write "praise" on the Connection Word sign. **Now let's do some more praising!**

When finished, walk around the Tree House site and read several of the butterflies. After you read (or describe, in case of a picture) each one, have the group call out: **Praise God!**

B. Prayer Connection

Have the kids get into circles in their *VeggieConnections Groups*, and have the *VeggieConnection Shepherds* lead a "round of praise" followed by a "round of applause." First the leader begins, **God we praise you for . . .** , and the kids quickly go around the circle calling out, in one or two words, something to praise God for. As soon as they've gone around the circle once, they all clap—give a round of applause to God for a few seconds. Then the Shepherd may have them go around again. Consider giving them categories of praise such as: **In creation we praise you for . . . At home . . . At school . . .** The different *VeggieConnections Groups* will be making their "rounds" at different paces, so there will be praises and applause all going on at the same time.

THE CHILDREN
will arrive with their *VeggieConnections Shepherds* from the opening Countertop Connections featuring Bob and Larry. Play the *VeggieConnections Music CD* as children enter the Tree House.

VEGGIE CONNECTION NEEDS:
- *VeggieConnections Music CD*
- CD player
- Colored markers
- Paper butterflies from site setup (one per child)
- Tape
- *VeggieConnections Bible Dictionary*
- Yellow highlighter
- Marker

BEFORE YOU START:
If your site doesn't already include paper butterflies, make one simple butterfly cut-out for each child. Distribute all the butterflies throughout the site, in trees, on bushes, along the path, and so on.

PART TWO:

Plugging In to God's Word

Connecting to God's Word in the Bible and understanding how that can help us to have a better relationship with him

A. God Connection: David's song of praise – 2 Samuel 22:1-51

GOD CONNECTION NEEDS:

- Bible
- Toy castle or house
- Phone
- Life ring or fireman's hat
- Big happy face poster
- Wet wipes
- Lamp (plugged in) or flashlight
- A musical instrument

TEACHER TIP:

Younger children may benefit from hearing the story before interacting with it. Explain to kids you'll read the story twice. For the first reading, they should listen carefully. For the second reading, kids will help tell the story.

Gather the kids on their "grass" carpets or blankets. Lead the group in saying the Program Verse, James 4:8. Then say: **David went through a whole lifetime of coming near to God. Another way of saying "coming near to God" is "walking with God." It doesn't really mean we stand up and walk, but it means that as we go through each day, we are remembering the Lord and talking with him in our hearts and following his ways.**

Point out the items from the needs list. **Remember that David wrote lots of songs about God. David liked to use pictures or everyday things to describe God, so as he walked through his day he'd have lots of things to remind him of God. Today we'll read parts of a long song that David wrote after God had brought him through many hard battles when he was king. We'll use these things to remind us of the joy of walking with God.** Show the kids in a Bible where the song is found, 2 Samuel 22.

The first thing David praised God for was for being his fortress, his stronghold, and his refuge. Hold up the toy castle for all to see. **What does that mean?** *(A strong, safe place of protection.)* **God is like a safe hiding place for us. When we're scared, we can pray to him and he'll give us peace.**

In this song David writes, "*I call to the Lord*" and "*I called out to my God.*" And then David writes things like, "*God heard my voice*" and "*my cry came to his ears.*" Hold up the phone. **What do you think David is talking about?** *(Praying, talking to God, and God listening and answering and caring.)* **We don't need a phone or e-mail with instant messaging to talk to God, but we always have an instant connection with him. We can call out to the Lord every time we need help or every time we want to praise him for something or just talk to him. That's what is so wonderful about having a relationship with him!**

David praised God for rescuing him and being his savior. Hold up the life ring or fireman's hat. **We know people with jobs who rescue others who could die without help. So what do you think David means when he says, "*You rescued me*"?** *(He was praising God for taking him out of a dangerous, scary situation, to save his life.)* **God rescued David from the enemy armies in hard battles. David knew that there was another way to be saved—he was forgiven. God forgave David for the wrong things he had done. That's being rescued from sin. God forgives us, too. When we accept his forgiveness and let go of guilty feelings, we feel great joy.**

David also said *why* God saved him. In verse 20, David says, "*He rescued me because he delighted in me.*" Hold up the big happy face. **God delights in you, too, and that's why he sent Jesus to die on the cross to save you. That's why you can be forgiven for things you've done wrong.**

David knew that another way to walk with God was to obey him. David called that keeping ourselves from sin and keeping ourselves "clean" in God's sight. Hold up the wet wipes. **It doesn't matter so much if our hands are actually clean, but when we say no to sin, it keeps our hearts clean.**

Here's an important way that David saw God walking with him. Turn on the lamp or flashlight. **In verse 29, David wrote, "*You are my lamp, O Lord; the Lord turns my darkness into light.*" What did David mean by God being our light?** *(When we're "in the dark"—need guidance, need to make a decision—God can "shed light" on it, help us make a good choice, show us how to follow his ways.)*

A great way that God shows us his light is through his Word, the Bible. Hold up the Bible. **How can the Bible help us walk with God?** *(By teaching us God's ways, by teaching us about salvation through Jesus, by teaching us how God stays close to us, and so on.)* **In verse 31, David wrote, "*As for God, his way is perfect; the word of the Lord is flawless.*" We can**

always trust God's Word because it never steers us wrong. We can trust what the Bible teaches to help us walk close to God.

David ends his song by showing how he felt about all these ways to walk close to God. He wrote, "*Therefore I will praise you, O Lord, among the nations; I will sing praises to your name.*" What did David do? *(He praised God.)* Hold up the musical instrument. **David praised God by singing and playing. We also can praise God in many ways. What could you do to praise God?** *(Sing, play instruments, clap, tell others, and so on.)*

In review, hold up each object and ask the kids how it can remind us of God or help us find joy in walking with God. Then ask: **What are ways that you can grow in your walk with God?** *(Get to know him better by reading the Bible and going to Sunday School, worship him at church and home, sing him songs, talk with him throughout each day, make a special time each day to pray, and so on.)*

B. Activity Connection

Choose from the following activities to help kids explore and remember that they can find joy in walking with God (approximately 10–15 minutes each).

1. High-Powered Game: Praise Stations

Divide kids into *VeggieConnections Groups* and gather groups in the middle of your playing area. **David praised God for everything that happened in his life, both good and bad. You're going to have an opportunity to do the same in this game.**

Station *VeggieConnections Shepherds* at each chair. If you have fewer than seven Shepherds (you can serve at one station), double up some card sets on chairs. Explain how kids in each group are to run to a chair of their choosing, pick up the card, and respond to the praise instructions on that card. Shepherds will ensure kids have said meaningful responses before sending them to another chair. Once they have said the praise, they are to keep the card and run to another chair and repeat the above. All kids will go to all eight stations and respond with eight praises.

After the game, tell kids that developing an ongoing pattern of giving God praise for all things is a practical application of the Program Verse, James 4:8.

2. Low-Powered Game: Walking & Singing with God

This is simply a game of musical chairs as a way of enjoying the music they have learned so far. Have everyone sit on a chair. Pick one of the kids' favorite new songs, and start the music. Ask a *VeggieConnections Shepherd* to be prepared to take away one chair. Without watching, stop the music. The person who is "out" gets to help with the music for the next time. Play several rounds, choosing as many songs you have time for.

Encourage the kids to sing along to the music. **God created us to enjoy music and singing. When we listen to praise music and enjoy the words and melodies to God's glory, we are praising God. Often God uses music to draw us near to him and deepen our relationship with him.**

3. Craft: CD Butterfly

A butterfly is a symbol of new life. Caterpillars build a cocoon, transform themselves, then emerge a beautiful butterfly. Madame Blueberry transforms herself as well by having a change of heart. The butterfly we will make today will remind you that when we have a relationship with God, we are made new when we believe in him.

Have the children gently overlap four compact discs to make a square. Secure with electrical tape. This makes the two wings. Glue a large craft stick down the center of the "wings" of the butterfly. This is the butterfly body. Cut small pieces of chenille wire and glue or tape them to the back of the butterfly head. Draw a face on the butterfly with markers.

Run a piece of fishing line through the two holes in the top wings and secure with a strong knot. This can be used to hang completed projects.

HIGH-POWERED GAME NEEDS:

- Praise Game cards on page 368 (one set per child)
- Chairs

BEFORE YOU START:

Copy and cut apart the Praise Game cards. Stack the same numbered cards together and place one set of cards on each of the eight chairs set in a circle around the perimeter of your room.

LOW-POWERED GAME NEEDS:

- Chairs set in a circle facing out (or "grass" carpets from site setup)
- VeggieConnections Music CD
- CD player

CRAFT NEEDS:

- Four blank CDs per child
- Electrical tape
- Large craft stick (one per child)
- Chenille wire stems
- Glue
- Scissors
- Markers
- Fishing line

PART THREE:

Plugging In to My Life

Life application of the lesson to lead kids to THINK–LINK–ACT and build a relationship with God every day

A. Cucumber Connection

CUCUMBER CONNECTION NEEDS:

- Pickle jar
- Pickles artwork from the *VeggieConnections Shepherd* pages (on the *VeggieConnections CD-ROM*)
- Green construction paper

Before kids arrive, enlarge and copy the pickles from the *VeggieConnections Shepherd* pages on the CD-ROM included in the *VeggieConnections Elementary Curriculum Kit* onto green construction paper. Cut them out and put in a pickle jar.

Let a volunteer draw a pickle from the Pickle Pot, and either the child or a Shepherd should read the dilemma out loud. Each Shepherd should then process the question with their group using the THINK—LINK—ACT phrase.

Tyler made a commitment to read his Bible and pray each night before bed. But lately he's been watching TV until he's so tired he can't keep his eyes open. What should Tyler do?	Sondra has been going to church with a friend. But the weather is getting nice and it's hard to give up Sunday morning every week. She feels like staying at home and playing outside instead of going to church. What should she do?	You are in a worship service, but none of your friends are singing. You want to worship, both because you know it's the right thing to do and because you love to sing praises to the Lord. What should you do?

B. Kid Connection: Joy Bags

KID CONNECTION NEEDS:

- Joy Bags (from *Lesson 1*)
- Plastic Easter eggs
- Lentils or other dried beans
- Colorful electrical tape
- *VeggieConnections Music CD*
- CD player

OPTION:

If you can't get plastic eggs, use egg cartons instead. Cut each egg holder part at right angles, so you have four tabs to tape together with masking tape after filling with beans.

Give kids their Joy Bags. To make the shaker, pop open the plastic eggs and put about a tablespoon of small beans inside. Snap it shut and run a length of tape around the seam to secure it.

Sing *THINK—LINK—ACT,* and have kids do the motions and use their shakers during the song. Then have kids pick other songs to sing as time permits. **Making music is one way to praise God. Put these music shakers in your Joy Bags to remind you to take the time to praise him each day.**

Collect Joy Bags for next week.

C. Christ Connection

CHRIST CONNECTION NEEDS:

- Objects from God Connection
- *VeggieConnections* take-home newspaper (one per child)

Set out the objects used in the God Connection Bible story. Have the kids form a line and walk by the objects. As they pass each item, tell them to stop by one or two, touch them, and say a sentence prayer, praising God for something that item reminds them of. If your group is large, divide the kids into their *VeggieConnections Groups*, and give each a set of the items to pass around as they pray.

Distribute the take-home newspaper, *VeggieConnections.*

Connecting to **Joy** by looking at **David's Life**
David's psalm of praise: **Psalm 145**

 **PART ONE:**

Plugging In at the Tree House

Introduction to the site and lesson focus

LESSON 8:
I want to share my joy in the Lord with others.

A. Veggie Connection

Dressed as the Deliveryperson, welcome the kids to the Tree House. Give each child a cup of colored candies. Be sure several colors are in every cup.

This is the last time you'll visit the Tree House. I've had fun telling you about joy and seeing Madame Blueberry's change. When you first came to the Tree House, Madame Blueberry was so blue. And she tried to become happy by buying stuff from StuffMart. Although she sure kept me busy delivering all that stuff, I'm much happier that she now has a very joyful heart. She realized true joy only comes from God, and sharing that joy is what Madame Blueberry does now.

These candies represent little pieces of joy, and your job is to share the joy. You need to give away all the colors in your cup but one. You can only give away one candy at a time, and it has to be a trade. You can only trade with one person at a time; so if you trade with someone, you have to go trade with someone else before you come back to that first person to trade again.

Give the signal to begin, and let the kids figure out their trading. With enough cooperation, the kids will each figure out a color they can collect enough of. Have the *VeggieConnections Shepherds* circulate to keep the efforts upbeat and resolve any problems. After a few minutes, let the kids be seated. Give everyone a fresh batch of candy to munch on.

We've been looking at the life of David. And we've seen how David wrote songs of prayers and praise to show his joy in God. Open a Bible and show kids the book of Psalms. **David is sharing his joy with everyone who reads the psalms. That is our Connection Word for today.** Let a volunteer look up the word *psalm* in the *VeggieConnections Bible Dictionary* and read the definition for the others. Let someone else highlight the number 8 button and write "psalm" on the Connection Word sign.

The joy of the Lord is a treasure we hide in our hearts, but it's one treasure that the more we can give away, the more we have! By connecting to each other with God's joy we connect to God.

B. Prayer Connection

Gather the kids into *VeggieConnections Groups*, and have the Shepherds lead prayer by naming a color. Then any kids who wish may thank God for something that color reminds them of. The leader should name all the colors in the candy game before closing the prayer time.

THE CHILDREN
will arrive with their *VeggieConnections Shepherds* from the opening Countertop Connections featuring Bob and Larry. Play the *VeggieConnections Music CD* as children enter the Tree House.

VEGGIE CONNECTION NEEDS:

- *VeggieConnections Music CD*
- CD player
- Cups of various colored candies (one cup per child) (check about possible food allergies)
- *VeggieConnections Bible Dictionary*
- Bible
- Yellow highlighter
- Marker

PART TWO:

Plugging In to God's Word

Connecting to God's Word in the Bible and understanding how that can help us to have a better relationship with him

A. God Connection: David's psalm of praise – Psalm 145

Gather the kids on their "grass" carpets or blankets. **This our last look at the life and work of David. We began our look at David by looking at some of the psalms he wrote. And we are going to end by looking at another psalm of David. But in addition to writing songs, David had an exciting life! I'll hold up a clue from each previous Bible story and ask you what you remember.**

Hold up the page showing the numbers 1–7 and then turn the page over. *(David was chosen from among 8 brothers to be king because of his heart for God.)* Hold up the sword. *(David fought Goliath, when everyone else was scared.)*

Hold up the piece of cut cloth. *(David was hiding from Saul and found him sleeping in a cave and cut off a piece of his robe, instead of killing him.)* Put the crown on your head. *(David became king after 20 years of waiting patiently for God's timing.)*

Next, hold up a crutch or picture of a wheelchair. *(David showed kindness to King Saul's handicapped grandson by giving him and his family a place to live.)* Lastly, show the sign "A life of joyful praise." *(David praised God his whole life.)*

Show the kids the book of Psalms in a Bible. **As we've seen, King David loved to sing and play the harp to praise God. The psalms are like David's journal or diary. They tell us about when David felt happy or sad, fearful or strong. Most of all, the psalms share David's joy in the Lord.**

Divide the class into two groups, explain that Group A will pop up and sit back down when they hear the words "praise", "exalt," or "extol." Group B will pop up and sit back down when they hear the words "tell", "speak," or "celebrate." You may want to write these words on the board to help the kids remember them. Psalm 145 is repeated below with Group A's words CAPPED and Group B's words underlined. As you read the psalm, pause and motion to the proper group when you read each marked word.

1   I will EXALT you, my God the King; I will PRAISE your name forever and ever.
2   Every day I will PRAISE you and EXTOL your name forever and ever.
3   Great is the Lord and most worthy of PRAISE; his greatness no one can fathom.
4   One generation will commend your works to another; they will <u>tell</u> of your mighty acts.
5   They will <u>speak</u> of the glorious splendor of your majesty, and I will meditate on your wonderful works.
6   They will <u>tell</u> of the power of your awesome works, and I will proclaim your great deeds.
7   They will <u>celebrate</u> your abundant goodness and joyfully sing of your righteousness.
8   The Lord is gracious and compassionate; slow to anger and rich in love.
9   The Lord is good to all; he has compassion on all he has made.
10 All you have made will PRAISE you, O Lord; your saints will EXTOL you.
11 They will <u>tell</u> of the glory of your kingdom and <u>speak</u> of your might,
12 so that all men may know of your mighty acts and the glorious splendor of your kingdom.

Pause at this point to ask: **Why did David want to share his joy in the Lord with others?** In answer, have all the kids repeat verse 12 after you, phrase by phrase. Then say: **Now David tells some of the reasons he finds joy in the Lord.** Continue to read, but neither group will stand up again until the last verse.

13 Your kingdom is an everlasting kingdom, and your dominion endures through all generations. The Lord is faithful to all his promises and loving toward all he has made.
14 The Lord upholds all those who fall and lifts up all who are bowed down.

15 The eyes of all look to you, and you give them their food at the proper time.
16 You open your hand and satisfy the desires of every living thing.
17 The Lord is righteous in all his ways and loving toward all he has made.
18 The Lord is near to all who call on him, to all who call on him in truth.
19 He fulfills the desires of those who fear him; he hears their cry and saves them.
20 The Lord watches over all who love him, but all the wicked he will destroy.
21 My mouth will <u>speak</u> in PRAISE of the Lord. Let every creature PRAISE his holy name for ever and ever.

Thank the kids for their participation and careful listening. Then discuss these questions: **What are some reasons David gives for having joy in the Lord?** Encourage the kids to draw their answers from the second half of the psalm, which they just heard. (*The Lord is faithful, gives food, is loving, comes near to us, watches over us, and so on.*) **What are some words David uses for sharing his joy in the Lord?** Encourage the kids to draw their answers from the first half of the psalm. (*Praise, extol, exalt, speak, tell, and celebrate.*) See if any kids remember any other words, such as *commend, proclaim,* and *sing.* **What are ways you can share your joy in the Lord with others?** Encourage kids to brainstorm ideas that would be practical for them. (*Talking, singing, inviting a friend to church or to watch a Christian video, and so on.*)

B. Activity Connection

Choose from the following activities to help kids explore and remember to share their joy in the Lord with others (approximately 10–15 minutes each).

1. High-Powered Game: Joy Target

BEFORE YOU START:

Attach Velcro hook pieces to table-tennis balls. Use fabric paint to create a felt target with "God" written in the center circle. Paint concentric circles with the words "friends," "family," "neighbors," "others." Tape the target to a wall or easel. Mark a start line with tape.

OPTION:

Instead of felt and Velcro, use newsprint or butcher paper and use double-sided tape wrapped around the table-tennis balls.

Explain to the kids that the balls represent the joy that they can share with God and others. Give each child three chances to hit the target. Whatever area of the target they hit they should complete the following sentence: **I can share my joy in knowing God with my neighbor by_____.** If they miss the target, allow them one rethrow per ball. Allow younger kids to stand closer.

There are so many places and people to share our joy in knowing God with. Let's not miss an opportunity this week to praise God and let others know where our joy comes from!

2. Low-Powered Game: Sharing the Joy

Have the kids sit in a circle or at a table with their three beads in front of them. It is best to play this game in groups of about six to eight. The child throws the three cubes at the same time. If they throw a 1 or a 2, one of their beads must be given to the person to their left. If they throw a 3 or a 4, their bead goes to the center. If they throw a 5 or a 6, their bead goes to the person on their right. So, if they roll a 1, 1, and a 5, two of their beads go to the person on the left and one to the person on their right. Pass the cube to the left after each child rolls.

Explain the goal of the game is to keep giving away your beads. **Just like we want to look for opportunities to share our joy, our goal is to give away our beads—not to collect them.** Keep playing until all the beads eventually end up in the center. A child should only roll as many cubes as he or she has beads. Remember that just because someone is without beads, it doesn't mean that some won't get passed their way as others take their turns. **Even though we kept giving our beads to each other, eventually all the beads ended up in the center. When we share our joy in knowing God with others in our lives, eventually all that sharing of joy is accepted by God as our praise offering to him.**

HIGH-POWERED GAME NEEDS:

- Table-tennis balls (Three per *Veggie-Connections Group*)
- Velcro with adhesive backing
- Fabric paint
- 2' x 2' piece of felt
- Masking/painter's tape

LOW-POWERED GAME NEEDS:

- Three number cubes for each *Veggie-Connections Group* (of approximately six to eight kids)
- Three beads or other small items for each child

3. Craft: God's Molded My Heart

CRAFT NEEDS:
- Bowls for mixing
- Measuring cups
- Vegetable oil
- Flour
- Food coloring
- Plastic sandwich bags
- Permanent marker
- Wet wipes

As we continue to build our relationship with God, we find joy in the fact that he loves us very much and has molded our hearts. That means that because we choose to know God, we give him the chance to make our hearts happy and full of joy. Today we are going to make some fun goop that we can also mold!

Divide kids into groups of three or four. Give each group a mixing bowl and measuring cup. Have the kids mix one-half cup of oil with three cups of flour. Let the children take turns kneading the concoction. Have a *VeggieConnections Shepherd* add a few drops of food coloring to the mixture. This may stain hands, be very careful of clothing.

As the dough becomes smooth, the kids can divide it up in their group and spend time molding shapes. Encourage the kids to think of things that bring them joy and show you what they make. When the kids are done, pass out plastic bags to take the project home in. You may want to label each bag with a permanent marker. Use wet wipes to clean up hands.

PART THREE:

Plugging In to My Life

Life application of the lesson to lead kids to THINK-LINK-ACT and build a relationship with God every day

A. Cucumber Connection

CUCUMBER CONNECTION NEEDS:
- Pickle jar
- Pickles artwork from the *VeggieConnections Shepherd* pages (on the *VeggieConnections CD-ROM*)
- Green construction paper

Before kids arrive, enlarge and copy the pickles from the *VeggieConnections Shepherd* pages on the CD-ROM included in the *VeggieConnections Elementary Curriculum Kit* onto green construction paper. Cut them out and put in a pickle jar.

Let a volunteer draw a pickle from the Pickle Pot, and either the child or a Shepherd should read the dilemma out loud. Each Shepherd should then process the question with their group using the THINK—LINK—ACT phrase.

Jenny received two of the same present for her birthday. She was angry. How can she act in that situation?	Bonnie sings in her church group and loves to sing praises to God. Her friend says she thinks that would be fun. What can Bonnie do next?	Some kids make fun of Marcia because she has trouble speaking clearly. She lives down the street from you, but if others see you playing with her, they might pick on you, too. What could you do?

B. Kid Connection: Joy Bags

KID CONNECTION NEEDS:
- Joy Bags (made in *Lesson 1*)
- Madame Blueberry on page 363 (one per child)
- Markers
- Gel pens
- Sequins
- Glue sticks
- Craft glue

The very first day that you came to the Tree House, we made a bag to fill with things to remind you of the joy you've learned at the Tree House. Have kids empty their Joy Bags and talk about what each joy reminder means. Point to the picture frame. (*I can be joyful for how God made me.*) Point to a giant head. (*God will help me face the giants in my life with joy.*) Point to a CONTENT key ring (*God will help me be content.*) Point to the horn of plenty book covers. (*I will be thankful to God for all things.*) Point to a collage heart. (*God wants me to show compassion to others in need.*) Pick up an egg shaker. (*I will joyfully praise God.*)

Madame Blueberry is now filled with joy, so we're going to decorate a happy picture of her to put on the back of the Joy Bags.

Distribute bags, a Madame Blueberry copy, and remaining craft supplies. Have kids cut out the picture and glue it to their bags. Then have kids use the other supplies to decorate Madame Blueberry as they wish. Have kids get one of the butterflies used in the Tree House opening from *Lesson 7* and put it in their bags. Then send the bags home with the kids today.

C. Christ Connection

Divide into *VeggieConnections Groups* for prayer. Ask the kids to think of two friends or relatives who don't know Jesus and say their names in their head. Then they should close their eyes and hold out their hands. They can imagine one of these people holding their right hand and the other holding their left. Allow a minute for silent prayer for these people.

Have kids say the Unit Memory Verse, Psalm 16:11, aloud by memory if possible. Then have the *VeggieConnections Shepherds* close-by thanking God for each child by name and for the time they've had learning about joy and David's life.

Distribute the take-home newspaper, **VeggieConnections.**

CHRIST CONNECTION NEEDS:
- *VeggieConnections* take-home newspaper (one per child)

Lesson 8 - Madame Blueberry

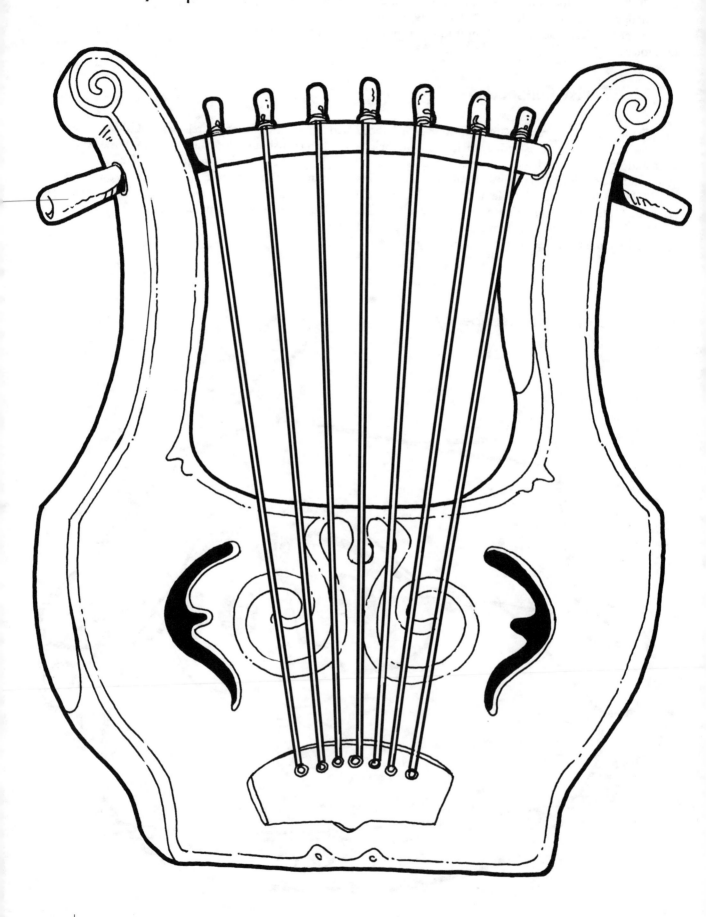

Lesson 4 – David and Saul Script

David: King Saul had tried to kill me so often that I had to run into the rocky, hilly desert to hide and live. But I had lots of good, fighting men with me. We managed to survive. I often wondered, "When would the Lord keep his promise to let me be king?"

Saul: Kill David! My kingdom will not be safe until I get rid of him! I must kill David!

David: We know Saul's army has been following us, but we are keeping our distance by staying in desert.

Saul: I heard that David was in the desert, so my 3,000 soldiers and I have set up camp here, near David. But now we need to rest.

David: I sent men to discover where Saul was and they gave me a good report. So I asked for a volunteer, and Abishai and I went down to Saul's camp and found him sleeping. I came up to Saul, and Abishai wanted to kill Saul. But I told him Saul was God's king and he couldn't kill him. So I grabbed his spear and water jug and we left his camp. Then I stood a distance from the king and called out to him.

Saul: Is that you, David?

David: King Saul, why are you trying to kill me? I have done you no wrong. I took your spear but did not kill you with it as I could have.

Saul: I have sinned. Because you saved my life I will not try to hurt you again. I have been a fool!

David: Here is your spear. Have one of your men come and get it. The Lord rewards those living for him. I would not kill you, and I ask the Lord to bless me.

Saul: May the Lord bless you, David. You will be a great man, and God will give you victory in your life!

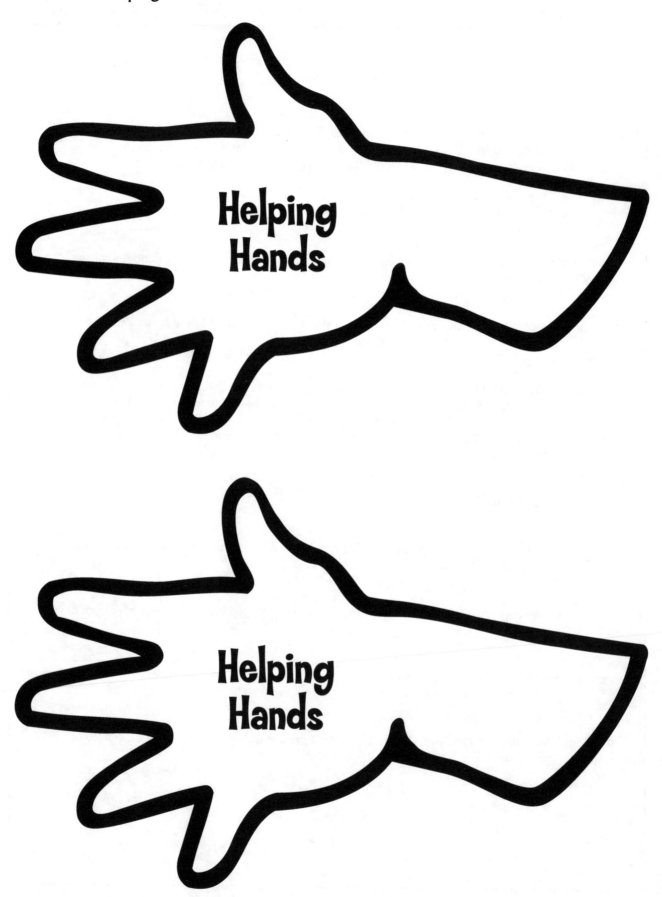

Compassion Coupon

Compassion Coupon

Compassion Coupon

Compassion Coupon

Compassion Coupon

Compassion Coupon

Compassion Coupon

Compassion Coupon

1.

Praise God for
a family member and
give a reason.

5.

Praise God for
helping you handle a
hard time in your life.

2.

Praise God for
a friend and
give a reason.

6.

Praise God for
a way he has shown
his love for you.

3.

Praise God for something
in God's creation and
give a reason.

7.

Praise God for
a way he
gives you hope.

4.

Praise God for
something good that
has happened to you.

8.

Name a
characteristic of God
to praise him with.